# REGULATING FAMILY RESPONSIBILITIES

# Regulating Family Responsibilities

*Edited by*

JO BRIDGEMAN, HEATHER KEATING AND CRAIG LIND
*University of Sussex, UK*

Routledge
Taylor & Francis Group
LONDON AND NEW YORK

First published 2011 by Ashgate Publishing

2 Park Square, Milton Park, Abingdon, Oxon OX14 4RN
711 Third Avenue, New York, NY 10017, USA

*Routledge is an imprint of the Taylor & Francis Group, an informa business*

First issued in paperback 2016



**British Library Cataloguing in Publication Data**
Regulating family responsibilities.
1. Domestic relations.
I. Bridgeman, Jo. II. Keating, Heather M. III. Lind, Craig.
346'.015-dc22

**Library of Congress Cataloging-in-Publication Data**
Bridgeman, Jo.
Regulating family responsibilities / by Jo Bridgeman, Heather Keating and Craig Lind.
p. cm.
Includes index.
ISBN 978-1-4094-0200-8 (hardback)
1. Parent and child (Law)--Great Britain. 2. Domestic relations--Great Britain. 3. Responsibility. I. Keating, Heather M. II. Lind, Craig. III. Title.
KD772.B75 2011
346.01'7--dc22

2010053032

ISBN 978-1-4094-0200-8 (hbk)
ISBN 978-1-138-26062-7 (pbk)

# Contents

# List of Figures

# Preface

This is the final volume of essays arising from a series of events hosted by the Sussex Law School at the University of Sussex between 2005 and 2008. The first volume arose from a symposium organized by the Child and Family Law Research Group held in September 2005 which brought together philosophers, sociologists and lawyers to explore *Responsibility, Law and the Family*. The following year, a second symposium took place, focused upon state responsibility for the family which led to the publication of a special issue of the *Journal of Law and Society* (co-edited by Heather Keating and Craig Lind, simultaneously published as an edited collection by Blackwell, 2008).

In 2008, an international and interdisciplinary conference on *Gender, Family Responsibility and Legal Change* at Sussex encouraged us to approach Ashgate with a proposal for a further publication. We were absolutely delighted that they were prepared to publish two volumes of the many excellent papers that contributed to the success of that conference. The first, *Taking Responsibility, Law and the Changing Family* was published early in 2011; this, its companion volume, is now before you.

As this is the third volume we have written and edited for Ashgate we would like to take this opportunity to express our gratitude to them for believing in the work that we have been engaged in on family responsibilities. They have been wonderfully supportive, extremely efficient and generously patient. We could not have asked for more a more caring approach to our work.

We would also like to thank all of the contributors to the symposia and the conference and we are only sorry that we could not publish more of the papers that were presented. Finally, we would like to thank the contributors to the volumes for their enthusiasm for the project and for their patience with our editorial demands. We very much hope that they, as well as those who read these collections, will think that it was worth it and that we have made a contribution towards understanding the nature of family responsibility.

Jo Bridgeman
Heather Keating
Craig Lind

Centre for Responsibilities, Rights and the Law
Sussex Law School
University of Sussex

# Notes on Contributors

**Shalhevet Attar-Schwartz** is a lecturer at the School of Social Work and Social Welfare at the Hebrew University of Jerusalem. Her research and teaching focus on the well-being and welfare of children and youth. She is particularly interested in intergenerational relationships and their contribution to child well-being, children's outcomes in various family structures, and children's quality of life in out-of-home settings. Shalhevet has recently won a grant from the Israel Science Foundation (ISF) for a large-scale study on grandparenting and adolescents' well-being from the perspective of Jewish and Palestinian youth in Israel. This study may allow a better understanding of the interplay between culture and intergenerational relationships and will help fill a considerable gap in existing literature. The findings of the Israeli study will be compared with the findings of the UK National Grandparenting Study, in which Shalhevet was involved. Shalhevet was lead author in several publications in leading social work and family psychology journals resulting from the latter study.

**Jo Bridgeman** is a senior lecturer in the Sussex Law School, University of Sussex. She is a founder member of the child and family research group and the Centre for Responsibilities, Rights and the Law. Jo has researched and published in books and journals in the field of healthcare law and the law regulating the care of children. This includes work on the healthcare of teenagers, a range of publications analysing the issues arising from the Bristol Royal Infirmary Inquiry and a monograph which offers a critical analysis of moral, social and legal responsibilities for the healthcare of babies, infants and young children, *Parental Responsibility, Young Children and Healthcare Law* (2007). She has developed this work in a number of publications considering different aspects of the legal regulation of the care of children, drawing upon the feminist ethic of care in order to develop a conceptual framework of relational responsibility. She was co-editor (with Heather Keating and Craig Lind) of *Responsibility, Law and the Family*, published by Ashgate in 2008, and *Taking Responsibility, Law and the Changing Family* (Ashgate, 2011).

**Ann Buchanan** is currently the Director of the Centre for Research into Parenting and Children, at the Department of Social Policy and Social Work, University of Oxford, and she is a fellow of St Hilda's College. Before entering academic life in 1990, she spent 10 years working as a child psychiatric social worker in an inner urban area. Her current research interests are promoting well-being in children, especially those at risk of social exclusion, and outcomes for children of divorce. Some of her earlier work was based on longitudinal data from the National Child Development Study. This was informed by her field studies and research eliciting the views of children. In 2009 she was the principal investigator of the UK National Grandparenting and Adolescent Well-Being Study funded by the ESRC, together with Dr Eirini Flouri, who was the co-investigator, Dr Jo-Pei Tan, Dr Julia Griggs and Dr Shalhevet Attar-Schwartz, who were co-researchers in that study. Prof. Buchanan was appointed to the Council of the ESRC in 2007 and in 2009 she chaired the group responsible for updating the ESRC Framework for Research Ethics. She was reappointed to the Council in 2010 and will chair the Evaluation Board. She became an Academician of the Academy of Social Sciences in 2009. She is currently serving on the University of Oxford Research Committee. In 2009 she was invited to talk on her 17 years of research to the Cabinet Office Strategy Unit.

**Ruth Cain** is Lecturer in Law at the University of Kent, Medway, having previously lectured in law at Keele University from 2007–2010. Her particular areas of interest are family, criminal, medical and mental health law, especially where law intersects with the politics of gender and reproduction. She is a member of the Centre for Law, Gender and Sexuality and the interdisciplinary Parenting Culture Studies group at the University of Kent. Her recent research has focused on the law and politics of motherhood in the contemporary UK, looking at the criminalization and condemnation of certain types of maternal conduct and subjectivity from regulatory and cultural perspectives. She is now preparing a monograph on this subject, provisionally entitled *Unspeakable Mothers: Maternity and Anxiety in Contemporary Law and Culture*, to be published by Zed Books in 2011.

**Richard Collier** is Professor of Law at Newcastle University. He has published widely in the area of law and gender and his books include *Men, Law and Gender: Essays on the 'Man' of Law* (Routledge, 2010), *Fragmenting Fatherhood: A Socio-Legal Study* (with Sally Sheldon, Hart, 2008), *Masculinities, Crime and Criminology: Men, Corporeality and the Criminal(ised) Body* (Sage, 1998), *Masculinity, Law and the Family* (Routledge, 1995) and *Fathers' Rights, Activism and Law Reform in Comparative Perspective* (edited with Sally Sheldon, Hart, 2007). He is presently researching the book *Family Men: Fatherhood, Law and Gender from the Late Nineteenth Century to the Present* and is conducting a project on male lawyers, fatherhood and work–life balance in the legal profession. Richard is an editorial board member of *Social and Legal Studies: An International Journal*.

**Susanne Fahlén** is a PhD candidate in Sociology, Stockholm University, with a multidisciplinary background in cultural anthropology and demography. Her doctoral project concerns gender and social politics in a European perspective with a special focus on parental work–life balance, childbearing intentions and realized fertility. She is part of the large European Research Network of

Excellence, RECWOWE, which has a strand devoted to tensions within work–family reconciliation. She is involved in several book projects and has published an article in the *ANNALS of the American Academy of Political and Social Science*, with Barbara Hobson, on fatherhood in Europe and agency inequalities in work–life balance in a capabilities perspective.

**Eirini Flouri** is Professor in Developmental Psychology at the Department of Psychology and Human Development, Institute of Education, University of London. She is interested in modelling risk and resilience patterns in both typical and atypical child populations. She has extensive experience in modelling longitudinal data, is on the Scientific Committee for the British Cohort Studies and is a Foundation Member of the Society for Longitudinal and Life Course Studies. Before joining the Institute of Education in 2005, she was Research Fellow at the Department of Social Policy and Social Work, University of Oxford, and College Lecturer in Statistics at St Hilda's College. Most of her externally funded research since 2000, when she was awarded her doctorate in psychology, has used longitudinal data from the British Birth Cohort Studies to investigate the role of parenting in children's development by fitting both additive and (especially since 2005) multiplicative models, and to test the effect and the moderation of contextual risk on children's emotional and behavioural problems. She has published a monograph (*Fathering and Child Outcomes*, 2005, Wiley) and some 100 scholarly articles, book chapters and reports. She is on the Editorial Board of the *International Journal of Behavioral Development*. She has held a visiting scientist appointment at the Mailman School of Public Health, Columbia University, and is currently collaborating with the School of Public Health, Harvard University. She is the Programme Director of the Master's in Child Development, Department of Psychology and Human Development, Institute of Education, and is a member of the Economic and Social Research Council Grant Assessment Panel.

**Robert H. George** has been Lecturer in Law at Jesus College, Oxford since 2006, where he teaches tort, trusts and EU Law. He also teaches family law for the Oxford Law Faculty, running an annual seminar series on the policy underpinnings of family law. He has strong links with Otago University in New Zealand and Melbourne University in Australia, as well as with the English Family Bar. Since January 2011, he has been case notes editor of the *Journal of Social Welfare and Family Law*. With a background in law and social policy, his research interests are mainly in child and family law, both in England and internationally. He has published widely on various aspects of child law, as well as on prenuptial agreements and cohabitants' property rights. He was also the lead author on a recent policy briefing paper about media access to the family courts, commissioned by the Nuffield Foundation, commenting on what is now the Children, Schools and Families Act 2010. Between 2007 and 2010, Robert H. George was engaged in doctoral research on relocation disputes, comparing the legal approaches in England and New Zealand. This work was funded by the Arts and Humanities

Research Council, and combined doctrinal analysis with empirical research in the form of qualitative interviews with family law practitioners in the two countries. This work has led to a number of publications, and has contributed to his chapter in this collection.

**Jonathan Herring** is a fellow in law at Exeter College, Oxford University and University Lecturer in Law at the Law Faculty, Oxford University. He has written on family law, medical law, criminal law and legal issues surrounding old age. His books include: *Older People in Law and Society* (Oxford University Press, 2009); *European Human Rights and Family Law* (Hart, 2010, with Shazia Choudhry); *Medical Law and Ethics* (Oxford University Press, 2010); *Criminal Law* (4th edition,Oxford University Press, 2010); *Family Law* (4th edition, Pearson, 2009); and *The Woman Who Tickled Too Much* (Pearson, 2009).

**Barbara Hobson** holds a chair in Sociology, with a specialization in comparative gender studies at Stockholm University. For the past five years, she has been a Strand Coordinator within the EU Network of Excellence, Reconciling Work and Welfare (RECWOE; FP6) She is task leader for a research project that applies a capabilities and agency approach to work–life balance with a multi-dimensional framework, considering household, policy and workplace organizational levels. She has published widely on gender and welfare states concerning themes of gender and citizenship, men and social politics, and social movements and gender diversity in welfare states, including three books: *Recognition and Social Movements: Contested Identities, Agency and Power* (Cambridge University Press, 2003), *Making Men into Fathers: Men, Masculinities and the Social Politics of Fatherhood* (Cambridge University Press, 2002) and *Gender and Citizenship in Transition* (Macmillan, 2000).

**Heather Keating** is Senior Lecturer in Law at the Sussex Law School, University of Sussex and a founder member of the child and family research group and the Centre for Responsibilities, Rights and the Law. She is co-author (with Chris Clarkson and Sally Cunningham) of *Criminal Law: Text and Materials* (7th edition, Sweet & Maxwell, 2010). She has also written widely on issues relating to criminal law and child law and her research now focuses upon children and the criminal law. She was co-editor (with Craig Lind) of a special issue of the *Journal of Law and Society*, *Children, Family Responsibilities and the State*, published in March 2008, which was simultaneously published by Blackwell as a book. She was co-editor (with Jo Bridgeman and Craig Lind) of *Responsibility, Law and the Family*, published by Ashgate in 2008 and *Taking Responsibility, Law and the Changing Family* (Ashgate, 2010). Her current project is a monograph on children, responsibility and the criminal law.

**Eva Feder Kittay** is Distinguished Professor of Philosophy at the State University of New York, Stony Brook, where she has taught since 1979. She is a graduate of

Sarah Lawrence College and the Graduate School of the City University of New York. She has taught and written on issues pertaining to women since her first appointment and has expanded that work into questions of disability since the 1990s. She is the mother of a woman with severe and multiple disabilities. She is also interested in ethics and social and political philosophy. She is an expert on metaphor and the philosophy of language. She was a founder of The Women's Committee of One Hundred (an organization of feminist women speaking out against punitive welfare reform) and chaired the American Philosophical Association Committee on the Status of Women. She was honoured by the Eastern Society of Women in Philosophy as Woman Philosopher of the Year in 2003. She helped found and also serves as the Chair of the Board of Philosophy in an Inclusive Key Summer Institute, a summer institute for undergraduates from underrepresented populations in academia.

**Ruth Lamont** has been a lecturer in law at the University of Liverpool since 2010, having previously lectured at the University of Sheffield. Her work examines the development of private international family law in the EU context, focusing specifically on international child abduction. Ruth has previously published on the implications of domestic violence for child abduction disputes and the mainstreaming of gender equality norms into private international family law by the EU. She has also published work on the interpretation of the concept of habitual residence in European law, applied specifically in the context of international child abduction and the Brussels II Revised Regulation.

**Craig Lind** holds law degrees from the University of the Witwatersrand (in Johannesburg) and the London School of Economics. He has taught at the University of the Witwatersrand, the University of Wales in Aberystwyth and is now a senior lecturer in law at the University of Sussex in Brighton. He teaches (amongst other subjects) family law and constitutional law. He also teaches courses in family and child law on a Master's programme aimed at exploring the legal regulation of family responsibility. His major research interests lie in the areas of family law and sexuality and have a strong cultural focus and a comparative slant. He is currently completing a book, *A Global Family Law?*, in which he explores the relationship between culture, sexuality and the legal regulation of the family.

**Kiran Pohar Manhas** is currently a doctoral candidate at the University of Calgary, Alberta, Canada. Prior to her PhD studies, Kiran completed undergraduate degrees in pharmacy and law, as well as a graduate degree in health research methodology. She articled at a national law firm prior to beginning doctoral work. Her training has facilitated her interest in bioethics and health law, particularly as it relates to professions, responsibility, paediatrics and non-institutional settings. Her dissertation research examines understandings of legal and ethical responsibility in the transition from hospital-based care to home-based care for young, ventilator-dependent children in Alberta, Canada. Kiran has presented locally and nationally, as well as internationally, on topics related to paediatric bioethics, responsibility, feminist ethics and justice. Her research is interdisciplinary and pulls from the disciplines of law, qualitative research and ethics. Along with her research, Kiran is committed to teaching and service. She is a sessional instructor in the Law and Society Program, Department of Communication and Culture, Faculty of Arts, University of Calgary. She is also the co-organizer of the Interdisciplinary Ethics Rounds: a bi-monthly seminar series open to health professionals and academics. She is the lawyer member of the Home Care Ethics Committee, Alberta Health Services – Calgary Health Region. Her research is generously funding by a studentship from the Alberta Heritage Foundation for Medical Research (now called Alberta Innovates – Health Solutions), as well as a research grant from the Alberta Centre for Child, Family and Community Research.

**Alexander Masardo** is a research fellow at the School of Health and Population Sciences, University of Birmingham. While pursuing his existing research interests in fatherhood, changing family forms and the post-separation care of children, he is also supporting a range of collaborative projects between the Centre for Biomedical Ethics and Centre for the Study of Global Ethics. Alex is also a visiting fellow at the Centre for the Analysis of Social Policy, University of Bath, where he was awarded a Master of Research in European Social Policy and later his doctorate in the Department of Social and Policy Sciences. He sits on the editorial board of *Social Policy and Society* and has contributed to taught undergraduate and graduate courses in the areas of sociology of the family and family policy, healthcare ethics and law, and the relationship between research and policy. Alex is co-investigator on the Arts and Humanities Research Council research network grant: 'Post-separation families and shared residence: setting the interdisciplinary research agenda for the future', which runs until September 2012.

**Joanna Miles** is a university lecturer in the Faculty of Law and a fellow of Trinity College, University of Cambridge, where she teaches on several undergraduate and postgraduate courses related to family law. Her research interests lie principally in the area of adult family relationships, family property and financial remedies following relationship breakdown, including prenuptial and other agreements concerning the financial consequences of relationships and their ending. She was seconded to the Law Commission for England and Wales for two years to work on its project 'Cohabitation: The Financial Consequences of Relationship Breakdown'. She is co-author, with Sonia Harris-Short, of *Family Law: Text, Cases, and Materials* (Oxford University Press), due to appear in its second edition in 2011. She has co-edited, with Rebecca Probert, an inter-disciplinary volume, *Sharing Lives, Dividing Assets* (Hart, 2009), which explores a wide range of empirical data – from economists, psychologists, sociologists, socio-legal scholars and others – pertinent to the law's treatment of family property and finances. She has recently completed a Nuffield Foundation-funded project examining the first three years' operation of new Scottish remedies between cohabitants, with

Professor Fran Wasoff and Dr Enid Mordaunt at the University of Edinburgh: 'Legal Practitioners' Perspectives on the Cohabitation Provisions of the Family Law (Scotland) Act 2006'.

**Annika Newnham** is a senior lecturer at the University of Portsmouth, teaching child law, family law and equity and trusts. Her chapter is rooted in her DPhil research comparing courts' approach to shared residence orders in England and Sweden. She is particularly interested in law's self-referential nature, its over-reliance on rigid definitions and abstract presumptions, and its inability to recognize the true value of care.

**Paula Távora Vítor** teaches family and succession law at the Faculty of Law of the University of Coimbra, where she has earned a Master's degree and is a PhD candidate. She has written on family law and medical law, mainly on adult family relationships and on issues concerning people with diminished capacity and old age. She is a member of the Direction Board of the Family Law Center and of the Scientific Board of 'Lex Familiae – Revista Portuguesa de Direito da Família' (Lex Familiae – Portuguese Family Law Review).

# Chapter 1

# Supporting, Fostering and Coercing? The Legal Regulation of the Exercise of Family Responsibilities

Jo Bridgeman, Heather Keating and Craig Lind

This volume is the fourth in a series in which we have been exploring the conceptualization of responsibility in families and family law. In the first, *Responsibility, Law and the Family* (Bridgeman, Keating and Lind 2008) we set out to explore different conceptualizations of responsibility in family life, law and policy. The second, *Children, Family Responsibility and the State* (Lind and Keating 2008) focused upon the role of the state in fostering and meeting the responsibilities owed to children. The most recent, *Taking Responsibility, Law and the Changing Family* (Lind, Keating and Bridgeman 2011a) explored the role of the law in the acceptance, avoidance and allocation of family responsibilities in an era of increasing diversity in family life.

This volume develops our ideas about responsibility in relation to the transforming landscape of family life. It is a companion volume to *Taking Responsibility* but, whereas in that volume we were interested in the law's more formal or overarching role in the recognition of the responsibilities that people took for one another outside the bounds of traditional families, in this volume we are interested in the effects that legal regulation (and its absence) have on the day-to-day responsibilities that people in family relationships actually undertake (or wish to avoid). In other words, our focus in this volume is on the legal (or other) regulation of the exercise of family responsibilities. Although the distinctions we have drawn in focusing these volumes are neither firm nor inevitable they are, we believe, useful; they have allowed us to develop ideas about the roles that law plays (or wishes to play) in relation to family responsibilities; they have focused our attention at particular points across a spectrum of concerns that occupy commentators on family law and family life (ranging from law's recognition of family types to its involvement in regulating the detail of their living arrangements). Whereas in *Taking Responsibility* we analysed the power of the law to affect family status by allocating formal responsibilities to people in particular relationships with one another, in this volume we explore the effectiveness of law in the regulation of the care people actually take (or should take) of their loved ones.

Perhaps most importantly, the chapters in this volume highlight the limited reach of the law in the regulation of the caring responsibilities family members assume for one another. As Mavis Maclean and John Eekelaar have observed: '[W]hen members of a family are living together, the law is strangely reticent in articulating and enforcing the obligations they may owe to one another. That does not mean that they do not have duties to one another. But these duties may be only indirectly recognised or enforced by the law. Indeed, they may not be legal duties at all' (Maclean and Eekelaar 1997, 1–2; see too Vitor in this volume). The sense of obligation that people feel for one another and the work to which this gives rise may derive not from law but rather from their ethical position in relation to one another: a family ethic instilling a moral obligation of care. And that care is often left to family members to get on with, without legal acknowledgement and with little in the way of practical (or even notional) support (see Newnham in this volume). What legal regulation there is seems, at best, to be peripheral to the actualization of care.

But, of course, the law has both historic and prospective purchase (Cane 2002). People seek to use its power – or rather, its perceived power – when things go wrong; and their aim is to use it to control and police family responsibilities. In this volume we have set out to explore the role of the law in regulating family responsibilities when the people concerned are unable to resolve them (see Cain, Miles, Newnham, George, Lamont, and Manhas in this volume). We are also interested in the impact that legal regulation has on the care that people actually take in family settings when the law has no immediate, material purchase on their day-to-day lives (see Hobson and Fahlén, Collier, Masardo, Attar-Schwartz et al., Vitor, Keating and Bridgeman, Herring, and Kittay in this volume), and in whether or not the law ought to be changed to create a different impact.

Our interest in the concept of responsibility remains at the heart of this volume. But in this volume we focus on the way in which responsibility and regulation interact. Superficially we are minded to think that regulation – when approached by lawyers – implies legal regulation. In the context of family responsibility, particularly given our acceptance of the difficult boundary that exists between ideas of legal and moral or ethical responsibility, we are interested in the extent to which responsibility in families is regulated by law. The chapters in this volume thus explore the extent to which the law attempts to involve itself in the regulation of family responsibilities and its shortcomings and failings in doing so. To what extent are the responsibilities taken within families determined by moral or ethical norms, social expectations, economic regulation, for example, and to what extent does the law reinforce these rather than create them? But our authors are aware that, even where law appears to fail fully to 'regulate' responsibility, its attempts have an effect in the regulation of responsibility that emerges. As Paula Vitor (in this volume, 216) says: 'We might say that the law acts in an indirect way, assuming pre-existing family ethical and social values and rules, and taking advantage of its consequent behaviour, while accepting that there is not a strong enough foundation upon which to base a duty.'

Our focus in this collection is upon the legal regulation of responsibilities *within* family life. To paraphrase Alison Diduck in her chapter in our first volume, in this collection we ask what shape family law gives to our responsibilities to care for family members (2008, 265). In this introduction we consider the nature and content of responsibilities rather than obligations, duties or rights; the privatization of, and limits of public responsibility for, care; financial and caring responsibilities; the gendered nature of caring responsibilities; and fulfilling responsibilities in separated and fragmented families. We conclude with some thoughts on the role of the law in the regulation of family responsibilities.

## Responsibilities, Obligations, Duties and Rights

We have previously explored the concept of responsibility in the context of liberal, communitarian and relational approaches (Bridgeman and Keating 2008, 3–8; Lind, Keating and Bridgeman, 2011b); here we consider, in light of the chapters in this collection, the distinctions between the concepts of responsibility, obligation, and duty.

In relation to their families, people often draw no distinction between the concepts of responsibility, obligation and duty; academics likewise may consider them to be interchangeable. In his detailed analysis of legal and moral responsibilities, Peter Cane advances the view that duties and responsibilities are 'consistent'; 'A person under a legal duty has a prospective responsibility to fulfil that duty, and can be held historically responsible for failure to do so' (Cane 2002, 31). And in Cane's view, the relationship between responsibility and legal obligation is that '[t]he law's ethic of responsibility is an ethic of obligation, not of aspiration; of acceptable behaviour, not virtuous or supererogatory behaviour' (Cane 2002, 33–4). For Cane, therefore, responsibility is legally onerous. It has legal consequences that can take the form of sanctions. For John Eekelaar (2006, Chapter 5), on the other hand, the extent to which responsibilities and legal duties or obligations overlap is, at best, partial. For him responsibility necessarily imports an ideal of extra-legal obligation. It is both what people do by virtue of legal obligation and what they do beyond the requirements of the law. In other words, responsibility includes an aspirational element. Our view, expressed in *Taking Responsibility*, is that 'whilst family responsibility includes obligations and duties, it is more than the sum of these' (Lind, Bridgeman and Keating 2011b, 13). The tension between duties and obligations on the one hand, and responsibilities on the other, is central to the analyses offered by many of the authors in this volume. Jo Miles uses the distinction in her analysis of the financial consequences of relationship breakdown to demonstrate the way in which more powerful legal duties and obligations are attached to responsibilities that have more subtle legal consequences. Paula Vitor is concerned with this distinction in her analysis of the way in which we conceptualize the care owed to older people in our societies. In their chapter, Jo Bridgeman and Heather Keating also demonstrate a more tenuous relationship between ideas of responsibility and obligation (in which 'legal' obligation or duty seems to be the smallest part of what people do for their loved ones).

The relationship between responsibilities and rights has been at the heart of much social and political debate in recent years. In *Taking Responsibilities* we made much of the political interest in reasserting the need to counter the move towards rights by reawakening a communal sense of responsibility (Lind, Bridgeman and Keating 2011b, 8–10). In any examination of the way in which people, in their day-to-day care of one another, meet and fail to meet the responsibilities they owe other family members, the issue of rights cannot fail to be near at hand. Recognition of the rights of people has come to be used as a device through which we foster better conduct in others (Zander 1985; Dworkin 1990). In relation to the family that trend has been spelled out most significantly (and successfully) in relation to the rights of children (Freeman 1983; Eekelaar 1986; Fortin 2009). This, of course, could be taken yet further: in their chapter, for example, Shalhevet Attar-Schwartz, Ann Buchanan and Eirini Flouri report on their research finding that grandchildren would like to see their relationship with grandparents supported by a doctrine of rights – in which the right would be seen, not least, as the children's right to a relationship with their grandparents.

In several chapters in this volume the desire to foster responsible family behaviour by embracing a notion of rights is discussed and analysed. Exploring the promotion of responsibility through rights has led to questions both about possible extension of the contexts in which rights could be used and the success of such endeavours in areas where the rights discourse has already taken hold. The chapters by Paula Vitor, Jonathan Herring, Eva Kittay, and Shalhevet Attar-Schwartz et al. in this volume all, in various ways, consider the way in which rights – and legal rights, in particular – might be used to give recognition to and further foster and/or support responsibilities. Kittay, for example, comments in relation to responsibilities already being undertaken, that 'it is interesting that caregiving has been viewed primarily as a responsibility and not as a right' (307). Rather than seeing the relationship between rights and responsibilities as dichotomous, she argues for 'the right to meet those responsibilities' which arise from connections with others (304). In a similar vein, Attar-Schwartz, Buchanan and Flouri argue that the responsibilities that grandparents demonstrate they already take for their grandchildren would benefit from better legal recognition in the guise of 'rights'; once again, something akin to a 'right to be responsible'.

Other chapters consider areas where the rights discourse has already had an impact and where the emphasis is upon rights to foster or promote family responsibility. The rising importance of 'fathers' rights' discussed by Richard Collier in this volume, and the uses to which the state has put this momentum to re-engage parents in their responsibilities, may be seen to have had a positive impact on the way in which fathers do (increasingly, perhaps) take responsibility for their children. In her chapter, Annika Newnham points out how the advent of claims to rights has affected both the actual and perceived sharing of care when couples separate. The idea of responsibilities being less gendered – of there being a shift to more gender-neutral parental responsibilities – is fostered but without, she argues, a corresponding shift in the real responsibilities to provide actual day-to-day care. She concludes that rights affect responsibilities rhetorically but have less of an impact in the real allocation of care in family relationships. In contrast, Alex Masardo argues that, in cases in which shared residence is negotiated rather than asserted as of right, the responsibilities of parents are more evenly distributed. But it is also clear that rights cannot do all of the work that responsibility does in fostering better family care.

We remain of the view, therefore, that responsibility incorporates more than the duties and obligations that are owed to people; rights cannot account for all the responsible conduct that does and should occur within contemporary family relationships. And they can, therefore, only go some way towards providing the regulatory framework for responsibility. Vesting rights in people will create a minimum level of responsible conduct (as Cane suggests it should), but it will continue to fail to account for our grander ambitions to foster more responsible care, to support responsible caring and to recognize where responsible care has been taken. This is especially true where people accept and actually take responsibility for those to whom they are related and for those to whom they have a 'lesser' connection. In either case we, as a society, rely on the fact that people often choose either *not* to exercise their legal rights or choose to go beyond their legal obligations (Eekelaar 2006, 128) in providing care. There will, therefore, remain an ambit of caring activity that is responsible but that is beyond the scope of any rights discourse. And the questions we should ask ourselves revolve around the extent to which that conduct is beyond (legal or social) regulation.

Some have argued for a reframing of rights in the family context. In this regard the views of Martha Minow and Mary Lyndon Shanley, in their response to critiques of rights as abstract and individualistic, are instructive. They advocate '[a] theory of relational rights and responsibilities [which] would encompass not only individual freedoms but also rights to enter and maintain intimate associations consistent with public conceptions of the responsibilities those associations entail, underscoring the connection between families and the larger community' (Minow and Shanley 1997, 103). The two central features of their conceptualization of relational rights are, first, that rights are 'claims grounded in and arising from human relationships of varying degrees of intimacy' and secondly, it ensures that there is recognition of the connection between the family and its social, cultural and political context:

> Each intimate relationship is in turn embedded in ties among members of neighbours, religious and ethnic groups, fellow citizens, all of which are deeply affected but not entirely determined by the political system and economic circumstances. Connecting these relationships to a vibrant sense of responsibility would engage wide circles of people, including even public-policy makers and voters, who would need to consider what social and economic structures are

> necessary to permit continuous, caring human relationships especially responsive to those most dependent on such care. (Minow and Shanley 1997, 102)

Whilst this conceptualization of rights acknowledges the connections between individuals and the impact of social, economic and political contexts upon the fulfilment of their rights, its limitations remain in a focus upon entitlement – what the right-holder can make a claim to – and not upon care and concern for the other which is a normal feature of family relationships.

One of the best warnings against an over-reliance on rights as a mechanism for fostering better interpersonal conduct (and care, in particular) is contained in Onora O'Neill's critique of children's rights (O'Neill 1992). In the last third of the twentieth century, a powerful and unstoppable movement towards the legal inscription of children's rights had taken hold both in the domestic jurisdictions of Western nations and in the international community. O'Neill cautioned against thinking that this trend would foster a world in which children would live better lives in which they were provided with better care and more protection. Central to O'Neill's argument was the simple observation that 'children's fundamental rights are best grounded by embedding them in a wider account of fundamental obligations' (O'Neill 1992, 24). And although she acknowledged that rights could be the basis upon which obligations were founded, her concern was that only particular 'perfect' or 'complete' obligations could be derived from a framework of regulation that was based on rights. In other words, a right could only arise if a general obligation to particular individuals or groups was identifiable. Where the object of the obligation was less clear – where it was owed more generally, or where its better quality was something we wished to see fostered – only 'imperfect' or 'incomplete' obligations could be said to arise. And these, she argued, could have no counterpart in rights. In relation to children's rights O'Neill says:

> If we care about children's lives, we will have a number of good reasons not to base our arguments on appeals to children's fundamental rights. Some of these reasons are the theoretical difficulties of theories of fundamental rights. To look at rights is to look at what is ethically required indirectly by looking at what should be received. Constructivist accounts of what should be received are radically indeterminate, hence blurred. All rights-based approaches are incomplete in that they tell us nothing about what should be done when nobody has a right to its being done: they are silent about imperfect obligations. The view we get from the perspective of rights is not merely indirect, but blurred and incomplete. (O'Neill 1992, 39)

This sentiment can, we submit, be expanded to all rights claimed in family relationships. In this volume, therefore, although rights and their perfect obligation counterparts are considered, we are more interested in the impact of law on the imperfect obligations to which O'Neill pays so much attention. For us, responsibility in family life is often about people trying to meet those imperfect obligations and the personal and social discussions that surround their attempts to do so. What requires analysis – the kind of analysis our authors offer here – is the role of law in fostering, supporting or attempting to coerce this kind of responsibility.

## Taking Care Within Families

### *The privatization of care*

In her analysis of American law, society and policy which is to a degree, but by no means wholly, applicable to modern Britain, Martha Fineman exposes the extent to which 'the autonomy myth' ('ideas about autonomy and self sufficiency'), the allocation of the primary responsibility for dependency to the family and the institutions which support the privatization of care, operate to mask inevitable dependencies and the derivative dependencies of carers (2004, xiii). She presents a 'theory of collective responsibility for dependency' through which the social debt owed to carers would be recognized by the provision of financial and structural supports. In this volume Jonathan Herring echoes that call:

> Care work needs to be valued, acknowledged and rewarded effectively. That involves making it part of the wider community's responsibility. Care of those unable to care for themselves should be seen as one of society's most important tasks (Herring 2007, 244).

This assertion follows directly from his view that:

> Dependency itself is not undesirable. Dependency is often regarded as causing a loss of freedom and dignity. This is not, and should not, be so. We are all, or virtually all, dependent on others; and others are dependent on us. It is true that at different stages of life the extent and nature of dependency may vary. Further, it is often far from apparent in a caring relationship who is dependent on whom. In truth there is often give and take in the "carer" and "cared for" relationship. Their relationship is marked by interdependency. The "cared for" provides the "carer" with gratitude, love, acknowledgement and emotional support. Indeed often a "carer" will be "cared for" in another relationship. (Herring 2007, 244)

It is apparent that for both Fineman and Herring there are both public and private dimensions to the care that people provide for one another in family relationships. Alison Diduck has argued that family law should be understood as both private law – identifying which relationships count as family for the purposes of private regulation – and as public law: 'To be sure, family law is about promoting some idea of justice and welfare for, and perhaps even the rights of, individual members of the "family" group, but it is also about the nature and public value of dependence and independence and about regulating the balance of political, social and economic power in society as much as in the family' (Diduck 2008, 255). As both Diduck and Fineman point out, the principal purpose of family is the care of dependants (Diduck 2008, 255); publicly invested support institutions and structures and the expectations that they create have a profound impact upon the shape and activity of families (Manhas, Keating and Bridgeman, and Herring in this volume). The family is the primary location for the care of children. The essential maintenance, and emotional support, of the 'productive' worker occurs within the family. The ill are tended back to health, the elderly and frail are cared for and the long-term sick and disabled are nursed, all largely within the confines of the family. This essential work of care, upon which the operation of the public sphere depends, takes place in the privacy of the home. It is expected but unacknowledged, essential but unvalued, indispensible but invisible. Because of the way in which family life has changed (discussed further in *Taking Responsibility*) the private nature of caring is also often an individualized obligation: elderly spouses are interdependent; mothers provide personal care for children with extraordinary needs; women care for both children and parents (Lewis 2006, 105); the care of children is shared by people in two households. The view of care as a private, individual responsibility thus becomes further entrenched.

Particular challenges arise where caring responsibilities have to be discharged across separated households (Newnham, Masardo in this volume), or continents (Lamont in this volume) or, as is increasingly common, where the responsibilities are both to ascendants and to descendants or where they are particularly intense because of the particular needs of the dependant. In her chapter, Kiran Manhas argues that the judiciary, in the two Canadian cases which are the focus of her discussion (*Dassonville-Trudel (Guardian ad litem of) v Halifax Regional School Board*, 2004 NSCA 82; *McQueen v Nova Scotia (Coordinator for Home Care)*, 2006 NSSC 127), reinforced existing expectations of maternal care of children with extraordinary needs. She argues that the law, through the judgments in these two cases, perpetuated the privatization of caring responsibilities and the devaluation of care. A similar interest in the context of care is to be found in the chapter by Heather Keating and Jo Bridgeman. They examine intensive caring activity, privatized to the family with limited public support and with societal obstacles to individual fulfilment of caring responsibilities as the context for compassionate killings. Questions of societal responsibility are evaded, just as in cases of elderly abuse explored by Jonathan Herring, who argues that the explanation for elder abuse in terms of carer stress places responsibility for the abuse with either the older person or their carer, individualizing and privatizing the abuse. This is done at the same time as limits have been (and will continue to be) placed on public provision and support for care: the Equality and Human Rights Commission Report, *How Fair Is Britain?*, recently noted that the proportion of formal home care provided to older people had halved in England between 1994 and 2008 with local authorities concentrating upon the provision of critical, urgent or substantial needs and older people increasingly relying upon their spouses, children, friends and neighbours for the 'ordinary' day-to-day support they require (Equality and Human Rights Commission 2010, 528–32). But older people do not only require care: many are also relied upon as providers of care. Despite the recent policy to increase formal childcare, many parents are unable to afford the cost of good formal childcare or prefer for their children to be cared for by someone within their family; grandparents fulfil most of this (informal) need. They provide 26 per cent of all childcare (Equality and Human Rights Commission 2010, 564). However, as Shalhevet Attar-Schwartz, Ann Buchanan and Eirini Flouri comment in their chapter, grandparents' involvement in their grandchildren's lives – where they act as carer, mentor or confidante – has yet to receive formal recognition in law. It is time, therefore, that the issue of giving legal rights to grandchildren, which the Conservative Party promised to review in its 2010 manifesto and which is under consultation as part of the Family Justice Review initiated by the coalition government (Cabinet Office 2010, 20; Conservative Party 2010, 42; Ministry of Justice 2010, 6), was properly resolved.

Of course, devoting time to caring work has consequences for people's paid employment, their income, health, leisure and life plans. The Equality and Human Rights Commission concluded that further research is required into questions of 'autonomy (choice, control and empowerment)' in the division of responsibilities for paid and unpaid work (Equality and Human Rights Commission 2010, 563). But whilst caring for someone we care about is the demonstration of a choice, it is not an unconstrained choice; it is not a choice in the sense of the rational economic choice which is often assumed by policy makers. It is, we suggest, a moral or ethical choice arrived at in the context of social expectations of the 'proper thing to do' (Finch 1994; Barlow and Duncan 2000, 38).

### *Money and care-giving responsibilities*

In *Moral Boundaries*, Joan Tronto separates care into its component parts of caring about (identifying need), taking care of (taking the responsibility for caring), care-giving (providing the care) and receiving care (Tronto 1993, 105–8), each involving, respectively, the values of attentiveness (in order to recognize the needs of the other), responsibility, competence (resources) and responsiveness (127–36). Seeing family responsibilities in financial terms is, Joan Tronto suggests, a form of 'taking care of'. Money alone does not fulfil needs; it must be converted into care (107). Many of the chapters in this volume explore questions about the relationship between caring and financial responsibilities. Is family responsibility primarily a matter of care? Can it be met – in part, at least – by financial arrangements which see particular people making particular payments? Can we fulfil our family responsibilities by paying those to whom we owe responsibility? Or by paying others to fulfil our obligations for us? Do we behave responsibly where we pay others to fulfil our caring roles?

One concern evident in many of the chapters in this volume is the role of the husband/partner/father as financial provider or breadwinner in family contexts.

This concern arises as problematic because of our changing expectations of family member labour market participation and our changing attitude towards the way in which parenting should be conducted. Fathers are said to desire a more actively involved, hands-on caring role in raising their children (or, at least, policy is informed by that belief). Policies aimed at promoting 'good' or 'responsible' fatherhood have, therefore, become the order of the day (Hobson and Fahlén, Cain, Collier, Lamont, Masardo, Miles, Newnham in this volume).

In this context, we must question the extent to which providing financial support for family members still constitutes an adequate performance of family responsibilities. If it is, what is the role of the state in intervening to establish and enforce those responsibilities? One recent illustration of government policy provides at least some insight into this problem. There is no doubt that the Child Support Act 1991 was introduced to effect a seachange in terms of attitudes regarding the continuing responsibility of non-resident fathers for their children (whether they have separated from them or never lived with them) (Keating 1995). However, while many would strongly endorse the principle that fathers should contribute towards the maintenance of their children (and much had been wrong with the pre-existing court-ordered maintenance system), the legislation took a narrow view of what responsibility entailed: parenting equalled paying (ibid.) The law would be coercive in promoting responsible behaviour. The tension between this and the policy aims operating in other areas of family law discussed in this volume was clear: what mattered was that child support was paid irrespective of whether this meant that the father, for example, would be left with too little money to travel to have contact with and play a part in the life and development of his children. But since nearly all mothers using the child support scheme were on benefits, the money collected went to the state to offset the benefits paid; under the original scheme the child would be no better off at all.[1] In this sense, then, the father's (forced) responsibility seemed to be to the state; it might certainly have been experienced as such.

The difficulties which beset the original scheme and its subsequent modifications have been well documented (see, for example, Wikeley 2006) and demonstrate vividly the obstacles the state faces in regulating this aspect of family responsibility. But the latest manifestation of the scheme provides a further opportunity to consider the relationship between responsibility, care and finance. The aim of the Child Maintenance and Enforcement Commission (established by the Child Maintenance and Other Payments Act 2008), which has taken over the running of the Child Support Agency, is to maximize the numbers of children whose parents live apart and for whom effective support arrangements are in place. But, under this scheme, the preference is for parents to agree the terms of support.

1 This is no longer the case: following a series of changes, from April 2010 all child support paid by the non-resident parent goes to the child with no deductions from benefits paid to the family. Whether this policy can survive given the government's plans to reduce spending remains to be seen.

As Jo Miles notes in her chapter, despite the development of policy encouraging private agreements, the law denies these agreements legal force and completely takes over control of assessment and enforcement if the parents are unable to agree (94). From the increased use being made by the Child Support Agency of its (improved) enforcement powers, it seems reasonable to infer that parents are no more likely to be able to agree now than they have been in the past (CMEC 2010).

In her chapter, Jo Miles focuses upon financial responsibilities which adults owe one another upon relationship breakdown. She examines the balance between autonomy and protection (96) and considers questions of family responsibility through the 'axes' of individual, relational and state responsibilities. The provision of care, and paying for it, are, she demonstrates, inevitably intertwined. Individual decisions, relational agreements and state determinations about family finances inevitably reflect the value attributed to the provision of care.

*The gendered nature of caring responsibilities*

Jo Miles' examination of individual, relational and state responsibility post-separation also reveals the gendered nature of caring responsibility and the enduring lack of value given to caring activity. Despite many significant changes to family life, family responsibilities remain deeply gendered (Diduck 2008; Equality and Human Rights Commission 2010, 558–60). Despite the introduction in the UK of measures affecting working and family life (including the introduction of paternity leave, the right to request flexible working and investment in childcare) which can be understood to support a shift from a single breadwinner to a dual earner model, the gendered nature of care work endures (see also Hobson and Fahlén in this volume). These policies are, as Jane Lewis explains, directed at increasing women's employment rather than being concerned to support the fulfilment of caring responsibilities (Lewis 2006, 106). There is a substantial body of research which indicates that whilst women undertake more paid work outside the home, the contribution of men to domestic work and childcare in the home has not altered to the same extent (Lewis 2001; Lewis and Campbell 2007). It is predominantly women who take time off to look after sick children, including 60 per cent of women who earn the same or more than their partners. Working mothers with children put twice as many hours into housework as their partners despite the possibility of 'role reversal' in earnings (Harkness 2005, 1).

Inevitably, because caring responsibilities are gendered, many of the chapters examine the gendered nature of family responsibilities; they do this in the context of post-separation residence (Newnham), migration (George, Lamont), the care of children with exceptional needs (Manhas, Keating and Bridgeman), and the care of the elderly (Vitor, Herring). Ruth Cain's discussion of responsible motherhood is situated within research which shows that women undertake the majority of domestic work and childcare, whether they undertake paid work or not. This has an impact upon the wage levels they command, the leisure time available to them and to their sense of devaluation in the performance of both roles. In the context of the family policy of the New Labour government, she sets out to expose the 'affective burdens of feminisation and the care vacuum in neoliberalism' (83).

Robert George's analysis of relocation cases in England and Wales also exposes gender problems. Because mothers are primary carers in the majority of post-separation cases, the outcomes and the legal reasoning found in them are almost inevitably gendered. Ruth Lamont's chapter engages with gender in a slightly different way. She criticizes the failure of the EU to address the nature of, and reasons for, 'child abduction' within the EU, resulting from changing family forms and changing patterns of migration. She suggests that EU law is guided by the belief that child abduction commonly involves a father snatching his child whereas the reality is that it more often involves a mother returning to her country of origin to facilitate fulfilment of her caring responsibilities for her child: either by extending the network of care by returning to her wider family or by removing herself to a jurisdiction in which she can find paid work.

Several chapters address the way in which the gendered nature of fathering is itself changing. Alex Masardo's interviews with fathers in France and England with shared residence of their children post-separation provide examples of fathers who, at least in those circumstances, wished to be actively involved in the day-to-day care of their children. Richard Collier offers a more general reflective retrospective of the family policy of the New Labour government in the UK between 1997 and 2010. He reviews policy changes which 'challenge the assumption that families are synonymous with mothers' with respect to, for example, birth registration, early years care and parental responsibility (47). There is a gap, he suggests, between family policy directed at supporting and encouraging the involvement of fathers and the reality of fathering which lies in the 'emotional and affective dimensions' of fathering as a 'daily, emotional, intimate practice' (59). As the chapters by both Richard Collier, and Barbara Hobson and Susanne Fahlén demonstrate, the factors affecting the ability and willingness of fathers to spend less time working and more time engaged in care of their children are manifold (and include, for example, the organizational culture of the workplace). The power of the state to overcome these 'silent codes and shared sets of assumptions' (Hobson and Fahlén, 35) (such as a culture of overtime being an indicator of productivity) is, at best, limited.

### *Care and responsibility in the fragmented family*

The law's engagement with responsibility and the family has, perhaps, been most profoundly affected by changes to family life that have occurred in the last 50 years. The advent of easier divorce, multiple marriages, unmarried cohabitation and extramarital parenting have all created new tensions in family life. The fragmented family has required a more thorough analysis of family responsibility. And the rise in intra-familial disputes is heralded not only by fragmenting families, but also by growing acceptance that family responsibility is a matter of public importance and that the public/private dichotomy is an unacceptable determinant of the boundaries of state interest and of legal regulation. Whereas caring responsibilities in intact families (in the absence of significant harm to children or other serious harm to other family members) were seen as a matter of private regulation, the advent of the fragmented family has seen a rise in the need for those responsibilities to be subjected to external scrutiny. Indeed, Mavis Maclean and John Eekelaar have reflected that the closer in relationship people are, the less likely is the law to be involved in sorting out differences as these are resolved within 'the dynamic of the entire relationship' such that '[r]esorting to law has negative implications which outweigh the benefits of the interactive relationship'. Where the relationship has broken down, however, differences take on greater significance and the reasons against resorting to law in order to resolve them diminish (Maclean and Eekelaar 1997, 2).

The law has, therefore, become more profoundly and more regularly involved in family disputes. And yet, perhaps most interestingly, its tendency to privatize family responsibilities has not abated. As Jo Miles notes in her chapter, the courts are now much more willing to uphold a prenuptial agreement (most recently affirmed in the Supreme Court decision in *Radmacher v Granatino* [2010] UKSC 42), and consent orders (where the parties negotiate their own agreement in the shadow of the law that is then ratified by the court) after divorce are still very common. The failed Family Law Act 1996 provides a further illustration of the way in which law has tried to exhort people to make their own responsible arrangements (in that case, in relation to divorce). Even the latest version of the child support system – which was once so coercive – now encourages parents to make their own arrangements for the support of their children (see also Miles in this volume). In this volume Annika Newnham's chapter provides perhaps the best illustration of the law's (in her view misplaced and failed) aspiration to limit its own intervention in the regulation of the actual care provided in fragmented families. In the context of the care of children after parental separation, the law wishes to enforce a shared care ethic (in the way that it believes there to be one in intact families). But it holds back from enforcing that ethic in the day-to-day care that is necessary in a fragmented family setting. In a similar vein, Ruth Lamont's chapter exposes the impact of the summary return principle that operates under the Hague Convention when children are abducted to or wrongfully retained in a country by one parent in contravention of the custody rights of the other. Such abductions are more frequently by mothers seeking to return to their own countries yet 'the control exercised over how the responsibility for post-separation care is carried out may effectively hinder the carrying out of care responsibilities' (Lamont 185) by the parent with care, by denying her access to the informal support networks that would enable her to work to fulfil her responsibilities. And, as Robert George comments (in relation to domestic relocation disputes), 'the law's regulation of post-separation parenting is brought into especially sharp relief … where the issues at stake are so high, the parties so polarised, and the outcomes of the decision often irreversible' (George 154). But even in sharp relief the issue of the particular day-to-day care of children is not being addressed by the courts.

Instead it is only interested in settling broad living arrangements which will have a profound effect on the care given to – and the parental ability to provide care for – children.

This tension between law's involvement in the resolution of disputes, and its failure to grasp the particulars of the care issues that arise in those disputes, propel us to enquire into the nature of the legal regulation of the post-separation family. Clearly, regulation of post-separation families is occurring where the parties are unable to agree or one of them takes unilateral action. But in its response, is the law unable to see the obstacles it places in the way of those with caring responsibilities? Or is this part of a larger 'responsibilization' process, where parties are expected to 'get over' their differences and look beyond their own interests? In Alex Marsado's study, parents appear to do exactly that; in the light of a perception that the law requires them to cooperate they appear to cooperate fairly successfully to provide shared care for their children. In Annika Newnham's analysis, on the other hand, the imposition of shared residence regimes by courts seems to have little bearing on the way in which care is performed in the post-divorce families which these regimes are designed to govern. It is as if the law's encouragement of responsibility works on those who are responsive to its lessons, but fails to work on those who are not.

In her analysis of both divorce and parental responsibility Helen Reece (2003; 2006) has argued that a transformation has taken place: 'responsibility has become a mode of thought. In the context of parenting, this means that to a large extent there is no longer a right way to parent: good parenting is now an attitude, and an important part of that attitude is being prepared to learn' (Reece 2006, 470). She warns that as responsibility has now become an attitude, it is a continuum and that this means 'one's attitude can be more or less reflective but it can never be reflective enough' (2006, 483). In her view, this means parents can always be found lacking and this enables the law to be 'uniquely interventionist' (2006, 483). In this volume our authors have attempted to address the ways in which that interventionism works.

## Conclusion: The Regulation of Family Responsibilities

Day after day, year in, year out, parents, grandparents, adult children, spouses and partners act responsibly in providing care for members of their families. Most of this work is invisible to the law. In this volume we hope to shine some light on the fulfilment, the *taking*, of family responsibilities. But we wish to do more than just to 'notice' what people do. Our ambition is to examine the extent to which the law is involved in shaping that caregiving. We wish to explore the nature of the law's attempt to open up the family to scrutiny and to regulate it for *responsible* care. We have argued that responsible conduct is behaviour beyond the reach of legal obligation. But we have also noted – as our authors note – the impact that law and legal structures have on the care that people provide for their families.

The law is a social institution which – with others – creates the expectations against which family members negotiate their family responsibilities even when it does not directly intervene in their daily lives. In 2003 Helen Reece made this argument thoroughly and convincingly in relation to the state's attempt to reform divorce law (Reece 2003). In this volume Alex Masardo makes a similar argument. The approach the law takes to shared residence influences the way in which the parties to a potential dispute about childcare after separation resolve their differences in that regard. He observes that the law's (historical) support for a resident/non-resident dichotomy presents a goal that encourages conflict between parents as they both attempt to achieve the stronger parental role; the one who achieves residence obtains the trump card. He tries to demonstrate that this tension can be averted if the law embraces shared residence. Where parents feel an inevitable move towards the formal sharing of care, he argues, they are less likely to be involved in the kind of conflict that is recognized as damaging to both adults and their children. Barbara Hobson and Susanne Fahlén (in this volume) make a similar argument in relation to paid work and the progress that has been made towards the equalization of the male and female roles in childcare. Where the state embraces a policy along these lines and transforms the law to reflect that policy – by making generous parental leave provisions which require both parents to take part – it changes the pattern of care in the direction of the transformed policy.

Law, reflecting family policy, can therefore attempt to influence the approach to private family ordering; law is fulfilling a 'responsibilizing' ambition. However, we should be cautious of thinking that law's ambition to encourage responsibility is translated easily or directly into an ability to frame negotiations about the way in which care will be shared between family members. If, as we have argued above, responsibility extends beyond legal obligations and duties and the ability of the state to affect changes in behaviour through law and policy is limited, we cannot hold out too great a hope for its success in achieving these ends. As Newnham (in this volume) shows, we have to embrace a degree of scepticism about the power of law to influence behaviour in this way. Whereas the law may wish to see parenting shared after separation, a nominal (legal) sharing of care will not necessarily make people take their caring responsibilities any more seriously than they already do. Even in Hobson and Fahlén's analysis of 'successful' family policy we are warned that the degree of uptake of gender neutral parental leave is not a safe indicator of a greater equality in the actual sharing of care. Law like that envisaged in the Shared Parenting Bill 2010 – which tries to compel the sharing of care after separation – may, therefore, be misguided.

Of course, that is not to suggest that law has no impact. Indeed Masado's and Hobson and Fahlén's work demonstrates empirically that some impact is felt in the way in which responsibility is borne. Family policy promoted in law will filter down into practice; legislation is advertised and provides privileges and punishments for particular behaviour, while court-based rulings – although fact-based, particularistic determinations – provide legal principles that are filtered into popular practice (at least in part) because of the legal advice provided by practitioners. As Robert George (in this volume) observes, whilst family responsibilities may exceed obligations, the law can regulate who gets to fulfil those responsibilities and hence whose way of fulfilling them is to be privileged.

There is a further dimension to law's engagement with family responsibilities that is not captured by any discussion of intra-familial disputes. Problems around family responsibility often involve people other than those within the family. They may, for example, take the form of challenges to the public support provided to fulfil them (Manhas in this volume). Or they may not be about disputes at all. They may be about practices of responsibility which involve people outside the family that are, as yet, beyond the scope of legal regulation. Law's reach is not universal in this regard. The state may not yet have recognized the importance of regulating particular ways of fulfilling family responsibilities (Kittay in this volume). The way in which disputes are resolved involving others and debates about the state's role in the broader provision of care and support for families will all contribute to setting the parameters for family care and responsibility. It remains possible that some of the responsibilities discussed in this volume will be allocated to the state. Others will be revived in the hands of family members who have either fulfilled those roles traditionally, or to family members who will find themselves incorporated into new categories of responsible family members. The chapters in this volume inform our understanding of how in all these ways – in allocating formal care, in structuring frameworks for the provision of care, and in providing dispute resolution – the law continues to participate in the fostering, supporting and coercing of responsible family behaviour.

## References

Barlow, A. and Duncan, S. 2000. Supporting families? New Labour's Communitarianism and the 'Rationality Mistake': Part I. *Journal of Social Welfare and Family Law*, 22, 23–42.

Bartlett, K. 1988. Re-Expressing Parenthood. *Yale Law Journal*, 98, 293–340.

Bridgeman, J. and Keating, H. 2008. Introduction: Conceptualising Family Responsibility, in *Responsibility, Law and the Family*, edited by J. Bridgeman, H. Keating and C. Lind. Aldershot: Ashgate, 1–17.

Bridgeman, J. Keating, H. and Lind, C. 2008. *Responsibility, Law and the Family*, Aldershot: Ashgate.

Cabinet Office. 2010. *The Coalition: Our Programme for Government*. London: Crown Copyright.

Cane, P. 2002. *Responsibility in Law and Morality*. Oxford: Hart.

CMEC. 2010. More than 800,000 children benefit from child maintenance payments. (http.//childmaintenance.org/en/news/article13.html) (27 January 2010).

Conservative Party. 2010. *Invitation to Join the Government of Britain: The Conservative Manifesto 2010*. London: Conservative Party.

Diduck, A. 2008. Family Law and Family Responsibility, in *Responsibility, Law and the Family*, edited by J. Bridgeman, H. Keating and C. Lind. Aldershot: Ashgate, 251–68.

Dworkin. R. 1990. *A Bill of Rights for Britain*. London: Chatto and Windus.

Eekelaar, J. 1986. The Emergence of Children's Rights. *Oxford Journal of Legal Studies*, 6, 161–82.

Eekelaar, J. 2006. *Family Law and Personal Life*. Oxford: Oxford University Press.

Equality and Human Rights Commission. 2010. *How Fair Is Britain? Equality, Human Rights and Good Relations in 2010*. London: Equality and Human Rights Commission (www.equalityhumanrights.com) (accessed 18 October 2010).

Finch, J. 1994. The Proper Thing to Do, in *A Reader on Family Law*, edited by J. Eekelaar and M. Maclean. Oxford: Oxford University Press, 63–98.

Fineman, M.A. 2004. *The Autonomy Myth: A Theory of Dependency*. New York: The New Press.

Fortin, J. 2009. *Children's Rights and the Developing Law*. Cambridge: Cambridge University Press.

Freeman, M. 1983. *The Rights and Wrongs of Children*. London: Frances Pinter.

Harkness, S. 2005. Employment, work patterns and unpaid work: An analysis of trends since the 1970s. ESRC Report (www.esrc.ac.uk).

Herring, J. 2007. Where Are the Carers in Healthcare Law and Ethics? *Legal Studies*, 27, 51–73.

Keating, H. 1995. Children Come First? *Contemporary Issues in Law*, 1, 29–44.

Kittay, E.F. 1999. *Love's Labor: Essays on Women, Equality and Dependency*. New York and London: Routledge.

Lewis, J. 2001. The Decline of the Male Breadwinner Model: Implications for Work and Care. *Social Politics*, 152–69.

Lewis, J. 2006. Employment and Care: The Policy Problem, Gender Equality and the Issue of Choice. *Journal of Comparative Policy Analysis*, 8, 103–14.

Lewis, J. and Campbell, M. 2007. UK Work/Family Balance Policies and Gender Equality, 1997–2005. *Social Politics*, 14, 4–30.

Lind, C. and Keating, H. 2008. *Children, Family Responsibility and the State*. Oxford: Wiley-Blackwell.

Lind. C., Keating, H. and Bridgeman, J. 2011a. *Taking Responsibility, Law and the Changing Family*. Aldershot: Ashgate.

Lind. C, Keating, H. and Bridgeman, J. 2011b. Introduction: Taking Family Responsibility or Having It Imposed?, in *Taking Responsibility, Law and the Changing Family*, edited by C. Lind, H. Keating and J. Bridgeman. Aldershot: Ashgate.

Maclean, M. and Eekelaar, J. 1997. *The Parental Obligation: A Study of Parenthood Across Households*. Oxford: Hart.

Ministry of Justice. 2010. *Call for Evidence: Family Justice Review*. London: Crown Copyright.

Minow, M. and Shanley, M.L. 1997. Revisioning the Family: Relational Rights and Responsibilities, in *Reconstructing Political Theory: Feminist Perspectives*, edited by M.L. Shanley and U. Narayan. Cambridge: Polity Press, 84–108.

O'Neill, O. 1992. Children's Rights and Children's Lives, in *Children, Rights and the Law*, edited by P. Alston, S. Parker and J. Seymour. Oxford: Clarendon.

Reece, H. 2003. *Divorcing Responsibly*. Oxford: Hart.

Reece, H. 2006. From Parental Responsibility to Parenting Responsibly, in *Law and Sociology: Current Legal Problems 2005*, Volume 8, edited by M. Freeman. Oxford: Oxford University Press.

Tronto, J. 1993. *Moral Boundaries: The Political Argument for an Ethic of Care*. New York: Routledge.

Wikeley, N. 2006. *Child Support: Law and Policy*. Oxford: Hart.

Zander, M. 1985. *A Bill of Rights?* 3rd edition. London: Sweet and Maxwell.

# PART I
# The Gendered Nature of Family Responsibility

# Chapter 2
# Parent's Work–Life Balance: Beyond Responsibilities and Obligations to Agency and Capabilities

Barbara Hobson and Susanne Fahlén[1]

Throughout much of the last century legal interventions around parenting responsibilities were highly gendered: responsibilities for care were accorded to mothers and breadwinning to fathers (Lewis 2002). The legal framing of fatherhood was constructed around men's economic responsibility to support children, whether they were born in wedlock or not, married or divorced, whether they were biological fathers or social fathers (Hobson and Morgan 2002). However, in the last decades of the twentieth century the winds began shifting in the direction of extending care-giving rights/policies to men and employment rights/policies to women.

This chapter explores the impact of such policies upon parental aspirations to share parenting responsibilities and the abilities of fathers and mothers to change their working practices. Adopting an agency and capabilities perspective, this chapter analyses the findings of a number of studies across Europe and concludes that while the law has been instrumental in changing levels of aspirations among parents and norms for shared parenting, there has been much less of an impact upon the practices and responsibilities in the daily care of children. The gendered life course effects of this unequal division of unpaid work persist.

The shift towards the extension of care-giving rights/policies to men and employment rights/policies to women occurred first in Scandinavian societies in the 1970s. The Swedish case is a good example of how the state's role in the shaping of family responsibilities changed dramatically, from interventions to enforce fathers' economic obligations to laws ensuring fathers' caring rights. As early as the 1920s and 1930s, there were laws that required mothers to name the father in order to receive state support, and the creation of special agencies to track down delinquent fathers to make them pay (Bergman and Hobson 2002).[2]

1 This research has been supported by a European Science Foundation grant administered through the Swedish Research Council and by the FP6 Network of Excellence REWOWE.

2 In some respects these laws and interventions were not unlike those put into effect in the US and UK to force fathers to pay child support ('deadbeat dad' initiatives),

However, by the 1970s a new set of policies emerged in Sweden to promote women's participation in employment and men's participation in care-giving, a response to social demographic changes: rising divorce rates, low marriage rates with correspondingly high levels of cohabitation, and labour shortages (Bergman and Hobson 2002; Hobson 2003). The result of numerous government commissions on the family, children, and women's employment (Klinth and Johansson 2010) was a sweeping set of policies and incentives for reconciling employment with care: individual taxation being the most radical as it treated each individual in a couple separately in the system and tax deductions for dependent wives and children were eliminated. This meant that families were rewarded for every krona women earned (Gustafsson and Bruyn-Hundt 1991). Other policies supporting the dual earner family included publicly supported day-care services, the right to reduce working hours during the first eight years, and the first gender-neutral parental leave scheme.

The interventions to promote a dual earner family model set in motion a reconfiguration of state, market and family relations, what is known as the welfare triangle in comparative studies of welfare regimes (Esping-Andersen 1990; Hobson and Morgan 2002). Within the family the strong incentives for having two earners, particularly the individual taxation, signalled the demise of the full-time housewife;[3] though most mothers of young children were working a part-time 20–25 hour week (Sundström 1991). From the municipal/state side of the triangle, the expansion of and state subvention of day-care centres for children under three years implied a dramatic shift in the sharing of responsibilities for the care of young children between the state and family. Regarding the rights and responsibilities of fatherhood, cohabitant fathers were given the same rights as married fathers and expected to take on the same caring responsibilities, which we analysed as a shift from cash to care (Hobson and Morgan 2002).

The dual earner family would become the family norm in most European societies, but the bundle of family friendly policies in the Scandinavian policy packages have not necessarily transferred to other societies; including publicly supported daycare, generous care leave benefits and flexible work options. Nonetheless, the weakening of the male breadwinner norm that began in Scandinavian countries in the 1970s and 1980s presaged new rights and interpretations of gendered responsibilities for care and employment that would spread across European societies, reaching even strong male breadwinner societies, such as the Netherlands, Germany and the UK (Lewis 1997; Hobson et al. 2006). As was the case in Scandinavian countries, activating women into the labour force was a crucial driver for the weakening of a single male breadwinner model. But there were also other factors in the 1990s, recognized as a period of welfare state retrenchment and global economic pressures that would contribute

---

but as was true in Sweden in the 1930s, they were difficult to implement (Hobson and Morgan 2002).

3 By the end of the 1980s the number of full-time housewives was below 10 percent.

to the declining salience of a male breadwinner norm (Lewis et al. 2008). These factors included the unsustainability of pension systems built around a single earner (Esping-Andersen 1990), low fertility rates in countries with few policies that supported mothers' ability to reconcile family with employment (Hobson and Oláh 2006) and the diminishing number of protected male jobs over one's lifetime as well as declining male wages (Walker et al. 2000).

Unlike the evolution of family policies in Scandinavian countries in the 1970s, in which work/family policies emerged from specific coalitions of political actors – feminists, social democratic party members and unions – and were seeded in institutions, in the 1990s, a supra-national actor, the EU, played a key role in the creation of new rights and discourses for women's care-giving and men's employment, such as EU directives addressing the rights for care leave as well as the Barcelona Summit that created targets for childcare places that would facilitate women's activation into the labour market. In addition, EU laws removed some of the formal barriers against equal treatment of women workers (Hervey and O'Keefe 1996) and fathers' rights to care were underscored in the Parental Leave directive.

The EU became a forum for new actors to put forward new agendas and discourses and created norms for a dual earner family model. A new discourse emerged in Europe on work–life balance (WLB) that acknowledged the rights and responsibilities of a family with two adult earners. A range of innovative WLB policies were developed by different national governments, including job sharing and flexible work arrangements and working time accounts, which allow workers to build up time credits during periods in the life course in which workers have fewer care-giving responsibilities. Policy documents affirmed the importance of men's participation in care and women's participation in employment as EU goals for creating a gender balance in work and family life. The balanced participation of women and of men in both the labour market and in family life is an essential aspect of the development of society, and maternity, paternity and the rights of children are eminent social values to be protected by society, the member states and the European Community (2000/C 218/02, 5).

Work–life balance has become a discursive refrain in EU discourse and policymaking that assumes optimal outcomes: that a better balance in work and family life will result in *greater productivity*, *efficiency*, *gender equality*, and *child well-being*. However, greater productivity and efficiency (market goals) do not always fit neatly with goals of gender equality and child well-being. Activation of mothers into the labour market (efficiency) without WLB policies that allow them to reconcile employment with having a family do not result in optimal conditions. Considering the well-being of children, we see a growing number of lone mothers who have lost their benefits to be full-time carers and face coercive activation policies (welfare to work strategy) without corresponding affordable care services. Hence the increasing levels of time poverty and economic poverty among lone mothers across European countries (Goodin et al. 2008). Considering gender equality, we see two patterns that reflect the disjuncture between WLB goals and the possibilities to combine employment and care-giving. For women who are unable to combine employment with having a family, the choice is often not to have children. The low fertility rates in many countries with weak WLB policies have been analysed as the incoherence effect (McDonald 2000; Hobson and Oláh 2006), the incompatibility between rising aspirations for gender equality in the family and employment and weak institutions to support these aspirations. For men, the incoherence effect can be seen in the gap between the rising expectations of fathers who seek to become more engaged in care of their children, that have led to new rights for fathering and care, and the barriers standing in the way of exercising them.

Despite the emergence of rights and discourses for work–life balance in which women and men are expected to be both carers and earners, there remain wide variations in work–life balance policies across European societies, even when European rights exist. From the policy level, these rights may not be implemented or may only be given inadequate protection in national laws. From the workplace organizational side, research shows that the pressures for increased productivity and competitiveness in the global economy can undercut the ability of workers to make claims for WLB (Fagan et al. 2006; Perrons et al. 2006). These pressures translate into greater work intensification, precarious work situations and unstable futures for individual workers and their families (Perrons et al. 2006). Seen from the individual parent within a household, we see an agency gap between WLB rights and policies and the abilities of mothers and fathers to exercise them. This agency gap not only varies across countries but also within them, reflecting resources and means in situated agency: including differences by gender, ethnic/minority groups and class (economic and educational resources) and their intersections.

In this chapter we analyse the agency gap between the existence of WLB policies and the ability of parents to exercise their rights using a framework derived from Amartya Sen's theory of capabilities and agency in which agency is nested within institutional, and societal/cultural contexts (Sen 1992; 2003). In the first section, we apply Sen's capabilities approach in the context of WLB and family responsibilities. Then we focus on two policy areas applied in European societies that have emerged from European law and discourse for WLB: rights to reduce hours and to parental leave. Parental leave in our era embraces paternity leave and daddy quotas which aim to redistribute parenting responsibilities, that is, to promote a greater sharing of care-giving responsibilities. As gendered norms are important conversion factors in the capabilities framework, in the final section we analyse the growing gap between norms/values and practices for WLB. We conclude with a discussion of the possibilities for change.

## Shifting the Theoretical Terrain

The policy and discourse on family responsibilities have revolved around the obligations and rights of parenting. Our purpose in presenting an alternative paradigm is to shift the debates from responsibilities to capabilities and the agency of mothers and fathers to achieve a work–life balance that allows them the choice to be carers and earners. Although WLB in political discourse is a strategy for supporting instrumental goals of increasing labour force activity and incentives for higher fertility (EC 2002; 2003; MacInnes 2006), from a capabilities perspective it is a value in itself in which quality of life is at its core. Weak capabilities for WLB can be seen in work–family conflicts, ill health, and lack of contact with children. In this chapter, with its focus on shifting familial responsibilities, work–life balance policies are defined as those that both (1) enable parents to participate in employment and care; and (2) create a more equitable division of care-giving responsibilities.

*A dynamic model*

Much of the research on WLB, both time budget studies and analyses of policy outcomes, suggest that there has not been much change in the organization of carework within the family. Women still bear the responsibility for caring and men the responsibility for earning, despite the dramatic rises in women's labour force participation and the new proactive polices to increase men's share of carework (Blossfield and Drobnic 2001; Gornick and Meyers 2008) and the gender equality discourse for WLB at the European and national level. Alongside this ostensible stasis in WLB, there is actually more fluidity than is reflected in the outcomes or statistics on the division of paid and unpaid work responsibilities in families.[4] Not only the declining salience of the male breadwinner norm, but also the meaning of fatherhood have moved more toward both norms for active fathering and men's expressed values to be more engaged fathers (Hobson and Morgan 2002). This is especially true in Northern European countries (Smith 2008). In those countries with proactive policies for men to take up carework, we can begin asking the question: what are men's capabilities to be earners and carers?

The capabilities approach poses a frontal challenge to preference theory, which often assumes unchanging situations (Becker 1991; Hakim 2000). In the case of preferences that shape employment and family choices, Catherine Hakim has argued that there are a priori cultural values and lifestyles that determine whether mothers are career or family oriented. Yet her account belies the fluid and dynamic aspects of the organization of care and breadwinning in families over the life course, which are recast and renegotiated (Man Kee 2007). Moreover it does not recognize the universe of constraints (both structural features of employment or the moral rationalities and normative frameworks that inhibit change (Crompton

4 For example, in our current survey, Hobson and Fahlén (2009a) found that many fathers who are not taking formal parental leave work around the system, for example leave work early or work from home. One Norwegian research team found that fathers of young children reduced their actual hours, though not their contractual hours (see Dommermuth et al. 2007).

and Harris 1998; Duncan 2005). Hence it is important to develop an agency framework that asks different questions about potential freedoms. Would women and men systematically prefer different options if they had real opportunities to choose? (Sen 2003; Lee and McCann 2006; Hobson and Fahlén 2009a).

### *A multi-layered approach*

The capabilities approach is essentially multi-layered as it nests individual agency and capabilities within the institutional and societal/normative context, what Sen calls the capability set. Our analysis of capabilities for WLB within a European context includes individual/household, institutional, and societal/cultural factors. It acknowledges differences in situated agency (variations in resources and means); however, it underscores the importance of institutional context for entitlements and their implementation. Furthermore, the capability framework recognizes that institutional contexts not only shape access to resources, but also the subjective experiential level of agency (Hobson et al. 2011). In our studies of gender and WLB, we operationalize this level of agency as the ability to claim one's rights to a WLB, which can often challenge gendered norms in the family and workplace (Hobson and Fahlén 2009a; 2009b).

There are institutional path dependencies in the gendered construction of different policies around caring and earning that shape and are shaped by gendered norms of care, which have been characterized as 'gender cultures' (Pfau-Effinger 2005; Gregory and Milner 2009). Yet this concept ignores the differences in 'gender cultures' among mothers and fathers across and within different societies in their values around breadwinning and care and attitudes toward gender equality in care (Smith and Williams 2007; Smith 2008). Societal/cultural factors affect the agency of individual mothers and fathers to make claims for WLB in the household and workplace. But norms/values can change with the emergence of new discourses and policies. In fact, new rights and entitlements themselves can seed new norms (Barnard et al. 2001).

## European Policies to Promote WLB

When considering the role of the state in supporting families, the vast research on welfare states has concentrated on economic well-being and redistribution of economic resources. However, analysing work–life balance, the ability to combine earning and caring, involves considering time as a redistributive resource in law and policies.

In the following section we focus on two policies that aim to create a WLB in which time is a redistributive resource in the workplace and family: the right to reduce hours and the Parental Leave directive; their application across European societies reveals the agency gap between rights and capabilities to exercise them and the gendered assumptions and consequences that are connected to them.

*Rights to reduce hours/working time regimes*

In the Directive on Part Time Work (97/81),[5] European citizens were not given the right to request reduced hours, but it provided a strong proviso: it 'recommends' that employers facilitate part-time work at all levels and that member states adapt their social security systems to accommodate part-time work (Fagan 2004). There are marked differences across EU countries in the extent and form of the rights of employees to reduce hours. The right to reduce hours has been most relevant to mothers' reconciliation of employment and family, and many studies note the double-edged nature of part-time work. It allows many women to have jobs who otherwise would not have been able to combine employment with raising children, yet this option affects women's earnings, and lifetime earnings (Fagan 2004), understood as the maternal motherhood penalty (Gash 2009).

From a capabilities and agency perspective, considering the long-term prospects for a more equal sharing of earning and care-giving, one needs to pose the question as to whether mothers who have reduced hours when children are small have the possibility to return to full-time work. The research of Fagan and Walthery (forthcoming) shows that there is wide variation at the workplace organizational level as to whether parents (mainly mothers) can make claims to move between part-time and full-time work. Agency inequalities can be seen at the level of work organizational culture (between public and private) and individual resources (skills matter), but also statutory protections make a difference. Sweden and the Netherlands stand out as countries with most protection for full reversibility (the ability to move back and forth between part- and full-time work). In Sweden, where the right to reduce hours when children are small has been in place for decades, the statutory right for full reversibility is widely accepted and used in Swedish firms (Fagan and Walthery forthcoming). In the transition to market economies (Central Eastern European countries), this is not an option (Hobson et al. forthcoming).

Why this right is almost exclusively used by women reflects the structural features of part-time jobs. Full-time jobs offer higher salaries and job advancement, whereas part-time jobs often do not. But as recent studies have shown, this is not necessarily inherent in the job tasks, but expresses a work organizational culture (the ever-present employee) that in the past and today assumes a full-time male breadwinner model (Den Dulk and Ruijter 2005; Den Dulk and Peper 2007).[6] Very few fathers in Europe voluntarily choose part-time work because of its gender coding and the structural features of part-time jobs (Crompton and Harris 1998).

There are few policy measures that specifically encourage men to reduce hours. The Dutch case is an exception. A job sharing initiative was put in place

5 The Directive provides statutory protection for equal treatment of part-time workers on a pro-rata basis with comparable full-time workers (see Eklund 2001).

6 One out of five women in the EU has a part-time job compared to one out of twenty men (Mutari and Figart 2001).

in the 1990s to encourage couples to seek a more equal division of family and work (Knijn and Selten 2002). The policy sought to allow men to reduce paid hours of work to spend more time caring for children, while their partners could increase their labour market work. However, few couples took up this option. Defining job share as 32 hours each per week, studies show that the number of couples using this option had decreased from 9 percent in 2001 to 5 percent by 2004 (SCP 2004, Emancipatiemonitor).[7] Though the decision whether to accede to requests to reduce hours is at employers' discretion, according to Den Dulk et al. (forthcoming), few employers would reject such a request. Other studies show that many fathers would choose this option. In a qualitative study, Widener (2006) found that 81 percent of Dutch fathers said that they would like to work part-time in order to take a greater role in care-giving of children but that only 33 percent of those in the survey did reduce their hours.

One explanation for fathers' reluctance to reduce working times is that of informal workplace organizational cultures: unwritten rules and codes that penalize men who care. Another is that it is disconnected from other agency and capabilities inequalities: the lack of policies and infrastructures for creating more gender-equal sharing of work and care; and the institutional and cultural context in which Dutch women have one of the highest proportions of short working time hours (a 1¼ breadwinner model). This agency gap between men's working hours and working times that they would choose is shown in our analysis of working time capabilities hours.

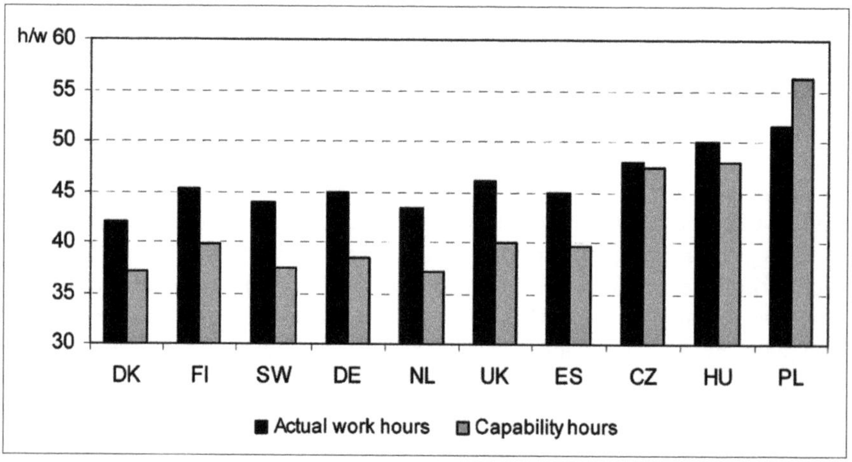


**Figure 2.1 Fathers' time differentials**

7 As in other countries, it is mainly mothers who choose to reduce hours (over 60 percent).

Using ESS data from 10 European countries representing different welfare regime paradigms we found that, with the exception of Central Eastern European (CEE) countries, fathers with children under 13 years of age would choose to work shorter hours even if it meant a loss in hourly pay.[8] We analysed the difference between fathers' average working times (reflecting the working time regime) and the hours that they would choose to work if it meant a loss or gain in hourly pay (Hobson and Fahlén 2009b), which we called capabilities hours. This indicator reveals not only what they would choose but also the economic constraints in choices. We assume that the high average capabilities hours of Polish and Czech men, as high as 47 and 55.4 (Figure 2.1) hours per week if it means an increase in pay, reveal more about the economic pressures in their lives than what they might actually choose if they had alternatives. In these countries, families' time poverty is often conjoined with economic poverty. This is most obvious among Polish men who appear to be the most time poor. Many men are not only working over 50 hours a week but would increase their hours by five hours if it meant increasing their pay, while women's average hours are already above 40 hours and yet they too would increase this further.

Fathers in Sweden, Germany, and the Netherlands would reduce their hours substantially, below the 40 hour work week (Figure 2.1). Danish men get the prize for the fathers who work the least hours and would want to work the least hours. Men in the UK are among the most time poor among the EU 15 countries; they would choose to reduce their hours by six hours, even if it meant a consequent hourly loss of income.

Individual working times vary, influenced by the family economy and by work organizational cultures. However, as our analyses on working time capabilities suggest, we find country-specific working time patterns: these are defined as working time regimes that reflect different legal and social norms of expected working times in different societies and work organizations within them (Bruning and Plantenga 1999). Working time regimes are gendered in most European countries (Bruning and Plantenga 1999; Hobson and Fahlén 2009b), so that in countries where mothers of young children tend to leave the labour market or work very short part-time hours, one would expect to find long working time regimes for men. However, there is not a neat fit between men's working time regimes and women's working times (Hobson and Fahlén 2009a; 2009b). The existence of organizational cultures in the private sector, government regulatory systems and collective bargaining agreements all play a role in shaping the working time regime. The working time regime circumscribes what individuals can claim for altering work hours, but one cannot ignore the economic pressures in certain families and the low paid, poor quality of jobs (so that fathers may have to work two jobs to support a family). The long working time regimes of fathers in CEE countries are only slightly lower for working mothers in these countries, who

8 For a fuller description of the data set we used in our analysis of ESS 2004 module on work and family, see Hobson and Fahlén 2009b and Hobson et al. 2006.

have a much higher average of working hours than mothers in other European countries. Both have weak capabilities for decent working times (Hobson and Fahlén 2009b).[9]

*Parental leave*

Maternal leave has been a long-standing policy for allowing mothers to reconcile employment with family. Both the EU directive based upon the health and safety of the mother and numerous EU court cases have affirmed this right irrespective of type of contract and employment.[10] Compensatory levels are fairly high.[11] The Parental Leave Directive gave all parents, mothers and fathers, the rights to three months' leave each after a child is born.[12] By making parental leave gender-neutral (in contrast to maternity leave), the EU Directive (96/34) gave men in several countries their first opportunity to exercise a right to take parental leave. Still, in most countries this is not a social right to care given the minimal levels of replacement for men's income (Moss and Deven 1999; Ferrarini 2003; Plantenga and Remery 2005). Our capabilities and agency approach for WLB brings into focus two questions on parental leave. What effect can leave policies have on the distribution of family responsibilities around care-giving? Can specific policy incentives aimed at men's care leave result in new norms for fathering and care-giving?

Duration, generosity and flexibility are all dimensions that shape who takes the leave and how long. Care leaves can reinforce gendered work–life patterns (women as carers and men as earners) over the life course, if they have little or no compensation and are fitted into a set of policy formulas in which long stays out of the labour force are assumed (Gauthier 2004). Women who take long leaves are often least likely to return to employment. Our study of parental leave in Hungary, a country with a long history of the dual earner family, showed that the policy of three-year leave had adverse affects on women being able to return to employment after parental leave (Hobson et al. forthcoming). According to one EU study, more than 75 percent of Hungarian parents on parental leave, mainly mothers, said that they had planned to continue working in their old job after their leave is over. However, the actual return rate is less than 45 percent (Plantenga and Remery 2005).

---

9 The ILO defines long working times as above 40 hours per week (ILO 1999).

10 *Elisabeth Johanna Pacifica DekkervStichting Vormingscentrum Voor Jong Volwassenen (VJV-Centrum)* C-177/88 and *Habermann-Betterman* C-412/92 and *Webb* C-32 93.

11 Maternity benefit levels range between 60 to 100 percent of previous income in most countries (Gauthier and Bortnik 2001).

12 In June 2009 this agreement was updated to four months for each parent (European Alliance for Families 2010).

Parental leave is a policy most often analysed in relation to mothers' care-giving roles; however, more and more attention is now being paid to fathers' leave and its effects on gender roles and the division of care in the family (Bruning and Plantenga 1999; Deven and Moss 2002; Hobson and Morgan 2002; Gornick and Meyers 2008; Haas and Hwang 2008), as well as its effect on workplace organizational cultures (Fagan et al. 2006; Den Dulk et al. forthcoming; Hobson et al. forthcoming). A growing interest in men's leave has been sparked by the emergence of policies directed at fathers: at the national level there are numerous EU countries that have adopted polices for paternity leave, exclusively for fathers (in most cases, this is a short portion of the leave, a few days or a couple of weeks at most). However, in three countries (Sweden, Norway and most recently Germany), there are specific policy incentives that encourage men to take leave: a 'use it or lose it' ('daddy quota') policy, ranging from six weeks to two months[13] so that if one parent (in most cases the father) does not take the reserved leave, the family loses the higher benefit.

The policy discourse on daddy leave carries with it many expectations; that men's greater use of the leave would result in more equitable sharing of care, that it would enable women to devote more time to paid work (Hobson et al. 2006); it would raise fertility (Henninger et al. 2008); and within the labour market lead to the weakening of the statistical discrimination against women in job recruitment and the gendered care penalty in wages and career trajectories (Hobson and Morgan 2002).

When we consider fathering in terms of agency and capabilities, it is the take up of these rights that reveal most about the cultural coding of fatherhood in society, as it reveals the constraints and incentives for men's claims for care. Plantenga and Remery (2005) show that in only five countries out of the EU 27 do men's take up rates reach over 10 percent. Ray et al. (2010) conclude that there is a relationship between generosity and gender-equality design in policy. Long leaves with low compensation are those in which men have the lowest take up rates, reflecting the cultural coding of fathering and mothering (as breadwinning and care). Targeted leave for men and specific incentives for men's leave (the use it or lose it policy) have been shown to increase the number of men taking leave and the proportion of men's leave. For example, in Portugal, only 150 men took any leave in 2000 as the leave was unpaid. Three years later the Portuguese government set aside two weeks of paid leave for fathers at full replacement for this leave: 27, 000 men took the leave. Germany is an example in which a shift in the policy design to promote men's fathering resulted in a dramatic uptake in the leave. Whereas in the 1980s Germany had an exclusive maternal leave policy (see the challenge in *Hofmann* C-184/83), from 1996 mothers and fathers could share the leave up to three months after the birth of a child with a means tested benefit. The number of men using leave was at a low level, between 2.1 and 3.3 percent.

---

13 Denmark had a similar policy, but it was removed and most recently replaced with a two-week father leave.

A new leave policy was introduced in 2007 in which there is a daddy quota and the level is 67 percent wage replacement. About 8.8 percent of all children born in 2007 had fathers that took parental leave, and the most recent figures in 2009 show that the take up rate has increased to 18 percent (Reich 2010).[14]

Sweden has been characterized as having one of the most father friendly parental leave schemes as it has one of the most generous and flexible schemes among European societies (Plantenga and Remery 2005; Gornick and Meyers 2008; Ray et al. 2010). Swedish mothers and fathers have 16 months that they can use up until the child is eight with 80 percent replacement and a high ceiling (910 SEK: 92 Euros per day). Moreover, many large firms top up men's wages to 100 percent (all public sector employees have a 90 percent replacement). As is true of other countries, highly educated men tend to use the leave more than those with lower levels of education (Hobson et al. 2006) and those in the public sector more often than men in the private sector. Since the daddy leave months were introduced in the mid 1990s, the vast majority of fathers take some leave (84 percent) and the proportion of the leave has doubled from 10 to 22 percent (Swedish Social Insurance Agency 2009). More recently a new law, the equality bonus, was enacted as an economic incentive to encourage more equitable sharing of the parental leave. If one takes more than the two months' leave reserved for each parent (in nearly all cases the father), parents will receive a maximum SEK 100[15] a day extra for each day on parental leave during the first year after the child is born (maximum of SEK 13, 500). To date, there is little evidence that this has had much effect on the division of parental leave, which may be the result of few knowing about this right.[16] It is more likely that the equality bonus does not carry the sense of entitlement for using caring rights that the daddy leave rights do. In the latter it is a generalized right for all fathers and fathers lose months of leave if they do not take it so they have a stronger claim in the workplace and family. In the former the incentives for claims for more leave are in the form of an extra payment, not a loss of rights.

Returning to our question whether proactive polices can alter the use of the leave: there is evidence that supports this. The number of men using the leave in Norway, Sweden, and even more recently Germany, increased exponentially since the daddy months were enacted. In Sweden the proportion of the leave doubled in the years since the policy was enacted. However, it is more difficult

14 As the national official statistics are based on completed benefits for the year parental allowances benefits are applied for, these figures probably underestimate the take up rates as fathers can use the second year after the birth (Reich 2010).

15 100 SEK=11.2 €, rate for 04.01.2011, ECB.

16 In February 2010 the Social Insurance Agency estimated that a total of 13,500 parents were entitled to the equality bonus, but 34 percent of these did not apply. The main reasons why they did not apply were 'difficult rules, difficult form, unawareness of the bonus' existence' (Swedish Social Insurance Agency 2010).

to assess whether these policies will ultimately lead to a redistribution of care responsibilities in the family over the life course.

Current research suggests that the Swedish daddy leave has not changed substantially the sharing of tasks and overall responsibility in the daily workings of the family. The official statistics show that women have cut down their hours doing domestic tasks, but there has been almost no change in the hours spent by fathers in unpaid work in the home (SCB 2003) since the daddy leave. Nonetheless, in Sweden the gap in weekly hours spent on housework between fathers and mothers is one of the lowest (4.7 hours), as shown in European Social Survey data. Other findings reveal that the length of leave fathers take actually has an effect upon feelings of closeness to children and satisfaction with fathering (Haas and Hwang 2008; Klinth and Johansson 2010). Moreover, research has shown that families in which men take more parental leave are less likely to end in divorce (Oláh 2001). Most recently there is evidence that indicates that even after divorce there is greater father contact with children. More equal sharing of children's care can be seen in the rise in the number of children living for half of their time with fathers and mothers after divorce, which increased from 4 percent in 1993 (before the introduction of the daddy month) to 28 percent in 2007 (Lundström 2010). This stands in contrast to current research in many countries that suggests a polarization in men's care: married fathers spending more time care-giving and divorced fathers reducing contact (O'Brien and Shemilt 2003).

Parental leave rights illustrate the importance of what Sen refers to as conversion factors: conversion of rights into capabilities is often dependent upon whether rights are social rights (Deakin 2003) (i.e. well compensated), clearly shown in the take up of parental leave rights for men, more often the main breadwinner in families. Gender equality discourses in employment as well as gendered norms for both mothering and fathering responsibilities also make it easier for individual mothers and fathers to make claims for rights to care and WLB in the family and workplace. Other institutional resources, such as whether rights are protected in collective agreements, act as conversion factors. Job security regulations are another example. In a qualitative survey of 100 individual parents with at least one child under seven conducted in Budapest and Stockholm, we found that these conversion factors underpin differences in agency for exercising care-giving rights (Hobson et al. forthcoming).

In the results of this survey, specifically designed for a capabilities approach, we concluded that there was a vast divide between Swedish and Hungarian fathers' capabilities to convert resources in agency to rights to care (Hobson et al. forthcoming). Though, compared to most European countries, Hungary has a fairly generous parental leave policy available for fathers even before the regime change, only 5 percent of Hungarian men take any leave. Fathers not only had little entitlement to make claims for fathering and care in the household or workplace, but also many were not aware of their rights under European law or protection in national law for exercising them. By contrast, Swedish fathers were aware of their rights, and expressed a strong sense of entitlement to make a claim for leave at their workplaces and within the family.[17] Few Swedish men noted any discriminatory treatment towards themselves or others as a result of taking their daddy leave; often referring to laws protecting family rights and protections through collective agreements (Hobson et al. forthcoming).

Barnard et al. (2001) and Deakin (2003) argue that rights can lead indirectly to the development of a different ethos or 'seed' new norms that can have a destabilizing effect on conventional assumptions around paid and unpaid work.[18] The Swedish case is an example of the seeding of new norms for fathers' care-giving that has come into fruition after decades of gender equality discourse and fathers' involvement in care. There is an institutional and discursive embeddedness of fathers' rights to care, which first came on the agenda in the 1970s when the parental leave was implemented as the first de-gendered care policy. At that time it was debated whether men should have a portion of leave reserved for them (Bergman and Hobson 2002), although it took over 20 years for the daddy leave to be enacted. Our survey of Stockholm fathers and other national surveys found that at least one-third of the fathers would have liked to have more leave, though there is little support for a mandated equal sharing of the leave (Hobson et al. 2006; Hobson et al. forthcoming).

Given our capabilities perspective, we are interested in how this seeding mechanism operates in other societies: what is the effect of the institutional/policy level in which it is implemented? How are rights converted into agency and capabilities to make claims? We assume that the seeding mechanism involves conversion factors that are multi-layered. Entitlements can emerge from the supra-national and are implemented at national policy level. They are mediated and interpreted in work organizations and negotiated in families.

Model 1 (below) seeks to present the complex processes involved in converting resources from rights into a sense of entitlement. The conversion factors discussed above for parental leave rights can be applied more generally to WLB claims (welfare regime contextual variables in which rights are converted into social rights). Gender equality discourses give legitimacy to claims for exercising one's rights. These resources bracket situated agency (individual resources) and workplace organizational culture. As discussed above in the Swedish parental leave example, the institutional embeddedness of a right to care weakens the importance of individual resources for making a claim (situated agency) including gender, human capital and

---

17 Lee and McCann (2006) note that the right to refuse is an indicator of working time capabilities.

18 Using the example of the protection of pregnant women from dismissal from work, Barnard et al. (2001) suggest the existence of such laws can motivate women to increase their human capital, knowing that they will be able to retain their jobs after becoming pregnant. Yet these laws did not lead to an ethos or 'seed' new norms that had a destabilizing effect on conventional assumptions about the division of paid and unpaid work, nor overturn employers' discrimination against women workers, which operates informally in many workplaces.

economic means and resources as well as one's partner's resources and means. We found that the sense of entitlement for the Swedish parental leave and its use cut across educational groups (Hobson et al. forthcoming).

As the model illustrates, the workplace/firm level is where these rights are mediated. In the case of parental leave, rights to reduce hours and flexibility in working times and workplaces (whether one can work at home or has to be ever present at workplace) is a crucial dimension that needs to be incorporated in models and analysis of WLB and policies for the redistribution of care-giving within families. Workplace organizational cultures have been emphasized in several studies to explain why men do not exercise their rights to care leave (Widener 2006; Hobson and Fahlén 2009a).

Many studies underscore the importance of workplace organizational cultures in the implementation of fathers' capabilities to care (Den Dulk and De Ruijter 2005; Perrons et al. 2006). Fagan has argued that organizational cultures can be seen as sites for converting rights into capabilities (Fagan 2004). A study in Sweden of fathers' use of parental leave in firms supports this thesis. Bygren and Duvander (2006) found that the use and proportion of leave was dependent on how many in the firm had already taken the leave. Organizational cultures are more often characterized as creating barriers against fathers' caring time. This is true not only of the structuring of working times, but also the expectations and understandings of the costs and risks for parents exercising their rights to care in different workplaces. There are silent codes and shared sets of assumptions that operate in workplaces, such as an overtime culture being a sign of productivity (Fried 1999). Lewis (1997) argues that care-related entitlements for extended

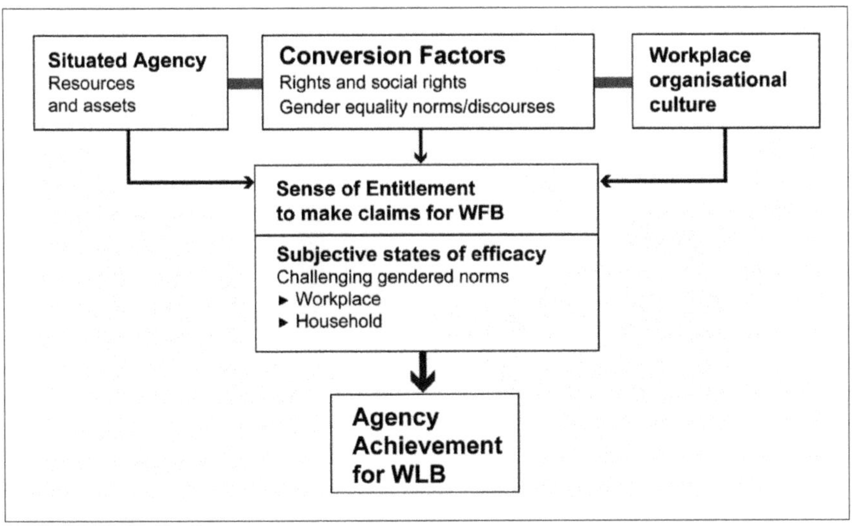


**Figure 2.2 Converting rights into agency for work–life balance**

leave or other working time adjustments have a low take-up rate among fathers, particularly when the policy is not underpinned by a statutory entitlement and where such policies are perceived to be 'symbolic statements' that are undermined by conflicting workplace norms and practices.

As Figure 2.2 highlights, the sense of entitlement is the agency space between the existence of rights and capabilities to exercise them. The sense of entitlement is the cognitive level of agency that enhances self-efficacy to challenge gendered norms operating in the workplace and household, which still assume that care is the main task of mothers and breadwinning is men's obligation. Both conversion factors, including institutional/discursive resources and the sense of entitlement, effect agency freedom for work–life balance that can lead toward more equitable shares of women and men in earning and caring.

## Prospects for Change: Toward a More Equitable Division of Caring and Earning?

The data and state of the art research on WLB suggest that the glass appears to be half empty regarding the gendered division of care-giving. Mothers experience a care penalty to a much greater degree than men in terms of career possibilities, their ability to make use of their education and skills, human capital in jobs (Sjöberg 2004) and the wage differences (Gash 2009). They also bear the greatest risks as seen in the high levels of lone mother poverty after divorce (Miller and Rowlingson 2008). Fathers' long working time regimes inhibit change; in fact, a higher proportion of fathers than mothers express work–life conflict than mothers in seven of the ten European countries we have analysed in our research (Figure 2.3).

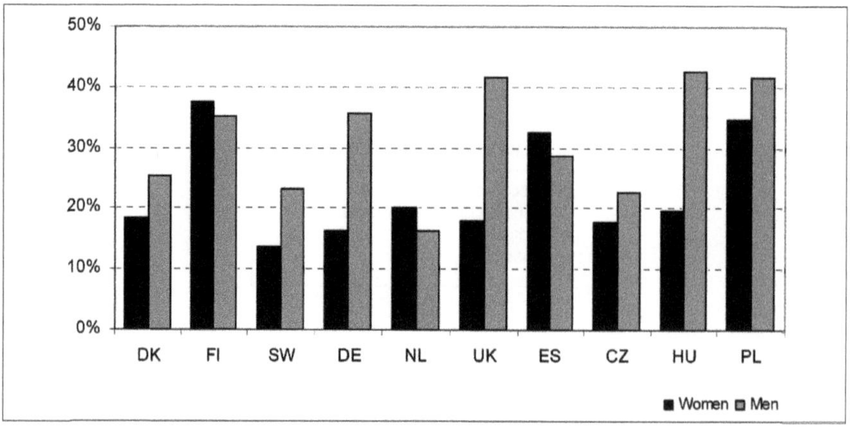


**Figure 2.3 Proportion of working parents who always/often feel that the job prevents them from giving time to their family/partner**

Nevertheless, we see growing expectations and aspirations among fathers and mothers for WLB. This can be seen in the extent to which WLB has become a widely accepted norm in European societies. In Sen's terminology it can be seen as a core value (or functioning). It is part of the EU's evaluative space on gender equality and family well-being as discussed above, having emerged through dialogues on many levels: policy discourse and norm construction, mobilization of actors beneath and above the state; advocated by NGOs, and epistemic communities. We can see the seeding of these norms in responses of parents in the European Social Survey (2004).

We find a growing consensus among families across Europe that parenting responsibilities should be shared. Both mothers and fathers agree that men should take as much responsibility for home and family as women; around 80–90 percent of both men and women take this position, though women on average are slightly more positive (see Figure 2.4). One finds the same high proportion of men and women who agree that family should be your main priority in life.

Most relevant to WLB are the responses that reveal the prioritizing of family in job choice (see Figure 2.5). Not just women, but the overwhelming majority of men said that they place importance on being able to find jobs that allow them to combine employment with family responsibilities. Here we can see a visible gap between norms and practices.

Although we are seeing a convergence and consensus on WLB, we still find differences across our countries around whether a mother's role and responsibility should primarily be that of the care-giver. When asked if a *woman should be prepared to cut down on paid work for the sake of family*, in four countries (three Scandinavian countries and the Netherlands) we found that less than one-third

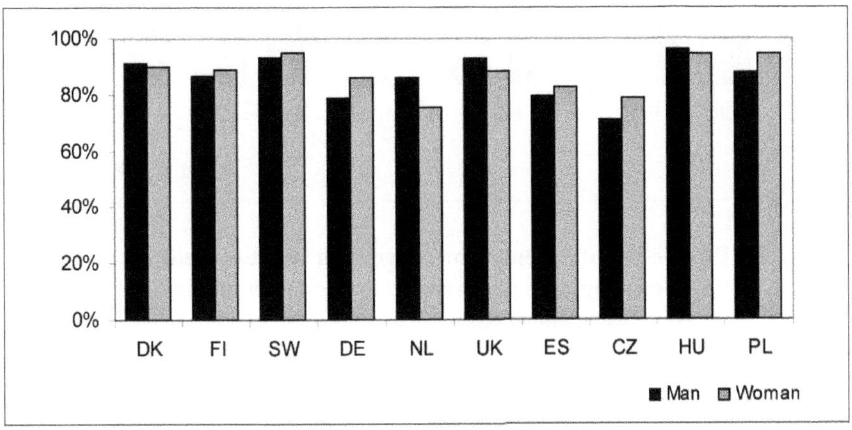


**Figure 2.4 Proportion of parents who agree that men should takes as much responsibility as women for home and children**

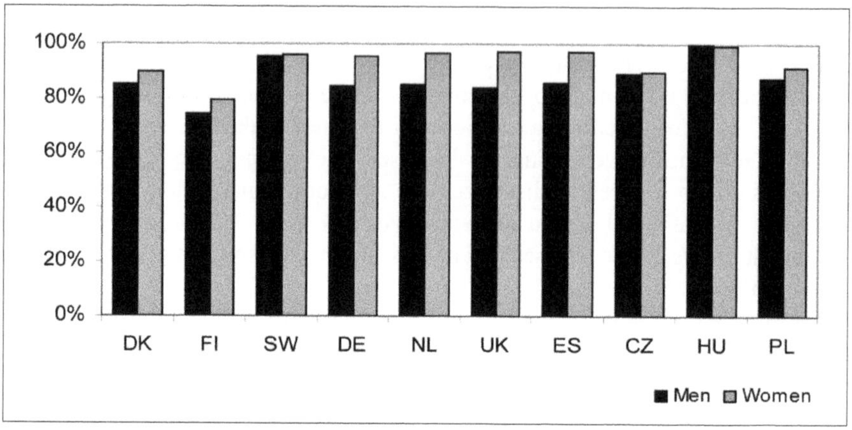


**Figure 2.5 Proportion of working parents stating that it is important, when choosing a job, that work allows them to combine work and family life**

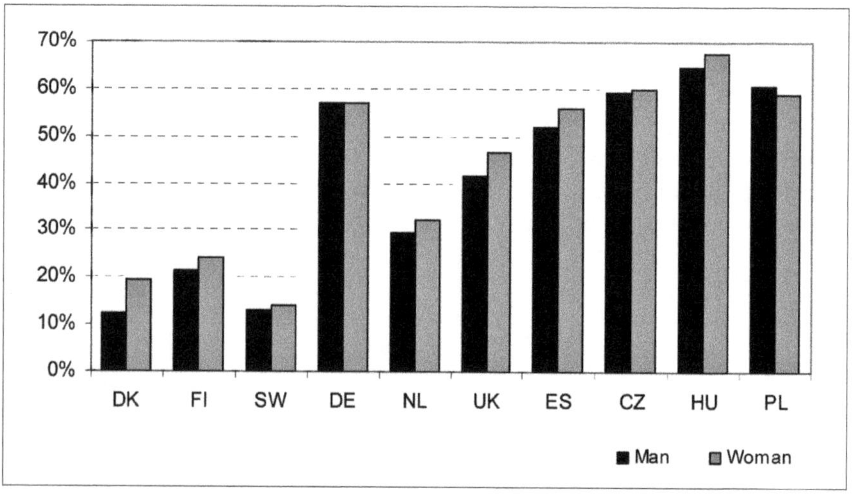


**Figure 2.6 Proportion of parents who agree with the statement: 'Women should be prepared to cut down on paid work for the sake of the family'**

of men and women agreed with this statement. In Germany, Spain, the UK and the CEE countries, more than half of the parents thought that women should be prepared to cut down on paid work for the sake of the family (Figure 2.6).

At the same time, there is recognition of women's rights to employment. Our data shows that the majority of European men and women do not agree with the statement that men should have the jobs when they are scarce (Figure 2.7). This reflects increases in female labour force participation, but it also lends support for the view that European law and discourse play a role in seeding norms for gender equality in employment (Walby 2004). Among the CEE countries, the most recent members of the EU, we find between 40 and 60 percent still hold on to the norm of men's rights to employment when jobs are scarce.

We see convergence across these European societies in the growing aspirations of men and women to have a WLB. In addition there are differences across and within European societies in the ability to exercise rights and policies for WLB, even those that are legitimated in European law and discourse. The CEE countries have the weakest capabilities for WLB in which both time poverty and economic pressures are conjoined as seen in the long working hours and capability hours. Significant proportions of fathers and mothers have working hours that exceed the EU Directive on working time limits (48 hours) and the majority do not meet the ILO formula of decent working times of a 40-hour week. These outcomes need to be understood in relation to the high proportion of men and women who feel economically vulnerable in these transition economies (about 40 percent in the CEE countries compared to 4–11 percent in the Nordic countries). Here we need to ask what are the substantive freedoms to choose alternatives? The fathers and mothers in these transition market economies cannot consider reducing hours, and feel that they have no sense of entitlement to make claims for WLB. A Hungarian

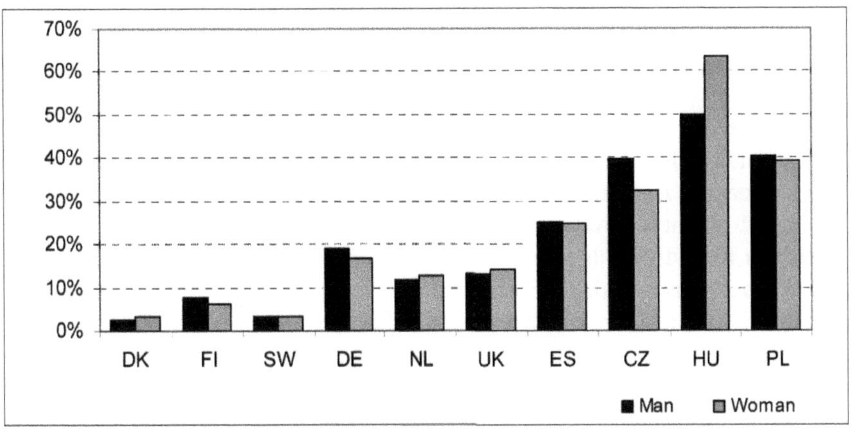


**Figure 2.7 Proportion of parents who agree with the statement: 'Men have more right to a job than women when jobs are scarce'**

father from our qualitative survey gave voice to this in his response to our question about whether he could ask for more flexible working times: 'Obviously, one must support his/her family so working is a must. *You have no choice.* Well, I wouldn't mind to leave earlier sometimes. However, we don't have a say in this matter.' A Slovenian study on parents' ability to make claims for WLB mirrors the same lack of self-efficacy to make claims for care that we found among our Hungarian parents. This study underscores the dominance of work demands in Slovenia that shade out all claims for all other spheres of life for both men and women (Kanjuo Mrčela and Černigoj Sadar, forthcoming).

Even in the best case scenario, Sweden, with the high proportion of shared leave and least support for traditional views about who should be responsible for care in the family, we still see an agency gap among fathers for WLB: over 40 percent of fathers with young children work more than 40 hours per week (Hobson and Fahlén 2009b). Mothers with young children express the time squeeze in vivid images of feeling as if one is running around like a chicken without a head (from data archive of Capabilities Survey 2008). Nonetheless, in comparison with many dual earning couples across Europe, Swedish mothers and fathers have greater agency and capabilities for WLB, even among the less skilled and educated. Fathers have a strong sense of entitlement to make claims for care; Swedish mothers have rights to reduce hours that allow them full reversibility and strong protection to return to their previous employment before they had children. The embeddedness of these rights to care enhance the capabilities and agency to make changes and possibilities for the future.

Central to this volume is the role of the state in the reshaping and regulation of family responsibilities. To understand the extent to which laws and policies make a difference in redistributing care responsibilities, one has to focus on how individuals are able to convert institutional resources into agency for WLB (Sen 1992). In our research, we can see these conversion factors involve specific policies at the state and firm level that legitimate a sense of entitlement to make a claim for care needs and, more broadly, for family time. For example, variations in conversion processes can be found in the legal formulation of policies as to whether flexible work arrangements are regulated by law, collective agreements or negotiated at the workplace. Another example is the indisputable right to reduce hours when children are small in some countries, versus the more generalized EU right to request a reduction in hours (Eklund 2001) or if there is statutory protection for individuals to move between part-time and full-time work (Fagan and Walthery forthcoming). Furthermore, whether a right can be converted in agency achievement often depends on whether it is a social right (Deakin 2003), particularly relevant to parental leave. Finally, the workplace level is a crucial dimension for understanding whether rights are exercised. Indeed, a workplace and organizational culture can show sensitivity to WLB. However, in the post economic crises period, will it be even more difficult for firms to promote WLB or individual parents to feel entitled to make claims for care-giving?

**References**

Barnard, C., Deakin, S. and Hobbs, R. 2001. Capabilities and rights: An emerging agenda for social policy? *Industrial Relations Journal*, 32, 464–79.

Becker, G.S. 1991. *A Treatise on the Family*. Cambridge, MA: Harvard University Press.

Bergman, H. and Hobson, B. 2002. Compulsory fatherhood: The coding of fatherhood in the Swedish Welfare State, in *Making Men into Fathers: Men, Masculinities and the Social Politics of Fatherhood*, edited by B. Hobson. Cambridge: Cambridge University Press.

Blossfield, H.P. and Drobnic, S. 2001. *Careers of Couples in Contemporary Society*. Oxford: Oxford University Press.

Bruning, G. and Plantenga, J. 1999. Parental leave and equal opportunities: Experiences in eight European countries. *Journal of European Social Policy*, 9, 195–209.

Bygren, M. and Duvander, A.-Z. 2006. Parents' workplace situations and fathers' parental leave. *Journal of Marriage and the Family*, 68, 363–72.

Crompton, R. and Harris, F. 1998. Explaining women's employment patterns: 'Orientations to Work' revisited. *British Journal of Sociology*, 49, 118–36.

Deakin, S. 2003. Social rights and the market: An evolutionary perspective, in *Systems of Production: Markets, Organizations and Performance*, edited by B. Burchell, S. Deakin, J. Michie and J. Rubery. London: Routledge, 74–88.

Den Dulk, L. and De Ruijter, J. 2005. Explaining managerial attitudes towards the use of work–life policies in the UK and the Netherlands. Paper presented at *the International Community, Work and Family Conference*, 16–18 March, Manchester, UK.

Den Dulk, L. and Peper, B. 2007. Working parents' use of work–life policies. *Sociologia, Problemas e Práticas*, 53, 51–70.

Den Dulk, L., Peper, B., Černigoj Sadar, N., Lewis, S., van Doorne-Huiskes, A. and Smithson, J. forthcoming. Work, family and managerial attitudes and practices in the European workplace: Comparing Dutch, British and Slovenian financial sector managers. *Social Politics*.

Deven, F. and Moss, P. 2002. Leave arrangements for parents: Overview and future outlook. *Community, Work & Family*, 5, 237–55.

Directive 96/34/EC. Council Directive 96/34/EC on the framework agreement on parental leave concluded by UNICE, CEEP and the ETUC. 3 June 1996. <http://eur-lex.europa.eu/smartapi/cgi/sga_doc?smartapi!celexplus!prod!DocNumber&lg=en&type_doc=Directive&an_doc=1996&nu_doc=34> (accessed 10 September 2009).

Directive 97/81/EC. Council Directive 97/81/EC of 15 December 1997 concerning the Framework Agreement on part-time work concluded by UNICE, CEEP and the ETUC – Annex: Framework agreement on part-time work. <http://eur-lex.europa.eu/LexUriserv/LexUriserv.do?uri=CELEX: 31997L0081:EN:HTML> (accessed 10 September 2009).

Dommermuth, L. Kitterod, R.H. and Nymoen, E. 2007. Fathers' employment in a father-friendly welfare state. Does fatherhood affect men's working hours. Paper presented at the workshop. *Changes in family structures, fertility trends and parenthood practices in the Nordic countries: Empirical evidence and challenges to public policy*, 11–12 October, Klaekken, Norway.

Duncan, S. 2005. Mothering, class and rationality. *Sociological Review*, 51–76.

EC (2000/C 218/02). Resolution of the Council and of the Ministers for Employment and Social Policy on the Balanced Participation of Women and Men in Family and Working Life. Official Journal of the European Communities. <http://eur-lex.europa.eu/LexUriserv/LexUriserv.do?uri=CELEX:32000Y0731(02):EN:NOT> (accessed 9 September 2010).

EC. 2002. *Increasing Labour Force Participation and Promoting Active Ageing*. European Commission. Brussels: COM, 9 Final.

EC. 2003. *Scoreboard on Implementing the Social Policy Agenda*. European Commission. Brussels: COM, 57 Final.

Eklund, R. 2001. The Chewing-Gum Directive – part-time work in the European Community, in *Festskrift till Hans Stark*. Stockholm: Liber Amicorum, 55–78.

Esping-Andersen, G. 1990. *The Three Worlds of Welfare Capitalism*. Cambridge: Polity.

European Alliance for Families. 2010. Social partners sign updated agreement on parental leave. Newsletter, Issue 6, January 2010.

European Social Survey. 2004. Round 2. <http://ess.nsd.uib.no/ess/> (accessed 31 July 2007).

Fagan, C. 2004. Gender and working-time in industrialized countries: Practices and preferences, in *Finding the Balance: Working-Time and Workers' Needs and Preferences in Industrialized Countries*, edited by J. Messenger. London: Routledge/Institute for Labour Studies of the International Labour Organization, 108–46.

Fagan, C. and Walthery, P. forthcoming. Individual working-time adjustments between full-time and part-time working in European firms. *Social Politics*.

Fagan, C., Hegewisch, A. and Pillinger, J. 2006. Out of time: Why Britain needs a new approach to working time flexibility. Research Paper for the Trades Union Congress.

Ferrarini, T. 2003. *Parental leave institutions in eighteen post-war welfare states*. PhD dissertation. Stockholm: Institute for Social Research.

Fried, M. 1999. Parental leave policy and corporate culture. *Women and Work*, 1, 11–26.

Gash, V. 2009. Sacrificing their careers for their families? An analysis of the penalty to motherhood in Europe. *Social Indicators*, 93, 569–86.

Gauthier, A.H. 2004. Choices, opportunities and constraints on partnership, childbearing, and parenting: The policy responses. Background paper for the European Population Forum. Geneva.

Gauthier, A.H. and Bortnik, A. 2001. Comparative maternity, parental and childcare database. Version 2, University of Calgary, online.

Goodin, R., Rice, J.F., Parpo, A. and Eriksson, L. 2008. *Discretionary Time: A New Measure of Freedom.* Cambridge: Cambridge University Press.

Gornick, J.C. and Meyers, M.C. 2008. Creating gender egalitarian societies: An agenda for reform. *Politics and Society,* 36, 313–49.

Gregory, A. and Milner, S. 2009. Editorial: Work–life balance: A matter of choice? *Gender, Work and Organization*, 16, 1–13.

Gustafsson, S.S. and Bruyn-Hundt, M. 1991. Incentives for women to work: A comparison between the Netherlands, Sweden and West Germany. *Journal of Economic Studies*, 18, 30–65.

Haas, L. and Hwang, P. 2008. The impact of taking parental leave on fathers' participation in childcare and relationships with children: Lessons from Sweden. *Community, Work & Family*, 11, 85–104.

Hakim, C. 2000. Work–Lifestyle Choices in the 21st Century: Preference Theory. Oxford: Oxford University Press.

Henninger, A., Wimbauer, C. and Dombrowski, R. 2008. Demography as a push toward gender equality? Current reforms of German family policy. *Social Politics*, 15, 287–314.

Hervey, T. and O'Keefe, D. (eds). 1996. *Sex Equality Law in the European Union.* Chichester: Wiley.

Hobson, B. (ed.) 2003. *Recognition Struggles and Social Movements: Cultural Claims, Contested Identities, Power and Agency.* Cambridge: Cambridge University Press.

Hobson, B. and Fahlén, S. 2009a. Two scenarios for European fathers: Adversity and risk? Opportunities and agency for a work family balance. *The Annals of the American Academy of Political and Social Science*, 624, 214–33.

Hobson, B. and Fahlén, S. 2009b. Applying Sen's capabilities framework to work family balance within a European context: Theoretical and empirical challenges. Working Papers on the Reconciliation of Work and Welfare in Europe. REC-WP 03/2009.

Hobson, B. and Morgan, D. 2002. Introduction: Making men into fathers, in *Making Men into Fathers: Men, Masculinities and the Social Politics of Fatherhood*, edited by B. Hobson. Cambridge: Cambridge University Press, 1–24.

Hobson, B. and Oláh, L.Sz. 2006. Birth strikes? Agency and capabilities in the reconciliation of employment and family. *Marriage & Family Review*, 39, 197–227.

Hobson, B., Duvander, A.-Z. and Halldén, K. 2006. Men and women's agency and capabilities to create a worklife balance in diverse and changing institutional contexts, in *Children, Family Policies and Welfare State Change*, edited by J. Lewis. Cheltenham: Edward Elgar, 267–97.

Hobson, B., Fahlén, S. and Takács, J. 2011. Agency and Capabilities to Achieve a Work-Life Balance: A Comparison of Sweden and Hungary. *Social Politics*, forthcoming.

Hobson, B., Fahlén, S. and Takács, J. forthcoming. Tensions in the aspirations, agency and capabilities to achieve a work-life balance in two institutional contexts: Sweden and Hungary. *Social Politics.*

ILO. 1999. *Decent Work.* Report of the Director-General to the International Labour Conference, 87th Session. Geneva: International Labour Office.

Kanjuo Mrčela, A. and Černigoj Sadar, N., forthcoming. Social policies related to parenthood and capabilities of Slovenian parents. *Social Politics.*

Klinth, R. and Johansson, T. 2010. *Nya Svenska Fäder* [*New Swedish Fathers*]. Stockholm: Borea.

Knijn, T. and Selten, P. 2002. Transformations in fatherhood in the Netherlands, in *Making Men into Fathers: Men, Masculinities and the Social Politics of Fatherhood*, edited by B. Hobson, Cambridge: Cambridge University Press, 168–90.

Lee, S. and McCann, D. 2006. Working time capability: Towards realizing individual choice, in *Decent Working Time: New Trends, New Issues*, edited by J.-Y. Boulin, M. Lallement, J.C. Messenger and F. Michon. Geneva: International Labour Office, 65–91.

Lewis, J. 2002. Gender and welfare state change. *European Societies*, 4, 331–57.

Lewis, J., Knijn, T., Martin, C. and Ostner, I. 2008. Patterns of development in work/family reconciliation policies for parents in France, Germany, the Netherlands, and the UK in the 2000s. *Social Politics*, 15, 261–86.

Lewis, S. 1997. 'Family friendly' employment policies: A route to changing organizational culture or playing about at the margins? *Gender, Work and Organization*, 4, 13–23.

Lundström, K. 2010. Växelvis boende ökar bland skilsmässobarn. *Välfärd.* Publication of Statistics Sweden, 3, 1–3.

MacInnes, J. 2006. Work–life balance in Europe: A response to the baby bust or reward for baby boomers? *European Societies*, 2, 223–49.

Man Kee, Y. 2007. Work orientation and wives' employment careers. An evaluation of Hakim's preference theory. *Work and Occupations*, 34, 45–66.

McDonald, P. 2000. Gender equity, social institutions and the future of fertility. *Journal of Population Research*, 17, 1–16.

Miller, J. and Rowlingson, K. (eds). 2008. *Lone Parents, Employment and Social Policy: Cross-National Comparisons*. Bristol: Polity Press.

Moss, P. and Deven, F. 1999. *Parental Leave: Progress or Pitfall?* Research and Policy Issues in Europe. Brussels: NIDI/CBGS Publications.

Mutari, E. and Figart, D. 2001. Europe at a crossroads: Harmonization, liberalization and the gender of work time. *Social Politics*, 1, 36–64.

O'Brien, M. and Shemilt, I. 2003. *Working Fathers; Earning and Caring.* Manchester: Equal Opportunities Commission.

Oláh, L.Sz. 2001. *Gendering family dynamics: The case of Sweden and Hungary.* PhD dissertation. Stockholm, Sweden: Demography Unit, Stockholm University.

Perrons, D., Fagan, C., McDowell, L., Ray, K. and Ward, K. (eds). 2006. *Gender Divisions and Working Time in the New Economy: Changing Patterns of Work, Care and Public Policy in Europe and North America*. Cheltenham: Edward Elgar.

Pfau-Effinger, B. 2005. Culture and welfare state policies: Reflections on a complex interaction. *Social Policy*, 34, 1–18.

Plantenga, J. and Remery, C. 2005. *Reconciliation of Work and Private Life: A Comparative Review of Thirty European Countries*. European Expert Group on Gender, Social Exclusion and Employment (EGGSIE). Luxembourg: Office for Official Publications of the European Communities.

Ray, R. Gornick, J. and Schmitt, J. 2010. Who cares? Assessing generosity and gender equality in parental leave policy designs in 21 countries. *Journal of European Social Policy*, 20, 3, 196–216.

Reich, N. 2010. Who cares? Determinants of the fathers' use of parental leave in Germany. HWWI Research Paper, 1–31. HWWI Research Programme Economic Trends. Hamburg Institute of International Economics.

SCB. 2003. Tid för vardagsliv – Kvinnors och mäns tidsanvändning 1990/91 och 2000/01 [Time for everyday life – Women's and men's time use 1990/91 and 2000/01]. Living Conditions, Report No. 99. Statistics Sweden. SCB-Tryck: Örebro.

SCP. 2004, Emancipatiemonitor. Centraal Bureau voor de Statistiek.

Sen, A. 1992. *Inequality Re-Examined*. Oxford: Oxford University Press.

Sen, A. 2003. Continuing the conversation: Amartya Sen talks with Bina Agarwal, Jane Humphries and Ingrid Robeyns. *Feminist Economics*, 9, 319–32.

Sjöberg, O. 2004. *Attitudes related to fertility and childbearing in the EU countries*. Report presented at the Swedish Institute for Futures Studies.

Smith, A.J. 2008. Working fathers as providers and carers: Towards a new conceptualisation of fatherhood, in *Social Policy Review*, 20. Bristol: Policy Press, Chapter 14.

Smith, A.J. and Williams. D. 2007. Father-friendly legislation and paternal time across Western Europe. *Journal of Comparative Policy Analysis*, 9, 175–92.

Sundström, M. 1991. Sweden: Supporting work, family and gender equality, in *Parental Leave, and the Under 3s: Policy Innovation in Europe*, edited by S.B. Kahn and A. Kamerman. New York: Auburn House, 171–99.

Swedish Social Insurance Agency. 2009. Föräldrapenning över län och kommun 2008 <http://statistik.forsakringskassan.se/portal/page?_pageid=93, 225513 &_dad=portal&_schema=PORTAL> (accessed 27 April 2009).

Swedish Social Insurance Agency. 2010. Orsaker till att föräldrar inte ansökte om jämställdhetsbonus år 2010. Socialförsäkringsrapport 2010: 15.

Walby, S. 2004. The European Union and gender equality: Emergent varieties of gender regime. *Social Politics*, 11, 4–29.

Walker, R., Goodwin, R. and Cornwall, E. 2000. Work patterns in Europe and related social security issues, in *Changing Work Patterns and Social Security*, edited by D. Pieters. London: EISS Yearbook, 5–43.

Widener, A.J. 2006. 'Doing it together': Mothers and fathers integrating employment with family life in the Netherlands, in *Reconciling Family and Work: New Challenges for Social Policies in Europe*, edited by G. Rossi. Milan: FrancoAngeli, 162–82.

Chapter 3

# The Responsible Father in New Labour's Legal and Social Policy

Richard Collier

## Introduction

> Policies focused on children and families have tended in the past to operate on the assumption that families are synonymous with mothers … However, fathers are becoming increasingly involved and their involvement with their children is important in contributing to child development, as well as being good for mothers. The Government wants to support and encourage fathers' involvement. (DCSF 2010, 113, para. 6.6)

The relationship between fatherhood and law is the subject of a rich international literature exploring the plural, often contested, ideas about fatherhood that circulate across institutional and cultural contexts pertaining to law and social policy (see, for example, Hobson 2002; Collier and Sheldon 2008; Featherstone 2009). Set against the backdrop of a growing interdisciplinary research base concerned with fathers and fatherhood, and considerable media interest in the subject, the issue of fathers' *legal* rights and responsibilities has been linked to diverse concerns about the changing nature of families and 'family life' (O'Brien 2004; Burgess 2007). In the area of fathers' rights, divorce and separation especially, debates about fatherhood and law reform have become the focus of much academic and political attention, both in the UK and internationally (Collier and Sheldon 2006; Collier 2009b; Smart 2004). The interconnections between fatherhood and law is also a recurring theme within discussion of the rights and responsibilities of parents and the shifting terrain of equality projects in law (Fineman 2004; Bridgeman et al. 2008; Hunter 2008; Ruxton and Baker 2009; Wallbank et al. 2009).

Drawing on themes within the above literature, this chapter presents a 'snapshot' of how, in the period of New Labour government from 1997–2010, social and legal policies sought to challenge 'the assumption that families are synonymous with mothers' and refocus social policy on supporting and encouraging father involvement. I argue that, throughout this period, social, economic, political and technological shifts brought about a new constellation of ideas about what constitutes responsible fatherhood in law. These developments have transformed in significant, complex and contradictory ways, legal understandings of what it now means to be a 'good' dad.

## New Labour, Fathers and Families

The development of New Labour thinking in family law and policy over the period from 1997–2010 has been subject to extensive academic discussion. This is the case in terms of both general political-theoretical analysis and with specific regard to the idea of responsible parenting (see, for example, Annesley 2001; Henricson 2008; Lind and Keating 2008). Socio-legal scholarship has traced, from the early *Supporting Families* Green Paper of 1998 (Home Office 1998) through to the pre-election January 2010 *Families and Relationships* consultation (DCSF 2010), a range of 'mixed messages' in the approach to parents' legal rights and responsibilities underscoring New Labour's family policy and welfare reforms (Dey and Wassoff 2006). Distinctive 'phases' have been identified within policy development, reflecting the shifting emphasis given, at different moments, to ideas of equality and social justice, economic efficiency and responsible citizenship. Within and beyond the field of family law a tendency towards authoritarianism and (class-inflected) moral judgment of 'bad' parents (Wallbank 2009b) has co-existed uneasily with New Labour's desire to promote justice, equality and social inclusion, and avoid the allocation of moral blame (Gillies 2006; 2008).

Locating New Labour's approach to parenting in the context of a commitment to the 'social investment state' (Bonoli 2005; Lister 2006), social policies, in particular those directed at lone mothers and aimed at encouraging women's employment were marked, some critics suggest, by problematic assumptions about the 'gendered rationalities' of women and men (Barlow et al. 2002). In particular, institutionalizing paid work as a main route to responsible citizenship, an implicit gender bias has been detected in policies that have sought to reshape the citizen as worker, parent and carer (Rake 2001). Premised on an adult-centered understanding of family life, New Labour was preoccupied, Fiona Williams has argued, by a (gendered) ethic of paid work rather than an ethic of care (Williams 2001). More recently, aligned to new sociological studies of parenting cultures (Changing Parenting Culture 2009/10), it has been argued that legal policies have increasingly constructed, and in turn pathologized, all parents as an 'at risk' social group (see further below) whereby mothers and fathers are positioned as potentially vulnerable and, crucially, as in need of expert advice and information provided by the state (Furedi 2003; 2008).

Much of the focus of this sociological and socio-legal work has been on mothers and motherhood. Yet fatherhood, if less explored, has also been regendered in distinctive ways during the period of New Labour government and rendered subject to law's governance as a distinctive kind of social problem. Before discussing further the position of fathers within these debates, it is necessary to consider, first, how the relationship between fatherhood, responsibility and law might be approached within discussion of New Labour's family policy. Three points are relevant in 'setting the scene' for the analysis of the specific policies to follow.

## Approaching Fatherhood, Law and Men's Responsibilities

First, it is important to note the diversity of the areas of law in which the responsibilities of fathers are potentially relevant to a discussion of parenting cultures. Concerns about fatherhood encompass a wide range of ethical, social, psychological and medical issues. Most obviously, the legal regulation of marriage, divorce and cohabitation involves an array of questions about the content and scope of fathers' rights and responsibilities. Discussion of fathers' responsibilities in law might also involve consideration of the legal regulation of birth, raising issues about contraception, the relationship between men and health care, the significance of abortion, the role of service providers and the implications of treatment decisions within pregnancy for men (Collier forthcoming). Between 1997 and 2010, social policies around work–life balance (Kilkey 2006; Lewis and Campbell 2007), New Labour's expansion of provision for parental and paternal leave, attempts to promote gender equality and social justice and tackle crime and social exclusion each envisaged a key role for law in radiating normative messages about what it means to be a 'good' dad.

Second, a note of caution is required in analysing substantive changes in the law. New Labour reforms bearing on the legal responsibilities of fathers, and related shifts within case law and legal practice, drew upon and developed an established legal trajectory with regard to the responsibilities of parents. A reconfiguring of Parental Responsibility (PR), for example, as a distinctive legal concept, was by 1997 already well established within family law following the enactment of the Children Act 1989 (Gilmore et al. 2009). The Children Act, setting out the broad scope of what PR entailed, aligned to the explicit commitments contained in the Act to gender neutrality, formal equality and a model of 'parental responsibility for life', entrenched the paramountcy of the welfare of the child in law (Reece 1996). During the 1990s the development of what has been termed a 'pro-contact' culture saw a reconceptualization of the desirable post-separation relationship between fathers and their children, a paradigm shift in thinking about fathers and families (see further Smart 1997; Smart and Neale 1999b).

From the mid 1980s, therefore, through the Children Act 1989 and to the late 1990s, the embedding within case law and legal practice of a distinctive kind of desirable paternal responsibility for fathers reflected, on the surface, a wider narrative of a historical move from (paternal) rights to (gender-neutral) responsibilities in law. On closer examination, however, these developments drew on multi-layered policy shifts within family law around the balance of discretion and rules (Dewar 2000), shifting ideas about rights and care and, of particular importance for the political debates around fatherhood that followed, the embedding in law of formal gender equality and gender neutrality. Bound up with what Robert van Krieken suggests has been a longer-term historical shift in the form of law's governance of families, based upon the idea of 'civilizing' parents (Van Krieken 2005), the heightened focus on *paternal* responsibility in law over this period can thus be seen as part of a broader shift in understanding of law's role in relation to families and the state.

Nonetheless, contemporary family law debates concerned, for example, with judicial interpretations of the Children Act, as in relation to the issue of shared residence (Gilmore 2006; Cain, Newnham and Masardo in this volume) or the allocation of PR to unmarried fathers (Reece 2009), reflect how, in the intervening years, a conflation of social, economic and cultural shifts during the specific period of New Labour government, including the political resonance of an increasingly vocal fathers' rights lobby (below), have also redrawn at a social and cultural level ideas about what being a 'good' father entails.

Finally, interlinked with the rethinking of paternal responsibility in family law, fatherhood has become increasingly *politicized* within the legal arena. Debates in this area have been shaped by a bifurcation between the ideas of the 'good/bad father' (Furstenberg 1988), a division with a long history in law and criminology (Collier 1998). In the recent period, however, the political dimensions of fatherhood have been heightened, not least in relation to the areas of reproductive technologies, divorce and separation. Discussion during the early 1990s about the 'troubled masculinities' of boys and young men shaped a policy at the time about 'father-absence' and 'feckless' fathers (Williams 1998). The lineage of New Labour's promise to be 'tough on crime, tough on the causes of crime' derives from concerns and events of this period, not least the depiction of much contemporary fathering as a potential social, and ethical, problem. The problem of fathers was also central, in particular, to discussions around the enactment of the Child Support Act 1991 (Wallbank 1997).

In retrospect, however, these controversies were a sign of what was to come in the later campaigns around contact and residence laws undertaken by fathers' rights groups, especially following the formation of the pressure group Fathers 4 Justice in 2002 (Collier 2005; Jordan 2009; Collier 2010a, Chapter 7). One result of the increasingly high public and political profile of fathers' protests during the latter years of New Labour government has been a broader repositioning of the father as a potential 'victim' of law, a development that has prompted responses from politicians, judges and policy makers and has had significant implications for organizations (such as the Fatherhood Institute) operating within the family and children's sector (Collier 2010a, Chapter 7). Questions about fathers' rights and responsibilities were, notably, a significant feature of the period preceding the enactment of the Children and Adoption Act 2006 (see Wallbank 2002), legislation which sought, in part, by amending the Children Act 1989, to facilitate and enforce contact between non-residential parents (the majority of whom are fathers) and their children.

With these observations in mind, in the remainder of this chapter I explore the concept of fatherhood underscoring these debates. I shall, first, outline examples of New Labour's social and legal policies aimed at 'engaging fathers' in families and promoting paternal responsibility. I proceed, secondly, to unpack the 'good father' ideal implicit in these developments, and how the emergence of a new father figure in law rested upon complex and contradictory ideas about the nature of men's family responsibilities.

## Supporting Fathers, Supporting Families

Within New Labour's social policy around fatherhood a key role has been envisaged for law, government and voluntary organizations alike in making men 'better' fathers (Williams and Roseneil 2004). This has been linked to a belief that experts, expert knowledge and evidence-based research have much to contribute to debates about contemporary parenting (Bristow 2009a; 2009b). Supported by a growing research base charting fathers' own needs and expectations, engaging with fathers, a wide range of policy documents argue, will encourage men to 'hit the ground running' in accepting their responsibilities and promoting future participation in family life. For politicians, policy makers and a myriad of other organizations alike, law has had a crucial role to play in providing a more 'modern' progressive infrastructure of economic and social support that might facilitate the caring commitments of *both* parents (O'Brien 2005).

The framework of paternal involvement that emerged as a result of these policy agendas has been described within sociological work as part of a wider move from 'cash to care' in refocusing of UK social policy towards fathers (Hobson 2002). To give no more than a flavour of the reforms introduced since 1997, and alongside New Labour's proposed changes to the law around the allocation of parental responsibility to unmarried fathers (DWP 2007; 2008; Sheldon 2009; see Welfare Reform Act 2009), work–life balance and the expansion of provision of paternal leave, well documented elsewhere, the Childcare Act 2006 requires local authorities in England and Wales to identify parents and prospective parents considered unlikely to use early childhood services (with fathers specifically mentioned) and work to facilitate access to those services. *Every Parent Matters* (DES 2007) reinforces this concern with fatherhood, stating that fathers should be offered as a matter of routine, irrespective of the degree of involvement they have had in the care of their children, the support and opportunities they need to play their parental role effectively.

National Service Frameworks and practice guidance, aimed at a wide range of organizations, have similarly placed specific requirements on the need to include fathers and prioritize work with young and vulnerable fathers, in particular in the development of service provision around pregnancy and birth (DH and DCSF 2007; DCSF 2009). The 2009 Child Health Strategy saw further recommendations about fathers' involvement in maternity services, including the provision of an 'Early Years Life Check' and use of an internet-based self-assessment tool for new dads (DH 2009). In January 2010, just months before the General Election, *Support for All: The Families and Relationships Green Paper* (DCSF 2010) saw enhancing provision for fathers in relation to birth as integral to government support for families and family relationships (para. 6.6). The Green Paper set out extra support from midwives, the provision of information packs on being a father, a father awareness campaign, the 'Think Fathers' best practice guide and greater support from Children's Centres as key initiatives that might further encourage father involvement (DCSF 2010, 114; see also Department for Education 2010). New

Labour polices and clinical guidelines, in short, have sought to encourage health and family services to engage proactively with fathers from the point of pregnancy onwards. The aim of these reforms has been clear. What is less evident, however, is what this has meant for understandings of fathers' responsibilities in law.

## Unpacking the 'Responsible Father' in Law

Social and legal attitudes to fathers have been shaped by an array of assumptions about gender, sexuality and the role of law in regulating parents. I have argued elsewhere that legal constructions of the rights, obligations and responsibilities of fathers at particular moments must be economically and politically grounded within the historical context of longer-term changes within family structures, adult/child relations, configurations of gender and forms of law's governance (Collier and Sheldon 2008, Chapter 1; Collier 2010a, Chapter 5). With regard to the social policies of the New Labour government, however, the figure of the father in law in recent years has been subject to some further and significant, if subtle, shifts. The result is a set of contradictory beliefs about fatherhood, particularly evident in relation to fathers, law and marriage, that runs through contemporary debates about fatherhood in the legal arena. This point requires clarification.

### *Do families 'need' fathers? Fatherhood, marriage and heterosexuality*

Marriage remains central to the determination of a father's legal status, playing a pivotal and well-documented role in how law has sought to attach men to their children. The legal 'ties that bind' men to children have linked beliefs about fatherhood to normative assumptions about heterosexuality, social policy and the 'natural' social roles of women and men (Carabine 1996). Law, over a period of time, evolved new ways of attaching men to children and allocating parental responsibility. Marriage is no longer the sole vehicle used in family law to safeguard (legal) fatherhood. However, bound up with law's concern to radiate normative messages and promote parental responsibility, three interrelated developments were particularly significant in refiguring the place of the father in law in the years 1997–2010.

First, the recognition in law of civil partnerships via New Labour's enactment of the Civil Partnership Act 2004, enmeshed with the embedding of equality agendas around same-sex relations in case law (as in the law relating to housing tenancies: *Fitzpatrick v Sterling Housing Association* [2000] 1 FLR 21) and statute law, for example around adoption (Adoption and Children Act 2002), has repositioned the father as 'family man' in the context of law's increasing openness to ideas of diversity in definitions of 'family life'. Recognition of this diversity was a core theme within the 2010 *Families and Relationships* Green Paper (DCSF 2010). Aligned to the refiguring of sex/gender in determining legal status contained within the Gender Recognition Act 2004, meanwhile, the idea of the legal 'family' as an, a priori, heterosexual institution has been challenged, if not wholly undermined, by these moves towards equality.

Some legal scholars have responded to the above developments with caution and a degree of scepticism, noting the continued hold of a tenacious 'form of thinking' about sex/gender in law (Stychin 2006; Cowan et al. 2009), the limited nature of the reforms and the still hierarchical nature of 'law's families' (Diduck 2003). Nonetheless, the period 1997–2010 did see an opening out of family life to ideas of diversity in reforms which constitute more than a cosmetic change in law's ideals of family life. Recalling how a traditional model of the 'good father' had rested upon particular assumptions about the normative nature of heterosexuality (Collier 1995), these reforms have, to degrees, challenged the assumption that the good father and 'family man' is a priori heterosexual.

Second, interlinked to the above, legislative changes to the law regulating assisted reproduction have reframed hitherto normative ideas about legal parenthood and heterosexuality. In a recent insightful account of the Human Fertilization and Embryology Act 2008, McCandless and Sheldon (2010) chart the background to and contradictory ideas about mothers and fathers that inform legislation concerned, in a number of ways, with the relationship between gender and parenting in law. The new parenthood provisions set out in Part 2 of the 2008 Act have removed the requirement contained in the Human Fertilisation and Embryology Act 1990 that clinicians consider the future child's 'need for a father' when deciding whether a woman should be accepted for treatment services. The Act has also introduced changes to the 'status provisions' which mean it is now possible for two women to be recognized as a child's legal parents.

In assessing the impact of this change, McCandless and Sheldon argue, it is certainly important not to downplay the 'tenacious hold' of a model of the 'sexual family form' in developments 'which might appear at first sight to herald its decline' (McCandless and Sheldon 2010, 177). However, this reform has also redrawn, even if it may have not fundamentally challenged in the way some critics would wish, a hitherto hetero-normative understanding of family life and the ideas about gender and parenting that shaped the traditional model of the father figure in law as outlined in much earlier socio-legal work. The controversy surrounding this legislation reflects how the Human Fertilisation and Embryology Act 2008, for all its entrenching, in some respects, of a hierarchy of law's families (McCandless and Sheldon 2010), has reframed the relationship between fatherhood, child welfare and heterosexuality in potentially significant ways.

Third, and finally, these developments can be seen as part of a wider rethinking in law of the place of marriage as primary determinant of paternal rights, a process that has led to what Sally Sheldon and I have suggested elsewhere is a 'fragmentation' of fatherhood in the legal arena (Collier and Sheldon 2008). Each of the above pieces of legislation must be set in the context of, and exist in a complex and at times contradictory relationship to, an increased emphasis within law on biological fatherhood and the biological and relational bonds between men and children. Bound up with a heightened focus at a policy level on the social and psychological importance of legally recognizing the genetic link between parent and child, and the cultural and legal importance of father involvement (for children, relationships, and society), there has occurred a twofold fragmentation and geneticization of fatherhood in law. Put simply, if it was the case that in the past all aspects of fatherhood were assumed to unite in the person of one man (the mother's husband and child's genetic and social father, albeit based on a number of social and legal presumptions), contemporary law is marked more by an enhanced focus on the genetic link as grounding the rights and responsibilities traditionally associated with fatherhood (Lind and Hewitt 2009).

This theme has played out in different ways across different areas of law. A desire to accord recognition to the genetic link between father and child has informed in recent years, for example, the development of case law around the allocation of parental responsibility to unmarried fathers (Reece 2009; Sheldon 2009; Wallbank 2009b). It is a theme also evident in the legislation, guidance and policy frameworks aimed at engaging fathers in families outlined above, as well as in case law around contact and residence. In relation to each, there has been a heightened focus on the biological link between father and child, reflected in attempts on the part of the judiciary and policy makers to validate and recognize fathers. This is not to suggest that this genetic link is by itself necessary or sufficient to claim the rights associated with fatherhood. Rather, in a series of cases that have cut across family law, informed also by the rights framework resulting from the Human Rights Act, the genetic link has been legally accepted as forming an important basis on which a father may then claim the right to develop a relationship with his child (see for example, *Re D* [2006] 1 FCR 556; Reece 2009). This has resulted, in some cases, in an effective 'splitting' of the rights and responsibilities associated with parenthood between different men, producing a fragmentation of the earlier model of fatherhood discussed above (*Leeds Teaching Hospitals NHS Trust v Mr A, Mrs A and others* [2003] EWHC 259; see further Collier and Sheldon 2008, Chapter 3).

These developments provide the backdrop against which concerns about responsible fathering, and the scope of fathers' legal rights, moved centre stage within family policy and public debates during the years of New Labour government. The activities of fathers' rights groups in the UK gave their grievances a particularly high profile in the years between 2002 and 2008. Central to those grievances was the perceived disjuncture between the messages law now sends out about responsible fatherhood (that families do need fathers) and what remain, for many men, the realities of their experiences of law and the legal process, especially following separation and divorce (for discussion Collier 2009a; 2009b; 2010a). Looking closer, however, these debates reflect the paradoxical, uncertain status of fatherhood itself in law. In the final section of this chapter, I shall discuss this conceptual basis of fatherhood, and consider what this can tell us about the contemporary political terrain around fathers' responsibilities in law.

## Rethinking Fathers and Fatherhood in Law

No one model of the 'new' fatherhood (or, indeed, paternal masculinity: Collier 2010a) underscores the approach within New Labour thinking towards the responsibilities of fathers. Rather, Jonathan Scourfield and Mark Drakeford (2002) argue, in their analysis of how a distinctive 'problem of men' informed an early phase of New Labour policy, there are differences in how the benefits of father engagement are deployed across areas of law. In relation to the perinatal period, and family law generally, for example, there has been 'policy optimism' about fathers. In the home and family, New Labour tended to focus on encouraging and facilitating father involvement in birth, underscored by the assumption, reflected in numerous ministerial and policy statements, not only that men *are* changing but also that men *want* to change. Such a perspective highlights, in turn, the institutional and organizational barriers to change, the cultural and legal obstacles to achieving 'active fathering' (Stanley 2005).

Outside the home, however, debates around fathers and responsibility have been informed by rather different ideas about men and masculinity. Far from finding optimism about 'changing men' in the context of youth crime, criminality and anti-social behaviour (Squires 2006), for example, we find more traditional ideas of fathers as disciplinarians and gendered masculine role models circulating within policies around working with men (Featherstone et al. 2007). If a deficit model of fathering inside the home was rejected by New Labour, outside it, and across diverse media and areas of academic and political discourse, a key concern has been to address men's individual and collective failure and lack (of ability, of commitment) to engage in their families. Different ideas about good fatherhood, in other words, have come to shape legal policy debates in different ways, depending on the context.

This reveals the open-ended and conceptually contested nature of fatherhood within these debates about men's responsibilities. The idea of the new fatherhood, much discussed within sociological, legal and popular cultural studies of fathers since the 1970s, is, Carol Smart and Bren Neale suggested in 1999, an undifferentiated social phenomenon made up of distinct elements in how men and 'what men do' are understood (Smart and Neale 1999a). At the same time, the construction of a 'problem of fathers' within New Labour's social policy – as, simultaneously, a barrier to social change, as a source of danger and risk, as an economic resource for families and so forth – is not a unitary discourse. The construction of this social problem of fatherhood 'does not arise from a homogeneous set of concerns. It comes from several different directions' and focuses on a wide range of behaviour (Scourfield and Drakeford 2002, 621). The debates discussed in this chapter encompass, for example, ideas about securing fathers as psychologically beneficial role models for children, as economic resources for their family, as full and active participants in the care of children, and, in other contexts, as potential perpetrators of social harm, of men as a 'source of danger and disorder, an anti-social influence' (Scourfield and Drakeford 2004, 621).

Each theme tracks, in different ways, to law's varying ideas about whether families do, or do not, 'need' fathers because of the distinctive gendered qualities that men bring to the parenting role. In one context, where a gender-neutral model of parenting has tended to dominate understandings of child welfare, fathers appear broadly interchangeable with mothers. Here, men have been positioned in policy debates as pushing for change, as embracing a new paternal role and, with it, the new cultural ideas of masculinity with which the role is associated. In other contexts, however, law's attempts to promote responsible fathering are pitched more in terms of tackling men's actual or potential irresponsibility and, in particular, the distinctive gendered qualities of the fathering role that are to be provided by a man, and ideally are located with the biological, genetic father. In debates about unmarried fathers (Sheldon 2009; Wallbank 2009b) and around crime, boys, in particular from lower socio-economic groups, are especially seen to require 'traditional' masculine values in their socialization, the presence of a male disciplinarian, an authority figure, a man who will provide something women, alone, it is presumed, cannot.

Each theme draws upon different (and of course, by no means mutually exclusive) strands within feminist thought whereby, in some contexts, it is the self-interest of fathers and men's collective commitments to maintaining a gender order that is seen as a significant impediment to social change. At the same time, however, a rethinking of the responsible father can be tracked to progressive readings of developments around fatherhood in law. In short, fundamentally different approaches to families, gender and parenting shape the identification of fathers as a social problem for law, and with it understandings of fathers' responsibilities.

In the following section, by way of concluding remarks, I shall briefly reassess the political terrain of fathers' responsibilities in law by drawing upon recent work that has questioned these changes in parenting cultures.

## Concluding Remarks

I have charted a tension between the messages about gender-neutrality embedded in law and the continued existence of gendered ideals of parenting. Set in the context of broader themes within New Labour thought around equality, social justice, responsibility and citizenship, contradictions exist between, for example, ideals of gender neutrality and the attempts within service delivery in practice, working with fathers 'on the ground', to value different styles of parenting, recognize the gendered dimensions of social experience and the need for gender-sensitive practice within specific contexts. With regard to the relationship between fatherhood, responsibility and law, I shall make three points by way of concluding remarks.

First, the concept of 'fatherhood' in debates about fathers and law needs to be interrogated more closely. Writing in 2003 in the book *Men and Masculinities:*

*Theory, Research and Social Practice*, Haywood and Mac an Ghaill observed how the very question of the existence of the 'new fatherhood' is one that reveals much about the poverty of contemporary thinking about fathers, reflecting an ultimately reductionist model based on ideas about bad (traditional) and good (new) categories of behaviour (Haywood and Mac an Ghaill 2003). Historical research points, in contrast, to the diversity of paternal attitudes and the plurality of fathering experiences, as well as the dangers inherent in reading fathers' practices in the past through the gaze of the present (Broughton 2007). This should lead us to guard against any assumption that the relationship between fatherhood and law can usefully be understood in terms of stark dichotomies between progress and regress (or stasis) – or in terms of 'new' and 'old', or 'good' and 'bad' fathers. Social practice is rarely so clear-cut.

Second, the model of responsible fatherhood outlined in this chapter relates in complex ways to the politics of equality and the ideas of gender neutrality contained in law. The dominant framework of engagement shaping New Labour's policy agenda around fatherhood has in some contexts, as in relation to work–life balance, been one in which men, like women, need to be 'freed' from dominant oppressive gender categories (Ashe 2007, 63–9). Such an approach begs the question, however, not only of whether men – and women – do want qualitatively different kinds of relationships with their children (see below), but also about the way the responsibilities of mothers and fathers are depicted in these debates. Notwithstanding policies aimed at engaging men in social and health care provision around the perinatal period, it would appear significant numbers of fathers do not see themselves as in need of support (Edwards and Gillies 2004; Gillies 2005). Contemporary experiences of 'intimate fathering', to use the sociologist Esther Dermott's term (2008), suggest that fatherhood continues to involve, for many men, a significant temporal and spatial trade-off between the domains of work and family (Crompton and Lyonette 2008) and, for many fathers, an experientially significant commitment to a (broadly defined) breadwinner role.

It is precisely such attitudes, of course, that the engaging fathers' agenda developed over the years 1997–2010 sought to address in promoting men's responsibilities and encouraging 'active fathering'. However, I have argued elsewhere, there are dangers in pitching a policy aimed at changing men in terms of men's 'choice' to change (Collier 2010a). What remains difficult to see in legal-political exhortations about the promotion of a new responsibility for fathers is how individual choice is socially and structurally constrained, bound up within gendered rationalities and social practices shaped by the relational networks and material circumstances in which particular fathers live (Lewis and Guillari 2005; Smart 2007). For some critics, therefore, the engaging fathers' agenda and the model of paternal responsibility with which it has been associated have been premised more on an individualized, moral exhortation of change in the parenting practices of women and men, not on any significant disruption of the unity of the 'sexual family' ideal in law itself (Fineman 1995).

It is particularly significant that the social and legal developments outlined above have occurred in the context of broader neo-liberal economic trends and the evolution of new 'intensive' parenting cultures marked by a reconstitution of the family as a site for the moral reassessment of the behaviour of *both* parents. A political concern to promote the privatization of economic responsibilities in families has run through debates which have positioned fathers as, simultaneously, both *cause of* and *solution to* a wide range of social problems. Further, it is noteworthy that, at a moment when gender-neutral social care agendas have expanded and individualized ideas of parental responsibility, other, more established, social policies around care have contracted (Lewis 2007).

This sheds intriguing light on the shift in the form of law's new governance of fatherhood, a paradoxical legacy of New Labour policies that have sought, simultaneously, to empower fathers and promote equality, and yet also regulate fathering in new ways. A re-gendering of the relationship between men and care, central to the new model of fathers' responsibility in law, has emerged as much at a nexus of these developments in politics and society as from any clear consensus in medical and scientific thinking about what constitutes 'good' fatherhood. Set in the context of the growing medicalization of birth, fathers have been encouraged to take on greater responsibility not just for children but also for their own personal lives, not least their health (see, for example, Fatherhood Institute 2010). However, cultural and legal exhortations for fathers to 'be responsible' may themselves, research suggests, be carving out a new context for fatherhood, rendering the risks and vulnerabilities associated with paternity increasingly psychologically indeterminate and experientially problematic. This new consciousness of risk and vulnerability amongst fathers is bound up with a growing social concern about men's health that can be linked, for example, to social constructions of fathers' self-doubt and worth as fathers, as evident in recent debates about paternal depression (Lee 2009). This is part of the new political terrain of fatherhood in law, raising important issues about a reshaping of fathers' experiences and expectations in relation to law and legal practice, and fathers' perceptions of formal equality, concerns that go beyond recent debates around fathers' rights in the field of contact and residence (Collier and Sheldon 2006).

Finally, it is important to reconsider the position of mothers and children in these debates and the complex relationship the legal promotion of 'active fathering' has with gender equality. Brid Featherstone has observed how it is most unlikely that 'good outcomes for children will … be promoted by forcing father involvement against the wishes of mothers' (Featherstone 2009, 131). There has been in law and practice a tendency, rather, Featherstone suggests, to downgrade the role and significance of mothers (who, in this model, need the importance of the father explained to them) and the needs of children (who appear simply as outcomes of good parenting: Jenson 2004; Lister 2006). Thus we find the view, not only that 'men need compensatory policies', but also that 'women [are] to blame for not allowing men to care' in the first place (Featherstone 2009, 145). The evolution of a pro-fathers social policy agenda during the years of New Labour, in other words, would appear to have had the paradoxical effect, in some contexts at least, of marginalizing the views and experiences of women and children (Featherstone and Trinder 2001).

With regard to legal studies, the latter is a theme that has had a particular resonance within some recent socio-legal scholarship. Both New Labour's proposals concerning the reform of the law on unmarried fathers and birth registration (DWP 2007; 2008; Sheldon 2009; McCandless, forthcoming), for example, developments in case law around fathers and the 'degradation of parental responsibility' (Reece 2009) and policy attempts to manage the 'problem' of contact (Wallbank 2009a) have each been seen by critics as exemplifying, in different ways, something more than simply the belief in law that 'fathers matter'. They illustrate the growing recognition in law that paternal responsibility has an important *symbolic* element within the context of broader therapeutic attempts to affirm fathers' identities as good parents of their children (Reece 2009).

In the book *Fragmenting Fatherhood*, Sally Sheldon and I argue that the micro-political realities of fatherhood, the everyday experiences of, say, breadwinning, domesticity and child nurturing, 'occur at the interface of structure and individual agency within specific situated contexts' (Collier and Sheldon 2008, 133). Men's experiences of caring and the social responsibilities culturally associated with fatherhood are, sociological research suggests, mediated by individual biographies and life histories in complex ways. This raises issues about the psycho-social dimensions of fathers' experiences in relation to birth, early years care, marriage and divorce, the parenting of teenagers or, in later life, their experience as a grandfather and so forth. Yet these dimensions of fatherhood are all too often absent from legal and socio-legal accounts of parenting and law. Questions of social class, race and ethnicity, health and disability, meanwhile, and even family size and whether fathers are parenting a boy or a girl, mediate experiences of parenting in particular ways. Recent sociological work, in focusing on the emotional and affective dimensions of the interconnected lives of women, children and men, suggests that the shifting investments during the life course that women and men can have in relation to gendered categories around parenthood and intimacy are highly complex (Smart 2007).

These concerns question the spaces and tensions between the normative messages about responsible fathering being conveyed by law and the experiential realities of men's 'everyday' fathering practices: experiences of, for example, joy, love, desire, pain, anger, fear and vulnerability. What has been so difficult to see in much of the discussion of the institution of fatherhood at a policy level is precisely this engagement with fathering as a daily emotional, intimate practice. Rather, there has tended to be a 'gap', Jennie Bristow (2009b) has observed, between assumptions on the part of policy makers about what fathers *should* do and feel, and the realities of what are, for many men and women, their 'everyday' family practices. Looking towards the 'bigger picture' of complex changes in parenting cultures, these developments illustrate the way fatherhood has become a new object of political intervention and focus of concern about the changing nature of family life and adult–child relations. Taking this longer view, the reframing of the relationship between fathers, law and responsibility should be seen as part of a broader reconstruction of fatherhood as a social problem.

This process pre-dates, and will not stop with, the election of the Coalition Conservative and Liberal government in 2010 (Bartlett 2010). In the context of deep cuts in public sector spending, however, cuts heavily gendered and classed in their effects, there is reason to believe socio-legal scholars may well look back at the years 1997–2010 as something of a 'golden age' in parenting policy. New Labour sought, if not without contradiction, to weld ideas of equality, justice and economic efficiency to model a new form of 'democratic family life'. At the time of writing, the future of numerous initiatives in service delivery aimed at promoting father involvement in families is, at best, uncertain, as are the consequences of these cuts for many mothers, fathers and children.

## References


Annesley, C. 2001. New Labour and Welfare, in *New Labour in Government*, edited by S. Ludlam and M.J. Smith. London: Macmillan.

Ashe, F. 2007. *The New Politics of Masculinity: Men, Power and Resistance.* London: Routledge.

Barlow, A., Duncan, S. and James, G. 2002. New Labour, the Rationality Mistake and Family Policy in Britain, in *Analysing Families: Morality and Rationality in Policy and Practice*, edited by A. Carling et al. London: Routledge.

Bartlett, D. 2010. Thinking About Fathers. *Parenting UK: News Bulletin.* Issue 25, June 2010, 2–3.

Bonoli, G. 2005. The Politics of the New Social Policies: Providing Coverage Against New Social Risks in Mature Welfare States. *Policy and Politics.* 33(3), 431–49.

Bridgeman, J., Lind, C. and Keating, H. (eds). 2008. *Responsibility, Law and the Family*. Aldershot: Ashgate Publishing.

Bristow, J. 2009a. Deconstructing Dads <http://www.spiked-online.com/index.php?/site/reviewofbooks_printable/6306> (accessed 28 March 2009).

Bristow, J. 2009b. *Standing up to Supernanny.* London: Societas.

Broughton, T. 2007. *Gender and Fatherhood in the Nineteenth Century*. London: Palgrave.

Burgess, A. 2007. *The Costs and Benefits of Active Fatherhood: Evidence and Insights to Inform the Development of Policy and Practice.* London: Fathers Direct.

Carabine, J. 1996. Heterosexuality and Social Policy, in *Theorising Heterosexuality: Telling It Straight*, edited by D. Richardson. Buckingham: Open University Press.

Changing Parenting Culture 2009/10, a seminar series funded by the Economic and Social Research Council <http://www.parentingculturestudies.org/seminar-series/index.html> (accessed 28 March 2009).

Collier, R. 1995. *Masculinity, Law and the Family.* London: Routledge.

Collier, R. 1998. *Masculinities, Crime and Criminology*. London: Sage.

Collier, R. 2005. Fathers 4 Justice, Law and the New Politics of Fatherhood. *Child and Family Law Quarterly.* 17, 511–33.

Collier, R. 2009a. The Fathers Rights Movement, Law Reform and the New Politics of Fatherhood: Reflections on the UK Experience. *Journal of Law and Public Policy.* 20, 65–110.

Collier, R. 2009b. Fathers' Rights, Gender and Welfare: Some Questions for Family Law. *Journal of Social Welfare and Family Law.* 31(4), 357–71.

Collier, R. 2010a. *Men, Law and Gender: Essays on the 'Man' of Law.* London: Routledge.

Collier, R. 2010b. Masculinities, Law and Personal Life: Towards a New Framework for Understanding Men, Law and Gender. *Harvard Journal of Law and Gender.* 33(2), 431–77.

Collier, R., forthcoming. Fathers and Birth, in *Birth Rights and Rites*, edited by F. Ebtehaj, J. Herring, M. Johnson and M. Richards. Oxford: Hart.

Collier, R. and Sheldon, S. (eds). 2006. *Fathers Rights, Activism and Legal Reform.* Oxford: Hart.

Collier, R. and Sheldon, S. 2008. *Fragmenting Fatherhood: A Socio-Legal Study.* Oxford: Hart.

Cowan, S., Sandland, R. and Sharpe, A. 2009. Debate and Dialogue: The Gender Recognition Act. *Social and Legal Studies.* 18(2), 241–63.

Crompton, R. and Lyonette, C. 2008. *Who Does the Housework? The Division of Labour Within the Home: British Social Attitudes 24th Report.* London: National Centre for Social Research/Sage.

Department for Children, School and Families. 2009, *Getting Maternity Services Right for Teenage Mothers and Young Fathers.* 2nd edition. London: DCSH.

Department for Children, School and Families. 2010. *Support for All: The Families and Relationships Green Paper.* London: DCSF.

Department for Education and Skills. 2007. *Every Parent Matters.* London: Department of Education and Skills.

Department for Education. 2010. *Parenting and Family Support: Guidance for Local Authorities in England.* London: Department of Education.

Department of Health. 2009. *Healthy Lives, Brighter Futures – The Strategy for Children and Young People's Health.* London: Department of Health.

Department of Health and Department for Children, School and Families. 2007. *Teenage Parents Next Steps: Guidance for Local Authorities and Primary Care Trusts on Improving Outcomes for Teenage Parents and their Children.* London: DH and DCFS.

Department for Work and Pensions. 2007. *Joint Birth Registration: Promoting Parental Responsibility.* Cm 7160. London: DWP.

Department for Work and Pensions. 2008. *Joint Birth Registration: Recording Responsibility.* Cm 7293. London: DWP.

Dermott, E. 2008. *Intimate Fatherhood: A Sociological Analysis.* London: Routledge.

Dewar, J. 2000. Family Law and its Discontents. *International Journal for Law, Policy and the Family.* 14, 59–85.

Dey, I. and Wasoff, F. 2006. Mixed Messages: Parental Responsibilities, Public Opinion and the Reforms of Family Law. *International Journal of Law, Policy and the Family.* 20, 225–48.

Diduck, A. 2003. *Law's Families.* London: Lexisnexis Butterworth.

Edwards, R. and Gillies, V. 2004. Support in Parenting: Values and Consensus Concerning Who to Turn to. *Journal of Social Policy.* 33(4), 623–43.

Eekelaar, J. 2006. *Family Law and Personal Life.* Oxford: Oxford University Press.

Fatherhood Institute. 2010. *Fathers and Family Health in the Perinatal Period.* London: Fatherhood Institute.

Featherstone, B. 2009. *Contemporary Fathering: Theory, Policy and Practice.* Bristol: Policy Press.

Featherstone, B. and Trinder, L. 2001. New Labour, Families and Fathers. *Critical Social Policy.* 21(4), 534–6.

Featherstone, B., Rivett, M. and Scourfield, J. 2007. *Working with Men in Health and Social Care.* London: Sage.

Fineman, M. 1995. *The Neutered Mother, the Sexual Family, and Other Twentieth Century Tragedies.* New York: Routledge.

Fineman, M. 2004. *The Autonomy Myth.* New York: New Press.

Furedi, F. 2003. *Therapy Culture: Cultivating Vulnerability in an Uncertain Age.* London: Routledge.

Furedi, F. 2008. *Paranoid Parenting.* 2nd edition. London: Allan Lane.

Furstenberg, F. 1988. Good Dads–Bad Dads: Two Faces of Fatherhood, in *The Changing American Family and Public Policy*, edited by A.J. Cherlin. Washington, DC: Urban Institute Press.

Gillies, V. 2005. Meeting Parents Needs? Discourses of 'Support' and 'Inclusion' in Family Policy. *Critical Social Policy.* 25, 70–90.

Gillies, V. 2006. *Marginalised Mothers: Exploring Working Class Experiences of Parenting.* London: Routledge.

Gillies, V. 2008. Perspectives on Parenting Responsibility: Contextualizing Values and Practices. *Journal of Law and Society.* 35(1), 95–112.

Gilmore, S. 2006. Court Decision Making in Shared Residence Order Cases: A Critical Examination. *Child and Family Law Quarterly.* 478–98.

Gilmore, S., Herring, J. and Probert, R. 2009. Introduction: Parental Responsibility–Law, Issues and Themes, in *Responsible Parents and Parental Responsibility*, edited by R. Probert, S. Gilmore, and J. Herring. Oxford: Hart.

Haywood, C. and Mac an Ghaill, M. 2003. *Men and Masculinities: Theory, Research and Social Practice.* Buckingham: Open University Press.

Henricson, C. 2008. Governing Parenting: Is there a Case for a Policy Review and Statement of Parenting Rights and Responsibilities? *Journal of Law and Society.* 35(1), 150–65.

Hobson, B. (ed). 2002. *Making Men into Fathers: Men, Masculinities and the Social Politics of Fatherhood.* Cambridge: Cambridge University Press.

Home Office. 1998. *Supporting Families: A Consultation Document.* London: Home Office.

Hunter, R. (ed). 2008. *Rethinking Equality Projects in Law: Feminist Challenges.* Oxford: Hart.

Jenson, J. 2004. Changing the Paradigm: Family Responsibility or Investing in Children. *Canadian Journal of Sociology.* 24(2), 169–92.

Jordan, A. 2009. 'Dads Aren't Demons. Mums Aren't Madonnas.' Constructions of Fatherhood and Masculinities in the (Real) Fathers 4 Justice Campaign. *Journal of Social Welfare and Family Law*. 31, 419–33.

Kilkey, M. 2006. New Labour and Reconciling Work and Family Life: Making it Fathers' Business? *Social Policy & Society.* 5, 167–75.

Lee, E. 2009. Pathologising Fatherhood: The Case of Male Post Natal Depression in Britain, in *Men, Masculinities and Health: Critical Perspectives*, edited by S. Robertson and B. Gough. Basingstoke: Palgrave.

Lewis, C. and Lamb, M. 2007. *Understanding Fatherhood: A Review of Recent Research.* York: Joseph Rowntree Foundation.

Lewis, J. 2007. Balancing Work and Family: The Nature of the Policy Challenge and Gender Equality: Working Paper for GeNet Project 9. *Tackling Inequalities in Work and Care Policy Initiatives and Actors at the EU and UK Levels, 2007.* <http://www.genet.ac.uk/projects/project9.htm> (accessed 18 October 2008).

Lewis, J. and Campbell, M. 2007. UK Work–Family Balance Policies and Gender Equality. *Social Politics.* 14(1), 4–30.

Lewis, J. and Guillari, S. 2005. The Adult Worker Model Family, Gender Equality and Care: The Search for New Policy Principles and the Possibilities and Problems of a Capabilities Approach. *Economy & Society.* 34(1), 76–104.

Lind, C. and Hewitt, T. 2009. Law and the Complexities of Parenting: Parental Status and Parental Function. *Journal of Social Welfare and Family Law.* 31(4), 391–406.

Lind, C. and Keating, H. 2008. Introduction: Responsible Parents and a Responsible State. *Journal of Law and Society.* 35(1), 1–2.

Lister, R. 2006. Children (But Not Women) First: New Labour, Child Welfare and Gender. *Critical Social Policy.* 26(2), 315–35.

McCandless, J. forthcoming. The Changing Form of Birth Registration?, in *Birth Rites and Rights*, edited by F. Ebtehaj, J. Herring, M. Johnson and M. Richards. Oxford: Hart.

McCandless, J. and Sheldon, S. 2010. The Human Fertilisation and Embryology Act 2008 and the Tenacity of the Sexual Family Form. *Modern Law Review.* 73(2), 175–207.

O'Brien, M. 2004. Social Science and Public Policy Perspectives on Fatherhood, in *The Role of the Father in Child Development*, edited by M.E. Lamb. New Jersey: John Wiley.

O'Brien, M. 2005. *Shared Caring: Bringing Fathers into the Frame*. Manchester: Equal Opportunities Commission.

Page, J. and Whitting, G. 2008. *A Review of How Fathers Can Be Better Recognised and Supported Through DCSF Policy.* DCSF Research Report DCSF-RRO40. London: DCFS.

Rake, K. 2001. Gender and New Labour's Social Policies. *Journal of Social Policy.* 30(2), 209–31.

Reece, H. 1996. The Paramountcy Principle: Consensus or Construct? *Current Legal Problems.* 49, 267–304.

Reece, H. 2005. From Parental Responsibility to Parenting Responsibly, in *Law and Sociology: Current Legal Issues*, edited by M. Freeman. Oxford: Oxford University Press.

Reece, H. 2009. The Degradation of Parental Responsibility, in *Responsible Parents and Parental Responsibility*, edited by R. Probert, S. Gilmore and J. Herring. Oxford: Hart.

Ruxton, S. and Baker, H. 2009. Editorial: Fathers' Rights, Fatherhood and Masculinity/ies. *Journal of Social Welfare and Family Law.* 31(4), 351–5.

Scourfield, J. and Drakeford, M. 2002. New Labour and the 'Problem of Men'. *Critical Social Policy.* 22, 619–40.

Sheldon, S. 2009. From 'Absent Objects of Blame' to 'Fathers Who Want to Take Responsibility': Reforming Birth Registration Law. *Journal of Social Welfare and Family Law.* 31(4), 373–89.

Smart, C. 1997. Wishful Thinking and Harmful Tinkering? Sociological Reflections on Family Policy. *Journal of Social Policy.* 26(3), 1–21.

Smart, C. 2004. Equal Shares: Rights for Fathers or Recognition for Children? *Critical Social Policy*, 24(4), 484–503.

Smart, C. 2007. *Personal Life: New Directions in Sociological Thinking.* Oxford: Polity.

Smart, C. and Neale, B. 1999a. 'I Hadn't Really Thought About It': New Identities/New Fatherhoods, in *Relating Intimacies: Power and Resistance*, edited by J. Seymour and P. Bagguley. Basingstoke: Palgrave Macmillan.

Smart, C. and Neale, B. 1999b. *Family Fragments?* Cambridge: Polity Press.

Squires, P. 2006. New Labour and the Politics of Anti-Social Behaviour. *Critical Social Policy.* 26(1), 144–68.

Stanley, K. 2005. *Daddy Dearest? Active Fatherhood and Public Policy.* London: Institute for Public Policy Research.

Stychin, C. 2006. Family Friendly? Rights, Responsibilities and Relationship Recognition, in *Feminist Perspectives on Family Law*, edited by A. Diduck and K. O'Donovan. London: Routledge Cavendish.

Van Krieken, R. 2005. The 'Best Interests of the Child' and Parental Separation on the 'Civilising of Parents'. *Modern Law Review.* 68(1), 25–48.

Wallbank, J. 1997. The Campaign for Change of the Child Support Act: Reconstituting the 'Absent' Father. *Legal Studies*, 191–216.

Wallbank, J. 2002. Clause 106 of the Adoption and Children Bill: Legislation for the 'Good Father'? *Legal Studies*. 22(2), 276–96.

Wallbank, J. 2005. Getting Tough on Mothers: Regulating Contact and Residence. *Feminist Legal Studies*. 15(2), 189–222.

Wallbank, J. 2009a. Parental Responsibility and the Responsible Parent: Managing the 'Problem' of Contact, in *Responsible Parents and Parental Responsibility*, edited by R. Probert, S. Gilmore and J. Herring. Hart Publishing: Oxford.

Wallbank, J. 2009b. 'Bodies in the Shadows': Joint Birth Registration, Parental Responsibility and Social Class. *Child and Family Law Quarterly, 267–82.*

Wallbank, J., Choudhry, S. and Herring, J. (eds). 2009. *Rights, Gender and Family Law.* London: Routledge-Cavendish.

Williams, F. 1998. *Troubled Masculinities in Social Policy Discourses: Fatherhood, in Men, Gender Divisions and Welfare*, edited by J. Popay, J. Hearn and J. Edwards. London: Routledge.

Williams, F. 2001. In and Beyond New Labour: Towards a New Political Ethics of Care. *Critical Social Policy.* 21(4), 467–93.

Williams, F. and Roseneil, S. 2004. Public Values of Parenting and Partnering: Voluntary Organizations and Welfare Politics in New Labour's Britain. *Social Politics*. 11(2), 181–216.

Chapter 4

# The Court of Motherhood: Affect, Alienation and Redefinitions of Responsible Parenting

Ruth Cain

> The judge pounds his gavel on the bench. He is getting larger by the minute and his old white face suffuses with scarlet like a syringe taking in blood. The defendant, meanwhile, is growing smaller and smaller. No bigger than a Barbie doll, she scrambles up on to the edge of the dock and balances there precariously in high heels. When she starts to shout at the judge, her voice is a gerbil squeak:
>
> "All right, you really want to know the truth? Guilty. Unbelievably, neurotically, pathologically guilty. Look, I'm sorry, but I have to go now. For heaven's sake, just look at the time." (Pearson 2002, 173)

During the ascendance of Western neo-liberal politics and its complex penetration into concepts of the 'good' citizen-self (Rose 1999a; 1999b; 2007; Lister 2003; Reece 2003), issues of affect, emotion and care occupy a rather confusing space within citizenship discourse. As Lynch and others have shown (Lynch 2009; Lynch, Baker and Lyons 2009), the productive citizen is practically 'care-less'; he has no obligations to others which are not fulfilled by someone else (Lynch and Lyons 2009). However, most notably during the Blair era in the UK, a new focus on 'responsible' parenting emerged (Lister 2003), emphasizing that the political burden on parents was now to police themselves effectively, as carers and producers of future citizens, with the state stepping in to provide re-education in the form of parenting classes and training and in the more intractable cases, coercive measures such as Parenting Orders and Anti-Social Behaviour Orders targeted at both parents and children (Holt 2008). The movement toward enforcing personal responsibility for children is part of a broader set of powerful communitarian ideals spanning both 'new' Labour and Conservative political spectrums (Giddens 1991; Etzioni 1993; Reece 2003; 2006a; 2009): the new citizen must be the best person he or she can be, embarking on a lifetime project of self-improvement and discovery, in order to show herself worthy of liberal freedoms (Reece 2003; 2006a; 2009). In similar vein, Nikolas Rose describes a 'complex of marketization, autonomization and responsibilization' which absorbs contemporary subjects (Rose 2007, 4). The disproportionate impact of the parental responsibility doctrine on mothers has already begun to be discussed by feminist commentators (Gillies 2005; 2007; Holt 2008). Part of this disproportionality has been theorized by feminists to be a result of new gendered parenting ideals which might not initially appear detrimental to maternal autonomy or status, as Susan Boyd summarizes:

> As the result of a rethinking of paternal responsibility in child welfare and development, and the emergence of new socio-legal norms around shared parenting, understandings about parenthood are being reshaped (Smart 1999). For instance, fatherhood has become a new policy concern, with initiatives to promote "good" fathering and social responsibility on the part of men, whether they are fathers within intact families or outside that structure. As Richard Collier and Sally Sheldon say, "[f]athers are now seen to have a more direct, unmediated relationship to their children" (2008: 117) than in the past. In other words, paternal relationships with children are no longer mediated by the type or quality of relationship that a father has with the mother. (Boyd 2010, 142)

The cases dealt with in the later part of this chapter tackle exactly this conception of 'involved' fathering in the era of the 'responsible citizen', and demonstrate its considerable impact on constructions of mothering and maternal responsibility. This chapter argues for the importance of a concept of *affective* (rather than simply socio-economic, or cultural) inequality in the exercise of law; what amounts to a very old message (mother-blaming versus the valorization of paternal involvement in the lives of children) is couched in new codes, citing persuasive doctrines of 'children's best interests', fairness, and progress away from old post-separation norms in which the separated or divorced mother got, or was left with, the children. While Carol Smart (2004) has already written of the disproportionate emotional and social impact on women of 'fifty-fifty' shared custody arrangements, and Susan Boyd notes how women's autonomy may in fact be reduced by the need to facilitate equal or near-equal contact with fathers, it is necessary to consider the affective impact of a post-separation environment in which both maternal autonomy *and* connectedness appear under threat (Boyd 2010). Given the large numbers of separated parents bringing up children and the amount of policy and media initiatives geared toward encouraging them to do this 'together', this is a huge personal and cultural as well as legal issue.

This chapter follows a previous article (Cain 2009) which theorized maternal depression and its 'biological' coding as, in part, a manifestation of a disturbed maternal affect which combines the biological with the social, legal and political, engendered by a complex of toxic factors such as the dominance of 'gender-neutral parenting' discourses, the economic pressures of the neo-liberal economy, and the continuing force of psychoanalytic and developmental assumptions about the fundamental role of mothers in the lives of children. This could be simplistically summarized as *the formalization of a 'do-it-all' model of responsible motherhood*, in which the mother is increasingly expected to manage the increasingly valorized role of the father in the child's upbringing *and* the difficult emotional issues which result from parental separation. While it is maternal 'hostility' or 'implacability' rather than depression which is the topic here, I suggest that this complex of damaging factors must be considered when assessing *any* form of negative maternal affect which is posited in legal reasoning and policy initiatives. It will be my argument here that legal scholars cannot examine maternal responsibility without taking account of the affective context of mothering, whether we describe the affective burdens of mothering as maternal depression, stress, or a more complex abstract set of 'problems with no name'. This chapter explores some of the cultural manifestations of maternal affective disturbance, stress, and 'hostility', and connects these to new and frequently coercive legal conceptions of good mothering. These are examined in the specific context of two recent UK Family Court cases where mothers were presented as failing to fulfil the role of the good gender-neutral parent in the fraught context of family break-up. My argument is that we must specifically connect the rise of legal scapegoats such as the 'no-contact mother' who frustrates or blocks paternal access to children (Rhoades 2002) with the difficult affective environment of neo-liberal or 'new capitalist' motherhood (Pitt 2002; Quiney (Cain) 2007). We must also take note of how the longstanding failure of the liberal, entrepreneurial subject to encompass mothering and, indeed, all forms of unpaid caring work is creating new disciplinary forms of 'bad parent', and that the majority of these 'bad parents' are women. I also argue that the function of law in producing 'bad mothering' from 'gender-neutral parenting' discourses demonstrates both the impossibility and the unfairness of excluding gendered affect from legal reasoning on family issues. As Richard Collier has recently written (2009: 366), the intensive study of 'emotion, gender and law' has never been more pertinent or necessary than in the era of 'responsible citizenship'.

## Motherhood, Affect and Neo-Liberalism

In order to examine maternity in law as a specific repository (and source) of negative affects, we need to explore two interconnected fields of scholarship before approaching some case law in detail. These are, first, the concept of the 'neo-liberal subject/citizen' as one determined by (to summarize a vast range of relevant factors briefly) vast consumer choice, increasing inequalities of wealth, corporatization, globalization and therapeutic culture (Rose 1999a; 2007), and the important and relatively critically neglected field of affect theory, most recently and originally expounded by Teresa Brennan (2004).[1] Both fields of study help us to understand a Western world in which it is increasingly the *psychological* self which is perceived as the source of every problem. Responsibility to the self

1 This chapter lacks space to discuss the detailed applications of affect theory to transdisciplinary work in the social and 'hard' sciences, and recent attempts to address and include the biological in cultural and social theory: nonetheless, I write on the assumption that to reference 'the biological' is not essentialist, but rather essential to a nuanced appraisal of contemporary subjectivity (see further Cain 2009; Papoulias and Callard 2010).

and to others, conceptualized as self-control and self-knowledge, is of central importance to therapeutic and confessional public cultures (Curk 2011). In such cultures, the 'feminized' emotional self may be encouraged to 'open up' for catharsis, examination and judgement, but its less controlled, destructive elements must be continually assessed and repressed by the responsible citizen-worker. The 'healthy' self controls its own emotions efficiently and does not burden others, and certainly not the economy/citizenry/state, with them (Swan 2008a).

Despite (or perhaps because of) the apparent emotional openness of media and literary cultures, it has been noted that workplaces and business locations remain areas of strictly limited and controlled affect in which 'feminized' expressions of emotion or personal openness are frowned upon (Swan 2008a; 2008b). In these contradictory environments, and under economic and social conditions which press women back to work while simultaneously valorizing intensive and perfectionist 'stay-at-home' motherhood (Hays 1998; Warner 2005; Quiney (Cain) 2007; Barker and Lamble 2009), women with children are placed in an exceptionally difficult and confusing position. They are in some circumstances urged to give vent to the emotions engendered by motherhood, its undoubtedly massive life changes, satisfactions and traumas; and at others they must forcibly repress such evidence of feminized affect (in many public arenas, but specifically in the workplace: see further Adkins 1995; 2005; Duxbury and Higgins 2001; Lewis 2001; Correll et al. 2007). In my previous article on post-natal depression I focused on depression as a contemporary 'habitus': the ways of being and feeling oneself to be a mother, good or bad (Cain 2009, 124). Here I expand discussion of ways of feeling and being a mother to encompass those feelings and identities which may lie beyond the mother herself, in the social, cultural and legal attitudes to her which she can never ignore or entirely exclude.

## Love Labour, Caring and Maternal Affective Inequality

Affect theory starts with mothers. Teresa Brennan's concept of affect transmission has the maternal body as its foundation; what she calls the 'foundational fantasy' is an early act of mother-blaming, originally performed by the infant:

> [T]he mother, especially, is seen as the natural origin of rather than the repository for unwanted affects. It is not that we dump on her (all our screaming rage and pain). It is rather that she dumps on us. For her occasional irritation or distraction she is held culpable, made the cause of all our rage and pain. We project onto her our helpless and unbearable passivity, our lack of agency. … Situating the mother as the passive repository for the child's unwanted raging affects is, perhaps, the first powerful instance of the transmission of affect. (2004, 12–13)

Thus the mother is the first taken-for-granted carer and dumping-ground for feelings the child-subject does not want to own (see also Kristeva 1982). As Brennan notes

(2004, 13), the 'foundational fantasy' positions the mother as producing negative effects rather than suffering them. (This is strikingly reproduced in the literature on maternal depression, which focuses almost exclusively on the potential damage to the child of the depressed mother (Kurstjen and Wolke 2001; Petterson and Albers 2001; Newport et al. 2002). Kathleen Lynch's (2009) analysis of the uncommodifiable, inalienable nature of 'love labour' gives a more positive view of maternal and other caring work (in that the male and female carers she surveyed were proud to identify themselves as carers and saw caring work as fundamental to their identities: but still she emphasizes the extent to which carers are devalued and disrespected (and thus feminized) in neo-liberal economies (Lynch 2007; Lynch 2009; Lynch and Lyons 2009). 'The idealised rational economic actor … model of the citizen, that valorises the entrepreneurial self, has taken hold and with it a new macho-masculinised public sphere has emerged' (Lynch and Lyons 2009), 92). In a context where caring is so frequently perceived as feminized and abject, while paid work partakes of 'macho-masculinised' cultural cachet, the status of the 'gender-neutral parent' is particularly fraught, as discussed below.

Similarly, as Maureen O'Brien writes, 'the taken-for-grantedness and intangibility of love labour and the emotional work it includes have meant that the resources and energies required for its production have been overlooked' (O'Brien 2009, 159). Lynch, however, makes clear that care is not an optional value in any society: '[w]hether people subscribe to other-centred, solidarity-oriented norms or not, their own existence is dependent on the successful enactment of such norms' (2009). The compulsoriness of care seems to entail *women's* compliance in particular, and the ingrained nature of intensive mothering norms (alongside a vast complex of gender-forming factors, including the education of young girls in caring behaviours and interpersonal relating) has much to do with this (Warner 2005; Quiney (Cain) 2007). Following the ideas of Carol Gilligan, O'Brien argues that '[t]hrough the internalisation of caring ideologies, and a moral imperative to care, mothers' identities, regardless of positioning and resources, become inescapably bound to emotional caring' (2009, 160). Although clearly it is important to 'avoid generating essentialist and romanticised' (2009, 160) images of maternal love, the emotional and iconic pull of maternal status within the culture of the neo-liberal individual remains striking (representing, I would argue, an area of experience in which all the unacceptable feminized affects which may not be expressible in other areas of life, such as the social, sexual or work-related, may be collected, shared and valorized). The private (and frequently unpaid) carer is more extensively required than ever, to clean up after and care for the bodies of the elderly, children, and the sick, and to service the unmet domestic needs of 'higher-level' workers in the neo-liberal society (see Kittay in this volume), yet s/he is arguably less respected than ever.

As love, care and solidarity involve work, affective inequality also occurs when the burdens and benefits of these forms of work are unequally distributed, and when this unequal distribution deprives those who do the love, care and solidarity work of important human goods, including an adequate livelihood and care itself (Lynch 2009).

Affective inequality thus appears to entail not only being ignored, but often actively denigrated: as the novelist Elizabeth Troop wrote in *The Woolworth Madonna* (1980), it is too often assumed that 'people who love people are the sickest people in the world' (37). This assumption also recalls the 'abjection' of the originary mother-figure, cast into a realm of non-signification in order that the subject may form in language, as theorized by Julia Kristeva (1982). To deploy a highly inelegant but accurate term, the 'dumpee' of difficult affects, particularly the working or single mother,[2] receives a negative image of herself from media, employers and others, as well as suffering the general strain of circumstances, dual work burden, time famine, and so on. Previously, I have explored the connection of depression not just with the immediate post-natal period but with maternity as a whole experience or identity (Cain 2009, see further Nicolson 1998; Thompson 2006). The evidence for depression in working mothers is particularly striking (Brown and Bifulco 1990).

## The Impossibility of the Gender-Neutral Parent

Thus, the overlap of uncommodifiable 'love labour' with economic labour appears to be causing particular problems for mothers of young children, problems which may be treated as 'post-natal depression' but which clearly have a more complex aetiology than hormonal or endocrine disturbance, as per the dominant medical model. I have previously (Cain 2009) mentioned the interactions of maternal distress with issues pertaining to the 'new economy', such as the need for two-worker families to support inflated household and personal debt, particularly in high-density urban areas, and the increasingly extreme demands of twenty-first century work environments in terms of hours, 'commitment', training and availability, which affect both women and men (Adkins 1995; 2005; Sassen 1998; Standing 1999). Any list of toxic cultural factors affecting mothers must now include the ascendance of the 'perfect', near-obsessive parent who utterly devotes herself to producing a 'rounded individual' and successful, adaptable future citizen-worker (Lister 2003; Warner 2005). UK parenting policies of the New Labour era, specifically the organization of parenting orders and classes, manifest these contradictions and anxieties, appearing to intrude into the lives of 'problem' families while failing to provide either adequate economic support or a coherent social strategy for workable, affordable childcare (Holt 2008). These inadequacies inevitably affect mothers more than fathers (despite the rhetoric of 'gender-neutral parenting' in which they are generally couched (Gillies 2005)) since a welter of statistics shows that mothers, whether they work or not, and whether or not the male partner works, continue to shoulder the majority of childcare and domestic

2 On the opprobrium routinely dealt out to single mothers since the Second World War and their popular and political association with poverty and the production of criminality, see further Fineman 1991; Silva 1996; Gillies 2005; 2007; Holt 2008.

work (National Statistics 2000; Crompton 2006; Crompton et al. 2007). There has recently been a new popular focus on the differentiation normally made in Family Court residence proceedings between a mother who stays at home and is thus recognized as the 'primary carer', and a mother who works (see further Reid 2009 for a typical media-spotlighted story; briefly, a mother who has stayed at home with her children all their lives and never worked is far more likely to be recognized as the primary carer of the children, with subsequent impact on decisions made about whether and how much they will reside with her). So while working mothers still tend to 'do it all', the partner of a full-time working mother will tend to have a far stronger claim to shared residence and possibly 'equal shares' of the children (Smart 2004).

The impressive empirical evidence of the disproportionate impact of working parenthood on maternal rather than paternal lives thus indicates a need to re-gender 'work/life balance' debates, which, like so many public debates on parenting issues, are usually couched in gender-neutral terms despite the highly gendered contexts in which they take place (Brown and Bifulco 1990; Duxbury and Higgins 2001; Lewis 2001). Powerful cultural discourses such as that of the selfish, materialist and uncaring working mother placing 'career' before children are clearly entrenched by continual media reports and high-profile psychiatric investigations into the 'damage' done to children by mothers' absence at work and increased stress at home (Brooks-Gunn et al. 2002). The chaotic, harassed and internally divided working mother who appears in popular novels such as the best-selling *I Don't Know How She Does It* (Pearson 2002) is an exhausted, disappointed and self-hating woman. Pearson's heroine regularly appears in a fantasy 'court of motherhood' to hear her harsh judgements of her own conduct played out, with her maternal 'conscience' rather aptly played by an 'old white' male judge (72). In the light of evidence that full-time employment actually increases vulnerability to depression in mothers, feminists perhaps need to look not only at the time-famine and stress factors (despite their undoubted contribution to depression) but to take good note of the contempt and anxiety 'dumped' on working mothers, who, I would suggest, are victims of forced signification: made to personify and manifest the stresses of socio-economic and cultural transformations of the family, with clear consequences for self-esteem.

## Working Mothers and Negative Affect

Consonant with the wage and leisure-time penalties disproportionately suffered by working mothers (Benard et al. 2007), studies suggest that they also suffer from a more general devaluation of themselves and their skills as workers *and* as mothers, by co-workers, employers and other peers (Cuddy et al. 2004). The working mother has become a powerful focus of coercive and confused legal/cultural anxiety, and individual women bear this negative affect. We should note here the splitting of working mothers into two equally coercive representational strands: the middle class, presumably married mother 'selfishly' choosing to work and the working class, often single mother 'selfishly' choosing not to (and claiming benefits) (Barker and Lamble 2009). Thus, the opprobrium attaching to working motherhood is organized around access to private funds (generally presumed to be provided by a (male) partner) which determines the 'appropriate' style of mothering to be adopted. Changes to the traditional male-breadwinner family thus appear to be forced into the private domain of negotiation within couples or (less frequently) other family members such as grandparents, with little if any governmental or legislative acknowledgment of the enormous and continuing stress and inequality, both at home and at work, faced by women with children. Thus, narratives of her misery and anxiety like *I Don't Know How She Does It* compete for public awareness and validation with stereotyped depictions of the working woman as a failed, incompetent mother (frequently in the form of investigations designed to measure deficits in the behaviour or 'adjustment' of children who spend time in nurseries or with other carers when their mother is at work: Bowlby 1973; Belsky 1986; Hays 1998; Brooks-Gunn et al. 2002; Leach 2003). Such portrayals clearly only serve to further entrench the marginalization and denigration of 'failing' mothers, and thus to pathologize 'problems with motherhood' as signs of weakness and poor citizenship.

## New Forms of 'Bad Mother'

While 'bad' mothering in its many forms has always been a focal point for condemnatory rhetoric and various practices of legal and cultural control (Roberts 1993; Ladd-Taylor and Umansky 1997; Quiney (Cain) 2007), the predominance of therapeutic culture, neo-liberal ideals of continuous self-regulation, and the rise of new types of gender 'equality' discourse such as that espoused by the 'fathers' rights' movement (Smart 2004; Collier and Sheldon 2006; 2008; Wallbank 2007; Collier 2009) are clearly creating new kinds of maternal blame-targets. I now go into some more detail on some examples recently highlighted in media and Family Court reports. These concern shared residence and the rights of each parent to involvement in and responsibility for their children's day-to-day lives after separation, themes already much discussed by many feminist family law commentators (Kaganas and Piper 2002; Rhoades 2002; Smart 2004; Smart and May 2004; Collier and Sheldon 2006; Wallbank 2007; McIntosh and Chisholm 2008; Smyth 2008; 2009).[3] Each presents a flawed version of (possessive,

3 Briefly, the use of shared residence orders, which were rarely used in the 1990s, has recently shown an increase in line with the rise of assumptions about the importance of increasing the value of ideas of parenting responsibility among fathers, and concern about contact with 'non-residential' parents (numerically far more often fathers): see Wallbank 2007 and Masardo and Newnham in this volume. At legislative level, the UK government has responded to the 'problem' of contact with the Children and Adoption Act 2006, Part

smothering, hysterical and/or 'greedy') motherhood, while at the same time deploying the 'gender-neutral' language of shared responsibility most recently favoured by the UK family courts. Current UK family law practice creates an expectation that agents will act rationally and even unemotionally in highly emotional situations (see further Reece 2003 on the expectation of 'reasonable' behaviour during divorce; Berns 2000; Cantwell 2004; Smart and May 2004). The reasonable mother thus actively facilitates access and even helps the father to cope with his duties as 'sharing' parent (Masardo and Newnham in this volume; Wallbank 2007; McIntosh 2009).

As Carol Smart writes on the 'micro-politics of child contact', the affective burden of residence decisions is undoubtedly greater for mothers because of the pressures of the 'good mother' trope which demands constant presence and involvement in the life of the child:

> It is empirically established that mothers do most of the caring for children – even if some fathers do a substantial amount. ... For mothers, reducing the amount of caring for children that they do is associated with guilt and loss ... giving up 'caring time' has emotional connotations for mothers. For fathers, love may not be so bound up with caring activities and responsibilities ... [T] he demand by fathers for caring time to be taken away from mothers creates emotional pain (especially if it is the father's new partner or mother who will do the work of caring). (Smart 2006, x)

Smart also notes that 'while fathers' anger has found a "legitimating" political voice [in the fathers' rights movement], mothers' anger has not' (ibid., xi). The lack of maternal 'voice' in family law discourse is a disturbing reproduction of traditional constructs of the silenced, sacrificial mother in philosophy, psychoanalysis and developmental psychology (Walker 1998; Quiney (Cain) 2007). The affective burden of repressed, unexpressed anger is thus a resonant one for the study of governmental, legal and cultural constructs of mothers.

## 'Parental Alienation Syndrome' as 'Evidence'

In this highly emotional context, and when women's unexpressed anger has so frequently been associated with the higher preponderance of psychiatric diagnoses such as depression and 'borderline personality disorder' (Chesler 1972; Ussher 1991; 1997), the deployment of psychiatric testimony in Family Court cases is an area of particular interest and concern for feminist analysis. Since the 1980s,

---

1 of which is concerned with facilitating and monitoring contact and with enforcing it if the residential parent fails to comply with court orders for contact (Wallbank 2007, 190). No duty is imposed on the non-residential parent who fails to comply with a contact order (Bainham 2003, 74–5; Wallbank 2007, 192).

syndromes have formed part of evidential arguments which postulate certain types of 'difficult' defendant or litigant, such as the battered wife (Downs 1996; Raitt and Zeedyk 2000). These defendants become legally comprehensible as representatives of a specific set of (frequently gendered) reactions, responses or actions.[4] In family law contexts, 'syndrome evidence' can appear to provide a 'scientific' explanation for the apparently inexplicable behaviour of a parent or child, which will provide a gloss of objectivity to any judgement based upon that explanation. The so-called 'Parental Alienation Syndrome' (PAS – a term coined in 1985 by an American psychiatrist, Richard Gardner, to describe his clinical impressions of cases he believed involved false allegations of child sexual abuse; see further Bruch 2001, 383; Johnston 2005) has not received official recognition as a psychiatric disorder, and has been deemed inadmissible by the British courts (Sturge and Glaser 2000; Fortin 2003, 263; Bainham 2005, 161). Nonetheless, its definitions and terminology recur frequently in high-conflict residence and contact cases. According to Gardner, PAS supposedly involves the effective 'brainwashing' of a child through a campaign of denigration of one parent by the other to which the child contributes in order to gain the 'alienating' parent's approbation (Gardner 1998). Gardner's recommended treatment for serious cases is

> to transfer custody of the child from the "beloved" custodial parent to the "hated" parent for deprogramming. This may entail institutional care for a transitional period, and all contact, even telephone calls, with the primary caregiver must be terminated for "at least a few weeks". Only after reverse brainwashing may the child slowly be reintroduced to the earlier custodian through supervised visitation. (Bruch 2001, 385 quoting Gardner 1991, 16–17)

The series of events described in *TE v SH* and the judicial remedies eventually adopted closely follow Gardner's description of PAS and his suggested 'cure' (*TE v SH, S (by his guardian ad litem, the National Youth Advocacy Service)* [2010] EWHC 192 (Fam)) despite the fact that, as already noted, PAS has been explicitly rejected as evidence in British courts.[5] The suggestions of alienation and the recommendation to remove S from his mother's care came initially from the child and adolescent psychiatrist in the case, Dr W, in a report which Bellamy J preferred to the opposing one of the National Youth Advocacy Service.

4 Raitt and Zeedyk (2000) discuss a number of 'syndromes' in their combined psychological and legal contexts and versions, arguing that the 'implicit relation' of psychology and law creates formats for legal actors into which individuals are inevitably forced, and that both disciplines reinforce each other's 'objective' hegemony in this process.

5 See further *TE v SH, S (by his guardian ad litem, Ms J)* [2010] EWHC B2 (Fam) and *In the matter of S (A Child)* [2010] EWCA Civ 325, two subsequent hearings in the case, in which counsel for S argued against his forcible removal from his mother's home and suggested that he might self-harm if transferred directly to his father. An order was eventually made for an interim 21-day stay with foster carers, after which S would be transferred to reside full-time with the father.

The case gives an insight into the hegemonic force of psychiatric testimony, even in a form that has been specifically barred from evidential use; an effect which, as Raitt and Zeedyk argue, is particularly likely where judgements about women and mothering are being made (2000). It would take another chapter to productively discuss the 'implicit relation' (Raitt and Zeedyk 2000) which so effectively enmeshes psychiatric testimony with the operations of law, and the specific authority of scientific expertise which imposes 'syndrome' and 'disease' models on supposedly dysfunctional personal behaviour. Ultimately, and as Raitt and Zeedyk note, productive shifts in the treatment of gendered individuals in the courts will not be achieved until psychiatrists and psychologists produce workable definitions of 'normal' behaviour in traumatic situations, such as sexual assault, abuse or family break-up, which impact upon women in specific, gendered contexts and ways (2000, 178–9). Until that time, it can fervently be hoped that legal practitioners will take increasing note of the 'medical model's' well-publicized tendency to pathologize women, in a much-needed step toward the 'epistemological transformation' for which Raitt and Zeedyk call (179).

Bearing in mind the affective burdens I have already mentioned, their primary impact upon mothers, and the inadmissibility of Parental Alienation Syndrome in the British courts, I turn to a recent case in which residence was transferred to the father of a child described as at risk of emotional harm due to his mother's apparent failure to facilitate contact with his father. The recent case of *TE v SH* is a particularly interesting example of the insidious gendering of 'gender-neutral' judgements about parents which, I suggest, illustrates the complex affective burden held by mothers and the peculiar power of 'syndrome'-based reasoning in high-conflict disputes where psychiatric evidence is introduced.[6] It is not my point here to claim that *all* or even a majority of mothers are thus treated in court, to argue on behalf of the mother in the case, or to claim that her behaviour was in any sense 'right', but to point out the strikingly contradictory ways in which this behaviour and her responsibilities were constructed by the court. The facts of the case are distressing. S, an 11-year-old boy, had grown up with his mother (M) who had separated from his father before he was born. Contact with his father, which had never been more than alternate weekends and shared holidays, had not occurred since 2006 because of the child's apparent wish not to see the father (F). There had been two previous orders for contact, but S refused to engage with them. The presiding judge, Bellamy J, noted 'a consistent theme of concern' about M's hostility to contact between S and F ([10]). Although Bellamy J's judgment criticized both parents, the assessment of M is far more detailed. M claimed to be open to contact, but failed to convince the judge of this.

S's mother had 'significant influence and power' ([11]) in his life according to S's guardian ad litem, who expressed surprise that M 'had not been able to persuade S to even look at a letter from his father' (*ibid.*). S claimed that his mother

6 A similar case, *In the Matter of R (A Child)* [2009] EWCA Civ 1316, was distinguished in *TE v SH*.

had in fact given him the choice whether to read it or not, but for the guardian ad litem this was not sufficient evidence of 'tough love', which (she suggested) would have meant making S write to his two half brothers and to F (ibid.). Thus, M had an obligation actively and even forcibly to encourage and facilitate contact, not merely to allow it. The judge made it clear that F did not fit contemporary 'bad' father stereotypes, and presumably was therefore deserving of better treatment by the mother of his child: he was 'not one of these feckless fathers often referred to by way of justification for the existence of the Child Support Agency' ([11]). The fact that M refused child support for S was regarded as 'specious' (ibid.) and as another attempt to cut F out of the boy's life by undermining the economically supportive actions of a normatively 'good' father.

Bellamy J conceded that F did not have insight into his own more troubling actions. These were mostly attempts to gain control of some kind, such as asking for a DNA test to be carried out on S, to change his surname and to have him privately educated. Bellamy J noted that it was 'unfortunate that the father did not have the foresight to contemplate the damage that might be caused by making these applications' ([7]). He also noted that 'the father's single-minded pursuit of [contact] is blind both to the risk of failure and to the potentially adverse impact on S of continuing the fight' ([8]). However, the judge's exploration of F's *lack* of insight into his actions ended in a favourable comparison with M, who, since she did in fact possess insight into *her* actions, could thus be expected to have done more to facilitate contact. Thus, the father was shown as impulsive and aggressive in his 'fight' for his son, but not as malignant, while M was calculating and immanent in her passive resistance to contact. M also appears as devious, while F is straightforward: 'her efforts have been intended to persuade the court that she has tried her best to make contact work' ([12]); 'I am not wholly convinced that she means what she says' ([11]).

M was assessed by various professionals, the most damning assessment being by a Dr W, a consultant psychiatrist specializing in high-conflict disputes. The phrase 'parental alienation' was specifically used by Dr W to explain S's intolerance of his father ([17]). S's expressed wishes to stay with his mother were ruled 'irrational' ([20]) by Dr W and implicitly by Bellamy J, and not expressive of his real needs and wishes; a conclusion the latter reached in the teeth of the report of the National Youth Advocacy Service representative who firmly believed it would be damaging for S to be moved to live with his father. (According to Bellamy J, this (female) officer had become 'emotionally involved' in the case and had lost objectivity ([21])). In his final decision, the judge said that M had 'behaved wilfully' in creating an antipathy to the father in S ([38]) (although, importantly, the court did not actually find that S had been exposed by M to distorted belief systems or false allegations ([45]). Bellamy J justified his decision to transfer residence to F by reasoning that permanent emotional damage would occur to S if he did not re-establish a relationship with F; that F, unlike M, was likely to maintain appropriate contact with the other parent; and that M admitted having 'lost control' of S in the matter of maintaining contact with F ([93]). In an intriguing and strongly worded assertion of the importance of the biological/genetic tie between father and son, Bellamy quoted from an earlier judgment stating that '[S] needs to be helped to come to terms with the fact that his father's DNA is in every cell of his body and what that implies for his own self-identity' ([73]). He also commented that 'both parents bear responsibility for … mistrust and tension … whereas in the father's case that was the result of lack of insight and empathy … in the mother's case it was more wilful' ([80]).

I have discussed *TE v SH* in detail, since it gives such an interesting description of the *mother's* responsibilities and failings in the context of 'responsible parenting'. As noted in the judgment, S had never actually lived with his father, and the parents had separated before he was born. In the judge's summation of the case, it was, however, clearly *M's* maternal duty actively to foster a contact relationship that would aid S's development as a full individual – conceptualized as a 'balanced' relationship with both parents, and one that would acknowledge the genetic link between himself and his father. Particularly striking is the portrayal of the mother throughout the judgment as quietly and cunningly duplicitous, 'wilful', and complacent. The father's unempathetic, insensitive but implicitly forthright attitude to the 'fight' is clearly preferred. The gendering of the portrayal is subtle but clear: the mother who has looked after the child from birth exerts a rather sinister power over S, which the nonplussed and excluded F is driven to battle against in order to re-establish the primal, genetic link to his son. The judgment resonates strongly with the arguments of critics such as Wallbank (2007), Rhoades (2002) and Featherstone (2010) who suggest that arguments for greater parental equality in the form of shared residence orders conceal a number of difficult gendered assumptions, including the image of the 'gatekeeping' mother. This mother holds too much (feminizing?) power over the children and tends to resist correct facilitation of relationships with the father until forced or persuaded by higher authorities (Featherstone 2010, 214). Brid Featherstone's recent research with fathers involved in contact disputes uncovered representations of mothers as 'powerful unpredictable women who were supported by feminized services' (*ibid.*, 223). The portrait of M in *TE v SH* presents a similar picture: M could not be relied upon to enforce previous contact orders with the 'tough love' apparently required. 'Feminized services' are strikingly represented by the NYAS worker who supported S's right to choose to stay with M, and was judged to be acting in a feminine, 'emotional' and unobjective way.[7]

7 It should be noted that in contexts where paternal conduct is considered to be less than ideal, a non-resident father's voicing of the assumptions named by Featherstone (that the mother has brainwashed his children, and that judges and other involved professionals are biased toward women/mothers) will tend to be sharply dismissed as 'obsessive behaviour': see further the damning judicial remarks in *Re O (Children, Contact: Permission to Appeal), Re B (A Child) (Contact: Permission to Appeal)* [2006] EWCA Civ 1199.

The case of *A v A (Shared Residence and Contact)* (2004), a case cited approvingly by fathers' rights groups,[8] demonstrates a slightly more measured judicial approach to the apparently possessive and manipulative mother (*A Father (Mr A) v A Mother (Mrs A), their Two Children (B and C) (Represented by the National Youth Advocacy Service (NYAS) and their Guardian Mrs P)* [2004] EWHC 142 (Fam) 2004). The case concerned two children, B and C, a boy aged 11 and a girl aged 9, who were living with their mother, Mrs A. Mr A had made an application for a joint residence order and defined contact order in 2002, complaining that Mrs A had been making unilateral decisions about the children's health and education. Mr A asserted that following his objection to a change of school for C, Mrs A informed him that C was frightened of him, and contact between Mr A and C ceased in March 2002. A consultant psychiatrist, Dr L, noted that C had previously been very fond of her father but had now turned against him and did not want any contact. Mr A then applied for a sole residence order in his favour, arguing that Mrs A would abuse a shared residence order. Wall J was not complimentary to either parent in his judgment, describing

> a virtual state of war … going on for over 5 years. It appeared that the first response of both parents in the event of even the most minor disagreement was to rush to solicitors or to make applications to the court … the bundle [of court papers] was a sad testimony that two intelligent people had lost all perspective and common sense in their hatred of each other and their need to battle and win over their ex-partner. I was clear that they had lost the focus on their primary role, which was to raise their children to adulthood … as best they could. ([23])

This warring couple represent vexatious divorce litigants, the antithesis of responsible agents in contemporary family law discourse (Reece 2003; 2006a; 2006b). Since the court made a finding of fact that Mrs A's allegations of sexual abuse were unfounded, Wall J decided to impose an order for shared care of the children with equal time in both parents' care. Although the judgment, including quoted sections from the report of Mrs P, the National Youth Advocacy Service representative involved in the case, criticized the parents both individually and jointly, and 'alienation' was not specifically mentioned as it was in *TE v SH*, it is still clear who is most at fault in creating the schism between father and daughter:

> [P]arents can impose their own wishes and feelings onto children and thus frustrate the formation or maintenance of a proper and loving relationship between the children and the other parent. C had been persuaded by her mother that she did not love her father and did not want to see him, when the opposite was the truth. ([24])

8 See, for instance, the Families Need Fathers website's review of case law on shared residence and responsibility: <http://www.fnf.org.uk/law-and-information/shared-residence>.

In addition, 'some of Mrs A's actions were particularly inappropriate and damaging to the children' ([25]). Once again, the circumstances surrounding the initial split and the events that led to Mrs A's initially having sole residence of the children are unclear, but Wall J does allude to the divorce being 'defended' initially; Mrs A is said to have 'distorted and misinterpreted entirely innocent activities' because of 'the intensity of her feelings towards her former husband' ([24]). In a particularly ironic twist, Mrs A is described as withholding C from contact with her father after she had heard Woman's Hour on Radio 4 debating the issue of children forced to continue to have contact against their will after disclosures of abuse.

With each party acutely aware of their own 'rights', Wall J makes it clear that responsibilities have been shirked on both sides. Over-emotionality is seen to be rife: the judgment takes a disapproving tone when it describes Mr A's continued attempts to achieve 'an acceptance that Mrs A had significant psychological problems, which were the primary causal factors in the family's previous difficulties' ([100]). Mr A is described as stating 'in an increasingly intemperate fashion' that he found Mrs A 'revolting', 'flesh-creeping' and 'a monster' ([102]). His antipathy represented a failure to 'focus primarily on the needs of the children', although it was noted that 'a man in Mr A's professional position would inevitably feel intensely bruised and battered by the allegations of sexual impropriety' ([103]). So, while Mr A is accused of intemperate behaviour, it is rendered at least partly explicable by the severity of the allegations Mrs A has made. No such mitigation is possible for Mrs A, who is portrayed as acting out of intense hatred for Mr A and a misguided sense of victimization which cannot be contextualized by the facts given in the judgment. In this context, Mr A's demands for her to acknowledge that she has a psychiatric disorder seems rather consonant with the tenor of the case as a whole. In the final parts of the judgment Wall J stresses further the need for each parent to relinquish their personal battle for control in favour of shared parenting practice in which 'the home offered by each parent [is] of equal status and importance to the children' ([121]). Wall J notes that he has 'no doubt at all that [Mr A] wishes to be in control' ([125]) and that 'this case has been about control throughout: Mrs A sought to control the children, with seriously adverse consequence for the family. She failed. Control is not what this family needs. What it needs is co-operation. By making a shared residence order the court is making that point' ([126]). Once again, although both parents are criticized as 'control freaks', stronger criticism falls on Mrs A as the instigator of the trouble.

It can be clearly seen that suffocation, excessive intimacy, hysterical imagination, possession, alienation, and selfishness are represented as specifically maternal affects in these high-profile residence and contact cases. For holding on too tightly to the children whose care is indisputably 'dumped' on them in broadly social terms (since they are women and the care burden falls more heavily on them in many ways), they may risk (at worst) imprisonment for defying contact orders (see, for example, *Re V* [2008] EWCA Civ 635). As noted, while fathers in high-conflict disputes certainly receive their share of criticism in the recent case law, it is far more muted than that meted out to mothers;[9] and as Wallbank (2007) notes, while mothers may be harshly punished by imprisonment or transfer of residence for disobeying contact orders, no such punishments exist for fathers who do not facilitate contact, implying that the law places less weight on paternal 'fecklessness' than maternal 'gatekeeping'. A particularly disturbing facet of recent case law involving high-conflict separations and children is the relative frequency of recorded claims by fathers that mothers have 'borderline personality disorder' (claims which are by no means always given psychiatric support (see, for example, *A v G* [2009] EWHC 1807 and *V v V* above). Borderline personality disorder is the notorious 'dustbin' diagnosis for difficult women who do not appear to be respecting established social or sexual boundaries (Ussher 1991; 1997). In this context, Teresa Brennan's remarks on an apparent increase in mother-blaming occurring in times of accentuated concern with boundaries and the loss of them are very pertinent. 'Boundaries, paradoxically, are an issue in a period where the transmission of affect is denied' (2004, 15). The child's boundaries are clearly portrayed as easily invaded in the PAS scenario, whereby its individuality and emotionality can be effectively possessed by the 'beloved' parent/mother. Since mothers, and especially the sinister and possessive caricatures that can be made of them, threaten the loss of subjective boundaries, it is perhaps small wonder that we see their relationships with children in particularly emotionally fraught scenarios portrayed in this way, just as the negative affects actually *borne* by divorcing or separating mothers (women who have probably shouldered the main burden of childrearing and its associated low status, even before separation or divorce) in particular are ignored.[10]

---

9 See further, V *v* V (Implacable Hostility) [2004] EWHC 1215, Re V (Children) [2008] EWCA Civ 635, Re C (A Child) [2007] EWCA Civ 866, A (A Child) (Change of Residence) [2007] EWCA Civ 899.

10 Wallbank (2007, 196) elaborates upon the situation in which a mother may in fact be in fear of actual abuse: '[t]he need to *prove* the violence sets a high bar for women'. She also notes that in all the cases she examines, where abuse is alleged by the mother, 'there is very little detail provided on the fathers' conduct or personalities … [t]here may also be a range of significant forms of behaviour that women identify as placing children at risk such as substance abuse or mental health problems, yet they are not necessarily taken as sufficient cause to negate the presumption of contact.' In such cases it could be argued that the mothers involved bear the burden of sometimes well-founded anxiety for their children as well as that of being portrayed as 'difficult', since the mere risk of violence is not sufficient to offset the presumption of contact with the father (Kaganas and Piper 2002). On feminist strategies for dealing with the problem of violence, abuse and parental conflict in divorce and separation, see further Reece 2006b.

## Conclusion

It is not the point of this chapter to claim that it is only mothers, or indeed women, who suffer the impact of abject affects such as to cause depression or excessive stress; such states are not restricted by gender, age, class or ethnicity. Nonetheless, they clearly tend to collect in the dumping-grounds of neo-liberal subjective hierarchies, where people perform low-status work, fail to 'create wealth', or bear the stigmatizing legacies of sexism, racism, colonialism and heteronormativity. I have tried to show here some of the ways in which women and particularly mothers may be left unable to give back 'what doesn't belong to them' (Caputi 2003) – to refuse the affective burdens of feminization and the care vacuum in neo-liberalism – and how legal language and assumptions around post-separation parenting are contributing to this. Mothers are being too often portrayed as the suffocating *agents* of negative-affect, modern-day Medeas destroying with too much misdirected 'love'. I would argue that such authoritative negative portrayals will inevitably feed back into affective disturbance: women are left with only impossible and contradictory maternal and other self-images to identify with (since previous self-images, as 'liberated' consumerist single woman or valued worker, will very likely suffer serious blows after having children: Cusk 2001; Quiney (Cain) 2007). There must be a point for practical legal reform to be made here: the family law courts would doubtless do a far fairer and more effective job of adjudicating disputes between separated parents if they dropped the pretence of gender-neutrality which creates distorted and frequently impossible expectations of parents, particularly, I would argue, the inevitably gendered mother. Sadly, with the concepts of the gender-neutral 'good parent' and responsible 'shared parenting' holding such powerful political sway across the world, such change seems far off.[11]

The almost complete exclusion of maternal suffering and even of maternal welfare[12] (Lister 2006) from legal and critical consideration (except in the 'disease model' format of depression validated by high-status psychiatric evidence)

11 See, for example, in Australia, The Family Law Amendment (Shared Parental Responsibility) Act 2006 (Cth) ('Shared Parental Responsibility Act') creating a presumption in favour of broadly equal 'shares' of time to be spent with each parent after separation; amending the Family Law Act 1975 (Cth), s 61DA (McIntosh and Chisholm 2008). See also outlines for reform of current Australian shared parenting policy, which has been heavily criticized (Rhoades 2010); for a therapeutic approach to high-conflict post-separation disputes over children in which alienation is alleged, see further Zeitlin 2007.

12 Smart (2004) argues that the overwhelming emotionality of divorce and separation is in fact denied to *both* parents by the legal process (as Reece (2003) emphasizes in her book on the construction of the reasonable and rational 'good divorce'), and that law must find a way to tackle the very gendered hatreds and entrenched positions fostered by relationship break-up (see further Berns 2000; Cantwell 2004; Featherstone 2010, ). I emphasize maternal affect here since, as Smart notes (2006), mothers' disappointment and anger are given so much less public expression at the current time.

revolves around its immeasurability and formlessness; the same deadening depersonalization, the sense of feelings impossible to expose and express to others, emerges in women's personal narratives (Cain 2009). The particular neo-liberal edge of perfectionism, competing demands and compulsory self-criticism which I have noted here is, I suggest, an inevitable accompaniment of forms of social organization which ignore and denigrate 'love labour' and caring relations, even as they demand them in order to operate profitably. Images of suffocation and alienation pathologize the too-powerful, alienating mother shown as seeking to monopolize her children. The negative affect attributed to such a mother represents her failure of responsibility to children, society and law and effectively negates possibilities for more open, productive narratives of care and relationality in the lives of adults and children. The 'dumping' of affect on mothers perceived as too powerful, devious and hysterical represents a dangerous further step toward the normalization of a destructive cycle of 'bad' maternal images. It is exceptionally difficult under current social and legal conditions for a mother to resemble the good gender-neutral parent beloved of responsible citizenship discourse. Too close, and she risks excluding the necessary paternal involvement; too distant, even at work, and she has forgone the few traditional privileges of maternal love labour – that is, the assumption of greater entitlement to the domestic care (and implicitly, love) of children.

## References

Adkins, L. 1995. *Gendered Work: Sexuality, Family and the Labour Market.* Bristol, PA: Open University Press.

Adkins, L. 2005. The new economy, property and personhood. *Theory, Culture and Society*, 22(1), 111–30.

Bainham, A. 2003. Contact as a right and obligation, in *Children and their Families: Contact, Rights and Welfare*, edited by A. Bainham, S. Day Sclater, M. Richards and L. Trinder. Oxford: Hart Publishing, 61–88.

Bainham, A. 2005. *Children: The Modern Law*. Bristol: Jordans.

Barker, N. and Lamble, S. 2009. From social security to individual responsibility: sanctions, conditionality and punitiveness in the Welfare Reform Bill 2009. *Journal of Social Welfare and Family Law*, 31(3), 321–32.

Belsky, J. 1986. Infant day care: A cause for concern? *Zero to Three*, 6, 1–6.

Benard, S., Paik, I. and Correll, S. 2007. Cognitive bias and the motherhood penalty. *Hastings Law Journal*, 59, 1359–76.

Berlant, L. (ed.) 2008. *Compassion: The Culture and Politics of an Emotion.* New York and London: Routledge.

Berns, S. 2000. Folktales of legality: Family law in the procedural republic. *Law and Critique*, 11(1), 1–24.

Bourdieu, P. 1990. *The Logic of Practice*, tr. Richard Nice. Stanford, CA: Stanford University Press.

Bowlby, J. 1973. *Attachment and Loss* (3 vols). New York: Basic Books.
Boyd, S.B. 2010. Autonomy for mothers? Relational theory and parenting apart. *Feminist Legal Studies*, 18, 137–58.
Brennan, T. 2004. *The Transmission of Affect*. Ithaca and London: Cornell University Press.
Brooks-Gunn, J., Hen, W. and Waldfogel, J. 2002. Maternal employment and child cognitive outcomes in the first three years of life: the NICHD study of early child care. *Child Development*, 73(4), 1052–72.
Brown, G.W., and Bifulco, A. 1990. Motherhood, employment and the development of depression: A replication of a finding? *British Journal of Psychiatry*, 156, 169–79.
Brown, S. and Lumley, J. 2000. Physical health problems after childbirth and maternal depression at six to seven months postpartum. *BJOG: An International Journal of Obstetrics and Gynaecology*, 107(10), 1194–201.
Bruch, C.S. 2001. Parental Alienation Syndrome: Junk science in child custody determinations. *European Journal of Law Reform*, 3(3), 383–404.
Cain, R. 2009. 'A view you won't get from anywhere else'? Depressed mothers, public regulation and 'private' narrative. *Feminist Legal Studies*, 17(2), 123–43.
Cantwell, B. 2004. In practice – CAFCASS and private law cases. *Family Law*, 24, 384–7.
Caputi, J. 2003. 'Take back what doesn't belong to me': Sexual violence, resistance and the 'transmission of affect'. *Women's Studies International Forum*, 26(1), 1–14.
Chesler, P. 1972. *Women and Madness*. New York: Doubleday.
Clarke, A.E., Shim, J.K., Mamo, L., Fosket, J.R. and Fishman, J.R. 2003. Biomedicalization: Technoscientific transformations of health, illness, and U.S. biomedicine. *American Sociological Review*, 68(2), 161–94.
Collier, R. 2009. Fathers' rights, gender and welfare: Some questions for family law. *Journal of Social Welfare and Family Law*, 31(4), 357–77.
Collier, R. and Sheldon, S. (eds). 2006. *Father's Rights Activism and Law Reform in Comparative Perspective*. Oxford: Hart.
Collier, R. and Sheldon, S. 2008. *Fragmenting Fatherhood: A Socio-Legal Study*. Oxford: Hart Publishing.
Correll, S.J., Benard, S. and Paik, I. 2007. Getting a job: Is there a motherhood penalty? *American Journal of Sociology*, 112(5), 1297–338.
Crompton, R. 2006. *Employment and the Family: The Reconfiguration of Work and Family Life in Contemporary Societies*. Cambridge: Cambridge University Press.
Crompton, R., Lewis, S. and Lyonette, C. (eds). 2007. Women, *Men, Work and Family in Europe*. Basingstoke: Palgrave Macmillan.
Cuddy, A.J.C., Fiske, S.T. and Glick, T. 2004. When professionals become mothers, warmth doesn't cut the ice. *Journal of Social Issues*, 60(4), 701–18.

Curk, P. 2011. Passions and dependencies: A theoretical account of relational responsibility, in *Taking Responsibility, Law and the Changing Family*, edited by C. Lind, H. Keating and J. Bridgeman. Farnham: Ashgate, 55–68.

Cusk, R. 2001. A *Life's Work: On Becoming a Mother*. London: HarperCollins.

Downs, D. 1996. *More Than Victims: Battered Women, the Syndrome Society and the Law*. Chicago: University of Chicago Press.

Duxbury, L. and Higgins, C. 2001. Work–life balance in the new millennium: Where are we? Where do we need to go? Canadian Policy Research Network Discussion Paper W/12. Ottawa: Canadian Policy Research Network.

Etzioni, A. 1993. *The Spirit Of Community: Rights, Responsibilities and the Communitarian Agenda*. New York: Random House.

Featherstone, B. 2010. Writing fathers in but mothers out!!! *Critical Social Policy*, 30(2), 208–23.

Fineman, M.L. 1991. Images of mothers in poverty discourses. *Duke Law Journal*, 274–95.

Fortin, J. 2003. *Children's Rights and the Developing Law*. Cambridge: Cambridge University Press.

Friedan, B. 1965. *The Feminine Mystique*. Harmondsworth: Penguin.

Gardner, R.A. 1991. Legal and psychotherapeutic approaches to the three types of Parental Alienation Syndrome families: When psychiatry and the law join forces. *Court Review*, 14(1), 14–21.

Gardner, R.A. 1998. *The Parental Alienation Syndrome*, 2nd edition. Cresskill, NJ: Donnin.

Giddens, A. 1991. *Modernity and Self-Identity: Self and Society in the Late Modern Age*. Cambridge: Polity.

Gillies, V. 2005. Perspectives on parenting responsibility: Contextualising values and practices. *Journal of Law and Society*, 35(1), 95–112.

Gillies, V. 2007. *Marginalised Mothers: Exploring Working-Class Experiences of Parenting*. London: Routledge.

Hamilton, J.A. and Russo, N.F. 2006. Women and depression: Research, theory and social policy, in *Women and Depression: A Handbook for the Social, Behavioral and Biomedical Sciences*, edited by C. Keyes and S.H. Goodman. New York: Cambridge University Press, 479–522.

Hays, S. 1998. *The Cultural Contradictions of Motherhood*. London: Yale University Press.

Hirsch, M. 1989. *The Mother-Daughter Plot: Narrative, Psychoanalysis, Feminism*. Bloomington: Indiana University Press.

Holt, A. 2008. Room for resistance? Parenting orders, disciplinary power and the production of 'the bad parent', in *ASBO Nation: The Criminalisation of Nuisance*, edited by P. Squires. Bristol: Policy Press, 203–22.

Johnston, J. 2005. Children of divorce who reject a parent and refuse visitation: Recent research and social policy implications for the alienated child. *Family Law Quarterly*, 38(4), 757–76.

Kaganas, F. and Piper, C. 2002. Shared parenting – a 70% solution? *Child and Family Law Quarterly*, 14(4), 365–84.

Kristeva, J. 1982. *Powers of Horror: An Essay on Abjection*, tr. Leon S. Roudiez. New York: Columbia University Press.

Kurstjen, S. and Wolke, D. 2001. Effects of maternal depression on cognitive development of children over the first seven years of life. J*ournal of Child Psychology and Psychiatry and Allied Disciplines*, 42, 623–36.

Ladd-Taylor, M. and Umansky, L. 1997. *'Bad' Mothers: The Politics of Blame in Twentieth Century America*. New York: New York University Press.

Leach, P. 2003. *Your Baby and Child*. London: Dorling Kindersley.

Lewis, S. 2001. Restructuring workplace cultures: The ultimate work–family challenge? *Women in Management Review*, 16(1), 21–9.

Lister, R. 2003. Investing in the citizen-workers of the future: Transformations in citizenship and the state under New Labour. *Social Policy and Administration*, 37(5), 427–43.

Lister, R. 2006. Children (but not women) first: New Labour, child welfare and gender. *Critical Social Policy*, 26, 315–35.

Lynch, K. 2007. Love labour as a distinct and non-commodifiable form of care labour. *Sociological Review*, 55(3), 50–70.

Lynch, K. 2009. Affective equality: Who cares? Available at <http: //74.125.155.132/scholar?q=cache:l1ur8AenyxcJ:scholar.google.com/&hl=en&as_sdt=2000> (accessed 10 April 2010).

Lynch, K. and Lyons, M. 2009. Care-less citizenship? Public devaluation and private validation, in *Affective Equality: Love, Care and Injustice*, edited by K. Lynch, J. Baker and M. Lyons. Basingstoke: Palgrave Macmillan, 78–92.

Lynch, K., Baker, J. and Lyons, M. (eds). 2009. *Affective Equality: Love, Care and Injustice*. Basingstoke: Palgrave Macmillan.

McIntosh, J. 2009. Legislating for shared parenting: Exploring some underlying assumptions. *Family Court Review*, 47(3), 389–400.

McIntosh, J. and Chisholm, R. 2008. Cautionary notes on the shared care of children in conflicted parental separation. *Journal of Family Studies*, 14(1), 37–52.

Naffine, Ngaire. 2004. Our legal lives as men, women and persons. *Legal Studies*, 24, 621–42.

National Statistics. 2000. UK time use survey. Available at <http: //www. statistics.gov.uk/timeuse/summary_results/housework_work.asp> (accessed 27 May 2010).

Newport, D.J., Wilcox, M.M. and Stowe, Z.N. 2002. Maternal depression: A child's first adverse life event. *Seminars in Clinical Neuropsychiatry*, 7(2), 113–19.

Nicolson, P. 1998. *Post-Natal Depression: Psychology, Science and the Transition to Motherhood*. London: Routledge.

O'Brien, M. 2009. The impact of economic, social, cultural and emotional capital on mothers' love and care work in education, in *Affective Equality: Love,*

*Care and Injustice*, edited by K. Lynch, J. Baker and M. Lyons. Basingstoke: Palgrave Macmillan, 158–79.

Papoulias, C. and Callard, F. 2010. Biology's gift: Interrogating the turn to affect. Body and Society, 16(1), 29–56.

Pearson, A. 2002. *I Don't Know How She Does It*. London: Vintage.

Petterson, S.M. and Albers, A.B. 2001. Effects of poverty and maternal depression on early child development. *Child Development*, 72(6), 1794–813.

Pitt, K. 2002. Being a new capitalist mother. *Discourse and Society*, 13(2), 251–67.

Quiney (Cain), R. 2007. Confessions of the new capitalist mother: Twenty-first century writing on the traumas of motherhood. *Women: A Cultural Review*, 18(1), 19–40.

Raitt, F.E. and Zeedyk, M.S. 2000. *The Implicit Relation of Psychology and Law: Women and Syndrome Evidence*. London and Philadelphia: Routledge.

Reece, H. 2003. *Divorcing Responsibly*. Oxford: Hart.

Reece, H. 2006a. From parental responsibility to parenting responsibility, in *Law and Sociology: Current Legal Issues*, edited by M. Freeman. Oxford: Oxford University Press, 459–83.

Reece, H. 2006b. UK women's groups' child contact campaign: 'So long as it is safe'. *Child and Family Law* Quarterly, 18(4), 538–61.

Reece, H. 2009. The degradation of parental responsibility, in *Responsible Parents and Parental Responsibility*, edited by S. Gilmore, J. Herring, and R. Probert. Oxford: Hart Publishing, 85–102.

Reid, S. 2009. The courts took my children away because I'm a working mother. *Daily Mail* online, 2 September. <http://www.dailymail.co.uk/femail/article-1209243/The-courts-took-children-away-Im-working-mother.html> (accessed 18 May 2009).

Rhoades, H. 2002. The 'no contact mother': Reconstructions of motherhood in the era of the 'new father'. *International Journal of Law, Policy and the Family*, 16(1), 71–94.

Rhoades, H. 2010. Revising Australia's parenting laws: A plea for a relational approach to children's best interests. *Child and Family Law Quarterly*, 22(2), 172–85.

Roberts, D. 1993. Motherhood and crime. *Iowa Law Review*, 39, 95–106.

Rose, N. 1996. Psychiatry as a political science: Advanced liberalism and the administration of risk. *History of the Human Sciences*, 9(2), 1–23.

Rose, N. 1998. *Inventing Our Selves: Psychology, Power, and Personhood.* Cambridge: Cambridge University Press.

Rose, N. 1999a. *Governing the Soul: The Shaping of the Private Self*, 2nd edition. London and New York: Free Association Books.

Rose, N. 1999b. *Powers of Freedom: Reframing Political Thought*. Cambridge: Cambridge University Press.

Rose, N. 2007. *The Politics of Life Itself: Biomedicine, Power, and Subjectivity in the Twenty-First Century*. Princeton and Woodstock: Princeton University Press.

Sassen, S. 1998. *Globalisation and its Discontents: Essays on the New Mobility of People and Money*. New York: New Press.

Silva, E.B. (ed.). 1996. *Good Enough Mothering? Feminist Perspectives on Lone Mothering*. London: Routledge.

Smart, C. 1990. Law's power, the sexed body, and feminist discourse. *Journal of Law and Society*, 17, 194–210.

Smart, C. 2004. Equal shares: Rights for fathers or recognition for children? *Critical Social Policy*, 24, 484–503.

Smart, C. 2006. Preface, in *Fathers' Rights and Law Reform in Comparative Perspective*, edited by R. Collier and S. Sheldon. Oxford: Hart, vii–xii.

Smart, C. and May, V. 2004. Why can't they agree? The underlying complexity of contact and residence disputes. *Journal of Social Welfare and Family Law*, 26(4), 347–60.

Smyth, B. 2008. Changes in patterns of post-separation parenting over time: Recent Australian data. *Journal of Family Studies*, 14(1), 208–23.

Smyth, B. 2009. A five-year retrospective of post-separation shared care in Australia. *Journal of Family Studies*, 15(1), 36–59.

Standing, G. 1999. Global feminization through flexible labour: A theme revisited. *World Development*, 27(3), 583–602.

Sturge, C. and Glaser, D. 2000. Contact and domestic violence – the experts' court report. *Family Law*, 30, 615–29.

Swan, E. 2008a. 'You make me feel like a woman': Therapeutic cultures and the contagion of femininity. *Gender, Work and Organization*, 15(1), 58–107.

Swan, E. 2008b. Let's not get too personal: Critical reflection, reflexivity and the confessional turn. *Journal of European Industrial Training*, 32(5), 385–99.

Thompson, T. 2006. *The Ghost in the House: Mothers, Children and Depression*. London: Piatkus.

Troop, E. 1980. *The Woolworth Madonna*. Harmondsworth: Penguin.

Ussher, J. 1991. *Women's Madness: Misogyny or Mental Illness?* London: Harvester Wheatsheaf.

Ussher, J. 1997. *Body Talk: The Material and Discursive Regulation of Sexuality, Madness and Reproduction*. London and New York: Routledge.

Walker, M.B. 1998. *Philosophy and the Maternal Body: Reading Silence*. London: Routledge.

Wallbank, J. 2007. 'Getting tough on mothers; regulating contact and residence' *Feminist Legal Studies*, 15, 189.

Warner, J. 2005. *Perfect Madness: Motherhood in the Age of Anxiety*. London: Riverhead.

Wolpert, L. 2001. *Malignant Sadness: The Anatomy of Depression*, 2nd edition. London: Faber.

Zeitlin, H. 2007. Acrimonious contact disputes and so-called Parental Alienation Syndrome: A model of understanding to assist with resolution. *Medico-Legal Journal*, 75(4), 143–9.

# Chapter 5
# Responsibility in Family Finance and Property Law

Joanna Miles[1]

## Introduction: The Three Axes of 'Responsibility'

'Responsibility' is a multifaceted concept in the family context and beyond (Eekelaar 2006a; Lind et al. 2011). However, it has not received direct judicial attention in England and Wales in relation to the financial and property implications of the breakdown of adult relationships. Recent House of Lords decisions regarding both spouses and cohabitants use the term 'responsibility' in relation to care of children, reasons for the relationship's demise and liability to pay mortgage and other household bills (*Miller v Miller, McFarlane v McFarlane* [2006] UKHL 24; *Stack v Dowden* [2007] UKHL 17). No mention is made of any 'responsibility' (as such), economic or non-economic, that might be owed between the parties following relationship breakdown. This may seem surprising: many consider it self-evident that spouses do and should have mutual financial responsibilities, certainly during marriage and, at least to some extent, on divorce.[2] More specifically, it may seem obvious to some that the economically stronger spouse has – or should have – some responsibility to alleviate the other's economic vulnerability or dependency, at least in certain cases. That said, the self-evidence or otherwise of this notion, particularly post-divorce, may be culturally specific as there is considerable diversity amongst European jurisdictions' post-divorce maintenance laws and practices.[3] Some further contend that those who are not spouses or civil partners but who live together in conjugal, or even non-conjugal, relationships should also carry such responsibilities.[4]

---

1 I am grateful to Rebecca Probert and the editors for comments on earlier drafts. The usual assumption of responsibility applies. This chapter was written before the Supreme Court decision on the appeal from *Radmacher v Granatino* [2009] EWCA Civ 649.

2 References to marriage, divorce etc. throughout should be taken to include their civil partnership equivalents, though we await any case law considering the issues addressed in this chapter in the civil partnership context.

3 Contrast, for example, the Swedish and German situations, described by Jänterä-Jareborg 2011 and Dutta 2011.

4 Space precludes extensive discussion of this issue here; from the extensive English

However, important as these issues are, the discussion so far assumes one axis of responsibility: the 'horizontal' responsibility of private individuals in a domestic relationship for each other's economic well-being even after that relationship ends. Family lawyers in this jurisdiction, perhaps reflecting conventions about the scope of 'family law' (cf. Probert 2007), tend more or less automatically to focus on that responsibility (for notable exceptions see Herring 2005; Diduck 2008; and from a Canadian perspective, Ferguson 2008). But, as Martha Fineman (2004) has demonstrated, it is essential that the issue is viewed in a broader context so that we do not overlook other candidates on whom we might place at least some responsibility for alleviating an individual's economic vulnerability. There are at least two contenders: first, the 'local' responsibility that I have for myself; and second, the 'vertical' responsibility of the state, or (put a slightly different way) the wider community, for the economic position of its citizens.[5]

The key task is to determine the appropriate distribution of responsibility between these three and so to determine the content of each type of responsibility. We need to attend to all three concurrently in order to achieve a coherent overall framework of responsibilities, since decisions about any one form of responsibility will necessarily affect, and be affected by, the others; greater emphasis on one axis of responsibility inevitably reduces the significance of others. So we cannot satisfactorily address the family lawyers' familiar inquiry about the nature and content of private individuals' horizontal responsibility for each other until we have taken at least a preliminary position on the importance, nature and content of the local and vertical responsibilities. These axes of responsibility can, of course, be arranged in several ways: as Diduck (2008) has observed, family law (and associated areas of legal regulation) plays a key role in 'shaping responsibility' for care and, in the present context, for the economic consequences of caregiving for the individuals concerned. Individual jurisdictions founded on differing political, economic and social philosophies, socio-economic conditions and cultural practices inevitably adopt distinctive positions. But while the conclusions may differ, the basic shape of the inquiry – the potential sources of responsibility which have to be evaluated and balanced – are likely to be common. This chapter explores the issues principally from the perspective of England and Wales.

One last note of introduction on the concept of 'responsibility': in this chapter I use the term in at least two senses reflecting my agreement with the editors of this volume that the notion of 'responsibility' can encompass both legally defined and enforceable duties and wider concepts of responsible action which are not reflected in any specifically legal obligation. In discussing the financial remedies that exist between spouses following divorce in the last part of this chapter, I use 'responsibility' to denote a straightforward legal responsibility (deriving from an

and Welsh literature, see Barlow et al. 2005; Bottomley and Wong 2006; Law Commission 2006; 2007; Glennon 2008; Lord Lester's Cohabitation Bill 2009 (HL).

5 Fineman also considers responsibility of the market; like her, I address these issues via the state's responsibility as labour market regulator.

underlying judgement of moral responsibility) imposed on one party to transfer assets to the other. However, in other parts of this chapter I use 'responsibility' in a broader sense, connoting a societal expectation (possibly shared or promoted in some manner by the legal system, the wider state or its agents) of certain behaviour. Failure to behave 'responsibly' in this sense may sometimes result in direct legal sanctions, such as the withdrawal of welfare benefits. But failure may otherwise simply result in the individual not being rescued (whether by the state or another private individual) from any adverse consequences that might arise from his or her conduct, or – least concretely, but no less powerfully – in being chastised as 'irresponsible'.

## The Local Axis: Responsibility for Self

If I am to be responsible for my own financial security several questions arise: who benefits from it? How does that responsibility arise? What does it entail? And how is it upheld? There are at least two beneficiaries (other than myself, where I positively want to take this responsibility): other private individuals and the state, either or both of whom might otherwise have been made responsible for addressing my economic vulnerability. Responsibility can instead be left with me by various routes. First, I could waive any responsibility that my partner might otherwise have towards me: for example, concluding an agreement forgoing claims for financial relief upon divorce; or (especially in a jurisdiction without remedies for parties to de facto relationships) agreeing to cohabit outside the legal framework of marriage. Secondly, family law itself might limit, or not afford me, the right to claim financial relief from another individual, thus making responsibility for self a matter of public policy and (unlike my first example) not a mere product of private arrangement. Thirdly, the state might inhibit my access to welfare support should I not make what it regards as sufficient effort to support myself, in particular through seeking paid employment, thereby requiring me – or (subject to the two points just considered) my family – to take responsibility for my situation.

### *Taking responsibility through private agreement and individual agency*

English law and policy are ambivalent about individuals' responsibility for their economic well-being, particularly in terms of allowing people to take responsibility for their fate via financial and property arrangements negotiated with intimate partners.

In some contexts, individuals are required or expected to take responsibility for themselves in this way. For example, couples buying a home together are encouraged to make an express declaration of the beneficial shares in which they own the property, on pain of being exposed to the tortuous law of implied trusts if they do not (*Carlton v Goodman* [2002] EWCA Civ 545). Such agreements are legally binding (*Goodman v Gallant* [1986] Fam 106), subject only to the courts' ample discretionary powers to redistribute property on divorce (but not, crucially, at the end of cohabitation). Many opponents of the introduction of financial remedies between cohabitants on separation urge instead that couples should either marry or take responsibility for securing their economic position as best they can within the current legal framework (see for example, the response of Christian Action Research and Education to Law Commission 2006, quoted at Law Commission 2007, para. 2.46). To that end, government-sponsored advice agencies encourage cohabitants to make 'living together agreements' that create and set out their financial responsibilities during the relationship and on its demise (<www.advicenow.org.uk/living-together/>). Other supporters of cohabitants' current legal position put their case more positively: that cohabitants should be *allowed* the responsibility to organize their own affairs free from state interference (for example, *Nova Scotia v Walsh* [2002] 4 SCR 325).[6] Meanwhile, separated parents are exhorted to reach private agreements relating to child support, rather than rely on the statutory agency to do it for them (DWP 2006, paras 21–2, leading to the Child Maintenance and Other Payments Act 2008). The clean break principle has, with various degrees of strength, extolled the individualistic virtue of self-sufficiency, or at the very least of seeking to mitigate one's economic situation, post-divorce (Matrimonial Causes Act 1973, s.25A).[7] Spouses are encouraged to negotiate and cement their post-divorce financial arrangements via consent orders (ibid., s.33).

In a different but not unrelated vein, parents (particularly lone parents) are increasingly encouraged to undertake paid employment to help alleviate child poverty and, it might be added, to prevent or alleviate poverty for themselves in the event of relationship breakdown, reducing dependence on state benefits (DWP 2008b; Welfare Reform Act 2009). The subtitle of a recent policy document – *Reforming Welfare to Reward Responsibility* (DWP 2008a) – reflects the emphasis in contemporary political rhetoric on the idea that individuals' welfare entitlements are contingent on their behaving responsibly, here by seeking to ameliorate their labour market position.

Taken together, to adapt Helen Reece's terminology (2003), all this might be said to amount to an agenda of partnering, parenting and (if it comes to it) separating responsibly. To adopt John Eekelaar's helpful distinction (2006a), it is about both *taking* responsibility for one's position and then *exercising* that responsibility in a particular way; about individual agency in light of (government-

---

6 This decision underpinned a pro-autonomy approach to enforcement of pre-nuptial agreements, *Hartshorne v Hartshorne* [2004] 1 SCR 550.

7 The strong clean break tendency of a series of Court of Appeal decisions was reversed by *Miller, McFarlane* [2006] UKHL 24; Canadian courts took a similar journey from *Pelech v Pelech* [1987] 1 SCR 801 to *Moge v Moge* [1992] 3 SCR 813 and *Bracklow v Bracklow* [1999] 1 SCR 420, and then, in relation to clean break agreements, *Miglin v Miglin* [2003] 1 SCR 303.

endorsed) information received, and state endorsement of certain modes of action and social engagement, notably with the labour market.

*Balancing individual responsibility, paternalism and state interest*

However, English law's willingness to let individuals take responsibility for themselves is not unlimited, particularly where it perceives a threat to welfare or the public purse. This is particularly evident in the area of pre-nuptial agreements. How should the three axes of responsibility be arranged: should some residual notion of the respondent's legal responsibility (notwithstanding the agreement) to make a payment to the other party – and potentially thereby to relieve the state of a welfare responsibility it might otherwise have – supersede the parties' attempt to take responsibility for their own fates through their agreement?

The Privy Council in *MacLeod* [2008] UKPC 64 and the Court of Appeal in *Radmacher v Granatino* [2009] EWCA Civ 649 have recently addressed the legal status of pre-nuptial agreements and associated policy questions, a discussion continued when a bench of nine Justices of the Supreme Court heard the appeal in *Radmacher* in March 2010. For the time being, despite the Court of Appeal's misgivings, pre-nuptial agreements (unlike post-nuptial agreements) remain void and so never straightforwardly binding. The courts have been giving increasing weight to pre-nuptial agreements, particularly following short marriages (*Crossley v Crossley* [2007] EWCA Civ 1491), even where there are minor children, at least to the extent that the agreement adequately provides for their arrival (*K v K (Ancillary Relief: Prenuptial Agreement)* [2003] 1 FLR 120; cf. *M v M (Prenuptial Agreement)* [2002] 1 FLR 654); and where foreign spouses have an agreement that is binding in another jurisdiction (*Radmacher*). However, the weight given to a pre-nuptial agreement is a matter for judicial discretion, operating within the wide parameters of section 25 of the Matrimonial Causes Act 1973. Paternalistically minded judges have ample room to order provision different from that agreed should they consider the bargain unfair.[8]

Baroness Hale, for the Privy Council, appeared to rest her policy distinction between pre-nuptial and later agreements on the risk that a pre-nuptial agreement might be extracted from the would-be spouse as the price for the prized goal of marriage; she contrasted post-nuptial agreements as the actions of 'grown-ups' which merit respect ([2008] UKPC 64, at [42]). While they readily acknowledged the difference of context, the Court of Appeal was respectfully unconvinced that that justified a different approach to pre-nuptial agreements, not least given the potential for post-nuptial agreements to be concluded under equivalent pressure: as the price for the continuation of the marriage (*NA v MA* [2006] EWHC 2900). Instead, by contrast with the Privy Council's approach, the Court of Appeal

8 Contrast the treatment of post-nuptial and separation agreements which, though they can be departed from by the family court, are contractually binding and form the court's starting point, *MacLeod v MacLeod* [2008] UKPC 64, see Miles 2009.

emphasized party autonomy, giving future spouses the right to take responsibility for their financial affairs:

> [T]he very basis of our present law … concerns me. Its usually unspoken premise seems to be an assumption that, prior to marriage, one of the parties, in particular the woman, is, by reason of heightened emotion and the intensity of desire to marry, likely to be so blindly trusting of the other as to be unduly susceptible to the other's demands even if unreasonable. No doubt in its application to each case the law must guard against the possible infection of a contract by one party's exploitation of the susceptibility of the other. But, as a general assumption, the premise is patronising, in particular to women; and I would prefer the *starting-point* to be for both parties to be required to accept the consequences of whatever they have freely and knowingly agreed. ([2009] EWCA Civ 649, at [127], per Wilson LJ)

However, affording parties the responsibility to reach even prima facie binding agreements would not necessarily exclude paternalism's potential to supplant this local responsibility. A paternalistic approach to the policing of formality requirements or to the exercise of a power to set agreements aside may allow one party to abdicate responsibility for the deal. For example, the Australian Family Law Act 1975 provides a scheme whereby pre-nuptial and other marital and cohabitation agreements can be made legally binding. But a recent decision adopted a strict interpretation of the formality requirements in preference to a 'substantial compliance' model. This rendered couples' agreements more vulnerable to judicial intervention and demanded more of those who wish to take responsibility for their own affairs without judicial intervention (*Black v Black* [2008] FamCAFC 7, Jessep 2011).[9] Even where private contracting is permitted, autonomy and protection must still be balanced: put another way, the extent of responsibility left with the parties and enforced in case of dispute must still be determined.

Similarly, in the sphere of child maintenance, despite governmental encouragement of private agreement, the law denies parents' agreements legal force. In the event of dispute, parents are required to submit to the statutory agency and are then deprived of any control over enforcement of either their own agreement or the agency's assessment (*Kehoe v UK* (App No 2010/06) ECHR).[10] Not least given the availability and widespread use of consent orders covering all other financial aspects of a divorce, it is unclear why parents should be denied any responsibility for enforcing child support, even though the maintenance is for the

9 Compare the relatively relaxed approach of the Canadian Supreme Court to questions of substantive fairness in *Miglin v Miglin* [2003] 1 SCR 303; *Hartshorne v Hartshorne* [2004] 1 SCR 550.

10 On the new balance of responsibility created by the Child Maintenance and Other Payments Act 2008, see Harris-Short and Miles 2011, Chapter 6.

benefit of the child and not the contracting parents. Indeed, children's interests are potentially more jeopardized by parents' freedom to agree that no support should be paid at all than they would be by the state permitting parents to enforce an agreed sum (particularly where the state is failing to do so itself).

*Obstacles to taking responsibility for self via private agreement*

As the Court of Appeal's observations in *Radmacher* indicate, discussion of party autonomy – of being afforded the opportunity to take responsibility for self via private bargaining – is often affected, rightly or wrongly, by concerns about gender, in so far as it is generally still women who are more economically vulnerable within relationships and so following relationship breakdown (see Fisher and Low 2009; Price 2009). Consider a cohabitant who comes out on the wrong side of a property law dispute with her ex-partner: having not made a formal agreement regarding her rights in relation to property acquired in his name during the relationship; having spent much of the relationship engaged in childcare, rather than paid employment; so having made little financial contribution to the household economy; and having little by way of private savings to support herself following separation. In the current state of the law, such an individual would be very unlikely to succeed in a claim to a beneficial interest in the property, and would be left to (rather limited and difficult to operate in practice) remedies for the benefit of any child of the couple under Schedule 1 to the Children Act 1989.

Some feminist commentators criticize such a woman for having 'abdicated responsibility' for her situation (cf. Auchmuty 2007, 190), misguidedly preoccupied by romance and concern for hearth and home, neglecting the stark realities of property ownership (under the law as it stands) and the need to engage with the labour market in order to avoid dependency. For them, family law should not rescue the damsel in distress with a claim for support from the ex-partner: that would only reinforce and endorse her vulnerability. Rather, from this viewpoint, women should be empowered by improved education, information and labour market participation to ensure they do not make that mistake: they must be encouraged to take responsibility for themselves – or to marry (see Deech 1980, and thoughtful discussion by Bottomley 2006).

Others, notably Justice L'Heureux-Dubé dissenting in *Nova Scotia v Walsh* [2002] 4 SCR 325, are conscious of the various obstacles and constraints encountered by those trying to protect their own position. Accurate information is essential to effective bargaining and other strategies for self-protection. Greater efforts must be made to dispel the 'common law marriage myth' which, social research shows, retains many adherents (Barlow et al. 2005 and 2008). Agents working within the legal system also have a responsibility here: research has revealed various aspects of conveyancing which may impede couples' ability to understand the significance of the actions they are taking and so to make informed choices about their property (Douglas et al. 2009). However, being armed with accurate information does not guarantee 'legally rational' (Barlow

2009), appropriately self-interested or responsible action. Cultural, relational and emotional factors can inhibit individuals' ability to protect themselves, particularly where the parties have different expectations about, and degrees of commitment to, their relationship (Law Commission 2006, para. 5.57; Douglas et al. 2009). Indeed, the very need to *reach agreement* may be precisely the problem. Gender difference may play a role here: Anne Bottomley (2006, 196), examining the case of Mrs Oxley, who failed to act on repeated and clear legal advice 'because she trusted her partner', has suggested that men and women approach and interpret discussions (and silences) about property and finances differently. In consequence, they both fail to reach a common understanding about their situation, and – perhaps more dangerously – fail to *realize* that they lack such an understanding until it is too late to renegotiate. In the absence of any family law financial remedies to redress any economic imbalance arising at the end of the relationship, the unlucky partner is left to shoulder her losses alone.

Protecting oneself via employment can also be problematic. Reliance on an independent source of income may – vagaries of the economy permitting – appear to offer a surer means of self-protection than reliance on a (former) family member. However, many obstacles – not least structural inequalities in the labour market and the home, the additional challenges of lone parenthood, lack of access to adequate, affordable childcare provision – inhibit labour market participation (Bellamy and Rake 2005; Bryan and Sevilla Sanz 2008; La Valle et al. 2008; and the compelling testimonies collected by Gingerbread 2008). UK labour market data indicate that a higher proportion of women than men are out of paid employment and economically inactive owing to domestic responsibilities, are working only part-time, or have requested flexible working patterns (ONS 2009, Chapter 4; Price 2009; Scott and Dex 2009). The responsibilities of the state to regulate this area are addressed in the next section.

The local axis of responsibility – taking responsibility for self – is complex. Competing concerns and influences produce a less than coherent overall picture in English law. Some individuals who would like to be able to take responsibility for themselves are frustrated in that endeavour by legal rules or systemic inequalities which deny them the agency that they seek. This is particularly evident in the context of marriage, where paternalism has the upper hand in regulating marital contracting. Conversely, in other contexts – cohabitants' relationships, and lone parents' 'responsibility' to engage with the labour market – a legal or policy expectation that individuals can, will or should take responsibility for their situation may neglect the real difficulties that individuals face, entirely blamelessly, in attempting to meet that responsibility.

## The Vertical Axis: Responsibility of the State

The discussion so far has identified one clear role for the state: facilitating individuals' ability to take responsibility for themselves. The state has a key educative function in providing basic information that individuals need to make informed choices regarding the legal consequences of different types of relationship, different types of property transaction, and so on. But there is a strong argument for imposing on the state rather more substantial responsibilities to support families and caregiving within them.

Martha Fineman – writing in the US context, in which conventional understandings of the state's role are (judged from a European perspective) starkly limited – provides a compelling case for placing responsibility on the state, and with it wider society, for alleviating the economic disadvantage of unpaid caregivers (2004, Chapter 2). We are all at some stage 'inevitably dependent' by virtue of the human condition, which necessarily entails vulnerable phases of infancy, youth, old age and infirmity. Caring for these inevitable dependants is a socially valuable and necessary function. Those who undertake that care unpaid within the family in turn render themselves 'derivatively dependent' (2004, 34ff.).[11] In social terms, individuals caring for their own children are not undertaking an essentially self-regarding task aimed purely at satisfying private preferences. They (like – in rather different ways – farmers or the armed forces, say) perform an essential 'society preserving' role (2004, 48), producing the next generation of which government and the market will be 'consumers' (2004, 43). Viewed in purely economic terms, caregiving in the UK contributes billions of pounds' worth of work to society, dwarfing NHS and social services' budgets (see Buckner and Yeandle 2007).

Yet, Fineman argues, despite the value which caregiving undoubtedly confers on society, the derivative dependency that carers experience consequent on their absence from the labour force continues to be viewed as a responsibility to be dealt with privately by families. Low-income, often lone-parent, families who cannot absorb these costs and so seek state assistance are chastised for becoming a burden on society. At this point in the argument, Fineman invokes a telling analogy, particularly resonant in the current climate, with governments' preparedness to bail out industries experiencing crisis, even if – it might appear today – those industries have to some extent brought that crisis upon themselves. Indeed, she notes, some sectors receive long-term subsidies described as 'investment'. So dependency on subsidy and regulatory support are not evils to be avoided, but universal and inevitable aspects of social existence (2004, 51–3). That being the case, we need to displace the rhetoric of individual responsibility and its abhorrence of dependence (cast as a 'failure to take responsibility') in the family context, and ask instead how the state could shoulder more responsibility for alleviating dependency that arises from the socially essential service of caregiving (2004, 49–54).

Fineman identifies two areas for state action: direct financial support to families; removal of structural inequalities in the labour market (and, by extension, in the

11 On the nature and extent of derivative dependency in the UK context, see Westaway and McKay 2007; Fisher and Low 2009; Price 2009: in addition to lower income and pension saving, women's lower non-pension savings record renders them more vulnerable to economic shocks such as divorce.

home) which impede individuals' efforts to balance and share caregiving and employment, rendering women (in particular) economically vulnerable. Flexible employment conditions, generous (in time and remuneration) maternity *and* paternity leave, parental/carer leave, and state-subsidized, high-quality childcare are all important tools for giving family members equal opportunity to undertake paid employment and to share childcare. The following sections address these techniques in the UK context.[12]

### *Welfare and fiscal support or private financial provision?*

In the UK, the state attempts to limit its responsibility to meet the needs of the economically vulnerable by imposing legal responsibility on family members, at least within intact families (see originally the Poor Relief Act 1601, s.7). Alison Diduck (2008) (who instructively classifies family law as a facet of public law) has argued that by expanding the legal concept of 'family', recently embracing same-sex couples, the state can relieve itself of welfare obligations, 'allocating responsibility for responsibility' onto more private individuals. Legal recognition as family therefore brings responsibilities (as a 'liable relative' within the social security system, Social Security Administration Act 1992, ss.105–8) as well as rights. Even cohabitants, while not formally liable for each other's needs as a matter of either public or private law, are subject to the aggregation rule in assessing eligibility for means-tested benefits (Social Security Contributions and Benefits Act 1992, s.137). This privatizes responsibility for alleviating needs for which the state might otherwise be responsible (see Diduck 2005).

Moreover, even though former spouses are, once divorced, no longer 'liable relatives' for social security purposes, the English courts – whilst not blind to the realities of low-income cases (see for example *Delaney v Delaney* [1991] 1 FCR 161[13]) have nevertheless been reluctant to allow an ex-spouse to cast his former spouse on the public purse where he can afford to provide support (*Peacock v Peacock* [1984] 1 All ER 1069). This alertness to state interests also features in judicial treatment of pre-nuptial agreements: one facet of public policy militating against their enforcement is a concern that individuals ought not to be able by agreement to place a burden on the public purse that ought to be borne privately (*MacLeod v MacLeod* [2008] UKPC 64 at [41]).[14] As I argue in the next section, however, the justification for private responsibility to alleviate need post-divorce is less than clear.

---

12 On the variation within Europe, see Lewis 2009.

13 This case casts interesting light on earlier perceptions of responsibility for first and second families, allowing an ex-spouse to prioritize the needs of a second family; cf. the seachange initiated by the Child Support Act 1991.

14 Some jurisdictions have set out that principle in legislation, enabling the court to order maintenance in such cases despite the existence of an otherwise binding private agreement, for example Family Law Act 1975 (Aus), s.90F.

The courts have gone further still in alleviating state responsibility. Even where there is no express or implied public or private law responsibility for one individual to support another, concern about welfare dependency may still influence private law outcomes. English trust law may be thought barren territory for references to responsibility towards family members, let alone the responsibilities of the state. Formally, the courts are concerned here simply to ascertain and give effect to the parties' intentions regarding property ownership. But consider Miss Fowler and Mr Barron [2007] EWCA Civ 377. They had bought a house in joint names, but made no declaration of their beneficial shares, so when they separated, in the absence of any statutory financial remedies, it fell to the court to determine what shares they intended. He had financed the house purchase and the running of the household alone, and (being retired) also cared for the children while she earned the money with which she bought clothing for herself and the children. Arden LJ noted that if Miss Fowler had no beneficial share in the property she might be dependent on state benefits and housing (ibid, at [46]). And, it might be added, the state would have no recourse against him to recoup its expenditure on her. This consideration could only be relevant as a matter of trust law in so far as it indicated the parties' intentions – so Arden LJ must be suggesting that the parties could not have intended Miss Fowler to become dependent on the state in the event of separation. Such a reading of these individuals' intentions might, with respect, be thought to be a little fanciful in so far as it is supposed to reflect intentions that they actually held. But the court's willingness to infer (or impute[15]) such an intention may reflect a norm which people are presumed to hold (in the absence of contrary evidence) that one ought not to leave one's factual dependants reliant on the state, even absent any direct legal responsibility to support them.

But the traffic is not all one way. Despite private law examples like *Fowler v Barron*, the trend over the last half-century and more in public law has been substantially to *narrow* the range of responsible family members by largely excluding kin from the liable relative category and focusing on the conjugal or quasi-conjugal family unit (see Wikeley 2007). Following enactment of the Child Maintenance and Other Payments Act 2008, the state now accepts a full role in alleviating child poverty following parental separation: from 2010, child maintenance will entirely supplement welfare benefits rather than result in a pound-for-pound reduction in state support (DWP 2008a, para. 4.12–4.16), alongside (for the time being, rather generously) means-tested tax credits.[16] Moreover, while various social security laws assume that cohabitants (and some

15 This rather fraught issue has preoccupied trust lawyers since the 1970s and since *Stack v Dowden* [2007] UKHL 17, see *Kernott v Jones* [2010] EWCA Civ 578.

16 Tax credits support both working and caring parents, alongside the rather low-level universal child benefit scheme: see CPAG's annual *Welfare Benefits and Tax Credits Handbook*. Cf. proposals for a guaranteed maintenance allowance for the then rather small number of lone-parent families, DHSS 1974. Proposals for 'wages for housework' have occasionally but unsuccessfully surfaced in this jurisdiction.

other family members) support each other while they are living together (see Wikeley 2007), no form of legal responsibility exists during or endures beyond the breakdown of such relationships (*pace Fowler v Barron*). This potentially – subject to individuals' responsibility to engage with the labour market, discussed above – leaves the state to pick up the tab.

*Re-structuring the labour market to improve work/care balance and sharing*

The UK has actively pursued the second aspect of the state's responsibility in this sphere by regulating the labour market on a more family-friendly basis – extending maternity leave; introducing a (limited) paid paternity leave and the right to request flexible working; subsidizing childcare, in particular via the tax credits system. But the orientation and adequacy of these initiatives have been criticized. As Jane Lewis (2009) has observed, UK policy has focused on facilitating mothers' involvement in the workplace and not on encouraging fathers to engage more with caring responsibilities (see also Scott and Dex 2009). The Equality and Human Rights Commission (2009) has persuasively argued that these well-intentioned, supposedly progressive developments have reinforced *traditional* role allocation: that it is for mothers to undertake care and so suspend or modify their paid employment, while dominant workplace culture and the regulatory framework leaves fathers – many of whom would like to play a greater care-giving role – still feeling obliged to live up to the 'ideal worker' model by forgoing their limited leave entitlements. Lone parents continue to cite, amongst other things, the lack of wrap-around, affordable childcare as a factor inhibiting their ability to work: even with tax credits, the sums simply do not add up for many families (Gingerbread 2008).

Clearly, more could be done to develop UK labour market and employment culture to make it more supportive of a work/care balance by both parents. But it is also worth noting reservations about 'solving' the problem of individual economic vulnerability by enabling female labour market participation. That solution could be said still to downgrade the socially and economically valuable function of caring in the home by implying that mothers (and fathers) ought to be out in the labour force instead (Mumford 2007). As Martha Fineman (2004, 40) has observed, there is not a little irony in the fact that many mothers training for the labour force in the US as a result of welfare reforms are training to become childcare workers. Moreover, as Eva Kittay (in this volume) highlights, when women in the developed world join the labour force, that often displaces caregiving to low-paid, migrant women, who may themselves be mothers of children left to be cared for (with financial support from the mother) by family on the other side of the world.

Our drive to get women out of the home and into the workforce, and children into institutionalized or at least non-familial childcare, may therefore come at substantial personal cost to certain individuals and – depending on our measure of welfare – questionable overall social benefit. The Secretary of State for Children stated in 2007 that:

> Staying at home or returning to work must be a choice for parents, and our role is to make that a real choice – to make both staying at home and returning to work practical and realistic, so that parents can do what is best for them and their children. (Speech to the Daycare Trust, 17 June 2007 quoted by Gingerbread 2008)

Rather more needs to be done by the UK to make that choice real for all families. The current 'welfare to work' policy for lone parents suggests that the current preference is for mothers to work and care, not to choose between them.

## The Horizontal Axis: Responsibility between Private Individuals

I return to my opening theme: private law responsibilities to alleviate economic vulnerability on relationship breakdown. By way of introduction, I shall quickly deal with the common complaint that private law remedies place different values on care: the housewife of a wealthy businessman will generally emerge with a rather larger award than the wife of an unskilled labourer. There are two things to say in response to this. First, that the relevant principles in private law are universal; it is their practical application which will necessarily yield awards of different sizes. This will certainly occur where one principle on which financial orders are quantified is based on entitlement to a share of a specified pool of assets (not, I argue below, a principle of responsibility at all). It will also occur where the extent of the assets means that more can be done to meet in full needs and losses which the universal principles identify but which in lower-value cases simply cannot be met from the available resources. The other response is that private law remedies are seeking to do justice (based on abstract, universal principles) between two individuals in the context of *their* relationship and lifecourse, not by reference to some objective measure of need (an issue explored further below) or market value of services rendered. Depending on the nature of the principles deployed, sensitivity to the living standard enjoyed by each party during and at the end of their relationship, or to the damage to earning capacity incurred (necessarily a function of that individual's qualifications and experience), may be necessary in quantifying the transfer of assets required.

### *Justifying the allocation of responsibility to support to the private individual*

We need good reason to ameliorate one individual's position by imposing a private law responsibility to pay one another. Any legal obligation must have a clear rationale (see also Ellman 1989). Otherwise, we have no secure basis for determining whether that other person is responsible to pay at all, in what amount, or for how long. On a practical level, this leaves courts uncertain of their task, risks inconsistent decisions, and leaves individuals attempting to settle disputes struggling to identify parameters within which to negotiate.[17]

Following the House of Lords decision in *Miller, McFarlane* [2006] UKHL 24, three 'strands' underpin the 'fair' resolution of financial disputes on divorce: need, compensation and equal sharing. Key aspects of all three principles remain unclear, as does the relationship between them (see *Charman v Charman (No 4)* [2007] EWCA Civ 503, Miles 2008). As explored below, the rationale for equal sharing may be thought (at least in part) to be grounded in the distinctive legal status formed on marriage, such that it cannot be translated (at least not in those terms) to the non-marital context.[18] But in so far as the principles base financial relief on functional arguments, in particular about relieving need, compensating for losses incurred or sharing gains accrued as a result of the division of functions, it can readily be argued that similar arguments – similar responsibilities and/or entitlements – should apply between non-spouses, particularly between parents.[19] Lisa Glennon (2008) has argued that discussion of the proper response to cohabitants and other non-married relationships in this jurisdiction has been 'over-determined' by adherence to the form-based distinction between marital and non-marital status, in place of a more flexible, functional approach. However, since space precludes detailed attention to that important issue here, I must risk accusations of perpetuating that over-determined convention by focusing on the nature and content of responsibility following divorce.

In considering the House of Lords' three strands of fairness, we must first distinguish arguments based on entitlement from those based on responsibility. As Bridgeman and Keating (2008, 8) note, nothing is gained by talking in terms of responsibility in relation to the simple correlative of a right vested in the other party which is of its nature exercisable only against the 'responsible' party. I proceed here on the basis that arguments of entitlement in this sphere rest on the notion that past events of one sort or another generate a right to a given share of assets, regardless of whether the entitled party is economically vulnerable in any sense. I reserve the concept of 'responsibility' to arguments that one party should be called upon to relieve the economically vulnerable, or disadvantaged, situation of the other following divorce.

---

17 See recent experience in Canada: *Moge v Moge* [1992] 3 SCR 813; *Bracklow v Bracklow* [1999] 1 SCR 420; Rogerson 1996; 2001; 2004; and in New Zealand: Property (Relationships) Act 1976, s.15 discussed in Miles 2003; 2004; 2005.

18 Cf. Glennon (2008), who advocates a reconceptualization of equal sharing (perhaps of living standard) post parental separation based on the duration not of marriage but of the continuing caregiving which allows the other parent to act as 'ideal worker'.

19 See the approach of Justice L'Heureux-Dubé to the basis of property sharing in the Canadian context in *Nova Scotia v Walsh* [2002] 4 SCR 325; Glennon 2008 in relation to co-parents; Sverdrup 2006. Cf. Law Commission 2006 and 2007 on cohabitants.

*Equal sharing: a principle of entitlement, not responsibility?*

Given that distinction between entitlement and responsibility, it is worth dealing briefly first with equal sharing because this principle does not obviously rest on a concept of *responsibility* to support (or even to share), but rather, it may be argued, on a simple entitlement arising from marriage and/or the (presumed) equal division of roles and contributions during it.

The notion of entitlement here is admittedly a weak one: English law has no rule of – and therefore no right to – equal division, rather a discretionary framework within which a strong equal sharing principle has emerged; and there may be debate, particularly after a short marriage, about the pool of property on which the principle bites. However, the operation of the principle is modified by reference to the quality of the parties' actual contributions to the partnership only in exceptional cases; it is more commonly, and simply, overridden pursuant to one of the other principles, not least need (see *Charman v Charman* [2007] EWCA Civ 503 on 'stellar contributions', Miles 2008). That being so, it seems right to treat equal sharing as a form of weak entitlement generally arising from the fact of the marriage partnership and/or the parties' presumed (very usually unmeasured) different but equal contributions to it.[20] As such, however, the equal sharing principle is entirely indiscriminate as a tool for dealing with the economic consequences of family role allocation: it potentially benefits a spouse who has not suffered economically from the marriage or its breakdown, and who has not contributed significantly either to the accumulation of assets now being distributed or to the welfare of the family in other ways.[21] An equal share of a particular pool of capital can undoubtedly have the *effect* of alleviating an economically weaker spouse's needs. But equal sharing is not just a methodology for dealing with economic vulnerability or otherwise allocating responsibility, whether for alleviating need or doing anything else. It has different conceptual foundations.

*Responsibility for alleviating need*

The other two strands of *Miller, McFarlane* – need and compensation – are more obviously grounded in a concept of responsibility. We need to know why responsibility to meet certain needs or respond to certain losses rests with the

---

20 Cooke 2007 provides an illuminating contrast between the partnership and valuation approaches to the equal sharing principle, see further Miles 2008, 385–6 and Sverdrup 2006.

21 Only extremes of misconduct (or exceptionally special contribution by the other spouse) deprive a spouse of his or her due share, *Miller, McFarlane* [2006] UKHL 24; *Charman v Charman* [2007] EWCA Civ 503.

putative payer. Yet the nature and content of those responsibilities in English law remain relatively obscure.[22]

The concept of need requires careful unpacking since the familiar language blinds us to ambiguity. What exactly do, or should, we mean by 'need' here? Need in an absolute/objective sense, or as related to the marital standard of living?[23] If we mean the latter, is the remedy really based on need, or is 'need' being used here as a proxy for a different, more compensatory style of relief – for loss of the marital standard of living, or even to mitigate 'the differential risk between the parties of the consequences of separation' (Eekelaar 2006b)? If we mean need in an absolute sense, is this properly a matter for private law remedies at all – of horizontal, specifically spousal responsibility – rather than the responsibility of the state (Ferguson 2008)?

An important underlying issue that casts light on the existence, nature and content of the responsibility here is the source of the need. The economically weaker party's inability to be self-supporting often reflects the fact that, in order to care for home and family, she withdrew from paid employment and so was unable to acquire the wealth and/or wealth-generating capacity that would have cushioned her on divorce. Here, the basis for relief may in truth not be need at all: need is a *symptom* of the true justification, which lies in the economic impact of that party's contributions to the relationship, and so on compensatory ideas (explored below). There is clear potential for this sort of (largely functional) argument to apply to cohabitants too.[24]

More difficult are cases where the applicant's need originates outside the conduct of the marriage, for example in illness or unemployment, or post-dates the divorce. Here, there is no causal connection between the putative payer and the need, and so any responsibility must originate in the parties' status or role as (erstwhile) spouses. The strongest case for imposing responsibility arises if the need arose and was evident prior to the marriage.[25] Then the other spouse might be said to have assumed responsibility for those needs by the act of marrying the needy party. But that begs the question, what responsibilities *should* we impose on those who marry. Indeed, why should *any* family member – and, if any, why the spouse in particular – be responsible for meeting such needs, rather than the

22 Contrast the more direct attention to these issues, though not to critical acclaim, in Canada by *Bracklow v Bracklow* [1999] 1 SCR 420; Rogerson 2001; Ferguson 2008, 72.

23 For an example of judicial disagreement regarding the scope of remedies based on 'need', see the New Zealand Court of Appeal in *M v B* [2006] NZFLR 641, at [128]–[129], [195] and [248]–[257].

24 Though note Glennon's concerns (2008) about this argument's focus on the caregiver's losses rather than the benefit conferred on the other party, who is enabled to play the role of ideal worker.

25 Cf. Lord Nicholls' and Baroness Hale's brief attention to this question in *Miller, McFarlane* [2006] UKHL 24 where the former talks in general terms about the relief of need from disability (at [11]), the latter contemplates either a causal or temporal relationship between the need and the marriage (at [137]).

wider community (Gray 1977, Chapter 6; Ferguson 2008)? The issue becomes all the starker when the substantial cause of need arises after separation. Is the other spouse, simply by virtue of having taken on the status of spouse, really to be treated as an insurer against all hazards for life? The practice of making nominal periodical payments orders for joint lives might make us think so (see in particular the use of such an order in *North v North* [2007] EWCA Civ 760). Whatever responsibilities are assumed before or during the course of the marriage, ought they to survive *divorce*?[26]

These questions must be answered in the light of the essentially no-fault basis of modern divorce law: answers which impose a heavy insurance responsibility on a former spouse may be particularly difficult to justify in that context (Miles 2003). It cannot be irrelevant that the former spouse ceases as a matter of social security law to be a 'liable relative' of the other spouse on divorce, suggesting that responsibility to meet basic needs has – pending a remarriage – prima facie reverted to the state and the needy individual. Needless to say, these questions arise even more starkly in the case of cohabitants where no explicit, formal commitment has been expressed. Can such responsibility arise from a developing de facto interdependency, absent formal commitment?

*Responsibility for sharing relationship-generated disadvantage*

Some jurisdictions and reformers have moved away from (or supplemented) needs-based relief in favour of compensatory ideas.[27] As noted above, need experienced on divorce – and inability to be self-supporting – is often merely a symptom of economic disadvantage arising from the division of functions within the marriage. This more clearly justifies the law imposing on the other spouse some form of responsibility to address the economically weaker party's position. The objective of compensatory approaches is generally to achieve a form of substantive economic equality between spouses following divorce, recognizing that simply dividing existing capital equally does not guarantee that the spouses start their new lives on an equivalent footing. While they may have equal capital, the allocation of care-giving responsibility during the marriage is likely to have had a differential impact on their earning capacities, such that their economic position will remain unequal. To the extent that the disparity between them is attributable to that role allocation, further financial adjustment – compensation – in some form may be considered necessary. The tendency has been to focus on making the economically stronger party responsible at least in part to compensate the weaker party in relation to

26 These questions are posed very starkly, and not answered entirely satisfactorily, by *North v North*, above, cf. *Seaton v Seaton* [1986] 2 FLR 398.

27 See *Moge v Moge* [1992] 3 SCR 813, interpreting s.15.2 of the Divorce Act 1985 (Canada), as amended; reforms in 2001 to the Property (Relationships) Act 1976 (NZ) and the Family Proceedings Act 1980 (NZ); American Law Institute 2000, §5; Law Commission for England and Wales 2006; 2007.

these losses. We might alternatively focus on the benefit derived by the stronger party from the fact that the weaker party has taken up the slack at home, enabling the former to flourish in the workplace unencumbered (cf. data on the 'marriage premium', discussed by Fisher and Low 2009, 248). Or, in response to concerns about the speculative nature of claims based on lost earning capacity, we might instead adopt John Eekelaar's preference (2006b; 2010) for relief based on the differential risk between the parties of the consequences of separation, given the simple fact of the disparity between them at divorce and the length of the marriage.

However, the basis of this responsibility somehow to compensate (in at least some cases) is not unquestioned. To begin with, given the social value of caregiving and the impact of structural inequalities on many caregivers' disadvantaged position (Ferguson 2008, 74–5), why should compensation for these losses be a matter for any private individual to bear, rather than the state? The state may properly be charged with supplementing family incomes and facilitating family-friendly employment. Does that preclude concurrent horizontal responsibility on divorce? Some would say so, as shown by media coverage (Laugesen 2006) of the first instance (New Zealand) decision of Judge Dale Clarkson in *X v X (Economic Disparity)* [2006] NZFLR 361 – overturned on appeal [2007] NZFLR 502, [2009] NZCA 399. A central issue was the court's statutory power under the Property (Relationships) Act 1976, s.15 to adjust the parties' shares of relationship property in order to compensate the applicant for economic disparity on divorce flowing from the division of functions within the marriage. Mrs X had given up paid employment to raise the couple's children. Given the parties' wealth, that had in no sense been necessary: Mr X could have bought in any amount of hired help, allowing Mrs X to continue to work – or, once the youngest child was in school, resume work – and achieve the professional career which she claimed she had sacrificed. Mrs X having therefore *chosen* caring over career, to Judge Clarkson's mind, precluded her from seeking compensation ([2006] NZFLR 361 at [147]–[149]). She also baulked at the idea that Mrs X should be able now to assert the disadvantage she had incurred by staying at home when she had accrued and would continue to accrue many (non-economic) advantages from doing so which her husband had not enjoyed and for which he could not now claim compensation (ibid at [160]).

Judge Clarkson presents a perspective that resonates with some UK government policy[28] and the views of some feminist commentators: that those able work should do so, and – by extension – if they choose not to do so, should not expect support from either the state or another individual when exposed to the economic implications of their choice on divorce (cf. Deech 2009). But Mr X had not opposed his wife's preference to stay at home: it seems that he supported it, so the decision was (or may be presumed to be ([2009] NZCA 399, at [104])

28 At least for lone parents and for those low-income families who are claiming benefits: see the new conditions requiring partners of benefit claimants to engage in work-related activity.

effectively joint, as in the leading English case of *McFarlane* ([2006] UKHL 24, [2009] EWHC 891). If parties choose to conduct their marriage (or, despite the state's efforts, feel constrained to doing so) in a manner that turns out to be economically detrimental to one of them on divorce, it is appropriate to augment with private remedies whatever support the state might provide. While society benefited from the caregiving, so too – it may be presumed – did the other spouse, whether materially or otherwise: there is a substantial element of self-regarding private enterprise here as well as 'society preservation' (noted by Hale J as she then was in *SRJ v DWJ* [1999] 3 FCR 153). The other spouse was freed, and may continue to be free, to play the role of 'ideal worker' whilst also enjoying the indisputable, lifelong (non-economic) benefits of having children, cared for day-to-day by his spouse, a form of care that they may be presumed to have regarded either as an economic necessity, or qualitatively superior to paid help. The carer's choice to care should not be equated with a choice to shoulder alone the associated economic losses to which the carer will be exposed in the event of divorce. In any event, as Fineman (2004, 42) cautions, characterizing these decisions as the product of unconstrained choice by the carer may be doubtful: if not financial or practical, then *cultural* pressures regarding the 'good mother' icon may influence women's decisions about work and care. State financial support is not going to provide realistic compensation (however measured) to carers whose sacrifices were large; and even the most flexible of labour markets may not enable caregivers re-entering the labour market post-divorce fully to recoup the opportunity costs earlier incurred.

Even if the validity of these types of argument for additional financial relief is accepted,[29] there remains the question of how to recognize and quantify such a claim. Compensation models raise difficult questions of principle,[30] and may be cumbersome and costly to implement. It is a 'truism' that women's earning capacity is habitually compromised by caregiving (*McFarlane (No 2)* [2009] EWHC 891, at [49]). But translating that into concrete awards at the end of individual marriages is not straightforward. This is particularly apparent when it comes to determining quantum.[31] These methodological questions have not been addressed by the English courts, largely because they have rebuffed attempts to calculate wives' losses, tending instead to acknowledge compensation-based arguments simply by ensuring that the applicant's needs are 'generously assessed' for the purposes of the award

29 See Miles 2008 for response to further objections based on concerns about compensation arguments' apparent neglect of respondents' position.

30 See, for example, the 'halving' debate in the New Zealand case law, not satisfactorily resolved in *X v X* [2009] NZCA 399.

31 See Atkin's concerns (2006, 473) about the costly nature of compensation claims, and the plethora of expert evidence adduced by the wealthy litigants in *X v X* [2009] NZCA 399, though the Court suggested that these cases could successfully be brought without such evidence, at [135] per Robertson J and [182] per O'Regan and Ellen France JJ.

(*McFarlane (No 2)*, ibid.),[32] or by taking the view that they are met by equal sharing (*Lauder v Lauder* [2007] EWHC 1227; *VB v JP* [2008] EWHC 112, at [82]).[33] In order to implement compensatory relief cost-effectively, 'individualised justice' and theoretical purity may have to be sacrificed in favour of the 'average justice' (Rogerson 2002, 6) provided by some sort of statutory formula, looser guidelines or a proxy measure for calculating the compensatory component of financial relief. Such approaches are commonly based on percentage sharing of the disparity in future income (cf. American Law Institute 2000; Department of Justice 2008; Eekelaar 2010). English judges' continued reliance on a discretionary, 'generous' assessment of 'need' is a more familiar, pragmatic (if arguably less satisfactory) way of overcoming the practical problems inherent in enforcing this form of responsibility.

## Why Locating Responsibility for Economic Vulnerability on Divorce Matters

The New Zealand *X* case raises basic questions about the nature and extent of individual, inter-personal and (in many cases) state responsibility in this field of human relationships. Many families – many women, lone mothers especially – daily face practical and emotional dilemmas created by the conflict between obligations to family and the workplace. Many will think that Judge Clarkson attached insufficient value to caregiving, effectively denying many women *and men* a choice which they should have. Opinion is clearly divided, but as Rodney Hansen J put it on appeal, 'it is not for the Court … to substitute a retrospective judgment of when it is reasonable for a person to re-enter the workforce for the joint decision of the parties' ([2007] NZFLR 502, at [116]).

Determining where and how to allocate responsibility for the consequences of those decisions is hard. As Craig Lind (2009) has observed, there is a potential trap here for those concerned to advance the position of women. If we acknowledge the still-gendered nature of family responsibilities by providing a compensation claim (and, we might add, extensive maternity leave), do we unwittingly entrap women in those roles? But to try to pursue gender equality by ignoring the situation of those who *do* take on such roles – by refusing to provide substantial state support for their work, by denying them a private law claim in the event of divorce, and instead charging them with the responsibility of self-help – would be to sacrifice those individuals on an altar of gender neutrality that belies social reality and

32 While he appears to focus not on the wife's losses but on the fruits of the parties' marriage (the husband's continuing earning capacity: see paras [44]–[45], [113]), Charles J's decision is ultimately needs-based.

33 The House of Lords in *Miller, McFarlane*, like the Canadian Supreme Court in *Moge*, offered no guidance on methodology for formulating orders based on these arguments.

the substantial social and economic value of care. We may not shed many tears for Mrs X, who – whatever the value of her compensatory claim – enjoys a half-share of a considerable pot of wealth. But reduce the figures, and we soon reach cases in which failure to enforce any measure of horizontal responsibility (whether articulated in terms of need or otherwise) against the other spouse could leave an individual who gave up paid work to care in considerable difficulty.[34]

What matters is not gender (or, arguably, the form of the relationship, spousal or otherwise), but the value of caregiving, whoever undertakes it; ensuring that those who care are not left to shoulder the economic consequences alone; and the wider problem of dependency. What sort of society do we want to be? How do we wish the socially inevitable responsibility of caregiving to be performed and by whom? And, whether the family stays intact or separates, how should responsibility for the economic consequences of care, or for economic vulnerability however arising, be shared between dependent individuals, their former partners and the state?

## Postscript

Since this chapter was written, the Supreme Court handed down its judgment in the further appeal of *Radmacher v Granatino* ([2010] UKSC 42). The Court held by a majority of eight to one that pre-nuptial agreements could no longer be held void on grounds of public policy, but that – whilst they may in theory now be enforceable (an issue that was not necessary for decision in this case) – both they and post-nuptial agreements remained subject to the overriding jurisdiction of the matrimonial courts to grant ancillary relief, a jurisdiction which no agreement may exclude. The majority largely affirmed the Court of Appeal decision, emphasizing the importance of upholding party autonomy where parties clearly intended that their agreement should be effective, holding that

> The court should give effect to a [pre- or post-] nuptial agreement that is freely entered into by each party with a full appreciation of its implications unless in the circumstances prevailing it would not be fair to hold the parties to their agreement. (At [75])

The central issue then is the parameters of 'fairness' for these purposes. The Court acknowledged that parties are free to make an agreement which makes provision different from that which a court would have ordered in the absence of an agreement: 'the fact of the agreement is capable of altering what is fair'. However, it is important to note that the 'horizontal responsibility' that exists between former spouses cannot be entirely excluded by agreement. This is because the Court essentially concluded that, while parties are free to disapply or modify the operation of the 'equal sharing' principle, it will readily be found that it would not

34 See the analysis of *CR v CR* [2007] EWHC 3334, at [92] in Miles 2008, 390–91.

be fair to hold parties to an agreement which precludes any financial relief based on need or compensation where that would leave one party 'in a predicament of real need, while the other enjoys a sufficiency or more' (at [81]). There is to that extent an irreducible core of marital responsibility – of horizontal responsibility – which private ordering may not exclude. This, of course, makes it all the more crucial to identify that core: the true nature and extent of needs-based relief and the compensation principle of *Miller, McFarlane* [2006] UKHL 24.

Baroness Hale's dissent, in some important respects concurred with the majority's treatment of nuptial agreements in ancillary relief proceedings whilst disagreeing with other important points of principle and with the result in the particular case. But she also made challenging observations about the gendered implications of any move to give pre-nuptial agreements greater prominence, remarking that 'there is a gender dimension to the issue which some may think ill-suited to decision by a court consisting of eight men and one woman' (at [137]). She appealed for the issues to be considered democratically following a comprehensive and careful review by the Law Commission. And so it is to the Law Commission that we must now turn. It published its consultation paper on marital agreements early in 2011.

**References**


American Law Institute. 2000. *Principles of the Law of Family Dissolution.* Philadelphia: ALI.

Atkin, B. 2006. Harmonising Family Law. *Victoria University of Wellington Law Review*, 37, 465–86.

Auchmuty, R. 2007. Unfair Shares for Women: The Rhetoric of Equality and the Reality of Inequality, in *Feminist Perspectives on Land Law*, edited by H. Lim and A. Bottomley. London: Routledge-Cavendish, 171–94.

Barlow, A. 2009. Legal Rationality and Family Property: What Has Love Got to Do with It?, in *Sharing Lives, Dividing Assets: An Inter-Disciplinary Study*, edited by J. Miles and R. Probert. Oxford: Hart, 303–20.

Barlow, A. et al. 2005. *Cohabitation, Marriage and the Law*. Oxford: Hart.

Barlow, A. et al. 2008. Cohabitation and the Law: Myths, Money and the Media, in *British Social Attitudes: The 24th Report*, edited by A. Park et al. London: Sage, 29–51.

Bellamy, K. and Rake, K. 2005. Money, Money, Money: Is It Still a Rich Man's World? An Audit of Women's Economic Welfare in Britain Today. Online: Fawcett Society <www.fawcettsociety.org.uk/?PageID=768> (accessed 12 May 2010).

Bottomley, A. 2006. From Mrs Burns to Mrs Oxley: Do Co-habiting Women (Still) Need Marriage Law? *Feminist Legal Studies*, 14, 181–211.

Bottomley, A. and Wong, S. 2006. Shared Households: A New Paradigm for Thinking about the Reform of Domestic Property Relations, in *Feminist*

*Perspectives on Family Law*, edited by A. Diduck and K. O'Donovan. London: Routledge-Cavendish, 39–58.

Bridgeman, J. and Keating, H. 2008. Introduction: Conceptualising Responsibility, in *Responsibility, Law and the Family*, edited by J. Bridgeman, C. Lind and H. Keating. Aldershot: Ashgate, 1–20.

Bryan, M. and Sevilla Sanz, A. 2008. Does Housework Lower Wages and Why? Evidence for Britain, ISER Working Paper 2008-3. Online: ISER <www.iser.essex.ac.uk/publications/working-papers/iser/2008-03> (accessed 12 May 2010).

Buckner, L. and Yeandle, S. 2007. *Valuing Carers: Calculating the Value of Unpaid Care*. <www.carersuk.org/Professionals/ResearchLibrary/Profileofcaring/1201108437> (accessed 12 May 2010).

Cooke, E. 2007. *Miller/McFarlane*: Law in Search of Discrimination. *Child and Family Law Quarterly*, 19, 98–111.

Deech, R. 1980. The Case against the Legal Recognition of Cohabitants. *International and Comparative Law Quarterly*, 29, 480–97.

Deech, R. 2009. What's a Woman Worth? *Family Law*, 39, 1140–45.

Department of Justice. 2008. Spousal Support Advisory Guidelines. Online: DOJ, Canada <www.justice.gc.ca/eng/pi/fcy-fea/spo-epo/g-ld/spag/index.html> (accessed 12 May 2010).

DHSS. 1974. Report of the Committee on One-Parent Families, Cm 5629. London: HMSO.

Diduck, A. 2005. Shifting Familiarity. *Current Legal Problems*, 58, 235–54.

Diduck, A. 2008. Family Law and Family Responsibility, in *Responsibility, Law and the Family*, edited by J. Bridgeman, C. Lind and H. Keating. Aldershot: Ashgate, 251–68.

Douglas, G., Pearce, J. and Woodward, H. 2009. Money, Property, Cohabitation and Separation: Patterns and Intentions, in *Sharing Lives, Dividing Assets*, edited by J. Miles and R. Probert. Oxford: Hart, 139–60.

Dutta, A. 2011. Marital Agreements and Private Autonomy in Germany, in *Marital Agreements and Private Autonomy in Comparative Perspective*, edited by J.M. Scherpe. Oxford: Hart.

DWP. 2006. *A New System of Child Maintenance*. Cm 6979. London: TSO.

DWP. 2008a. No One Written Off: Reforming Welfare to Reward Responsibility. *London: TSO.*

DWP. 2008b. Ra*ising* Expectations and Increasing Support: Reforming Welfare for the *Future. Cm 7506. London: TSO.*

Eekelaar, J. 2006a. Responsibility, in *Family Law and Personal Life*. Oxford: Oxford University Press, 103–31.

Eekelaar, J. 2006b. Property and Financial Settlements on Divorce: Sharing and Compensating. *Family Law*, 36, 755.

Eekelaar, J. 2010. Financial and Property Settlement: A Standard Deal? *Family Law*, 40, 359–67.

EHRC. 2009. *Working Better: Meeting the Challenges of Families, Workers and Employers in the 21st Century*. Online: EHRC <www.equalityhumanrights.com/uploaded_files/working_better_final_pdf_250309.pdf> (accessed 12 May 2010).

Ellman, I. 1989. The Theory of Alimony. *California Law Review*, 77, 1–82.

Ferguson, L. 2008. Family, Social Inequalities, and the Persuasive Force of Inter-Personal Obligation. *International Journal of Law, Policy and the Family*, 22, 61–90.

Fineman, M. 2004. *The Autonomy Myth: A Theory of Dependency*. New York: The New Press.

Fisher, H. and Low, H. 2009. Who Wins, Who Loses and Who Recovers from Divorce?, in *Sharing Lives, Dividing Assets: An Inter-Disciplinary Study*, edited by J. Miles and R. Probert. Oxford: Hart, 227–56.

Gingerbread. 2008. *There's Only One of Me: Single Parents, Welfare Reform and the Real World*. Online: Gingerbread <www.gingerbread.org.uk/portal/pls/portal/!PORTAL.wwpob_page.show?_docname=468171.PDF> (accessed 12 May 2010).

Glennon, L. 2008. Obligations Between Adult Partners: Moving from Form to Function? *International Journal of Law, Policy and the Family*, 22, 22–60.

Gray, K. 1977. *Reallocating Property on Divorce*. Abingdon: Professional Books.

Harris-Short, S. and Miles, J. 2011. *Family Law: Text, Cases, and Materials*, 2nd edition. Oxford: Oxford University Press.

Herring, J. 2005. Why Financial Orders on Divorce Should be Unfair. *International Journal of Law, Policy and the Family*, 19, 218–28.

Jänterä-Jareborg, M. 2011. Marital Agreements and Private Autonomy in Sweden, in *Marital Agreements and Private Autonomy in Comparative Perspective*, edited by J.M. Scherpe. Oxford: Hart.

Jessep. O. 2011. Marital Agreements and Private Autonomy in Australia, in *Marital Agreements and Private Autonomy in Comparative Perspective*, edited by J.M. Scherpe. Oxford: Hart.

Kittay, E. 2011. Why We Should Care About Global Caring, in *Regulating Family Responsibilities*, edited by J. Bridgeman, H.M. Keating and C. Lind. Aldershot: Ashgate, 303–317.

La Valle, I., Clery, L. and Huerta, M. 2008. *Maternity Rights and Mothers' Employment Decisions*. DWP RR 496. London: TSO.

Laugesen, R. 2006. Til dosh us do part. *Sunday Star-Times*. 12 March 2006. Wellington, New Zealand. <findarticles.com/p/news-articles/sunday-star-times-wellington-new-zealand/mi_8185/is_20060312/dosh/ai_n51655202/> (accessed 20 May 2010).

Law Commission. 2006. Cohabitation: The Financial Consequences of Relationship Breakdown, Law Com CP 179. London: TSO.

Law Commission. 2007. Cohabitation: The Financial Consequences of Relationship Breakdown, Law Com No 307. London: TSO.

Lewis, J. 2009. Balancing 'Time to Work' and 'Time to Care': Policy Issues and the Implications for Mothers, Fathers and Children. *Child and Family Law Quarterly*, 21, 443–61.

Lind, C. 2009. Conclusion: Regulating for Responsibility in an Age of Complex Families, in *Responsibility, Law and the Family*, edited by J. Bridgeman, C. Lind and H. Keating. Aldershot: Ashgate, 269–76.

Lind, C., Keating, H., and Bridgeman, J. 2011. Introduction: Taking Family Responsibility or Having It Imposed?, in *Taking Responsibility, Law and the Changing Family*, edited by C. Lind, H. Keating and J. Bridgeman. Aldershot: Ashgate, 1–21.

Miles, J. 2003. Dealing with Economic Disparity: An Analysis of Section 15 Property (Relationships) Act 1976. *New Zealand Law Review*, 535–68.

Miles, J. 2004. Theories of Financial Provision and Property Division on Relationship Breakdown: An Analysis of the New Zealand Legislation. *New Zealand Universities Law Review*, 21, 268–308.

Miles, J. 2005. Principle or Pragmatism in Ancillary Relief: The Virtues of Flirting with Academic Theories and Other Jurisdictions. *International Journal of Law, Policy and the Family*, 19, 242–56.

Miles, J. 2008. *Charman v Charman (No 4)* – Making Sense of Need, Compensation and Equal Sharing After *Miller/McFarlane*. *Child and Family Law Quarterly*, 20, 378–94.

Miles, J. 2009. Upping the Ante-Nuptial Agreement. *Child and Family Law Quarterly*, 21, 513–35.

Miles, J. and Probert, R. (eds). 2009. *Sharing Lives, Dividing Assets: An Inter-Disciplinary Study.* Oxford: Hart.

Mumford, A. 2007. Working Towards Credit for Parenting: A Consideration of Tax Credits as Feminist Enterprise, in *Feminist Perspectives on Family Law*, edited by A. Diduck and K. O'Donovan. Abingdon: Routledge-Cavendish, 189–210.

ONS. 2009. *Social Trends 39*. Online: ONS <www.statistics.gov.uk/social trends39/> (accessed 12 May 2010).

Price, D. 2009. Pension Accumulation and Gendered Household Structures, in *Sharing Lives, Dividing Assets: An Inter-Disciplinary Study*, edited by J. Miles and R. Probert. Oxford: Hart, 257–84.

Probert, R. 2007. *Family Life and the Law: Under One Roof.* Aldershot: Ashgate.

Reece, H. 2003. *Divorcing Responsibly*. Oxford: Hart.

Rogerson, C. 1996. Spousal Support After *Moge*. *Canadian Family Law Quarterly*, 14, 281–387.

Rogerson, C. 2001. Spousal Support After *Bracklow*. *Canadian Family Law Quarterly*, 19, 185–282.

Rogerson, C. 2002. *Developing Spousal Support Guidelines in Canada: Beginning the Discussion – Background Paper*. Online: DOJ, Canada <www.justice.gc.ca/eng/pi/fcy-fea/spo-epo/g-ld/ss-pae/pdf/ss-pae.pdf> (accessed 12 May 2010).

Rogerson. C. 2004. The Canadian Law of Spousal Support. *Family Law Quarterly*, 38, 69–110.

Scott, J. and Dex, S. 2009. Paid and Unpaid Work: Can Policy Improve Gender Inequalities? in *Sharing Lives, Dividing Assets*, edited by J. Miles and R. Probert. Oxford: Hart, 41–60.

Scottish Law Commission. 1981. *Report on Aliment and Financial Provision*, SLC 67. Edinburgh: HMSO.

Sverdrup, T. 2006. Compensating Gain and Loss in Marriage: A Scandinavian Comment on the ALI Principles, in *Reconceiving the Family: Critique on the American Law Institute's Principles of the Law of Family Dissolution*, edited by R. Fretwell Wilson. Cambridge: Cambridge University Press, 472–88.

Westaway, J. and McKay, S. 2007. *Women's Financial Assets and Debts*. London: Fawcett Society.

Wikeley, N. 2007. Family Law and Social Security, in *Family Life and the Law: Under One Roof*, edited by R. Probert. Aldershot: Ashgate, 97–116.

# PART II
# Regulating Responsibilities in Fragmented Families

# Chapter 6
# Negotiating Shared Residence: The Experience of Separated Fathers in Britain and France

Alexander Masardo[1]

## Introduction

One of the most striking developments to have taken place in post-separation care arrangements for children in recent times has been the rising interest in and practice of shared (dual) residence (also explored by Cain and Newnham in this volume). Here, children alternate their home life across the two households of their separated parents, reflecting the fact that a growing number of fathers are expressing a desire to be centrally involved in the care of their children post-separation. Though still a minority practice, shared residence can no longer be seen as marginal. Indeed, there are indications that such approaches make up a significant proportion of those practised by separated families in the UK (Skinner et al. 2007; Peacey and Hunt 2008), in France (Toulemon 2008) and across many other Western countries (Breivik and Olweus 2006; Skinner et al. 2007; Melli and Brown 2008; Smyth 2009; Spruijt and Duindam 2010). These studies, on balance, suggest that shared residence now accounts for around one to two in every 10 post-separation care arrangements. Establishing precise indicators remains difficult, however, given the non-comparability of studies and the disparity in definitions and reporting.

These difficulties are compounded still further given that the very notion of shared residence can be viewed through different lenses, depending on whether it is being considered as a judicial decision, a family practice, an administrative framework, a discourse, an aspiration, an ideology or a political tool.[2] In this sense, shared residence is neither an easily defined nor an easily identified parenting arrangement and one should be aware of its multidimensional character when considering the different ways in which law and policy attempt to understand and regulate responsibility for children in the wake of parental separation.

---

1 I would like to acknowledge the support of the ESRC for funding the research on which this chapter is based: Award No. PTA-030-2002-00230.

2 I am grateful to Christine Skinner for our previous discussions on this point.

As this practice has come under increasing scrutiny, the issue of shared residence has climbed the political agenda in a number of jurisdictions around the world (Rhoades and Boyd 2004; Collier and Sheldon 2006), and the legislative and policy responses have been both varied and controversial. Britain and France represent two interesting cases-in-point. Until recently, their respective legal frameworks governing the practice of shared residence could be seen to run on a similar trajectory, underpinned by a judicial acknowledgement of the possibilities of shared residence but a reluctance to implement orders in its favour because it was still seen as being contrary to the (best) interests of the child. However, when we look at recent changes to the laws governing 'parental authority' in France, marked differences are becoming apparent in their respective approaches. These differences are coming to shape our understanding of how, and under what circumstances, shared residence takes place. While the ways in which such approaches are regulated may not determine the way families arrive at particular arrangements, they may nonetheless act to make certain outcomes more likely than others.

In this chapter I draw on cross-national research which uses qualitative methodology[3] to explore and compare fathers' experiences of managing shared residence in Britain and in France (for an overview see Masardo 2009). Set against the changing legal and policy backdrops of each nation, I explore fathers' experiences of negotiating shared residence, look at the different ways in which law and policy are giving shape to such arrangements and argue that the capacity of regulation to foster change in our perceptions of gender and caring responsibilities is particularly strong in this type of multi-residence situation. Indeed, such practices bring the nomenclature of a lone–absent parent dichotomy into question by asking where this emerging model of family life should be situated.

## The Legal Contexts in Britain and France

In the UK,[4] the introduction of a legal 'presumption of equal contact' was considered as part of a wider review of issues relating to parental separation in England and Wales (DfES, DCA and DTI 2004). While 20 per cent of responses to its consultation favoured such a presumption, the subsequent governmental report on the consultation made it clear that it did not support such a change (DfES, DCA and DTI 2005, paras 11, 13, 42–5). These inter-departmental reports paved the way for legislation enacted in the Children and Adoption Act 2006, which has resulted in courts being given more flexible powers to facilitate child contact and enforce

3 Direct quotations from French respondents appear in their English translation only. Pseudonyms are used throughout.

4 While exploring the wider UK policy landscape, this chapter makes reference solely to the private family law context within England and Wales (English law).

court orders. While the key principle that children benefit from contact with both parents remains,[5] a presumption of equal contact was rejected, as 'impractical'.

Nonetheless, a review of recent case law in this area makes it clear that shared residence orders are now likely to be considered in a greater range of cases. There is no longer a need to show either 'exceptional circumstances' (*A v A* (*Minors*) (*Shared Residence Order*) [1994] 1 FLR 669) or a 'positive benefit' to the child (*D v D* (*Shared Residence Order*) [2001] 1 FLR 495). Neither is the distance between households, the strict division of parenting time (*Re F* (*Shared Residence Order*) [2003] EWCA Civ 592), nor past antipathy between parents (*Re G* (*Residence: Same-Sex Partner*) [2005] EWCA Civ 462) now just cause for a denial in making such orders. Indeed, in 2006, Thorpe LJ made the following observation in *Re C* when overturning the first instance judge and substituting a shared residence order:

> [T]he whole tenor of recent authority had been to liberate trial judges to elect for a regime of shared residence, if the circumstances and the reality of the case support that conclusion and if the conclusion is consistent with the paramount welfare consideration. The whole tenor of the authority is against the identification of restricted circumstances in which shared residence orders may be made (*Re C (A Child) (Shared Residence Order)* [2006] EWCA Civ 235).

The current position is that while s.11(4) shared residence orders are an option and judicial acceptance of such orders is increasing, they remain little used. What remains paramount in the development of such orders is that they continue to meet the underlying 'best interests of the child' principle.

Underpinning the current legal context in France is the notion of *coparentalité* (co-parenthood), which is based upon the indissolubility of ties between parents and children. With the introduction of the law of 4 March 2002, *résidence alternée* (shared or 'alternate' residence) is now an explicit option for separating parents within the French Civil Code and is placed symbolically before other forms of residence: 'the child's residence can be fixed on an alternating basis at both parents' domicile or at the domicile of one of the parents' (art. 373-2-9, para. 1).

Taking as its starting point the exercise in common of parental authority, each parent must not only maintain relations with the child, but also respect the ties that exist between the child and their other parent (art. 373-2). The role of the judge appears to have become one of enforcer in this regard; able to take measures to ensure that effective ties between the child and each of their parents are maintained.[6] This respect towards parental ties now extends in a similar way to grandparents; article 371-4 of the Code declares that children have a right to maintain personal relationships with their *ascendants* (someone from whom you are descended) and vice versa.

5 Under the Children Act 1989, there is no statutory presumption of contact.

6 A parent who disregards the child's right to contact with the other parent can now be sanctioned under article L.227-6 of the *Code pénal* (Criminal Code).

The new law respects the primacy of agreements made between parents, except where this does not sufficiently protect the interests of the child or where the consent of parents has not been given freely (art. 373-2-7). Where parents have reached an agreement on the issues of residence and maintenance, whether between themselves or through a lawyer, this is then 'ratified' by the judge. In this way the agreement then becomes official, though parents are able to agree shared residence without the need to go to court. Where parents are unable to agree, the judge may propose mediation.

At the request of one of the parents or where parents are unable to agree, article 373-3-9 (para. 2) provides that a judge may, unless the interests of the child are not best served, order *un titre provisoire* (a trial period of shared residence for a fixed term of which the duration is chosen by the judge), at the end of which time the judge will make a definitive ruling, choosing between shared residence or residence with one parent. Generally speaking, this term will not exceed six months. Judges are under no obligation to do this, however, and are able to grant shared residence without a trial period.

## The Policy Contexts in Britain and France

In France, the changes brought about in 2002 are now also supported through concrete policy measures aimed at facilitating the exercise in common of parental authority. They include requiring parents to register the addresses of both parents at the start of each school year; modifying the legislation on *sécurité sociale* (national insurance) so that children may benefit from social health insurance through both parents; and a greater recognition of the housing needs of both separated parents. Since 2002, the child of separated parents – whether or not they had been married – is now considered as living at the home of both parents in the calculation of resource ceilings relative to accessing social housing or in the payment of *supplément de loyer de solidarité* (a rent supplement for tenants).

Other special legislative provisions in cases of shared residence now include sharing in the benefit of the family general tax allowance[7] and the possibility of sharing state allowance paid to families with dependent children.[8] Since 2007, parents are now able to make 'a statement of division' with equal sharing of *allocations familiales* (family allowances). If one of them does not agree to the division, the case will be turned over to the *tribunal* (the Social Security court). Parents will also be able to continue to indicate a single allocation if they so wish. The calculation of the amount of the family benefits in the event of division will take into account possible changes in the configuration of the family, including further children and/or stepchildren.

7 Art. 196 of the *Code général des impôts* (General Tax Code).

8 Art. L.521-1 of the *Code de la sécurité sociale* (Social Insurance Code).

In respect of child maintenance, Moreau et al. (2004), reporting on a sample of judicial decisions taken in France in October 2003, found that no child maintenance was paid between parents in 70 per cent of shared residence cases and that in the remaining 30 per cent of cases, parents' earnings were substantially different. Martin and Math explain that the current system of *pension alimentaire* (child maintenance) in France does not have as its objective the reduction in possible costs to the state. Rather, '[a]n implicit objective may be to promote the negotiation between both parents to reach an agreement and thus make this arrangement more acceptable and stable' (2006, 6).

In the UK, policy measures concerning shared residence continue to move slowly through case law and precedent. The benefits system remains predicated upon the notion of one primary care-giver, resulting in a resident–non-resident parent dichotomy that can confer a profound disadvantage on the parent who is treated as non-resident. However, the level of interest accorded issues surrounding shared residence within the legal framework is increasing. For example, the manner in which discretion can be exercised in respect of Child Benefit – from which other forms of welfare for the purposes of childcare recognition flow – has been considered in relation to the practice of shared residence by the Administrative Court in the cases of *R (Barber) v Secretary of State for Work and Pensions* [2002] EWHC 1915 (Admin), [2002] 2 FLR 1181 and *Chester v Secretary of State for Social Security* [2002] All ER (D) 133. The concept of one 'primary carer' in social security legislation has also been challenged successfully in a landmark decision of the Court of Appeal in *Hockenjos v Secretary of State for Social Security* [2005] IRLR 471, in relation to a benefit supplement to Jobseeker's Allowance (available in 1997) payable in respect of dependent children. More recently, this issue has been looked at in terms of priority housing need in the light of a shared residence order made by consent, in *Holmes-Moorhouse v London Borough of Richmond upon Thames* [2007] EWCA Civ 970.

In terms of child maintenance, where parents share care equally, only the one who is claiming Child Benefit will be the so-called 'parent-with-care'. As a result, the non-resident parent may still have to pay nearly half of what they would have to pay if they never saw their child, regardless of whether or not the parent-with-care possesses a similar or higher salary than the non-resident parent. By the same token, payments are reduced to the parent-with-care according to the number of overnight stays.

What is clear is that policymaking in Britain remains predicated on a primary care-giver model, though it is significant that HM Revenue and Customs have recently made explicit reference to Child Benefit being able to be held by both parents in situations where there is more than one child and parents are in agreement (HMRC 2007).

## Research Methods and Respondent Characteristics

Between June 2005 and August 2006, qualitative (semi-structured) in-depth interviews were carried out with 15 French fathers and 20 fathers from England and Wales (making up the British sample) recruited using a 'snowball' referral process; whereby the social contacts between individuals are used to trace additional respondents. All participants had at least one biological child under 19 years of age in a shared residence arrangement, which for this research was defined in terms of time spent in each household; a minimum of 30 per cent over a year. While this sampling frame limited the scope to explore fully fathers' own perspectives on what shared residence means to them and how it might differ from contact arrangements, it nonetheless provided a useful framework within which to explore the intersection of resident and non-resident parenting. Other definitions would have been possible. However, the key issue here is not the precise definition but how and in what ways shared residence, as a family practice, is being shaped through its regulation and consequently what value there is in the concept of shared residence itself.

With regard to respondent characteristics, some clear similarities emerged between the two sample groups in relation to age, employment status, number and ages of children and the geographical proximity of homes. The majority of fathers were aged in their 30s and 40s, were in paid employment, had not repartnered and lived within five miles of their children's mothers. The only notable difference was that while the majority of British fathers had previously been married to their children's mothers, a greater proportion of the French sample had been cohabiting. Other similarities included fathers' claims that, for the vast majority, they had played a central role in the care and upbringing of their children prior to separation and that it had generally been the mothers that had instigated the separation. While we do not have the mothers' accounts here to compare, they are significant nonetheless, since fathers' perceptions of how the relationship had ended fed into the way arrangements developed.

These findings could suggest that fathers with shared residence are a particular subgroup, being more likely to exhibit certain common characteristics or that certain core conditions are more conducive to producing a shared residence outcome. While we should be wary in extrapolating these findings in such a way, given that this is a small qualitative study which has used a snowballing method of generating the sample, the issue would nonetheless merit further research.

Respondents also rarely had more than two children (although those that had repartnered tended to do so within the context of further children and/or stepchildren) and of the total number of 60 children with shared residence, all but four had been under the age of 11 when they first began alternating their residence, with nearly half of all children in each sample group having been under the age of five. Whether this indicates that shared residence is more easily established where younger children are involved is again difficult to say given the small sample size. However, there is other evidence suggesting that where shared residence proves problematic for children themselves, this is more likely to be the case for older children than for younger ones (Neale et al. 2003), and so this proposition is to some extent reinforced.

Given the recent legislative and policy changes in France outlined above, it is possible to speculate that, given time, we should start to discern differences in the make-up, characteristics and experiences of both fathers and families opting for shared residence in France. We would, for example, expect to find an increase in the numbers of younger parents and those on lower incomes with shared residence. It is also possible that the numbers of children with such arrangements in any one family group may also increase, given that the pro-natalist approach adopted in France more generally is now extended to post-separation situations. Finding ways of comparing the demographics of shared residence families cross-nationally over the coming years, though challenging, could lead to considerable advances in our understanding of the nature of the relationship between responsibility for family members and its regulation.

## Patterns of Care

Participants described a myriad of care arrangements together with the contexts within which they took place: whether, for example, they had been adopted from the outset or whether they had developed over time; whether they ran in parallel with residence arrangements for other children; how discernible patterns might vary over holiday periods; the extent of non-overnight caring; and whether or not respondents saw current arrangements changing, for instance, as their children got older.

While patterns of care tended to revolve around a one- or two-week cycle, fathers in the French sample also provided instances of children alternating their residence every two weeks, and a model of care known in the UK as 'nesting', in which the adults would alternate their own residence around the child's one home. While no other cycles of care took place within either sample, several French respondents indicated that they were aware of other families where children were alternating their residence every six weeks in line with the school term system.

Unsurprisingly, fathers revealed a great diversity within these 'cycles' in the actual day-to-day division of care. Even the most common patterns in the French and British samples – namely, alternate weeks and split-week arrangements respectively – exhibited great differences, not only in the days on which the changeovers occurred but also in their timing and logistics. Many arrangements would also include extra daytime contact for instance. The motivations and choices that participants gave for their particular approaches were often driven by a complex mix of reasoned considerations and trial and error. In this sense, arrangements were not static and could vary over time. However, this variation tended to concern the general pattern of care rather than a wholesale renegotiation of the care arrangement.

The most striking difference between the two sample groups was the length of time that parents were willing to agree to be apart from their children. A British respondent, Richard, echoed the sentiments of many fathers within both samples regarding the need for a comprehensible rhythm that both children and parents could keep track of:

> There's a minimum stay and there's a maximum stay. I think a pattern that left children moving from one night here and one night there on the odd fortnight would just … no one could keep track of that and confuse them. There needs to be a comprehensible rhythm […] and that usually means that you're dealing with more than a single day unit. On the other hand, I don't think that more than four or five nights without seeing your mum or your dad is good.

However, while for Richard and many fathers in the British sample this rhythm would generally be reflected in shorter three- or four-day blocks as a maximum period, for many in the French sample, three- or four-day blocks tended to be the point at which children would start to alternate their residence. There were, for example, no instances of alternate day approaches within the French sample, despite this being a fairly common occurrence among British respondents, particularly in the initial stages following parental separation.

Generally speaking, the French fathers described these longer periods of residence as stemming from a desire to limit the to-ing and fro-ing for the children that shorter periods would entail. The British fathers, by contrast, would generally see longer periods of time away from either parent as unhealthy for their children emotionally. Perhaps surprisingly, the length of residence did not appear to be related to the age of the child.

There were then striking differences in the way parents viewed the psychological well-being of the children among the sample groups. Although we are dealing with relatively small numbers, the fathers' accounts may nevertheless highlight wider cultural differences in the nature of the relationship between parents and children and the state with regard to what is considered appropriate for children at different stages of their development.

From what other evidence there is available, these respective differences in shorter and longer periods of residence are also borne out in wider British and French research. For example, Bradshaw et al. (1999), setting a minimum threshold of 104 nights over the year for the 'shared care' group they identify, found that the most common arrangement in their UK sample of non-resident fathers was for the child to spend half the week with the father and half the week with the mother. The second most common arrangement entailed children staying one night in the week, and then every weekend, or every other weekend.

By contrast, in France shared residence appears to some extent to have become equated with an alternate-weeks model of residence. When we look at statistics from the French Ministry of Justice, we see that since the 2002 reforms of parental authority came into force, when shared residence is applied for in the courts –

around one in 10 of all procedures concerning contact and residence of the child – weekly alternate residence is granted for eight in every 10 arrangements (Moreau et al. 2004, 6).

Again, reflecting the findings within the French sample of the current study, it is significant that weekly alternate residence in France does not appear to change appreciably according to the child's age, remaining at above 75 per cent of all children in each of the four age categories reported (0-4, 5-9, 10-14, 15+), including the very young It is also significant that an *à la carte* pattern of care, based upon a detailed parenting plan, still involved equal divisions of time in nearly 80 per cent of these cases, indicating that within a judicial framework at least, shared residence really does appear to equate to more or less equal divisions of time spent in each household.

What becomes clear from fathers' narratives in this cross-national context is that no 'one size fits all', neither are there any categorical rights or wrongs in approach. What might work for one family may not necessarily work for another. In addition, a certain amount of trial and error can be seen as an inevitable consequence of developing an arrangement that seeks to work well for all concerned.

## Negotiating Shared Residence – In the Shadow of Family Law

While three-quarters of fathers in the British sample had made arrangements privately without recourse to lawyers or the family courts, the French sample of fathers was more evenly split.[9] However, while the ability of couples to reach privately ordered agreements could be said to rest primarily upon a mutual respect for each other's parental role, other more pragmatic reasons were also evident among respondents, including the desire to avoid confrontation. Arrangements that had been privately ordered did not always mean that they had been worked out amicably or indeed that they had been in any way 'negotiated', as a British respondent, Bruce, highlighted in relation to his daughter, Sadie:

> [Her mother] turned round and said, you know, "I'm off!" And everything was on her terms. You know, she said, "look, this is it, you can see Sadie the weekends and that's that." I didn't want Sadie to go at all. There was no discussion. "This is what's going to happen. You will see her the weekends and weekends only." And as far as I was told there was nothing I could do about it.

Although Bruce would have liked a different outcome in the form of more contact and involvement on weekdays, he felt unable to 'rock the boat' for fear of antagonizing Sadie's mother and placing himself in what he saw as an even more vulnerable position as far as contact was concerned.

9 Reference is made here solely to issues of residence and contact and not in respect of divorce proceedings and/or financial issues.

While much is made of the fact that only 10 per cent of separating couples with children currently have their contact arrangements ordered by the courts in the British context (DfES, DCA and DTI 2004), a proportion of the remaining 90 per cent are likely to be party to arrangements that have not been worked out amicably or satisfactorily for all parties, if indeed a genuine arrangement has been worked out at all. While many might have reached amicable agreements that avoid the need to go to court, others might have been made under a certain amount of duress, principally in order to avoid potential confrontation. Fathers' accounts could often centre on appeasing the other parent in order to lessen any adverse impact on the children or, equally, avoid ending up in a worse position relative to the contact they did have.

Whether or not fathers had played an equal part in the care and upbringing of their children or indeed been the primary carer, there was a clear sense that parental separation had left them with a sense of becoming a 'second-class' parent. Fathers often felt mothers were able to act arbitrarily and that their own relationships with their children were now somewhat dependent on the mother's goodwill. Since this type of sentiment is more strongly associated with the accounts of non-resident fathers who have very little, if any, contact with their non-resident children, it was somewhat surprising to discover these feelings echoed so strongly among a significant proportion of fathers with shared residence.

Fathers expressed a strong desire to know where they stood on a day-to-day basis in relation to their children in order to be able to move on – in both emotional and practical terms – from the parental separation and begin to rebuild their lives and those of their families. The way they proceeded drew heavily on their perceptions (and misconceptions) of what family law could or could not deliver. The fact that many fathers indicated a preference for some form of court order, even in situations where arrangements had been made without recourse to lawyers or the family courts, or indeed where shared residence had been in place for several years, highlights how insecure some fathers felt in the arrangements they had with their children's mothers. Several indicated that their greatest security lay in their relationships with their children, who they felt would be able to have a greater say in arrangements as they got older. This desire for some form of official legitimation – in particular with regard to younger children – is perhaps a cause for concern in systems that ostensibly seek to promote parental cooperation and decision making over judicial decision making.

In contrast to the French sample, there were no instances in the British sample in which a shared residence order had been made. Several fathers spoke of how they felt a lack of access to such orders acted to legitimize one parent over the other despite the shared nature of their care arrangement, highlighting the symbolic importance fathers attached to them. In terms of shared residence more generally as a post-separation parenting solution, their infrequent use in the British context may also be acting to give a false sense of how parents are dealing with the post-separation care of children.

In this respect, there was also some evidence that consent orders were being used in place of shared residence orders. Colin explained that, after several appearances in court, he and his ex-wife had settled residence arrangements at a 'round-the-table' meeting with her solicitor. It was formally agreed that Colin would have his eight-year-old son Toby, six days out of 14 with slightly more time afforded Colin and Toby over holiday periods. The arrangement was to be set up under the auspices of a s.11(4) shared residence order and the Child Benefit was to be signed over to him. However, Colin went on to claim that despite having signed a consent order, no shared residence order had been forthcoming. Indeed, he had been confused as to whether or not the two orders were one and the same thing.

Whether a preference towards the use of consent orders – ostensibly employed for settling financial matters without the need to go to court – is now becoming more widespread with respect to the organization of where a child is to live is hard to say. It may nonetheless require further scrutiny, not least as such a preference would be likely to mask the levels to which de facto shared residence is taking place, potentially acting in some measure to influence not only the perceptions of the variety of family professionals engaged in such matters, for example, legal advisors and welfare officers, but also parents themselves.

## Regulating Shared Residence – Current and Future Challenges

Although this research has used a specific working definition within which to explore the intersection of resident and non-resident parenting, it in no way provides a definitive guide as to what might constitute such arrangements. Indeed, the point at which one arrangement may be considered a case of shared residence over one of contact is not at all clear and, as indicated in the introduction to this chapter, when viewed through different lenses is largely context-specific. Therefore, when considering how the regulation of shared residence may develop in future years it may be helpful to start by placing this model within the wider context of dynamic family patterns and the principle that policy should seek to help all parents care for their children after separation.

Such an approach presents something of a challenge for policymakers; there is already a struggle to implement policies in relation to financial support (child maintenance) and care issues are, arguably, even more complex and emotionally significant. However, where care is shared in roughly equal measure, a default primary carer model of post-separation family life that lies at the heart of current policy management may act to disenfranchise not only the non-resident parent but also any other members of that household, not least the children. A lack of recognition of childcare responsibilities can lead to multiple levels of disadvantage that can be particularly acute within low-income families. It will be important, therefore, for policymakers to identify and find ways of supporting the needs of separated parents to care equally for their children in ways that do not create disadvantage.

Similar situations vis-à-vis the interest in shared residence exist in France and Britain, though France can be said to lead the way in terms of facilitating policy. In large part, this can be seen as a result of the different ways in which the family is conceptualized. Maclean and Mueller-Johnson (2003, 123–4), for example, explain how the family in France is traditionally highly valued and seen as a cross-generational institution at the heart of society:

> [T]here is a strong school of thought in France that the purpose of contact lies in maintaining the concept of the family over time, through a line which flows from generation to generation. This conceptualisation of the relationship between parent and child argues for the provision of help and support in maintaining this relationship where there is no common household.

In the British context, the variability of possible configurations of family living arrangements and relationships has increasingly led to doubts about the usefulness of such frameworks over time. Rather, the very concept of *the* family as a unit for social observation has been considered as both value-laden and based on outmoded assumptions (Fox-Harding 1996; Hantrais 2004).

## The Dangers of Prescription

In both Britain and France, the notions of private ordering and *coparentalité*, respectively, are supporting the current evolution in the regulation of post-separation responsibility for children and in both contexts 'negotiation' is the key word for the success of these arrangements. The uncharted territory for fathers in the way shared residence is negotiated in this landscape is of utmost importance to future research.

Given the radical reforms adopted within France, it should be asked whether more could also be done to support shared residence approaches in the British context. While there has been considerable legal wrangling and interest group pressure applied to have a presumption of equal contact incorporated into judicial decision making under the Children and Adoption Act 2006, arguably little effort had been devoted to finding ways of supporting families who do share the care of their children or who may wish to do so. This may require more joined-up ways of thinking with regard to the ways in which family law articulates with family policy. Perhaps most importantly will be the need to find ways in which parents are able to come to terms with the nature of separation without setting themselves up in opposition to each other by needing to establish themselves as the resident parent.

More generally, being able clearly to identify shared residence as a distinct model of post-separation care through its regulation may well help to assist families and facilitate the development of policy in the future, where this is appropriate. However, the danger is ever present that as judges and policymakers attempt to pin down what constitutes such arrangements and what does not, its classification may become overly prescriptive. We need only look at the prevalence of an alternate-weeks model of care in the French sample and in wider French judicial statistics to suggest that shared residence may, to some extent, have become equated with such a model in France. Whether this is the result of public preferences having become reflected in judicial decision making or whether judicial decision making has come to influence the way couples proceed represents an important topic for further research, not least as it has the potential to offer wider explanatory power when exploring the nature of the relationship between parents, children and the state.

The dangers of becoming overly prescriptive are clear when we look at differences in the ways in which patterns of care have manifested themselves within the British and French sample groups; namely, through the adoption of shorter and longer blocks of residence respectively. These differences point to the need for flexibility in terms of definition as well as judgement on the part of parents. The fathers' accounts have shown us that there are no categorical rights or wrongs in approach. Therefore, a major challenge arises in the regulation of such practices to resist the temptation to become overly prescriptive in setting definitions that favour a particular pattern of care, however attractive an option this might seem. It will be equally important not to impose any subjective judgements on one type of arrangement over another, particularly since cross-national differences within the sample groups could be seen in part as stemming from differences in attitude regarding the psychological well-being of the children. Patterns of care were dependent on a multitude of factors and often developed through a process of trial and error, indicating that parents themselves are likely to be the best judge of their own family circumstances and the needs of their children at different stages of their development.

Crucially, in the French context, the law of 4 March 2002 provides that in the case of disagreement between parents on the mode of residence for the child, the judge may order a trial period of shared residence that, generally speaking, will not exceed six months. Thus, the main change introduced by the 2002 reforms resides in the power of the judge to impose shared residence on parents who have asked for exclusive residence and to take provisional measures where necessary. Leaving to one side the controversial nature of such a measure, it should be asked whether six months represents an adequate amount of time in which to assess the workability of such arrangements. This is questionable in light of the qualitative data, which suggests such negotiations are more open-ended. As such, these periods of time in themselves will require close monitoring in order to gauge their impact. More importantly still, will be a need to assess the criteria by which judges deem such arrangements workable or not. This will arguably represent a vital area of socio-legal research as the full implications of the 2002 reforms unfold, not least as it will provide us with a greater insight into how notions of *coparentalité*, as they relate to the (best) interests of the child principle, are measured and assessed within the French family law framework.

## Fostering Change through Regulation

The underlying principle of ongoing contact between children and separated parents is now generally accepted as being desirable. Indeed, provided that arrangements are safe and in the 'best interests' of the child, there is now a widely held view that frequency and regularity of child contact with their non-resident parent is associated with children's psychological well-being (Pryor and Rodgers 2001; Lewis and Lamb 2006). The old axiom that children need the stability of one home, though not abandoned, has begun to be called into question.

Nonetheless, the practice of shared residence is still viewed with caution among academics, policymakers, lawyers and the judiciary (for example, Newnham in this volume). Concerns centre on the way debates around shared residence tend to be framed in terms of parental rights rather than the needs of children: for example, the rights of fathers to equal parenting or the rights of mothers not to be forced to have ongoing relationships with their children's fathers (Collier and Sheldon 2006). A certain apprehension is perhaps inevitable given that such arrangements challenge the very basis upon which post-separation family life has traditionally been carried out; namely, that of a split-family–separate-roles (or primary carer) model.

Since the majority of resident parents are mothers and the majority of non-resident parents are fathers, this default model of care delivers gender-biased outcomes. In this context, fathers, in particular, are faced with a series of challenges in respect of negotiating shared residence, several of which have been drawn out within this chapter. These challenges, by implication, affect not only their children but also any other members of that household. It remains to be asked whether the practice of shared residence brings the nomenclature of a resident–non-resident parent divide into question in any meaningful way.

When attempting to respond to this question, it is important to recognize that these demarcations are, in the majority of cases, still reasonably clear-cut and that despite the growing consensus that parents should retain strong ongoing relationships with their children after separation, patterns of contact nonetheless remain variable (Cardia-Vonèche and Bastard 2007). However, although still a minority practice, shared residence appears to be more prevalent than previously thought as one of the ways in which parents care for their children post-separation. Moreover, it is possible to speculate that a rise in numbers of non-resident mothers (Kielty 2005) may additionally serve to influence the development, growth and acceptance of a shared residence model of family life.

The capacity of regulation to foster change in our perceptions of gender and caring responsibilities is particularly strong in the context of shared residence. Indeed, the different ways in which such practices are regulated are arguably playing a large part in determining broader societal understandings of what shared residence entails, that can lend or, equally, withhold a sense of legitimacy to such arrangements.

## Conclusion

Families stand at the intersection of a range of trends affecting society as a whole. Giddens (1998, 89–90), points to 'increasing equality between the sexes, the widespread entry of women into the labour force, changes in sexual behaviour and expectations, [and] the changing relationship between home and work'. There can be no doubt that these trends reflect a new willingness and openness in fathers' relationships with their children that are challenging the notion that men's lives are centrally located in the public rather than the private sphere. I would like to suggest that in the very practice of shared residence, we are looking at a microcosm of wider societal issues. Shared residence, arguably, provides a unique platform upon which the competing demands, expectations and aspirations of contemporary family life are being played out, precisely because it takes place on the periphery of normative roles and expectations – what it means to be a father, a mother, a family, and so on – to some extent free from the cultural scripts that tie us into certain pervasive family ideologies; the mechanisms through which representations of what family life should be like are promoted as normal or 'natural'. One French respondent, Claude, neatly sums up this idea when pointing to the advantages of shared residence:

> It's a dialogue all week and you're able to keep up with everything; the little cut on the hand … you're aware of everything that's going on, so you can play the full role of dad and the full role of mum and that's really important. We are really close. We are a united family – whereas before we were a family, but mum was one thing and dad was another.

Shared residence appears to have provided respondents with an opportunity to challenge certain external validations of their identities as fathers, largely allowing them to set out their own standards relative to care and family practices. These concern aspects of authority that might normally have been restricted within intact couple households or, equally, under more 'standard'-type contact arrangements (Smyth 2005) as they play out their social role as 'father'. In this way differentiated conceptions of family roles are brought into question. So while the capacity of regulation to foster change in our perceptions of gender and caring responsibilities is strong in this type of multi-residence situation, the different ways in which shared residence is regulated cannot be divorced from a growing cultural acceptance that surrounds it.

In this respect, it is worth pointing to a shared residence 'cluster' that was encountered through the sampling procedure, where a group of six fathers with shared residence was encountered within one school-class year group (equating to around one-fifth of the class). One of the four fathers who agreed to be interviewed remarked that he had no doubts that seeing how other parents were managing post-separation parenting had influenced his ex-wife's amenability towards such an arrangement when they separated.

While the extent to which these developing practices are causal in influencing wider parental decisionmaking is hard to say, it is nonetheless reasonable to suppose that the more widely accepted the practice of shared residence becomes, the more likely it is to be taken up as a serious option when parents separate. In this context, I would like to end this chapter by suggesting that through the very practice of shared residence itself, an opportunity is being created not only for such models of post-separation parenting to become more commonplace, but for engaged and participative parenting practices to 'spill-back' into wider communities and society more generally, acting as benchmarks with which to signal extended debate and change. This goes some way to counter arguments that gender equity in the context of family breakdown risks perpetuating wider inequalities in divisions of labour, without first addressing these issues within intact-couple households (Sottomayor 1999). While this does not necessarily mean that we should rethink the rejection of a presumption of shared residence to be made in law, it does, however, point to the fact that we should be mindful not to equate such a rejection with the practice of shared residence per se.

Appraising the ways in which shared residence is understood and regulated in different national contexts will be of the utmost importance to future research over the coming years if we are to contribute to a greater understanding of this phenomenon in particular, and the regulation of caring responsibilities within family life more generally.

## References

Bradshaw, J., Stimson, C., Skinner, C. and Williams, J. 1999. *Absent Fathers?* London: Routledge.

Breivik, K. and Olweus, D. 2006. Adolescents' adjustment in four post-divorce family structures: Single mother, stepfather, joint physical custody and single father families. *Journal of Divorce and Remarriage*, 44(3/4), 99–124.

Cardia-Vonèche, L. and Bastard, B. 2007. Why some children see their father and others do not: Questions arising from a pilot study, in *Parenting After Partnering: Containing Conflict After Separation*, edited by M. Maclean. Oxford: Hart.

Collier, R. and Sheldon, S. (eds). 2006. *Fathers' Rights Activism and Law Reform in Comparative Perspective*. Oxford: Hart.

DfES, DCA and DTI. 2004. *Parental Separation: Children's Needs and Parents' Responsibilities*, Cm 6273. London: HMSO.

DfES, DCA and DTI. 2005. *Parental Separation: Children's Needs and Parents' Responsibilities, Next Steps*, Cm 6452. London: HMSO.

Fox-Harding, L. 1996. *Family, State and Social Policy*. London: Macmillan.

Giddens, A. 1998. *The Third Way: The Renewal of Social Democracy*. Cambridge: Polity Press.

Hantrais, L. 2004. *Family Policy Matters: Responding to Family Change in Europe*. Bristol: Policy Press.

HM Revenue and Customs. 2007. *Child Benefit Statistics: Geographical Analysis 2006*. London: National Statistics.

Kielty, S. 2005. Mothers are non-resident parents too: A consideration of mother's perspectives on non-residential parenthood. *Journal of Social Welfare and Family Law*, 27(1), 1–16.

Lewis, C. and Lamb, M.E. 2006. Father-child relationships and children's development: A key to durable solutions?, in *Durable Solutions*, edited by Rt Hon Lord Justice Thorpe and R. Budden. Bristol: Family Law/Jordans.

Maclean, M. and Mueller-Johnson, K. 2003. Supporting cross-household parenting: Ideals about 'the family', policy formation and service development across jurisdictions, in *Children and their Families: Contact, Rights and Welfare*, edited by A. Bainham, B. Lindley, M. Richards and L. Trinder. Oxford: Hart.

Martin, C. and Math, A. 2006. *A comparative study of child maintenance regimes: Answers to the questionnaire for national informants for France*. Available at <http://www.york.ac.uk/inst/spru/research/childsupport/France.pdf> (accessed 31 May 2010).

Masardo, A. 2009. Managing shared residence in Britain and France: Questioning a default primary carer model, in *Social Policy Review 21: Analysis and Debate in 2009*, edited by K. Rummery, I. Greener and C. Holden. Bristol: Policy Press.

Melli, M.S. and Brown, P.R. 2008. Exploring a new family form – the shared time family. *International Journal of Law, Policy and the Family*, 22, 231–69.

Moreau, C., Munoz-Perez, B. and Serverin, É. 2004. La résidence en alternance des enfants de parents séparés. *Études et Statistiques Justice 23*, Paris: Ministère de la Justice.

Neale, B., Flowerdew, J. and Smart, C. 2003. Drifting towards shared residence? *Family Law*, 33, December, 904–8.

Peacey, V. and Hunt, J. 2008. *Problematic Contact After Separation and Divorce?: A National Survey of Parents*. London: One Parent Families/Gingerbread.

Pryor, J. and Rodgers, B. 2001. *Children in Changing Families: Life after Parental Separation*. Oxford: Blackwell.

Rhoades, H. and Boyd, S.B. 2004. Reforming custody laws: A comparative study. *International Journal of Law, Policy and the Family*, 18, 119–46.

Skinner, C., Bradshaw, J. and Davidson, J. 2007. *Child Support Policy: An International Perspective*. Research Report No. 405, Department for Work and Pensions: HMSO.

Smyth, B. 2005. Parent–child contact in Australia: Exploring five different post-separation patterns of parenting. *International Journal of Law, Policy and the Family*, 19(1), 1–22.

Smyth, B. 2009. A 5-year retrospective of post-separation shared care research in Australia. *Journal of Family Studies*, 15, 36–59.

Sottomayor, M.C. 1999. The introduction and impact of joint custody in Portugal. *International Journal of Law, Policy and the Family*, 13(3), 247–57.

Spruijt, E. and Duindam, V. 2010. Joint physical custody in the Netherlands and the well-being of children. *Journal of Divorce and Remarriage*, 51, 65–82.

Toulemon, L. 2008. Two-home family situations of children and adults: observation and consequences for describing family patterns in France. Paper presented at the 35th CEIES Seminar on 'New Family Relationships and Living Arrangements. Demands for Change in Social Statistics', Central Statistical Office, Warsaw, Poland, 24–25January 2008. Luxembourg: Eurostat.

Chapter 7

# Law's Gendered Understandings of Parents' Responsibilities in Relation to Shared Residence

Annika Newnham

## Introduction

In the family courts, parents are increasingly lectured by judges and told to behave more responsibly; they must recognize how their conflicts harm their children and take responsibility for co-parenting without further recourse to the courts (see, for example, *D v D* [2001] 1 FLR 495; *Re J* [2004] EWCA Civ 1188; *Re T* [2009] EWCA Civ 20; *Re R* [2009] EWCA Civ 358). It is in this context that the judiciary have overcome their earlier dislike of the shared residence order; what was rejected as prima facie wrong in *Riley v Riley* [1986] 2 FLR 429 'is nowadays the rule rather than the exception', according to Mostyn J in *Re AR* ([2010] EWHC 1346, at [52]). This chapter argues that the case law has, during this decade, developed too fast in an undesirable direction (see also Cain in this volume). The available empirical evidence cannot prove shared residence to be superior to any other arrangement. Children's outcomes depend on such a diverse range of known and unknown factors that it is well nigh impossible to draw clear conclusions, but it seems that formal orders have little impact (Breivik and Olweus 2006, 70; Gilmore 2006, 493).

However, English courts have not justified their increased use of this order by reference to the direct benefits to children, but the supposed indirect benefits that flow from using shared residence to make parents behave in a more responsible manner. This is premised on an inadequate, partial understanding of how parents do or should share the responsibilities of post-separation parenting. Shared residence is increasingly considered primarily in terms of status, while caring is invisible. This has contributed to the current unrealistic expectation that shared residence can be imposed to improve cooperation, which is likely to leave many children exposed to unwarranted risks of harm through exposure to conflict (Johnston 1995). Furthermore, the allocation of responsibilities under a shared residence order is implicitly gendered. In the individual cases, and in the wider context where these decisions both inform and are informed by policy concerns, regulation of responsibilities occurs predominantly through what is not being said.

The assumption is that primary carers, most of whom are mothers, will continue to support familial relationships within a new, binuclear structure.

The idea that shared residence should be used this way originates within legal discourse rather than the child welfare sciences. It is unlikely to be a coincidence that the newly discovered supposed side effects of a shared residence order (encouraging paternal involvement and co-parenting) fit perfectly with the ideals and objectives underpinning both the Children Act 1989 and subsequent practice. Although s.8 cases are private law disputes, they are not wholly disconnected from the political debate where separated fatherhood has come to be seen as a problem to be 'managed' by law (Collier and Sheldon 2008, 176; Collier in this volume). Thus, the family courts continue to search for potential solutions, frequently applying them 'with all the sensitivity of a sledgehammer' (Smart and Neale 1999, 180).

The next section of this chapter examines the judicial reinterpretation of the shared residence order's function, linking this not only to the insistence in the Children Act 1989 that parenthood is a permanent responsibility but also to law's inherently patriarchal nature and the focus on the right to have a say rather than the responsibilities of actually caring for children. The following section criticizes the use of shared residence to address the difficulties caused by contemporary family law's insistence that parents must continue to cooperate over their children's upbringing regardless of what it was that caused them to divorce or separate. The gap between the gender-neutral language of the legislation and implicit gendered understandings of parents' responsibilities is examined next. In conclusion, it is argued that the shared residence order should be restored to being about where children live, and that orders should only be made after the court has realistically evaluated the parents' ability to share the responsibilities of caring for their children in such a way that the latter are actually likely to benefit.

## The Dual Purposes of Shared Residence

Family courts' use of the shared residence order is determined to a large extent by legal understandings of what it is that is to be shared and how law is to be used in the regulation of these family responsibilities. In this respect, the cases have little to say; the only subject that is discussed in any detail is the identification of those minor decisions that can be taken unilaterally (*A v A* [2004] EWHC 142, at [133]). It is argued here that the legal preoccupation with decision-making (as well as the financial responsibilities regulated separately under the child support legislation) is not only a reaction to complaints made by applicant fathers, but also indicative of gendered legal understandings of fatherhood and motherhood, rooted in the public/private dichotomy. There is no discussion of the regulation of caring responsibilities under a shared residence order because these are hidden within the private sphere, associated predominantly with women and thus not perceived to be important enough to warrant legal regulation (Olsen 1990, 207).

*D v D* [2001] 1 FLR 495, the case at the start of the current chain of cases reinterpreting shared residence, was a welcome decision. It was held that shared residence cases should be assessed the same way as any other applications under s.8 of the Children Act 1989: through a careful, contextualized application of the s.1(3) welfare test. The case concerned three girls, aged between nine and 11, who spent 38 per cent of their time with their father. The Court of Appeal, overturning earlier precedent, stated that an applicant should not have to prove exceptional circumstances. The application of the s.1(3) checklist led to the conclusion that since the order would reflect the practical realities it would not confuse the children.

However, a less desirable development was that the Court saw the order as having dual purposes: both practical and symbolic. In relation to the latter, the Court recognized that a shared residence order 'removes any impression that one parent is good and responsible whereas the other parent is not' (*per* Dame Elizabeth Butler-Sloss, at [40]). The six years since the parents' separation had been marred by frequent disputes; the father had complained he felt like a second-class citizen and it was felt that the additional symbolic benefits of the shared residence order would enable him to 'go away and make contact work' ([43]). Responsible behaviour was encouraged through the symbolic granting of greater responsibility, which also signalled to the mother that she must not see herself as having the upper hand. Instead, she must prove herself responsible by not obstructing the father's involvement. Practical responsibilities are only mentioned briefly in an abstract observation that the capacity to make decisions while caring for children is 'part of care and part of responsibility' (*per* Hale LJ (as she then was), at [23]).

In subsequent cases, *D v D* [2001] is regarded as having significantly changed the law (see, for example, *Holmes-Moorhouse v Richmond LBC* [2009] UKHL 7, at [7]). Since 2001, there have also been further developments. The judiciary initially emphasized that orders must reflect practical realities; fathers who seemed too preoccupied with their own rights or were unduly confrontational received robust responses from the judiciary (see, for example, *Re R* [2003] EWCA Civ 597). However, once the application was past this first hurdle, courts became increasingly prepared to be swayed by arguments about messages regarding equal status (see, for example, *Re A* [2002] EWCA Civ 1343; *Re C* [2002] 1 FLR 1136). Furthermore, the granting of shared residence orders in cases where the geographical distances were so great that one parent's contact time must necessarily be during school holidays altered perceptions of shared residence and weakened any implicit link between this order and practical day-to-day caring (*Re F* [2003] EWCA Civ 592; *CC v PC* [2006] EWHC 1794; *Re N* [2006] EWCA Civ 872).

A gradual loosening of the tie between allocations of time and the classification of orders means the distinction between shared residence and sole residence with generous staying contact is now a question of degree; this was acknowledged in *Re K* [2008] EWCA Civ 526. Wall LJ has described equal division as 'rare', suggesting that most cases now depart from what could previously have been presumed to be the standard arrangement of 50/50 with weekly changes (*Re T* [2009] EWCA Civ 20, at [35]). In *Re W* [2009] Wilson LJ rejected the submission that shared residence orders should not normally be made in cases where there is a very unequal division of the child's time (in this case 75/25) (*Re W* [2009] EWCA Civ 370, at [13]). This is difficult to reconcile with the stipulation in *D v D* [2001] that orders must reflect reality since they could otherwise confuse children, and is also contrary to the intention of the drafters of s.11(4) of the Children Act 1989 who clearly saw this as an order about where children actually live. Shared residence has developed 'a special meaning' that is 'far removed from the statute' (Spencer 2008, 24).

It is interesting to note that this reinterpretation is purely judge-made; shared residence has changed gradually as members of the judiciary have linked their own comments with observations from previous cases into a self-reinforcing chain that associates shared residence primarily with the equal sharing of power or status. In *Re W* [2009] Wilson LJ quoted Sir Mark Potter P in *Re A* [2008]:

> It is now recognised by the court that a shared residence order may be regarded as appropriate where it provides legal confirmation of the factual reality of a child's life or where, in a case where one party has the primary care of a child, it may be psychologically beneficial to the parents in emphasising the equality of their position and responsibilities. (*Re W* [2009] EWCA Civ 370, at [11])

It seems that the two purposes, the practical and the symbolic, identified in *D v D* [2001] have been separated; in the quote they are linked with 'or', rather than 'and'. It is no longer necessary for the order to reflect a practical arrangement close to equal sharing before the supposed benefits of emphasizing parental equality can be considered. Instead, it appears that the symbolic side of the order has become the most important. Gilmore has justly criticized the suggestion that the order can be made purely for the benefits it offers parents (Gilmore 2010). Harris and George have complained that the shared residence order is currently undergoing a downgrading similar to the parental responsibility order's conversion from 'a thing to *do*' to 'a thing to *have*' (Harris and George 2010, 169). They have rightly criticized the courts' move away 'from the scheme devised by the [Law] Commission and the legislative intentions of Parliament' (ibid., 165).

The current reinterpretation of shared residence is, however, consistent with the objectives underpinning the Children Act 1989, particularly the desire to convert legal fatherhood from something contingent upon marriage into an immutable status 'unaffected by the vicissitudes of adult life' (Roche 1991, 349). There are echoes of 1980s neo-liberal discourse in current debate, when links are drawn between father absence, a wider increase in irresponsible behaviour, and perceived social disintegration (Geldof 2003). Collier and Sheldon have observed that although legal constructions of fatherhood vary across different branches of family law, they are characterized by continuity more than change; the breadwinner paradigm has not been supplanted, but exists 'alongside, and in tension with', the 'hands-on' ideal (Collier and Sheldon 2008, 136). Furthermore, law has been central to 'attempts to entrench, promote and shape the role of fatherhood' (ibid., 23). In this context, it is claimed that a shared residence presumption could help fathers stay involved, and thus strengthen family relationships (but see also Masardo and Cain in this volume).

Law's societal role as arbiter and neutralizer of conflicts makes it inherently conservative, keen to diffuse or obfuscate challenges to existing power structures (Luhmann 1989, 144). Feminist commentators have highlighted law's support for marriage and argued that this is because patriarchy is dependent upon the pater familias as inculcator of patriarchal values and defender of the status quo (Dowd 1995, 41). Recent changes in familial patterns are said to have 'exposed the fragility' of the nuclear paradigm (Silva and Smart 1999, 3). Within this framework, the conjugal family is constructed as timeless and essential to a healthy society, yet fragile; demographic change is presented as a symptom of moral decline (Nicholson 1994, 28). Motherhood, although idealized, is truly valued only when practised within this patriarchal framework; it has been described as 'a colonised concept', used to tame 'unruly women' into responsibility and conformity (Pogrebin 1993, 130; see also Cain in this volume). Family breakdown is, consequently, perceived to be a threat to the prevailing order. Law has responded by constructing binuclear families, which expand the definition of family in order to conceal demographic change and thus contain 'the anxieties that it engenders' (Reece 2003, 156). Although this new family is presented as progressive, it has been suggested that is in fact both conservative and repressive (Vonèche and Bastard 2005, 100). The new family is expected to conform to the nuclear ideal not only in terms of membership but also in the gendered distribution of rights and responsibilities and, then, it occupies a similarly privileged position.

In shared residence cases, the risk of paternal disengagement is now an overt justification for the making of orders. In *Re W* [2009] Wilson LJ stated that 'the deliberate and sustained marginalisation of one parent by the other' constitutes a sufficient reason to make a shared residence order where what is being ordered is, in substance, contact (*Re W* [2009] EWCA Civ 370, at [15]). The comparison has been made with an early twentieth-century compromise technique, which sought to reconcile the competing demands of fathers and the best interests standard (at that time guided by maternal preference rules) by separating legal custody from practical care and control (van Krieken 2005, 30). Similarly, contemporary cases appear only to demand of responsible fathers that they remain involved in decision-making. In both instances, family law's preoccupation with preserving patriarchal pre-separation familial structures is evident, and shapes understandings of what it is to be a responsible parent.

Nevertheless, the Children Act 1989 stipulates in s.1 that an order can only be made where it is in the relevant child's best interests; the aim of encouraging paternal involvement must be justified using welfare rhetoric. Constructing the appeasement of fathers as important for children's welfare is not, however, too difficult, given the malleability of the welfare test (Rejmer 2003), and what feminists have identified as law's 'male' form of reasoning: objective, and universal, with a tendency to organize information along hierarchical dichotomies (Gilligan 1982; Finley 1989).

The most important of these is perhaps the public/private dichotomy, which places anything associated with the female within a private, unregulated familial sphere. Traditionally, the family has been said to be too precious and fragile to be subjected to the blunt tools of legal regulation. Consequently, practical caring is understood as a private responsibility, beyond law's regulatory net; it is obfuscated further by the social construction of motherhood as a 'natural outpouring' of instinctive love (Tronto 1993, 111; Fineman 2001, 1042). In contested shared residence cases, this means that decisions are made without adequate recognition of how children benefit from receiving proper care. In *Holmes-Moorhouse v Richmond LBC* [2009] UKHL 7, Baroness Hale was disappointed by how little the court at first instance had actually known about the family ([33]). An order had been made for the equal division of time, primarily to support the father's claim for social housing. However, the outcome is likely to have been different if adequate consideration had been given to the fact that social workers had, during previous involvement with the family, not only investigated allegations of domestic violence but also concluded that the mother 'although working, did all the physical care of the children, running the house, collecting the two younger children after school, helping the children with their homework and preparing supper' ([35]). It is encouraging to see the absence of a discussion on practical caring responsibilities noted, albeit in this oblique way. In cases such as *Holmes-Moorhouse*, courts should recognize that decisions are more likely to be in children's best interest if the parent who has the insight developed through a significantly greater and closer involvement in their care is allowed to have a greater input.

However, in recent shared residence cases the benefits of maintaining parents' equal involvement in decision-making appear to be viewed as so obvious that they require no elucidation. A parallel can be drawn with the strong presumption in favour of contact, which developed during the 1990s. In all but a small minority of cases children's and resident parents' objections were held to be less important than the supposed long-term benefits of maintaining the father–child link, stated in the general abstract terms characteristic of legal discourse. Although there has been some retreat from the strong contact presumption since *Re L* ([2000] 2 FCR 404), this is chiefly in relation to domestic violence, which is treated as an exception to the general rule. In other cases, law's preference for the abstract and generalized has moved family law from the observation that a good relationship with a father is very important to some children to the assertion that all children need relationships with their fathers (Barnett 2009a, 50). According to Piper, the contact case law shows that 'in private law a focus on future benefits can lead to inappropriate attention being given to particular aspects of the child's future welfare'. She has argued for 'more *now-centred* decision-making about children' (Piper 2010, 1, emphasis in original). In the shared residence cases, there are unfortunately signs that the focus has shifted towards consideration of the supposed risks of growing up fatherless.

In *Re A* [2008] EWCA Civ 867, Adam J had, at first instance, told the litigants that the six-year-old boy needed 'a rounded future', which he said was 'achievable only with a father figure as well as a mother figure', and this surprising reinterpretation of the welfare test was repeated without further comment by Sir Mark Potter when the case reached the Court of Appeal ([35]). The applicant had only discovered that he was not the biological father some time after separation. The mother resisted shared residence and the Court of Appeal found some merit in her argument that her former partner was likely to be controlling. He had admitted to installing CCTV cameras for the purpose of spying on her while she was still living in their joint home. The shared residence order was, nevertheless, made since it would give the stepfather parental responsibility and would make it more difficult for the mother to exclude or marginalize him (*Re A* [2008] EWCA Civ 867, *per* Scott Baker LJ, at [100]). It was said to be particularly important to maintain the link with the appellant because the latter was 'the only father figure known' to the boy ([65]). In the welfare balancing exercise, the need for a male influence outweighed all other concerns, despite the lack of empirical evidence to support such a conclusion. This use of the shared residence order is not, it is submitted, in children's best interests.

## Can Shared Residence Help Litigants Take Responsibility for Co-Parenting?

The shared residence order is used for a second reason that is equally misguided and likely to put children at risk: to teach parents to cooperate in a more responsible way. Qualitative research has shown that shared residence is much more difficult and demanding than coordinating the many aspects of childrearing within an intact family, and that young adults whose parents have not managed to make this transition describe the arrangement in very negative terms (Socialstyrelsen 2004). Yet, the continued relegation of care to the hidden, private sphere and the consequent construction of responsible parenting as joint decision-making means orders are now made without any consideration of this, but as a solution to a different problem.

Contemporary law's insistence that post-separation families must continue across two households has resulted in increasing numbers of antagonistic parents appearing before the courts to seek the latter's assistance. The problem of high-conflict cases can no longer be managed by expecting the warring parents to execute a clean break and move on to new marriages. At the same time, there is an expectation that parents can and should negotiate their own arrangements and there is a well-documented 'settlement culture', where this message is conveyed by all professional groups (Bailey-Harris et al. 1999). It is against this background that shared residence has been identified as a tool for improving parental cooperation.

Shared residence is attractive because of its superficial fairness: if you give parents equal time, or at least equal status, they ought to have nothing left to fight over (see, for example *A v A* [2004] EWHC 142). Shared residence is also compatible with the dominant binuclear paradigm. As has been explained by Reece, post-liberal emphasis on reasoned decision-making has combined with communitarian influences; the result is a 'coercive slide' where the obligation to reflect is complemented by 'an additional duty to reach the right result' (2003, 171–2). Binary classifications of 'good' and 'bad' post-divorce behaviour have 'become entrenched through the cumulative effect of self-reinforcing professional received wisdom' (Bailey-Harris et al. 1999, 122). At the same time, the contemporary policy focus on investment in children to eliminate risks and ensure a future generation of healthy, productive citizens has increased expectations of parents; being a responsible parent now involves accepting that you need to be taught how to parent well (Piper 2010). Thus, in legal discourse, if a responsible parent always puts the child's need to know both parents over their own needs, and conflict per se is constructed as harmful, then parents who fight over residence are prima facie in the wrong. Consequently, their objections are often dismissed or trivialized. This has combined with private family law's current hazy understanding of what is involved in sharing the responsibilities of raising children to allow this order to be imposed in a dangerous attempt to instil responsibility.

In the case law before *D v D* [2001], good cooperation between parents had, quite correctly, been regarded as a prerequisite for shared residence, rather than a potential by-product of the order (see, for example, *A v A* [1994] 1 FLR 669; *H v H* [1997] 1 FCR 603). This limited courts' ability to use this order. The solution has been an undesirable reversal of the causal relationship between conflict and shared residence. A number of cases have cited *D v D* [2001] as having established that shared residence orders can be used to reduce the stakes in high conflict cases. This reasoning featured prominently in *A v A* [2004], where the shared residence order appears to have been a measure of last resort to try to end what the children's guardian had described as a 'virtual state of war' (*A v A* [2004] EWHC 142 at [23]).

Gilmore has expressed concern over the judicial tendency to refer only to other judgments and not to engage with the existing research (2006, 497). The justifications given for this use of shared residence do not withstand scrutiny. It is sometimes suggested that if shared residence is ordered the requirement for frequent communication will, '[i]n layman's terms', force parents to 'get their act together and keep it that way' (McIntosh 2009, 395). There may be some moral force in the common-sense assertion that since it was the parents who created the difficult situation through their decision to separate, 'they should be the ones who have to learn to cooperate for the best interests of their child' (Kipp 2003, 71). Nevertheless, there is no empirical evidence to support the idea that parents can be taught this way. McIntosh has concluded that while the assumption that parents will learn to communicate could possibly work in some instances, her research showed that '[t]his logic falters with complex, conflicted families' (2009, 395). Studies in several jurisdictions have shown that shared residence is often a reluctant compromise seen as the only way out of a stalemate (Maccoby and Mnookin 1994, 236; Smart and Neale 1999; Socialstyrelsen 2004; McIntosh 2009). Parents in such instances cannot be assumed to possess the mutual respect, flexibility and willingness to compromise which are essential prerequisites for a real sharing of the duties of parenting.

Consequently, shared residence is markedly less stable than sole residence, particularly when parents have been coerced into trying it (Smart and Neale 1999, 76; Socialstyrelsen 2004, 8; McIntosh 2009, 395; Masardo in this volume). Abandoned schedules, renegotiations, and further litigation are likely to have a negative impact on children. Where the arrangement does last, the need for more frequent and detailed communication may increase children's exposure to, and involvement in, their parents' disputes – something which is known with reasonable certainty to be harmful (Johnston 1995; Melli and Brown 2008, 252). As noted, family law's failure to understand parental responsibility primarily in terms of doing things for children means this is not taken into the s.1(3) welfare balancing exercise. In several qualitative studies, young people have also reported that the considerable practical inconveniences associated with shared residence can be exacerbated by inflexible parents whose hostility prevents the retrieval of homework, football kits or favourite toys (Smart and Neale 1999; Socialstyrelsen 2004). The fact that parents have 'exhausted the dispute resolution continuum' and appear before a judge should be seen as a strong contraindication of shared residence since such parents are extremely unlikely to be able reach joint decisions in the future (Freeman 2000, 460).

Yet, the family courts, intent on finding a solution to the problem of high-conflict families, have not been receptive where these kinds of arguments have been advanced by those with a child welfare science background. In *Re A* [2008] Adam J had taken note of the psychologist's concerns, but chose to rely on case authorities that held parental conflict not to be a bar, but rather a reason for granting the shared residence order (*Re A* [2008] EWCA Civ 867, at [58]). In *Re R* [2009] the psychiatrist had opposed shared residence on the grounds that it would increase the child's exposure to the parents' severe conflict. Wall LJ, however, stated that the shared residence order under s.8 'is a legal, not a psychiatric concept, in relation to which; (a) there is now a substantial jurisprudence; and (b) a psychiatric opinion, however distinguished its source, is not determinative' (*Re R* [2009] EWCA Civ 358, at [30]). Shared residence continues to be constructed as a cure for entrenched disputes so that, paradoxically, the recent emphasis on the harmful nature of conflict has increased its appeal.

Although the judiciary insist that parents must learn to work together, no detailed guidance is provided for how this is to be achieved; an indication that this is regarded as a private matter beyond law's concern. It appears from the case law that the required levels of cooperation are low; it is sufficient that parents refrain from interfering with each other's day-to-day parenting and that the child's passage between homes is 'relatively fluid' (see, for example, *Re P* [2005] EWCA Civ 1639; *Re C* [2006] EWCA Civ 235). This undemanding interpretation of collaborative parenting is likely to have allowed courts to order shared residence in cases where they would otherwise have been reluctant to do so.

In *A v A* [2010] EWHC 1282, a fact-finding hearing had been held in relation to 89 allegations, some trivial but some of domestic violence serious enough to constitute criminal offences. Nevertheless, Mostyn J expressed no concern that a shared residence order for an equal division of time had been made a few weeks later, 'effectively by consent'; in fact, he praised this as a 'sensible' order and the most likely outcome regardless of the veracity of the allegations and counter-allegations ([30]). There was, very worryingly, no consideration of the impact of frequent moves between two hostile households on the three small children aged between six and three. This case is a striking illustration of the potential dangers should shared residence, like contact, come to be viewed by professionals as 'an unquestionable good' (Trinder 2010, 246).

## Shared Residence and Gendered Expectations of Parenting

It is important to note that the recent use of the shared residence order to appease or encourage applicant fathers easily leads to an identification of mothers as the obstacle, or problem. Whilst no parent should be able maliciously to exclude the other, one lesson that should have been learned from the over-enthusiastic presumption in favour of contact is that mothers' objections should not always be dismissed as egotistical short-sightedness or implacable hostility.

In legal discourse, parents' rights and responsibilities in both intact and post-separation families are discussed in gender-neutral terms, creating an impression of equality and hiding the continued gendered nature of parenting (Barnett 2009b, 138). Empirical studies show that women's entry into employment has not been matched by anything like a commensurate change in the domestic sphere, where women continue to shoulder primary responsibility (Lader et al. 2006). The public/private dichotomy's classification of caring as a private matter beyond the reach of public regulation means that the law can remain 'habitually based' on an unequal allocation of parenting responsibilities, without any acknowledgement of 'the value of the [caring] work involved', since the latter is in law's self-created blindspot (McKie et al. 2001, 237). Furthermore, the taken-for-granted nature of mothering combines with law's desire to preserve patriarchal power structures to focus the welfare test on children's supposed need for fathers. Lawler has explained how a false link is produced between what is expected of responsible mothers and children's supposed intrinsic needs, which are in fact constructed within a particular socio-political context (1999, 70).

Research has shown that in intact families fathers' involvement is largely mediated through mothers; thus, the transition to post-separation parenting is difficult given the demands for new levels of practical and emotional involvement (Simpson et al. 2003). However, this is not discussed; legal debate remains focused on the problems of father absence and encouraging male involvement on the implicit assumption that mothers, as the primary 'meeters' of children's needs, will remedy any paternal shortcomings (Lawler 1999, 67). As Piper has observed, 'mothers may be expected to do more and be held accountable for more' (2010, 6). In contrast, fathers' participation in parenting is rarely subjected to the same levels of legal scrutiny; 'virtually any involvement' has 'come to be considered good-enough fathering' (Eriksson and Hester 2001, 791). Case law has clearly established that mothers with residence must not merely, as the statute stipulates in s.8, 'allow' contact, but also actively support and facilitate post-divorce fathering. A mother of young children 'ought to be able to influence them' to look forward to contact (*Re H* [1998] 2 FLR 42). The current interpretation of the welfare test, with its focus on the perceived dangers of both fatherlessness and exposure to parental conflicts, has resulted in mothers being recommended counselling to learn how to 'assist in supporting contact' (*Re P* [2008] EWCA Civ 1431, *per* Ward LJ, at [36]). In *Re M* [2003] the mother was justly criticized on several grounds. However, the suggestion that she had not pushed the issue of contact 'as far as she properly might', and had been giving in too easily to the 12-year-old boy's protests, extended resident parents' duties too far (*Re M* [2003] EWHC 1024). In the context of shared residence, it can be argued to be imperative that mothers are not made responsible for encouraging, manipulating or perhaps coercing children; according to Baroness Hale, children's views 'ought to be particularly important in shared residence cases' given the considerable sacrifices they are asked to make (*Holmes-Moorhouse v Richmond LBC* [2009] UKHL 7, at [36]).

As commented above, shared residence is known to be very demanding in practical, emotional and financial terms; any unequal allocation of the burdens of maintaining a binuclear family, therefore, becomes particularly significant. Spreading a child's school life, healthcare, sport, hobbies and toys across two households requires a coordinated effort. If there is not that coordination, in reality what happens is that the mother continues the caring work she had primary responsibility for in the intact family, while her own freedom may be quite severely curtailed by a regimented schedule. In this context, the use of shared residence orders for arrangements which are really generous weekend and holiday contact also give cause for concern. It allows, or even pushes fathers to opt out of the demanding, but ultimately more rewarding, primary carer role to merely spend fun time with children. This construction of shared residence will disappoint fathers who sought the order to avoid being relegated to Sunday 'McDads' (Kruk 1994; Trinder 2003; Simpson et al. 2003; Men's Hour 2005). It is also less likely to have the desired effects; empirical research suggests that it is day-to-day involvement that deepens relationships and is associated with better outcomes for children (Amato and Gilbreth 1999; Bauserman 2002).

Finally, this new legal understanding of shared residence, with its inequitable distribution of caring responsibilities, viz. decision-making capacity, is likely to be a source of resentment for mothers, particularly those who do not judge post-separation relationships to be good enough to justify the efforts necessary to maintain them (Smart and Neale 1999). Yet these efforts, like housework, go unnoticed until someone decides they are no longer prepared to make them (Smart 1991, 496). In case reports, mothers are almost exclusively mentioned when they are lectured over their failures to support contact or praised for their efforts in maintaining links with difficult fathers; references to single mothers' efforts in raising children are rare. It is, however, difficult for mothers to complain; 'good' motherhood is understood in terms of self-sacrifice (Lawler 1999, 67). Thus, mothers who reject the law's view of what their children need, and refuse to make the necessary adjustments, are condemned as selfish (Wallbank 1998, 361). In *Re C* [2007] EWHC 2312, the mother avoided a transfer of residence by explaining to the court that she now realized she had previously been wrong in thinking that maintaining the relationship between the father and child was 'up to the father': '[b]eing neutral', she conceded 'was not enough' ([78] and [99]). Mothers are likely to receive severe criticism for their perceived inflexibility if they continue to protest that co-parenting with their former partner is impossible or bad for their children even after a shared residence order has been made. Moreover, a change to sole residence in the father's favour may seem less drastic because residence is already shared. At the same time, the current use of the shared residence order is unlikely to satisfy increasing numbers of men, who wish to maintain their practical involvement from their intact families and do not conceptualize fathering primarily as a hands-off exercise of authority.

## Conclusion

Shared residence orders are made in an attempt to instil a sense of responsibility into parents and thus improve their co-parenting. This can be described as a triumph of hope over experience. Mostyn J recently advocated the use of shared residence orders to avoid 'the psychological baggage of right, power and control that attends a sole residence order' (*Re AR (A Child: Relocation)* [2010] EWHC 1346, at [52]). It should be noted, of course, that the same arguments were made when custody was replaced by residence. These changes in legal formalities do not seem to affect the complex problems of entrenched conflict families. Nevertheless, as is noted in the introduction, the construction of law as a tool to manage supposedly dangerous social change such as the growth of non-resident and disengaged fatherhood leads law to search for different solutions to solve the perceived problem (Collier and Sheldon 2008, 176).

While the alleged future benefits of maintaining binuclear families are, at the very least, uncertain, research does show that shared residence can expose children to real risks of present harm, particularly in the kind of high-conflict families that preponderate in the family courts. It is very challenging, and does not suit all parents, or children; courts should consequently be slow to impose this arrangement against family members' wishes (Socialstyrelsen 2004; Skjørten and Barlindhaug 2007, 383). If the order is to be made at all in contested cases, there must be, as stipulated in *D v D* [2001], a full and careful application of the s.1(3) checklist. There should be a pragmatic assessment of the parents' ability to cooperate, compromise and change arrangements where children's wishes change.

Moreover, adequate consideration must be given to children's present need to be properly cared for and the adults' joint responsibility to provide this care.

## References

Amato, P. and Gilbreth, J. 1999. Nonresident Fathers and Children's Well-Being: A Meta-Analysis. *Journal of Marriage and the Family*, 61(3), 557–73.

Bailey-Harris, R., Barron, J. and Pearce, J. 1999. From Utility to Rights? The Presumption of Contact in Practice. *International Journal of Law, Policy and the Family*, 13(2), 111–31.

Barnett, A. 2009a. The Welfare of the Child Re-Visited: In Whose Best Interests? Part I. *Family Law*, 50–54.

Barnett, A. 2009b. The Welfare of the Child Re-Visited: In Whose Best Interests? Part II. *Family Law*, 135–41.

Bauserman, R. 2002. Child Adjustment in Joint-Custody versus Sole-Custody Arrangements: A Meta-Analytic Review. *Journal of Family Psychology*, 16(1), 91–102.

Breivik, K. and Olweus, D. 2006. Children of Divorce in a Scandinavian Welfare State: Are They Less Affected than US Children? *Scandinavian Journal of Psychology*, 47(1), 61–74.

Collier, R. and Sheldon, S. 2008. *Fragmenting Fatherhood: A Socio-Legal Study*. Oxford: Hart Publishing.

Dowd, N. 1995. Stigmatizing Single Parents. *Harvard Women's Law Journal*, 18(1), 19–82.

Elrod, L. and Dale, M. 2008. Paradigm Shifts and Pendulum Swings in Child Custody: The Interests of Children in the Balance. *Family Law Quarterly*, 42(3), 381–418.

Eriksson, M. and Hester, M. 2001. Violent Men as Good Enough Fathers? A Look at England and Sweden. *Violence Against Women*, 7(7), 779–98.

Fineman, M. 2001. Fatherhood, Feminism and Family Law. *McGeorge Law Review*, 32(4), 1031–49.

Finley, L. 1989. Breaking Women's Silence in Law. *Notre Dame Law Review*, 64(5), 886–910.

Freeman, M. 2000. Disputing Children, in *Cross Currents: Family Law and Policy in the US and England*, edited by S. Katz, J. Eekelaar and M. Maclean. Oxford: Oxford University Press.

Geldof, B. 2003. The Real Love that Dare Not Speak its Name: A Sometimes Coherent Rant, in *Children and their Families: Contact, Rights and Welfare*, edited by A. Bainham, B. Lindley, M. Richards and L. Trinder. Oxford: Hart Publishing.

Gilligan, C. 1982. *In a Different Voice*. Cambridge, MA: Harvard University Press.

Gilmore, S. 2006. Court Decision-Making in Shared Residence Order Cases: A Critical Examination. *Child and Family Law Quarterly*, 18(4), 478–98.

Gilmore, S. 2010. Shared Residence: A Summary of the Courts' Guidance. *Family Law*, 285–92.

Harris, P. and George, R. 2010. Parental Responsibility and Shared Residence Orders: Parliamentary Intentions and Judicial Interpretations. *Child and Family Law Quarterly*, 22(2), 151–71.

Johnston, J. 1995. Research Update. *Family and Conciliation Courts Review*, 415–25.

King, M. and Piper, C. 1995. *How the Law Thinks About Children*, 2nd edition. Aldershot: Arena.

Kipp, M. 2003. Maximizing Custody Options. *North Dakota Law Review*, 79(1), 59–82.

Kruk, E. 1994. The Disengaged Non-Custodial Father: Implications for Social Work Practice with the Divorced Family. *Social Work*, 39(1), 15–25.

Lader, D., Short, S. and Gershuny, J. 2006. *The Time Use Survey 2005*. London: ONS.

Lawler, S. 1999. Children Need but Mothers Only Want: The Power of 'Needs Talk' in the Constitution of Childhood, in *Relating Intimacies: Power and Resistance*, edited by J. Seymour and P. Bagguley. Basingstoke: Macmillan Press Ltd.

Luhmann, N. 1989. Law as a Social System. *Northwestern University Law Review*, 83(1), 136–50.

Maccoby, E. and Mnookin, H. 1994. *Dividing the Child: Social and Legal Dilemmas of Custody*. Cambridge, MA: Harvard University Press.

McIntosh, J. 2009. Legislating for Shared Parenting: Exploring Some Underlying Assumptions. *Family Court Review*, 47(3), 389–400.

McKie, L., Bowlby, S. and Gregory, S. 2001. Gender, Caring and Employment in Britain. *Journal of Social Policy*, 30(2), 233–58.

Melli, M. and Brown, P. 2008. Exploring a New Family Form – The Shared Time Family. *International Journal of Law, Policy and the Family*, 22(2), 231–69.

Men's Hour 2005. *McDad Day Demo coming Friday 17 Jun 2005*. Available at <http://men.typepad.com/mens_hour/mcdad_day_demo_17_jun_2005/> (accessed 2 August 2010.

Nicholson, L. 1994. The Myth of the Traditional Family, in *Feminism and Families*, edited by H. Nelson. London: Routledge.

Olsen, F. 1990. Feminism and Critical Legal Theory: An American Perspective. *International Journal of the Sociology of Law*, 18(3), 199–215.

Piper, C. 2010. Investing in a Child's Future: Too Risky? *Child and Family Law Quarterly*, 22(1), 1–20.

Pogrebin, L. 1993. The New Father, in *Family Matters: Readings on Family Lives and the Law*, edited by M. Minow. New York: The New Press.

Reece, H. 2003. *Divorcing Responsibly*. Oxford: Hart Publishing.

Reece, H. 2009. The Degradation of Parental Responsibility, in *Responsible Parents and Parental Responsibility*, edited by R. Probert, S. Gilmore and J. Herring. Oxford: Hart Publishing.

Rejmer, A. 2003. *Vårdnadstvister. En rättssociologisk studie av tingsrätts funktion vid handläggning av vårdnadskonflikter med utgångspunkt från barnets bästa.* Lund: Lund Studies in the Sociology of Law.
Roche, J. 1991. The Children Act 1989: Once a Parent Always a Parent. *Journal of Social Welfare and Family Law*, 13(5), 345–61.
Silva, E. and Smart, C. 1999. Introduction, in *The New Family?* edited by E. Silva and C. Smart. London: Sage Publications.
Simpson, B., Jessop, J. and McCarthy, P. 2003. Fathers after Divorce, in *Children and their Families: Contact, Rights and Welfare*, edited by A. Bainham, B. Lindley, M. Richards and L. Trinder. Oxford: Hart Publishing.
Skjørten, K. and Barlindhaug, R. 2007. The Involvement of Children in Decisions about Shared Residence. *International Journal of Law Policy and the Family*, 21(3), 373–85.
Smart, C. 1991. The Legal and Moral Ordering of Child Custody. *Journal of Law and Society*, 18(4), 485–500.
Smart, C and Neale, B. 1999. *Family Fragments?* Cambridge: Polity Press.
Socialstyrelsen. 2004. *Växelvis Boende*, 2nd edition. Stockholm: Socialstyrelsen.
Spencer, S. 2008. Benchmarks: Family Residence. *Law Society Gazette*, 24–6.
Trinder, L. 2003. Working and Not Working Contact after Divorce, in *Children and their Families: Contact, Rights and Welfare*, edited by A. Bainham, B. Lindley, M. Richards and L. Trinder. Oxford: Hart Publishing.
Trinder, L. 2010. Talking Children into Being *In Absentia*?Children as a Strategic and Contingent Resource in Family Court Dispute Resolution. *Child and Family Law Quarterly*, 22(2), 235–58.
Tronto, J. 1993. *Moral Boundaries: A Political Argument for an Ethic of Care.* London: Routledge.
van Krieken, R. 2005. The 'Best Interests of the Child' and Parental Separation: On the 'Civilizing' of Parents. *Modern Law Review*, 68(1), 25–48.
Vonèche, L. and Bastard, B. 2005. Can Co-Parenting Be Enforced? Family Law Reform *and Family Life in France,* in *Family Law and Family Values*, edited by M. Maclean. Oxford: Hart Publishing.
Wallbank, J. 1998. Castigating Mothers: The Judicial Response to 'Wilful' Women in Disputes over Paternal Contact in English Law. *Journal of Social Welfare and Family Law*, 20(4), 357–76.

# Chapter 8
# Regulating Responsibilities in Relocation Disputes

Robert H. George[1]

A relocation dispute arises when one parent proposes to move with their child to a new geographic location and the other parent objects to the proposal. Defining relocation is complex, because the key issue is usually not the distance of the move itself, but rather the effect which it would have on the child's relationship with the other parent and others who would be left behind. Consequently, for one family, a move of hundreds of miles might have little effect on these relationships (if, for instance, the child was having only indirect contact with the parent anyway), while for another family, moving to the next suburb could significantly change existing relationships (such as in a shared care arrangement). Whether a move constitutes a relocation or not therefore depends more on interpersonal than on geographic factors.

Because of this relational nature of relocation, these increasingly common legal disputes challenge our understandings of two aspects of family responsibility. The first is part of the broader construction of the responsibilities of post-separation parenting which are also addressed by Alex Masardo, Annika Newnham and Ruth Lamont in this volume. The relationship between geographic location and caring responsibilities is complex, especially in light of the reasons why many applicants wish to move. As will be seen, parents often seek to relocate for family support, new jobs or new partners, but they also seek to move to discharge family responsibilities, such as to elderly parents or unwell relatives.

The second aspect of family responsibility engaged by relocation disputes concerns the law's role in regulating these responsibilities. While it is rightly pointed out that responsibilities go beyond legal obligations, and that, although obligations which coincide with responsibilities may be legally enforceable, the responsibilities themselves are not (Eekelaar 2006), it is nonetheless possible for the law to regulate the exercise of family responsibilities. When parents take a relocation dispute to court, the court must decide whether allowing or refusing

1 The work presented in this chapter is drawn from parts of my doctoral thesis; I am grateful to the Arts and Humanities Research Council for generously supporting that research (Grant No. 135597). I would like to thank Alison Diduck and Mavis Maclean who commented on an earlier draft of this chapter, and the editors for their help in developing the final version. The views expressed, and any errors, remain my responsibility alone.

the relocation is in the welfare and best interests of the child (Children Act 1989, s.1(1)). But another way of expressing that decision-making process could be to say that the court must decide which course of action will best enable the parents to exercise their (various and perhaps conflicting) family responsibilities. The law's regulation of post-separation parenting is brought into especially sharp relief by relocation disputes, where the issues at stake are so high, the parties so polarized, and the outcomes of the decision often irreversible.

Intersecting with both of these issues is the gendered nature of family responsibilities (see the editors' introduction to this volume; also Lamont in this volume; Diduck 2008), which is highly visible in relocation disputes. Indeed, almost all aspects of relocation cases raise gender issues, and the gendered impact of relocation disputes on family responsibilities – and on the law's regulation of these responsibilities – is a significant dimension as yet rather under-explored in the English literature (for a brief discussion, see Deech 1988, 30–31; in other counties, see Young 1996; 2010; Behrens 1997; 2003; Boyd 2000; 2010).

For various reasons, the English law on relocation is currently subject to a heated debate amongst academics (Hayes 2006; Herring and Taylor 2006; Freeman 2009; George 2009), judges (for example, *Re D (Children)* [2010] EWCA Civ 50; *Re AR (A Child: Relocation)* [2010] EWHC 1346 (Fam)), lawyers (Geekie 2008; Pressdee 2008; Judd and George 2010), pressure groups (for example, articles on <www.mckenziefriend.com> and <www.thecustodyminefield.org>, and the online campaign at <www.relocationcampaign.co.uk>) and policy makers (Hodson 2009, 164–7; Maclean 2009). That debate needs to be alive to the realities of those involved in relocation disputes, about whom we know very little.[2] This requires us to keep in mind the exercise of care-giving and other responsibilities of the families involved, including the gendered aspects of those responsibilities; and doing that may require us to look at the ways in which the courts regulate the exercise of those responsibilities in the relocation context. It is that dimension which this chapter seeks to add to the English relocation debate.

The chapter proceeds by explaining why relocation disputes raise gendered issues around the exercise of responsibilities. Looking then at the current law in England, we see why it is that many of those gendered concerns appear, at least superficially, to have been addressed or avoided by the English courts. However, we shall see that the current legal approach has been subjected to significant criticism. The question is whether an approach can be found which remains alive to the gendered realities of relocation disputes, while also meeting some of the more compelling criticisms. The chapter concludes by offering some first steps towards such an approach.

2 In Australia and New Zealand, longitudinal studies are underway, which will provide invaluable data in those national contexts: for early results, see Behrens et al. 2009; 2010; Parkinson 2010; Taylor et al. 2010.

## Relocation as a Gendered Issue

Why do relocation disputes give rise to particular gender considerations? As with many aspects of family law, the gender issues in relocation disputes are not usually explicit, but arise systematically from the effect the law has on litigants. A full examination of English relocation law is found below (at 000), but to understand the reasons why relocation disputes raise gender concerns, the legal powers in question must first be considered.

Unlike many countries, English law divides its approach between moves which are within the United Kingdom and those which cross international borders (for comparison, see George 2009; Judd and George 2010). For moves within the country, the court has power to control the child's geographic place of residence in two direct, and three indirect, ways. Directly, s.11(7) of the Children Act 1989 allows conditions to be imposed on a residence order which can include conditions about the child's geographic place of residence, or the court can make a prohibited steps order (Children Act 1989, s.8). Less directly, the court can make a shared residence order requiring frequent transfers between the parents; it can make a residence order in favour of one parent which is conditional on that parent continuing to reside in a particular location, with residence transferring to the other parent should the former move; or it can make a specific issue order requiring, for example, that the child continue to attend a particular school (Children Act 1989, s.8), thus limiting the distance which a parent with care of the child could move.

In cases involving overseas moves, on the other hand, the law imposes a prima facie restriction. Under s.13(1)(b) of the Children Act 1989, where a residence order is in force,[3] a parent wishing to relocate overseas with his or her child must obtain either written consent from the other parent or court permission before the child can be removed for more than one calendar month.[4]

Technically, these powers apply only to the relocation of the child. If the court imposes a condition on internal relocation or refuses permission for an international relocation, the parent remains free to move, so long as they do not contravene the order by taking the child with them. Understandably, few parents who have been caring for their child choose to move without their child (though it is not unheard of); many stipulate in evidence that they will not move unless they are also permitted to take the child too. This means that, in reality, the court's powers to restrict children's place of residence are also powers to restrict the resident

3 In cases not involving a residence order, a parent would still be well advised to obtain permission to avoid any potential difficulty; many reported cases involve children who are not the subject of a residence order.

4 A removal without consent or permission is child abduction, which is a criminal offence (Child Abduction Act 1984, s.1), and can invoke international law to secure the child's return under the Hague Convention on the Civil Aspects of International Child Abduction, 1980, if the removal is to a signatory country. On child abduction cases, see Lamont in this volume; for a broader overview, see Lowe et al. 2004, Chapters 12–18.

parent's place of residence. Parents who care for children and wish to move are subject to the court's power potentially to restrict their ability to do so.

Parents who do not have the care of their children, on the other hand, are subject to no such restriction. They are free to move as and when they wish (*Re B (Removal from Jurisdiction); Re S (Removal from Jurisdiction)* [2003] EWCA Civ 1148, at [12]), regardless of the effect on the child or, indeed, on the other parent.[5] Theoretically, the court could make a specific issue order requiring the parent to attend particular contact; but the Court of Appeal has explicitly denied any power to force non-resident parents to have contact with their children (*Re L, V, M and H (Contact: Domestic Violence)* [2000] 2 FLR 334, 364), and I am unaware of any case where this has even been suggested.[6]

This disparity in the court's power over resident and non-resident parents seems, at first sight, gender-blind: the difference relates to one's function in the child's life, regardless of gender. However, relocation is an example par excellence of gender-blind rules leading to potentially gender-biased outcomes. The fact that 90 per cent of children of separated parents are in the primary care of their mothers (Hunt 2004, 1) is sufficient to begin to illustrate why powers which affect resident parents but not their non-resident counterparts are potentially gender-discriminatory. The translation of this social fact to relocation cases appears from the fact that the vast majority of applicant parents are mothers.[7] The upshot is that relocation has potentially huge gender implications. As Juliet Behrens has said, 'restrictions on residence parents argued for by contact parents are usually restrictions on women argued for by men' (1997, 66).

However, the gender issues in relocation go beyond the mere fact that most applicant parents are mothers. With women continuing to provide the bulk of childcare in most cases (Dex and Ward 2007, especially 57 and 66–77), 'restrictions on relocation operate unfairly against the person who is likely to be providing the majority of care to a child. In doing so, they compound the social and economic disadvantages that accompany the provision of care, particularly where

5 For example, the remaining parent may have been reliant on the moving parent for assistance with childcare arrangements.

6 Compare the position in Australia: the approach of the High Court in *U* v *U* (2002) 191 ALR 289 opened the way to the possibility of direct restraint in a parent's place of residence, and was said by a majority of the Full Court of the Family Court to mean that the court had a broad injunctive power to make such orders, as long as they did not go beyond what was necessary to promote the child's interests: *Sampson* v *Hartnett (No 10)* [2007] Fam CA 1365. My thanks to Juliet Behrens for guidance on Australian relocation law.

7 In *Payne v Payne* [2001] EWCA Civ 166, at [31], Thorpe LJ said that relocation applications 'are only brought by maternal primary carers'. While this goes a little far, mothers are the applicants in almost all cases; those featuring fathers as applicant parents, such as *Re W (A Child) (Removal from Jurisdiction)* [2005] EWCA Civ 1614 and *Re J (Children) (Residence Order: Removal Outside Jurisdiction)* [2006] EWCA Civ 1897 are the exception, and tend to involve additional factors such as the mother suffering a mental illness.

the caregiver is a woman' (Behrens 2003, 584). When we add in the fact that the reason for most relocation applications is a return to family (which often provides help with childcare or relates to other caring responsibilities), a new partner or an employment opportunity – all of which mark considerable opportunities for women to escape poverty,[8] as well as to enhance their own happiness – the gender implications of relocation decisions begin to become clear.

It was also noted earlier that few resident parents will relocate without their children, and that most give evidence to this effect. Doing so creates something of a no-win situation for an applicant parent. If she says that she will not go without the child, the court may conclude that relocation is not critical to her well-being and that she can discharge her caring responsibilities adequately without moving; but if she says that she will go without the child, she falls foul of gendered stereotypes about 'good' and 'bad' mothers,[9] and about responsible and irresponsible attitudes to parenting. She also risks being seen as trying to hold the court to ransom, which could appear to be a challenge to the court's authority as the regulator of family responsibilities. This would seem to be another gendered risk which disproportionately affects mothers: the exercise of mothers' family responsibilities are subjected to court regulation in ways and to extents which fathers' rarely are (Wallbank 2007).

Susan Boyd has noted similar trends in Canada, and suggests that mothers' fears of losing the residence of their children has led to '[a] "disciplining" of mothers' behaviour ... with ... expectations that mothers behave in a more selfless manner than fathers' (2000, 252).[10] Looking at the Australian position on relocation, Behrens similarly concludes that the message coming from the law is that 'residence parents (usually mothers) should be expected to sacrifice their interests to what a judge perceives as being in their child's best interests, but contact parents (typically fathers) should not' (2003, 585). The result of this differential treatment, according to Boyd, is that 'the voices of [non-resident] parents (mostly fathers) [are] elevated to a position of equality with those of mothers, regardless of any differential in caregiving responsibility' (2000, 281).

---

8 The poverty rate for single women with children is well above average, and the average income for lone mothers in one survey of seven European countries was 42 per cent below the mean income: Daly and Rake 2003, 105). Re-partnering is the most effective way of rising out of poverty, but obtaining a more lucrative job or assistance with childcare also helps (Hetherington and Kelly 2002, 165 and 88 respectively).

9 The danger of 'stereotypical views as to the proper role of a mother' impacting on legal decision-making was highlighted in Gaudron J's dissenting judgment in the High Court of Australia's decision in *U v U* (2002) 191 ALR 289, 296.

10 It could be suggested that non-resident parents are also restricted from moving away if they wish to maintain a strong relationship with their child. However, it should be noted that this 'restriction' is not backed by legal powers in the way that restrictions on the movement of resident parents potentially is. This compares with the position in Australia where the courts consider that they do have the power to restrict non-resident parents as well as resident parents: see above.

It is for these reasons that relocation law might be seen as being particularly significant from a gender perspective. With these points in mind, we turn then to look at English relocation law and some of the criticisms levelled against it.

## English Relocation Law and its Critics

When it comes to relocation within the United Kingdom,[11] the English courts have been most reluctant to impose conditions on children's place of residence, with Thorpe LJ saying that such restrictions ought to be imposed only in 'truly exceptional' circumstances (*Re B (Prohibited Steps Order)* [2007] EWCA Civ 1055, at [7]). It has been stressed, however, that the primary carer's parenting ability does not need to be in doubt for a case to be exceptional (*Re S (A Child) (Residence Order: Condition) (No 2)* [2002] EWCA Civ 1795, at [17]). The House of Lords gave broad approval to this approach in *Re G (Residence: Same-Sex Parents)* [2006] UKHL 43, at [15], with reference to the earlier decision in *Re E*, in which Butler-Sloss LJ described such restrictions on movement as 'an unwarranted imposition upon the right of the parent to choose where he or she will live within the United Kingdom' (*Re E (Residence: Imposition of Conditions)* [1997] 2 FLR 638, 642). Consequently, restrictions on children's geographic place of residence within the United Kingdom are rare,[12] and, when it comes to domestic relocation, resident and non-resident parents are more or less equally free to move in practice.

On international relocation, the provisions in the Children Act 1989 mean that the initial onus of making an application to relocate overseas is on the parent seeking to relocate, since such moves are prima facie blocked by s.13. However, in general, the courts look favourably on well thought through applications to relocate (Hayes 2006; Geekie 2008). The leading case on international relocation, which discusses the approach to be taken to such applications in considerable depth, is *Payne v Payne* [2001] EWCA Civ 166 (hereafter, '*Payne*'), in which Dame Elizabeth Butler-Sloss P and Thorpe LJ both gave full judgments.

The facts of *Payne* are typical of relocation disputes. The mother was a New Zealander, the father British. The mother had been the primary care-giver, though by the time the case came to trial the child had substantially shared residence, spending 23 of every 56 nights with her father. The mother applied for leave to relocate to New Zealand, which the trial judge granted. The father appealed.

---

11 For a summary of the relevant authorities, see *Re L (Shared Residence Order: Internal Relocation)* [2009] EWCA Civ 20, discussed by George 2010.

12 It should, however, be noted that there is some discussion about whether restrictions ought to be made more readily (see the tentative suggestion to this effect by Ward LJ in *Re G (Contact)* [2006] EWCA Civ 1507, at [26], and the discussion in George 2010). This compares with the approach in New Zealand and Australia, where restrictions on moves within the jurisdiction are frequent: comparison is made in George (2009) and Judd and George (2010).

*Payne* is a complex decision, and there is a temptation to pick out only selected paragraphs and to treat them as if they reflect the entirety of the approach taken. However, despite this concern, there is much to be learnt from the key passages of the main judgments. In her summary, the President said that the following issues would likely be relevant:

> (a) The welfare of the child is always paramount.
>
> (b) There is no presumption created by s.13(1)(b) in favour of the applicant parent.
>
> (c) The reasonable proposals of the parent with a residence order wishing to live abroad carry great weight.
>
> (d) Consequently the proposals have to be scrutinised with care and the court needs to be satisfied that there is a genuine motivation for the move and not the intention to bring contact between the child and the other parent to an end.
>
> (e) The effect upon the applicant parent and the new family of the child of a refusal of leave is very important.
>
> (f) The effect upon the child of the denial of contact with the other parent and in some cases his family is very important.
>
> (g) The opportunity for continuing contact between the child and the parent left behind may be very significant.
>
> All the above observations have been made on the premise that the question of residence is not a live issue. If, however, there is a real dispute as to which parent should be granted a residence order, and the decision as to which parent is the more suitable is finely balanced, the future plans of each parent for the child are clearly relevant. (*Payne*, at [85]–[86])

In his judgment, Thorpe LJ said:

> To guard against the risk of too perfunctory an investigation resulting from too ready an assumption that the mother's proposals are necessarily compatible with the child's welfare I would suggest the following discipline as a prelude to conclusion:
>
> (a) Pose the question: is the mother's application genuine in the sense that it is not motivated by some selfish desire to exclude the father from the child's life? Then ask is the mother's application realistic, by which I mean founded

on practical proposals both well researched and investigated? If the application fails either of these tests refusal will inevitably follow.

(b) If however the application passes these tests then there must be a careful appraisal of the father's opposition: is it motivated by genuine concern for the future of the child's welfare or is it driven by some ulterior motive? What would be the extent of the detriment to him and his future relationship with the child were the application granted? To what extent would that be offset by extension of the child's relationships with the maternal family and homeland?

(c) What would be the impact on the mother, either as the single parent or as a new wife, of a refusal of her realistic proposal? [Where the mother cares for the child or proposes to care for the child within a new family, the impact of refusal on the new family and on the stepfather or prospective stepfather must also be carefully calculated.[13]]

(d) The outcome of the second and third appraisals must then be brought into an overriding review of the child's welfare as the paramount consideration, directed by the statutory checklist insofar as appropriate.

In suggesting such a discipline I would not wish to be thought to have diminished the importance that this court has consistently attached to the emotional and psychological well-being of the primary carer. In any evaluation of the welfare of the child as the paramount consideration great weight must be given to this factor. (*Payne*, at [40]–[41]).[14]

This final point of Thorpe LJ's discipline, emphasizing the importance of the applicant parent's emotional and psychological well-being and the impact on her of refusal of leave to relocate, has been reiterated in later cases. Trial judges have been criticized frequently for under-valuing this factor (for example, *Re B (Removal from Jurisdiction); Re S (Removal from Jurisdiction)* [2003] EWCA Civ 1149), and the suggestion that the child would not be particularly affected by the mother's unhappiness has been rebuffed by the Court of Appeal, saying that 'almost inevitable is the transference of unhappiness from primary carer to child' (*Re G (Removal from Jurisdiction)* [2005] EWCA Civ 170, at [24]). The Court of Appeal has also stressed that the burden on applicant parents in relation to their plans for relocation has to be proportionate to the factors which weigh against relocation (*Re W (A Child) (Removal from Jurisdiction)* [2005] EWCA Civ 1614, at [20]).

13 This addition was made by Thorpe LJ in *Re B (Removal from Jurisdiction); Re S (Removal from Jurisdiction)* [2003] EWCA Civ 1149, at [11].

14 In later cases, Thorpe LJ has said that this final paragraph would have been better expressed as part of para [40](c): *Re B (Leave to Remove: Impact of Refusal)* [2004] EWCA Civ 956, at [14].

While the English approach to relocation explicitly rejected a presumption in favour of relocation applications (*Payne*, at [25] and [82]), when it comes to the practical effect of *Payne*, there are some who claim that the English law 'is commonly perceived as walking and talking like a presumption' (Geekie 2008, 451–2; see also the New Zealand Court of Appeal decision in *D v S* [2002] NZFLR 116). This view might be supported by the remark of Charles J in *Re C* that *Payne* 'indicates that usually the harm that is likely to flow from a reduction in contact will not found a conclusion that the welfare of the child would be best promoted by refusing an application by the primary or custodial parent to take the child abroad' (*Re C (Permission to Remove from Jurisdiction)* [2003] EWHC 596 (Fam), at [24]).

It can be seen from this summary that the English law tends to look favourably on relocation, whether within the UK or internationally. In terms of the gender concerns discussed above, these outcomes suggest that the English courts may have minimized the extent to which 'restrictions on women argued for by men' (Behrens 1997, 66) are allowed to translate into restrictions on movement. Consequently, the English law avoids restrictions which 'operate unfairly against the person who is likely to be providing the majority of care to a child', and so reduces the potential for 'compound[ing] the social and economic disadvantages that accompany the provision of care, particularly where the caregiver is a woman' (Behrens 2003, 584).

However, the English approach has been subjected to a number of criticisms. While the critics are mostly focused on the legal reasoning adopted by the court, there are also possible implications for case outcomes in some of the critiques.

Jonathan Herring and Rachel Taylor (2006) criticize the English approach in legal terms by pointing to the court's disengagement from the rights dimension of relocation disputes. They argue that the human rights related to relocation have been given insufficient attention, but conclude that case outcomes would be likely to be unaffected by adopting the rights-based analytical framework which they suggest.

A different attack on the English law bases itself on the view that the Court of Appeal is too directive in relocation law, and thus restricts trial judges' ability to seek the welfare solution. Mary Hayes (2006), in a compelling analysis of the English case law, is highly critical of the Court of Appeal for being overly interventionist in relocation appeals, and argues that this approach undermines the welfare principle. Hayes' argument would, perhaps, lead one to consider that leave to relocate ought more frequently to be refused in the name of the child's welfare, though her concern is more with process than with outcomes.

Elsewhere, I have argued that the court's reading of s.13 of the Children Act 1989 may be open to doubt (George 2008). Section 13 requires the consent of all those with parental responsibility or of the court before a child is removed from the UK for more than one calendar month. At present, the courts purport to grant this leave by making an order under s.13 itself. However, it is not apparent that s.13 contains any such power, seeming to be merely prohibitive in nature. I suggest, therefore, that there is no such thing as 'a s.13 order', and that in granting leave to remove, the court should make a specific issue order under s.8. In practical terms, the difference between making a specific issue order and making a 's.13 order' is that the former must be made with regard to the *welfare checklist* under s.1(3), which includes aspects like the child's wishes and feelings, which are currently entirely sidelined in the Court of Appeal's thinking about relocation. Nowhere in *Payne*, which explicitly offers a full reconsideration of relocation law, are the wishes and feelings of the child even mentioned.

Finally, arguments are made against the English approach on the basis that its views on 'primary carers' and 'contact parents' are reflective of a past age, and are being interpreted in such a way as to 'disregard … modern views on the importance of co-parenting' (*Re G (Children)* [2007] EWCA Civ 1497, at [16], quoting Nicholas Mostyn QC's notice of appeal; Mostyn J made similar comments in *Re AR (A Child: Relocation)* [2010] EWHC 1346 (Fam), see also Geekie 2008; George 2010; Masardo in this volume). This perspective suggests that the court's approach of favouring relocation because of the impact of refusal of leave on the primary carer starts from a series of assumptions which no longer hold true. The response of these critics, therefore, is to seek to adjust these assumptions and 're-balance' the legal process of relocation disputes to reflect increasingly shared care-giving by parents more effectively. This view commands much support at present, though we need to be cautious about accepting its claims of significantly changing patterns of childcare at face value. While it is true that the court increasingly makes orders for shared residence (Gilmore 2006), this is often 'to choose one label rather than another' (as Wilson J put it in *Re F (Shared Residence Order)*[2003] EWCA Civ 592, at [32]), and says little about day-to-day parenting practices, which remain significantly gendered (Hunt 2004; Dex and Ward 2007; on the courts' use of shared residence orders which bear little resemblance to the actual allocation of care-giving responsibilities, see Harris and George 2010; Newnham in this volume).

These critics are not, of course, entirely united in their attacks, but it is apparent that the current law provokes considerable dissatisfaction from a number of quarters. We saw earlier that a gender perspective would have little difficulty with the *outcomes* of the English approach, since the concerns that we noted in the first part of this chapter appear largely to be avoided in an approach whereby relocation is generally allowed. It may be worth noting, though, that there may also be concerns about the *reasoning* employed by the English courts when considering it from a gender perspective.

First, in looking at the exercise of family responsibilities, the English law seems to focus only on the care-giving of the primary carer. This focus may be something of a double-edged sword: while it rightly gives due regard to the greater responsibility on the main carer, there may be a risk of perpetuating gendered parenting patterns. The relationship which a non-relocating parent has with his child can be hugely varied, but in general a parent who seriously opposes relocation is likely to be at the upper end of the contact spectrum, or to share the child's residence. Given this situation, the English approach may seem somewhat dismissive of the importance of contact, the loss of which, as we saw, will not normally justify refusal of relocation (*Re C (Permission to Remove from Jurisdiction)* [2003] EWHC 596 (Fam)).

Moreover, the English courts suggest that the loss of contact with a parent can be 'offset by extension of the child's relationships with the maternal family and homeland' (*Payne*, at [40](b)). Such a view is controversial, to say the least, especially since these new relationships are, by definition, with family members who do not currently live near the child. There is also little discussion of the fact that moving away may also affect existing relationship with other family members who are left behind.

Second, it could be said that the courts' regulation of relocation disputes displays only a superficial understanding of the gender issues at stake. The courts are aware that most applicants are women (*Payne*, at [31]), but have never explained why this factor is significant. There is no mention, for instance, of women's vulnerability to poverty after separation, or the impact of such poverty on the exercise of their care-giving responsibilities.

At the same time, in cases where there is a prima facie case made out that the child's relationship with the father is important enough to *consider* restraining the mother's freedom of movement, ought the court to give attention to whether it is a viable possibility for *both* parents to relocate (Weiner 2007)? If the exercise of parenting responsibilities requires the parents to be in the same location, a responsible regulation of those responsibilities by the court should ask about all possible ways of achieving that aim so as to avoid gender discrimination. As the New Zealand Family Court once explained, '[t]he party endeavouring to stop relocation … has as much an obligation to show why he or she cannot shift [that is, relocate] to the new place as to why the children should not be allowed to shift' (*NW v MW [Parenting Order]* [2006] NZFLR 485, at [10]).

For these reasons, as well as those expressed by others (especially Hayes 2006 and Herring and Taylor 2006), there are considerable difficulties with the current English approach to relocation. However, the challenge is to find an approach which takes adequate account of these criticisms while not losing sight of the gendered nature of the responsibilities involved.

## Reconsidering the Regulation of Relocation Responsibilities

A useful starting point in reconsidering the English approach to relocation is the analysis of the rights involved offered by Herring and Taylor (2006). Their work lays out clearly the separate interests of those involved in relocation insofar as they relate to the human rights which the court ought to be taking into account in a relocation dispute. However, there are two reasons why is might be necessary to go further than their rights-based approach allows.

One reason may be that a purely rights-based approach can be precarious in terms of supporting particular case outcomes. An approach founded on rights relies, for its substantive application, on an assessment of the weight and significance of those rights. Such an assessment is not fixed, but changes over time as our understanding and interpretation of the rights and their interrelationship changes (hence why human rights documents are said to be 'living instruments'). There is nothing to say, therefore, that the balance which Herring and Taylor think would be made, generally favouring relocation, would continue over time.

The second issue relates more generally to any rights-based approach in family law. Put shortly, my concern with such an analysis is that it focuses on only one aspect of family life, and not one that should necessarily be our main concern in family disputes. Responsibilities are, I suggest, a more appropriate analytical tool to use; and while responsibilities are probably fully inclusive of the obligations which make up the corollary of the rights in question, the responsibilities go much further (Lind et al. 2011). As John Eekelaar explains, 'to be fully responsible, people must sometimes refrain from doing what they are legally entitled to do, or do more than is necessary to comply with the law' (2006, 127). In other words, a rights-based analysis risks focusing on too narrow a range of issues, giving inadequate attention to interests and responsibilities which go beyond rights but which are at least as important in the family context. In particular, I wonder whether a rights approach may be apt to overlook the gendered division of family responsibilities.

Let me give just a couple of examples of the ways in which relocation responsibilities may go beyond rights (though many more could be suggested). First, we know that the English courts have been clear that the resident parent's emotional and psychological well-being is of great importance in deciding relocation disputes (*Payne*, at [41]; *Re B (Removal from Jurisdiction); Re S (Removal from Jurisdiction)* [2003] EWCA Civ 1149, at [12]). Herring and Taylor (2006, 523) rightly point out that refusing leave to remove the child can have a detrimental impact on the parent's mental well-being to an extent that 'may be sufficient to engage her private life under Article 8 [of the European Convention on Human Rights]'. What is missed by a rights analysis, though, is that even where the mother's *right* under Article 8 is not engaged, her mental well-being and its relationship to her ability to exercise her care-giving responsibilities is important, and should be weighed and considered explicitly alongside the other elements of the case.

To take another example, Herring and Taylor (2006, 530) note that 'where the child is old enough to form and express her own views, she may have a right under Article 8 for those views to be considered'. This view of what is required to engage the child's Article 8 rights may in any case be overly cautious (compare Taylor et al. 2007), but even if the child's *right* has not been engaged, parents (and courts) have a *responsibility* to explain the situation to the child in an age-appropriate manner, and to consider the child's views and perspective as part of the decision. Aspects like these risk being downplayed or overlooked if we focus too much on rights, at the expense of the broader considerations which are reflected in responsibilities.

To some extent, similar cautions could attach to the acceptance of Hayes' approach (2006), which calls for an unfettered welfare analysis in relocation cases. While this approach sounds attractive, there is much to be learned by looking at the approaches in other jurisdictions which have taken this line. In New Zealand, for instance, the guidance offered by *Payne* was rejected in favour of an 'all-factor child-centred approach' (*D v S* [2002] NZFLR 116), with no guidance offered to judges as to what factors should be taken into consideration. However, in the absence of guidance, trial courts have become increasingly varied in their practice, and particular factors have come to dominate the legal reasoning despite explicit instruction that all factors are presumptively equal in the analysis (Mackenzie 2009). The practical effect of this is a legal climate in which relocation is seen to be strongly disfavoured by the courts (Mackenzie 2009; Taylor et al. 2010), and where the well-being of the primary carer takes a very secondary role compared to the importance of contact with the other parent, even where this contact is playing a comparatively minor part in the child's life (George 2009).

It follows that we might consider that guidance of some kind would be beneficial in the relocation context. The welfare principle by itself has not always been able to take account of gendered family responsibilities (Kaganas 2007; Smart 2007), and clear guidance from the appellate courts can help trial judges to see the key issues which are involved in a child law dispute, as Hayes herself notes (2006, 372). The question may simply be how we create guidance which is not overly directive (Hayes 2006), but which still gives adequate attention to the rights of those involved (Herring and Taylor 2006) and to the broader family responsibilities concerned, as they are being exercised by the individuals involved in the case.

I suggest that there are lessons to be learned from *Payne* and the subsequent cases. There are, first, things which we can see that we need to avoid in future guidance, which I note briefly; but there are also positive lessons to learn, and I conclude by suggesting some factors which it may be worth considering when reassessing the English law.

One thing that needs to be avoided is the sense given by the current law that the considerations involved in determining relocation disputes are matters of law (Hayes 2006, 370–71). They are not. There is no element in the assessment which is not a pure question of fact. So, for example, while there is undoubtedly a connection between a child's welfare and the general welfare of a primary carer, it cannot be said as a generality that 'almost inevitable is the transference of unhappiness from parent to child' (*Re G (Removal from Jurisdiction)* [2005] EWCA Civ 170, at [24]). It is a question of fact for the trial judge to assess, with the assistance of appropriate guidance which reminds her that this is an issue to be considered (but does not dictate what answer she must reach). As the Supreme Court said in relation to children giving evidence in care cases, the balance of interests which the court has to consider 'may well mean that [a particular outcome is reached] in the great majority of cases, but that is a result and not a presumption or even a starting point' (*Re W (Children)* [2010] UKSC 12, at [22]).

Similarly, while it may be true in a particular case that an adverse impact on the applicant parent of refusing her leave to remove will affect the child more detrimentally than loss of contact with the other parent, that too is a question of fact, and cannot be decided in advance as a point of principle. It cannot be appropriate, therefore, for the Court of Appeal to say that '[o]nce the judge had recognised the mother as plainly the primary carer, *he had no option* but to recognise that her future lay with [her new partner] and that *necessarily* meant a South African future' (*Re B (Removal from Jurisdiction); Re S (Removal from Jurisdiction)* [2003] EWCA Civ 1149, at [15], emphasis added). The mere fact that the mother was the primary carer and was in a relationship with a South African man did not make a move to South Africa the best solution for the child – though of course it may have been, on the facts.

There are then some positive steps that can be taken in guiding trial judges towards all the considerations that are relevant in relocation cases. The court should make it clear, though, that all these matters are questions of fact and degree and that, as the New Zealand Court of Appeal put it, 'there will be no error of law if the decision … is based on the welfare of the children looking at all the relevant factors' (*D v S* [2002] NZFLR 116, at [47]). The Court of Appeal's task, in laying out guidelines, is to attempt to ensure that counsel and trial judges are equipped to identify 'all the relevant factors'. The court should guide judges towards factors which will be relevant in determining the issue before them. It might indicate that judges should be slow to reach certain conclusions without strong evidence to support that view; it may indicate that certain outcomes will be reached more frequently than others, on average (*Re W (Children)* [2010] UKSC 12); and it ought to advise judges to consider, in detail, the various possible outcomes of the case (not necessarily just those offered by the parties) and how they would affect the exercise of family responsibilities and, of course, the child involved.

So, what might those factors include? In a case note about internal relocation, I suggested a list of questions which might usefully be asked (George 2010, 78–9). Since the issues arising seem to be broadly similar whether the move in question is cross-border or not, I build on that work here in suggesting the following issues (in no particular order) as being likely to be amongst those relevant when determining a relocation application:

- The existing exercise of care-giving responsibilities by the parties, in particular to the child involved, but also to anyone else, and the different ways in which these responsibilities are affecting each person involved. The main focus of this enquiry may be on existing residence arrangements, but this aspect may be only one way in which parents are exercising their responsibilities, and the particular arrangements and contributions need to be borne in mind.

- The reasons for the proposed move, and the reasons for the opposition to the move, taking into account considerations like the value of autonomy and self-sufficiency and of maintaining and developing significant family relationships. Any family violence will be an important factor, and the link between the parents' reasons and their current and proposed future exercise of family responsibilities will also be relevant.
- The viability of the moving parent remaining where she is, and the viability of the other parent moving to the proposed new location; in cases where the child might realistically live with either parent, the effect on the child of remaining while one parent moves should be considered. For all these possibilities, the practicality of exercising family responsibilities will be important.
- The likely actual (rather than presumed) impact on each parent, and (both directly and indirectly) on the child, of allowing or refusing a relocation. This question will require a broad focus, looking at both material and non-material considerations, and at both short- and long-term consequences.
- The possibility for a realistic ongoing relationship between the child and the non-moving parent if the move goes ahead.
- The views of the child, taking into account that even older children may find it difficult to conceptualize the reality of life in a very different location.
- Relationships with wider family, friends and support networks (of the parents and of the child), both in the current location and the proposed new location.

It is, of course, difficult to know how any different approach would play out in practice. Applying this list of factors to the facts of an individual case would be difficult (because information relevant to these factors may not be provided in a judgment built around the current law), and of course the relative weight to be given to different factors would, to some extent, be a matter for the trial judge's discretion. In any case, though, it is worth stressing that these factors, like the questions posed in my earlier work (George 2010, 78–9), are intended as the start of a discussion about how we should develop the law, rather than as a conclusion. We need to think carefully and creatively about what matters in relocation disputes, and about how best to turn any list of the factors which are considered relevant into guidance which can be usefully employed by trial judges and legal advisors.

## Conclusions

In this chapter, I have sought to explain why relocation disputes raise particular gender-related concerns. I have attempted to demonstrate that, although the English law presently resolves relocation cases in a way which satisfies the substantive concerns of the gender critique in terms of case outcomes, the legal reasoning which underpins those outcomes is problematic. While there are several alternative solutions which might improve on the law's current position, one answer may be simply to offer different guidance to trial judges about the factors relevant to relocation disputes. A welfare approach which leaves trial judges free to make their own determination of the best approach for a particular family, but which guides them appropriately to all the relevant factors which they need to take into account to reach a sufficiently nuanced conclusion, has the potential to lead to rigorous legal analysis coupled with realistic, sensible outcomes.

## References

Behrens, J. 1997. A Feminist Perspective on B and B (The Family Court and Mobility). *Sister in Law*, 2, 65–89.

Behrens, J. 2003. *U v U*: The High Court on Relocation. *Melbourne University Law Rev*, 572–82.

Behrens, J., Smyth, B. and Kaspiew, R. 2009. Australian Family Law Court Decisions on Relocation: Dynamics in Parents' Relationships Across Time. *Australian Journal of Family Law*, 23, 222–46.

Behrens, J., Smyth, B. and Kaspiew, R. 2010. Outcomes in Relocation Decisions: Some New Data. *Australian Journal of Family Law*, 24, 97–103.

Boyd, S. 2000. Gendering the Best Interests Principle: Custody, Access and Relocation in a Mobile Society, in *Family Law: 'The Best Interests of the Child'*, edited by H. Niman and G. Sadvari. Toronto, Law Society of Upper Canada.

Boyd, S. 2010. Autonomy for Mothers? Relational Theory and Parenting Apart. *Feminist Legal Studies*, 18(2), 137–58.

Daly, M. and Rake, K. 2003. *Gender and the Welfare State: Care, Work and Welfare in Europe*. London, Polity Press.

Deech, R. 1988. The Rights of Fathers: Social and Biological concepts of Parenthood, in *Parenthood in Modern Society: Legal and Social Issues for the Twenty-First Century*, edited by J. Eekelaar and P. Šarčević. Dordrecht, Martinus Nijhoff.

Dex, S. and Ward, K. 2007. *Parental Care and Employment in Early Childhood: Analysis of the Millennium Cohort Study*. Working Paper No 57. London, Equal Opportunities Commission.

Diduck, A. 2008. Family Law and Family Responsibility, in *Responsibility, Law and the Family*, edited by J. Bridgeman, H. Keating and C. Lind. Aldershot, Ashgate.

Eekelaar, J. 2006. *Family Law and Personal Life*. Oxford: Oxford University Press.

Freeman, M. 2009. *Relocation: The Reunite Research*. London: Reunite (available online at <www.reunite.org>).

Geekie, C. 2008. Relocation and Shared Residence: One Route or Two? *Family Law*, 446–53.

George, R. 2008. Changing Names, Changing Places: Reconsidering Section 13 of the Children Act 1989. *Family Law*, 1121–25.

George, R. 2009. The Shifting Law: Relocation Disputes in New Zealand and England. *The Otago Law Review*, 12, 107–29.

George, R. 2010. *Re L (Internal Relocation: Shared Residence Order)* [2009] EWCA Civ 20, [2009] 1 FLR 1157 (casenote). *Journal of Social Welfare and Family Law*, 32, 71–80.

Gilmore, S. 2006. Court Decision-Making in Shared Residence Order Cases: A Critical Examination. *Child and Family Law Quarterly*, 18, 478–98.

Harris, P. and George, R. 2010. Parental Responsibility and Shared Residence Orders: Parliamentary Intentions and Judicial Interpretations. *Child and Family Law Quarterly*, 22, 151–71.

Hayes, M. 2006. Relocation Cases: Is the Court of Appeal Applying the Correct Principles? *Child and Family Law Quarterly*, 18, 351–72.

Herring, J. and Taylor, R. 2006. Relocating Relocation. *Child and Family Law Quarterly*, 18, 517–37.

Hetherington, M. and Kelly, J. 2002. *For Better or for Worse: Divorce Reconsidered.* New York, Norton.

Hodson, D. 2009. *Every Family Matters: An In-Depth Review of Family Law in Britain.* London, The Centre for Social Justice.

Hunt, J. 2004. *Child Contact with Non-Resident Parents.* Oxford, Department of Social Policy.

Judd, F. and George, R. 2010. International Relocation: Do We Stand Alone? *Family Law*, 63–8.

Kaganas, F. 2007. Domestic Violence, Men's Groups and the Equivalence Argument, in *Feminist Perspectives on Family Law*, edited by A. Diduck and K. O'Donovan. Abingdon, Routledge-Cavendish.

Lind. C., Keating, H. and Bridgeman, J. 2011. Introduction: Taking Family Responsibility or Having It Imposed?, in *Taking Responsibility, Law and the Changing Family*, edited by C. Lind, H. Keating and J. Bridgeman. Aldershot: Ashgate, 1–21.

Lowe, N., Everall, M. and Nicholls, M. 2004. *International Movement of Children: Law, Practice and Procedure.* Bristol, Jordans.

Mackenzie, F. 2009. Uneasy Trends in Relocation Law. Unpublished LLM thesis, Victoria University of Wellington.

Maclean, D. 2009. Early Day Motion 373: Relocation Cases. Available at <http: //edmi.parliament.uk/EDMi/EDMDetails.aspx?EDMID=39934&SESSION=903>.

Parkinson, P. 2010. What Happens When the Relocation Dispute Is Over? Findings from a Prospective Longitudinal Study. London Metropolitan University: International Child Abduction, Forced Marriage and Relocation Conference.

Pressdee, P. 2008. Relocation, Relocation, Relocation: Rigorous Scrutiny Revisited. *Family Law*, 220–24.

Smart, C. 2007. The Ethic of Justice Strikes Back: Changing Narratives of Fatherhood, in *Feminist Perspectives on Family Law*, edited by A. Diduck and K. O'Donovan. Abingdon, Routledge-Cavendish.

Taylor, N., Gollop, M. and Henaghan, M. 2010. Relocation Following Parental Separation in New Zealand: Complexity and Diversity. *International Family Law*, 97–106.

Taylor, N., Tapp, P. and Henaghan, M. 2007. Respecting Children's Participation in Family Law Proceedings. *International Journal of Children's Rights*, 15, 61–82.

Wallbank, J. 2007. Getting Tough on Mothers: Regulating Contact and Residence. *Feminist Legal Studies*, 15, 189–222.

Weiner, M. 2007. Inertia and Inequality: Reconceptualizing Disputes over Parental Relocation. *University of California Davis Law Review*, 40, 1747–834.

Young, L. 1996. Will Primary Residence Parents be as Free to Move as Custodial Parents Were? *Australian Family Lawyer*, 11, 31–9.

Young, L. 2010. The Interventionist Approach of the Australian Courts in Relocation Cases. London Metropolitan University: International Child Abduction, Forced Marriage and Relocation Conference.

# Chapter 9
# Child Abduction in the European Union: Recognizing and Regulating Care and Migration

Ruth Lamont[1]

## Introduction

The regulation of family responsibilities through law does not at first sight appear to be a subject upon which the European Union would, or should, have much influence. The EU has traditionally been regarded as an entity with a primarily economic role which should have little direct impact on family life. However, the policy of free movement of persons within Europe has encouraged both the formation and movement of families across European borders (Dethloff 2003, 37). The process of migration within Europe encourages the formation of 'international families' where the partners to the relationship are not in their home state, and/or may not be of the same nationality (Ackers 1998, 166) and also has the effect of increasing the diversity of family forms (Carlier and Sarolĕa 2007, 440). The international dimension of family life within Europe potentially extends the responsibility for care of family members across states. The interface between law, migration, family life, and the role of gender in these processes is, therefore, an important issue for European law (see Calavita 2006) and the question of responsibility for care within the family structure is central to effective legal regulation of family relationships across European member states.

Cross-border relationships present practical challenges of continuing family responsibilities for the care of children on the breakdown of the parental relationship. At this interface between family life and migration arise the difficulties of managing the continuing ties of family responsibility through law, which must respond to these continuing connections between individuals created by the need to provide effective care for children. The challenges of continuing care faced by parents generally following separation are potentially magnified by the added factor of physical distance and conflicting legal regimes, and demonstrate

1 I am very grateful to Helen Stalford and Heather Keating for their helpful comments on earlier drafts. I am also indebted to the participants at the Gender, Family Responsibility and Legal Change Conference at Sussex Law School for their contribution to the ideas and themes in this chapter. Any errors or omissions remain my own.

the gendered nature of care and the practical challenges of securing childcare across international borders. This chapter will examine the specific issue of child abduction, where a child is unlawfully moved between two EU member states, to explore how the management of cross-border family legal rights may have a significant impact on the broader care responsibilities of international families.

The EU is increasingly seeking to play a role in shaping international family law rules and this requires the EU to adopt a perspective on family relationships and behaviour. Despite its economic origins, the EU has been regulating the family through legislation adopted to secure the free movement of workers within the Community which permits a worker's family to migrate with the worker.[2] This intervention in family life attracted criticism for its gendered and instrumentalized nature (Ackers 1998), but there is evidence that this approach is evolving as the EU is increasingly aware of the changing nature of family life and the increasingly fluid nature of legal family ties (European Commission 2005). International migration may in fact create pressures on family life which contribute to the process of relationship breakdown (Boyle et al. 2009, 11) and since the EU has created an area in which free movement and migration are encouraged, it is appropriate that the EU takes a proactive approach to regulating family life in the area of cross-border relationships (Stalford 2003). The Brussels II Revised[3] Regulation addresses this need by creating EU rules on jurisdiction and recognition and enforcement of judgments on divorce and parental responsibility, and has also intervened to regulate the civil aspects of child abduction across internal European borders. Brussels II Revised, therefore, represents a more direct intervention in family life by the EU (see also Jones 2011).

The legal response to the breakdown of international families is not, therefore, shaped only by domestic law, but also by European law. However, as the child abduction provisions of the Brussels II Revised Regulation demonstrate, the EU has only limited awareness of the interaction between family responsibility for care of children, family connections across international borders and motivations for family-based migration. Changes in the family structure have made family life within Europe much more fluid, but the core notion of care within and by the family remains. Despite some negotiation of gender roles and the broader

2 Primarily regulated by Regulation (EEC) No. 1612/68 on the freedom of movement for workers within the Community, OJ Sp. Ed. 1968, No. L 257/2 p. 475, 15 October 1968. Now the right of citizens of the Union to move is governed by Directive 2004/38/EC on the right of citizens of the Union and their family members to move and reside freely within the territory of the Member States OJ [2004] L158/77. There is also legislation for the free movement of self-employed persons and for the provision of services but in this chapter the broad concepts of 'workers' and 'citizens' will be used.

3 Regulation (EC) No. 2201/2003 concerning jurisdiction and the recognition and enforcement of judgments in matrimonial matters and matters of parental responsibility, repealing Regulation (EC) No. 1347/2000, OJ [2003] L 338, 23 December 2003. Also known as Brussels II *bis*.

social changes in the practice of family life, women remain the primary carers of children especially following parental separation. In a migration context, responsibility for care and family ties may form a very important aspect of the decision to migrate abroad (Bailey and Boyle 2004, 236), yet neither the value of care, nor the need for support to care, have been recognized in the European context. Migration to access support and familial networks to help with caring responsibilities may form a rational response for women caring for their child following separation from their partner, but this form of migration may be restricted by the legal rights and obligations of, and the child's relationship with, that partner. The controls on international child abduction which operate when a parent, usually a mother, wishes to relocate to an alternative jurisdiction, despite the continuing relationship between their child and their former partner, has an impact upon the movement of children within the EU. The child's relationship with one parent means the movement of the other parent is also effectively controlled.

The Hague Convention on the Civil Aspects of International Child Abduction 1980 is based upon a male abductor model, directed at ensuring the return of children to their primary (female) carer and preventing an alternative jurisdiction being seized of the substantive custody decision. Evidence of the operation of the Hague Convention demonstrates that in the majority of cases mothers are the abductors of children (see Lowe and Horosova 2007). However, in adopting and reinforcing the remedy of the Convention, the EU has failed to re-examine the basis upon which the law is premised or question the reasons behind abductions of children. The provisions of Brussels II Revised act on gendered assumptions about the international movement of children on family breakdown and where the welfare of the child lies, informed by the Hague Convention. How the responsibilities of parents, and how they may choose to fulfil those responsibilities, are conceptualized clearly influences the legal response and rights available to family members. By acting on assumptions, rather than questioning and identifying the nature of the family-based phenomenon to be regulated, the law may give gendered responses and effectively hinder the fulfilment of caring responsibilities. In the case of international child abduction, the conflict of rights and interests is particularly acute and pressured and there are justifications for the approach taken in the Brussels II Revised Regulation in encouraging the return of the child to the state from which he/she was abducted. However, consideration of the wider factors which may motivate abductions by primary carer mothers demonstrate the significant links between migration behaviour and family responsibility. The approach adopted by the EU to the regulation of family life lacks informed reflection on the reality of this aspect of cross-border family life and the challenges that effective regulation may pose.

## Linking Post-Separation Care and Migration in the EU

### *Conceptualizing international family life in the EU*

How the law conceptualizes a family unit influences what is regarded as 'acceptable' behaviour in society and what constitutes a 'real' family. Changes in the way people define their family life can influence definitions embodied in law, which can in turn influence the way people live in a continual process that Diduck calls 'meaning-making' (Diduck 2008, 252). Although the law may not be consistent in privileging one form of family structure or defined family role, it does contribute to a stratification of desirable family forms (Wallbank 2001, 16). In legitimizing some family forms the law may also play a role in conveying and reproducing gender-based ideologies embodied within the more traditional notions of family life (Fegan 1996, 189). The traditional, privileged, family form is based around a heterosexual married couple with children, where the mother remains at home as primary carer, supporting a male breadwinner who participates in the market to maintain the family financially (Fineman 1995) and clearly embodies gendered expectations about responsibility for care of children. These ideologies can shape individual aspirations and behaviour in relation to family life and, although individuals make their own choices within this framework, it is important to expose how the roles which are constructed as socially desirable are exploited and to identify the gendered assumptions they embody. This has proved particularly relevant in the European context since, when regulating the family unit and the free movement of workers, the EU initially adopted a very traditional conception of family relationships based around the marital relationship. There has been some movement away from the very traditional European conception of family life but McGlynn (2006, 24) has argued that, in Europe, 'it is the dominant ideology of the family which pervades discussion of law and families and it is against this dominant ideology that the actions of all are measured, with varying disciplinary effects'.

In addition to social changes in the family structure, Diduck (2003, 23) notes that the nuclear family had its roots in a particular economic structure based on a man's 'family wage' which can no longer be sustained. Women have increasingly participated in the labour market, entering the 'public' sphere and contributing to the family financially, although the presence of children may affect women's labour market participation, particularly where the child is under five years old (Eurostat 2007, 13). The dual breadwinner model has been increasingly normalized as desirable and has been encouraged by the EU. This is in evidence across Europe as policymakers, including the EU, link employment and family policy to encourage women's labour market participation (Daly 2005, 392) altering women's relationship with the state by adjusting what, in policy terms, is expected of women (Lister 2006, 322).

Although women are now participating in the labour market, this has as yet had a limited impact on their caring responsibilities within the family, which remain broadly gendered. Eurostat's (2008) survey 'The Life of Women and Men in Europe 2008' notes that, across 14 member states in the EU, in a day women spend more time on domestic duties and childcare than men by approximately two hours and 40 minutes, even when both work. Women's public roles have changed but there has only been some renegotiation of the division of work in the private sphere. This has meant that, rather than the gendered role of care being transformed and shared equally between partners in a heterosexual relationship, women have assumed a 'dual burden' of work and care (Fineman 2001). Despite policies encouraging labour market participation by women, it remains difficult for both men and women to transcend the role of gender within the family structure. Even within the changing structures of family life, it is sometimes still difficult for women to resist or adjust their caring responsibilities. Windebank (2001, 286) states that: 'It remains the mother's, not the state's, and not the father's responsibility to organise and conduct domestic and parenting work and to maintain the complex and sometimes fragile balance of childcare arrangements which ensure the well-being in every respect of the child'.

However, the fluidity of family structures and relationships means that the management of care responsibilities may become less uniform and the personal and social consequences of such responsibility, as embodied in law (Diduck 2008, 255), may become more complex. In a European context, this complexity may be compounded by the additional factor of geographical distance and conflict between different family laws in the different member states of the EU. Although there is active pursuit of convergence and harmonization of domestic family laws in European states by the Commission on European Family Law (an academic body), historical differences remain, as do differences in the significance and interpretation of family relationships within the EU (see Antokolskaia 2007).

In regulating the family, European law has the potential to contribute to the ideology of family life, and therefore to influence individual behaviour. The EU may regulate and reflect on the conceptualization of family life for two main reasons: first, to regulate the free movement of families between the member states; and secondly, in managing the effects of differing domestic family law through private international law rules. The EU can thereby influence how families are defined in law by basing entitlements in European law, such as rights of residence, on specified family roles (Ackers 1998). This process produces responses to the legal structure by families, particularly in relation to their migration behaviour as the right to move and reside in another state is defined by worker and familial roles, such as 'spouse' in Directive 2004/38 on the free movement of citizens. Conforming to these roles will give the entitlement in European law and legitimacy to that family form and migration which those outside the model cannot achieve. If the conception of the family is very traditional, those who adopt family structures outside this model may be discouraged from migrating. The flexibility of family structures and cross-border responsibility for informal care and their coincidence with the legal concept of 'the family' may then have a marked effect on how people behave.

*Family motivated migration: moving to care or tied to location*

Despite the economic origins of the European policy encouraging the free movement of persons within the European space, individual choice to migrate is not solely based on economic imperatives. Family relationships can play an important role in migration behaviour (Bailey and Boyle 2004, 236). As Feijten and van Ham (2007, 646) state: 'Increasingly complex family structures, with second spouses, children, and stepchildren are likely to have spatial repercussions on the individual and societal level.' The connection between family changes, employment, care and migration has become more complex and new forms of migration have emerged in response to increasingly flexible family structures (Kulu and Milewski 2007, 575).

Individuals may migrate to facilitate care or have their movements restricted by care responsibilities due to family commitments and children. These family-based concerns are increasingly common factors in migration decisions, particularly for women (Feijten and van Ham 2007, 646). This reflects the reality that the family remains central to the provision of care within society. Silva and Smart (1999, 7) argue that despite the fluidity of families, the core notions of care, responsibility and obligation remain because: 'while there are new family forms emerging, alongside new normative guidelines about family relationships, this does not mean that values of caring and obligation are abandoned'.

Kulu and Milewski (2007, 581) use the concept of 'linked lives' to describe the interaction between relationships and migration behaviour, as the continuing link between two individuals can make a location necessary or desirable. For example, the requirement to facilitate child contact following the breakdown of a relationship could mean that migration may be restricted; whereas the desire to access informal care networks, such as grandparents' care for grandchildren, would encourage migration back to an individual's 'home' state. Such 'linked lives', where individuals do not live together but are connected through family ties or a former relationship and the provision of care, are an increasingly important influence on residential choices and, therefore, on spatial mobility patterns (Kulu and Milewski 2007, 576).

Family relationships may also be a significant factor for subsequent migration back home to the state of origin. Bailey and Boyle (2004, 236) have found that 'for many, the nature of their family relationships begins to dictate their migration behaviour, encouraging or preventing moves over long distances.' Responsibility for the care of children creates pressure on migration decisions, both in providing such care and facilitating opportunities for the child, including factors like access to education (see Ackers and Stalford 2007). Particular challenges in the provision of care may arise for migrant women in their host state as they may have limited access to affordable publicly available childcare and cannot necessarily rely on extended family or friendship networks to assist them in providing informal care (Stalford 2005, 370). The provision of informal care is particularly important for single parents and isolation from friends and family poses significant difficulties.

On the dissolution of the family, the caring responsibilities of those involved, or uncertain legal status, may encourage migration back to support networks elsewhere, or require individuals to remain in a state in compliance with a custody order. Pursuit of career or educational opportunities, access to welfare benefits and social networks, the wish to relocate home nearer to family and friends, or the desire to enable a new partner to pursue a career abroad may all form part of the decision to relocate on separation (Herring and Taylor 2006, 524; Morano-Foadi 2007, 14).

International families are more likely to migrate on family breakdown and the majority of those moving with children after the dissolution of a relationship in the EU appear to be women (Morano-Foadi 2007, 17). EU law has to acknowledge the increasing flexibility of the notion of 'family' and the importance of 'linked lives' on migration decisions so as to prevent inconsistent legal statuses in various member states or legal inhibitions on an individual's freedom of movement, and to assist in enforcing legal obligations such as maintenance.[4] The law should attempt to address the nature of those relationships, the continuing obligations and challenges of providing care and the circumstances of family breakdown so as to facilitate the protection of the rights and interests of the individuals involved.

### *The challenge of lawful relocation*

Migration following the breakdown of the parental relationship has significant implications for the movement of children across international borders, whether accomplished lawfully or unlawfully, as primary carers may attempt to relocate with their child following the dissolution of the family unit (Morano-Foadi 2007, 10–11). In England and Wales, the lawful relocation of a child across an international border requires consent to remove the child from the jurisdiction, either from the other individual holding parental responsibility or from the court (section 13(1)(b), Children Act 1989). The court will consider the request to relocate in the light of the welfare of the child (section 1(1), Children Act 1989, see George in this volume). In most applications to the court the mother wishes to relocate outside the jurisdiction which potentially has an obvious, and significant, impact on the child's relationship with their father, who will normally remain behind, and with any remaining extended family.

The fact that it is often primary carer mothers who wish to relocate abroad and return home has been recognized in England and Wales by Thorpe LJ in *Payne v Payne* ([2001] 1 FLR 1052). The judgment places considerable emphasis on the mother's ability to care for the child if relocation is refused as key to determining the child's welfare and hence whether the proposed relocation should be permitted (*Payne v Payne* [2001] 1 FLR 1052, 1063). Given that, in most cases, the mother

4 See Regulation 4/2009 on jurisdiction, applicable law, recognition and enforcement of decisions and cooperation in matters relating to maintenance obligations OJ [2009] L7/1, 18 December 2008.

is the child's primary carer, the reasoning in relocation applications places far more emphasis on her responsibility, attaching particular importance to evidence that her ability to care for the child may be inhibited by refusal of the application. The guidance given on relocation from the jurisdiction of England and Wales in *Payne v Payne* has been criticized as inappropriately favouring applications by primary carers (Hayes 2006) and, in recent cases, there has been a shift away from viewing the child's welfare through the prism of their mother's needs and back towards the individual child and their interests, particularly the loss of ongoing direct contact with their father (*Re H (a child)* [2007] 2 FLR 317). Although Herring and Taylor (2006) have suggested that an explicit human rights approach should be adopted in relocation cases, this would not necessarily adjust the reasoning of the court, which appears to be informed by expectations about post-separation caring by mothers and fathers. The exclusion of the father in these circumstances effectively ignores the father's responsibility for the child and is an approach which is not easily adjusted without a reassessment of the father's role (Collier 2010, 141). International migration decisions, therefore, demonstrate the challenge in accommodating expectations of caring relationships embodied in law with the reality and lived experience of post-separation care. The expectations of care may be gendered and significantly affect the relationship between parent and child, but the desire to relocate may be driven by the practical experience of fulfilling that responsibility and the need for greater support to provide that care.

One of the major reasons for the English approach to considering applications to remove the child from the jurisdiction is, therefore, to prevent unlawful removals of children. In *Payne v Payne* ([2001] 1 FLR 1052: 1061) Thorpe LJ stated that: 'There is a clear interaction between the approach of courts in abduction cases and in relocation cases. If individual jurisdictions adopt a chauvinistic approach to applications to relocate then there is a risk that the parent affected will resort to flight.'

This approach does not extend to other jurisdictions where permission to relocate is less likely to be granted (Worwood 2005). However, the EU does not have the competence to harmonize relocation law as this is a substantive family law issue and outside the scope of competence to legislate provided for by the EC Treaty. Relocation law, therefore, remains a patchwork across the member states and the permissions sought, and the likelihood of their being granted, remain subject to national approaches of which migrant parents will have to be aware. The EU has only had the competence to regulate the effects when a child has been relocated cross-border without the permission of the court or the holder of parental responsibility. Although English law on relocation acknowledges the difficulties posed by mothers' wishing to migrate with their children and the links to international child abduction, parents have to have knowledge of the need to seek consent or a court order before moving. Without the relevant permissions, if children are removed from their country of habitual residence by their mothers, this may constitute an unlawful abduction. Any legislation addressing the unlawful abduction of children should consider the best methods to counteract the pressures relating to care and the role of gender relations in family life, discussed above. The next section will, therefore, examine how the EU considered and addressed these factors when legislating on international child abduction.

## The EU and International Child Abduction

The ease of movement within the EU makes the movement of children across international borders and the removal of a child beyond the legal reach of a parent a significant problem. In adopting the Brussels II Revised Regulation the EU is potentially responding to the difficulties of free movement, but is also playing a role in the conceptualization of the responsibilities of parents in the care of children once the relationship has ended. The conflict of interests between the child and the parents on international relocation are forced into sharp focus in the situation where a child is removed or retained abroad without the permission of the court or the other parent. In these circumstances, it is important to ensure that family relationships are maintained, and that children are not prevented from having contact with a parent through the actions of the other by removing them to another state and into another legal jurisdiction. The difficulties in recognizing the pressures and needs motivating migration with a child whilst preventing unilateral action to prevent contact between a child and his or her parent represents a significant challenge in resolving the legal rights and obligations of the abductor and left-behind parent. The solution adopted by the EU is based on the Hague Convention 1980, which established the return remedy whereby the child is returned to his or her habitual residence prior to the abduction with the intention of securing the welfare of children whilst protecting also the rights of custody of the left-behind parent.

If children are removed or retained from their country of habitual residence in breach of another individual's custody rights, they have been unlawfully abducted contrary to Article 3, Hague Convention 1980. Given the trend towards awarding parental responsibility rights to both parents on the breakdown of the parents' relationship, it is likely that any parent removing a child across an international border will have custody rights as defined by Article 5, Hague Convention 1980. However, if the child's removal has been consented to (Article 13(a), Hague Convention 1980) or the court has given permission, the migration will be lawful. If a child has been removed in breach of custody rights under the Hague Convention 1980 a remedy will operate, whereby the child will be returned to his or her country of habitual residence by the courts of the state to which the child was abducted, under Article 12. This must be achieved as quickly as possible to prevent the child settling in the state to which he/she was removed. There are only limited exceptions to the principle of summary return under Articles 12 and 13: where the child has been present in the state he or she was removed to and has settled, or where there is consent or acquiescence to their removal, where there is a grave risk of harm to the child on return or where the child objects to being returned. In the vast majority of cases, the parent seeking to relocate will have to return the child to the child's habitual residence unless the parent has gained the consent of either the other party, or the court (see Lowe and Horosova 2007 on global practice in using the exceptions to return).

The purpose of the Convention is to return children to their 'home' environments as quickly as possible to prevent forced changes in jurisdiction over their welfare. The application for the return of the child is not a substantive hearing to identify where the child's welfare lies, or which parent can best secure the child's welfare, but is intended to be an almost automatic process to ensure the return of the child if the requirements of the Convention are made out. Any hearing concerning the welfare of the child should ideally take place in the courts of the country of habitual residence of the child. The return remedy is designed, therefore, not only to prevent artificial changes in jurisdiction and protection of rights of custody, but also to act as a deterrent to parental child abduction by preventing abductors from gaining any advantage from their actions. The return remedy thus acts in the interests of all children, not the individual child, except in the circumstances where the Article 12 or 13 exceptions to return are fulfilled (Beaumont and McEleavy 1999, 29). It is assumed that return is best for the child, whatever the circumstances (Silberman 2005, 1054).

The implicit assumption within the Hague Convention 1980, underpinning the notion of the child's return to the country of habitual residence, is that the child would be abducted by his or her non-custodial father following divorce with the aim of securing more favourable custody provision in another jurisdiction (Pérez-Vera 1982, 428). The model largely formed the basis of the Convention and debates over how to resolve unilateral changes in jurisdiction. It was presumed that the child would be returned to his or her primary carer, usually the mother, in the country of habitual residence. In this sense it was supposed to assist parents who previously had no consistent remedy if their child was taken abroad (Dyer 2000). The child's welfare would be secured by summary return, back to a place of familiarity where care would be provided until a substantive hearing could take place in the appropriate legal forum.

The child abduction provisions of Brussels II Revised were subject to intense negotiation between the member states, in part because of the existence of the Hague Abduction Convention. All EU member states were already signatories to that Convention and the risk of undermining its operation resulted in a compromise in Brussels II Revised whereby the Convention remains in force, but its operation is amended in cases of abduction between EU member states. Under Article 2(11), Brussels II Revised, if a child is removed from his or her country of habitual residence in breach of another person's custody rights over that child, the child has been unlawfully removed. Children will normally be returned to their country of habitual residence and the exceptions to the child's return under Articles 12 and 13, Hague Convention 1980 remain. However, Brussels II Revised now requires a child of appropriate age and maturity to be heard in return proceedings (Article 11(2)) and creates a new mechanism which operates when the return of the child is initially refused. If the return of the child is refused under the Hague Convention 1980, Articles 11(6)–(8) Brussels II Revised require that the courts in the child's country of habitual residence hear the substantive custody issues relating to the child and the resulting judgment may require the subsequent return of the child (see *HA v MB (Brussels II Revised: Article 11(7) Application)* [2007] EWHC 2016 (Fam); [2008] 1 FLR 289). This means that if the return of the child is refused, a substantive hearing in respect of the child's welfare can still take place in the country of habitual residence without the child's physical return to that state. If the courts of the state to which the child was abducted refused to return the child, this refusal can be 'trumped' by a subsequent substantive custody order made in the country of habitual residence which requires his or her return (see McEleavy 2005). The substantive hearing over the child's welfare takes precedence over the summary refusal to return and as such can be recognized and enforced to ensure the return of the child to the country of habitual residence. In this way, Brussels II Revised reinforces the application of the return remedy for the majority of children, even where concerns have been raised in the summary hearing under the Hague Convention 1980 exceptions to return because it is assumed that these concerns will be addressed and resolved in the substantive welfare hearing (see McEleavy 2005).

Brussels II Revised attempts to tackle the breakdown of international families and their subsequent migration within the Union by managing the relationship between member states' courts and legal systems. In addressing issues of family breakdown in Brussels II Revised, the EU is acknowledging that the policy of free movement of workers has an impact on its citizens: 'Given the increase in movement within the EU, there has been a concomitant increase in the number of marital and other family relationships between citizens and residents of EU Member States. Unfortunately, this has meant an increase in the numbers of divorce, annulments and separations involving citizens of different Member States' (Opinion of the Economic and Social Committee 2002, para. 1.2).

As such, Brussels II Revised is an explicit acknowledgment of diversity of family forms within Europe and aims to facilitate the effective management of relationships across borders following their dissolution. Despite this acknowledgment, the institutions failed to examine the nature of the problems to be regulated. It has become evident during the operation of the Hague Convention 1980 that the majority of abductions worldwide, 67 per cent, are accomplished by the mother of the child, not the father as was expected (Lowe and Horosova 2007). When the child is returned to the country of habitual residence in these circumstances it is likely that the mother, as the primary carer, will return with the child to care for him or her (Freeman 2001). It is now far more usual for circumstances such those occurring in *Re G (Abduction: Withdrawal of Proceedings, Acquiescence, Habitual Residence)* [2007] EWHC 2807 (Fam); [2008] 2 FLR 351) to form the background of the abduction. The mother had moved to the UK from Canada with one child, unlawfully retaining that child in England, whilst pregnant with a second child. In judgment, the English court acknowledged that the mother, who had spent most of her life in England but moved to Canada to be with her husband, had retained the elder child in England because she had not settled into life in Canada and felt isolated without family support networks. Sir Mark Potter stated that:

> This is one of those unhappy cases, frequently encountered within this jurisdiction, in which the court is confronted, not with the effective kidnapping and removal abroad of a child from the custody of the primary carer (the mischief which the Convention was originally concerned to remedy), but with the removal or retention of a child by a primary carer who, in a state of depression or desperation at her position in an unhappy marriage outside her country of origin, 'goes home to mother' in order to enjoy the support and sympathy of her own extended family, taking with her the child or children of the marriage. (*Re G* (2007) at [67])

This statement acknowledges both the original aim of the Hague Convention 1980, and the changing circumstances which have, in part, led to increased abductions by primary carer mothers.

Despite the evidence that women are the predominant abductors of children under the Hague Convention 1980, the European Commission, when proposing action on child abduction by the EU, used the non-custodial father 'type' of abduction as a justification for the introduction of rules reinforcing the application of the return remedy. The Commission did not examine any evidence identifying abductors as more commonly being mothers than fathers, and in the proposals laid out an example based on a non-custodial father, who wishes to modify a custody decision by creating an artificial link to a jurisdiction other than the child's habitual residence prior to the abduction (European Commission Proposal 2001, 2). The Commission's proposal adopts the same perspective as the Hague Conference 20 years before and, although identifying the wider social changes in family structure and the fluidity of family life, fails to engage more closely with the effects of these changes on international child abduction. The Brussels II Revised proposals do not acknowledge the situations giving rise to primary carer abductions, nor the fact that women are predominantly the primary carers of children even when there is not a traditional family form, and in doing so potentially reinforces a traditional ideology of the family. The wider factors of responsibility for care and the pressures of geographical distance in the provision of care are not identified. Care of children is a function of family life; the factors which facilitate or impede its provision are not identified as an aspect of regulating family life through EU law. The need to provide such care for the welfare of the child is recognized but the impact of this need on behaviour, particularly migration behaviour because of the ongoing challenge of 'linked lives', is not acknowledged. Silberman (2003) has argued that the Hague Convention 1980 has been manipulated in favour of primary carers in practice. Although the return of the child may be an appropriate remedy, the changed nature of abduction should perhaps be acknowledged alongside the desire to vindicate custody rights, protect private international law aims and the rigorous enforcement of the Convention remedy.

## Reconciling Care Responsibilities with Child Welfare

Using the Hague Convention 1980 as the basis of EU intervention eventually ensured political agreement by the member states, allowing the Brussels II Revised Regulation to enter into force, yet is underpinned by an assumption about female care of children. The presumption that the return remedy operates to secure the welfare of a child in his or her country of habitual residence is, at least in part, informed by the desire to return the child to his or her primary carer. On the issuing of a return order, mothers are expected to act in the best interests of children by returning with them to their country of habitual residence. For example, in *Re G* the elder child (X) had been wrongfully retained in England from Canada. A younger child (Y) had since been born in England and Wales and was habitually resident there and, therefore, not subject to the Hague Convention 1980. In ordering the return of the elder child, the court stated that: 'I start… upon the assumption that, if I order the return of X to Canada, the mother will feel herself compelled to accompany her and that, in doing so, she will also take Y who is only six months old and dependent upon her love and care'. (*Re G (Abduction: Withdrawal of Proceedings, Acquiescence, Habitual Residence)* [2007] EWHC 2907 (Fam); [2008] 1 FCR 1 at [26].)

Encouraging women to return with their children effectively ties women to their children's country of habitual residence, despite having separated from the children's fathers, because of the 'linked lives' created by their legal obligations. As an abductor who is not acting in the best interests of his or her child, a mother's view of the child's welfare is discounted. Smart (1991, 486) has argued that the ascendency of the welfare of the child has meant that mothers' caring role, and interest and knowledge of caring for their children, have lost standing in law. The separation and prioritization of needs is particularly problematic when embodied in law as it is difficult to alter, allowing assumptions to be made about a child and their interests (Piper 2000, 269). The norm of best interests is being imposed from outside the family, and is defined by law as being protected by return to the child's country of habitual residence. Abduction may harm a child (see Freeman 1998) but this is assumed to occur by Brussels II Revised whether the abduction is by a primary carer or not. Although Article 11(2), Brussels II Revised contains new guarantees protecting the right of the child to be heard in return proceedings, the wider issues of child welfare in these circumstances have not been addressed (see Lamont 2008). The effect of hearing the child may be limited given the reinforcement of the return remedy (Lowe 2007) and other factors relating to the abduction, including provision of care, will be discounted.

The 'moral obligation' to put the presumed nature of children's interests first has become unchallengeable and once it is established where this interest lies, parenting is judged against this standard (Ribbens et al. 2000). As parental care remains largely women's responsibility, this means that it is mostly women who are judged against this standard. Wallbank (2001, 8) argues that, 'As a result, the years of the mother's caring work are marginalized, with the law raising its own experience in similar cases to a position of prominence.' The welfare principle creates a standard which parents, and particularly mothers as primary carers, have to meet, which focuses solely on the risks to children and their needs, without considering the knowledge or interests of the child's carer (Reece 2006, 561). Women affected by the child abduction provisions of Brussels II Revised are potentially in the position of wishing to provide improved care for their child in another member state but, in the process of attempting to achieve this, abducting their child. The focus on children's rights and welfare, on returning to his or her habitual residence in Article 11, means that Brussels II Revised fails to consider or capture the links between gender, care and migration on the breakdown of the international family. This places women, whose children are summarily returned, in the unfortunate position of caring for children without the resources and facilities they would prefer to access to secure their children's welfare.

## Conclusions

At the core of family life remains the key relationship of care. Families are more fluid than they once were and, as well as being formed across international borders, relationships falter causing family obligations to stretch across national boundaries. Indeed, the stress of migration and life in a less familiar culture may in fact encourage the breakdown of international families. Caring responsibilities do not necessarily terminate with the end of a relationship and the ability to care can be made even more difficult across geographical distance. Given this social reality it is appropriate that the EU should have a role in regulating the consequences of movement of international families in Europe which its policies have a significant role in encouraging. In particular, following the breakdown of a relationship, it is necessary to ensure that the parties have secure legal status and the appropriate courts, those with the closest link to the family or child concerned, have jurisdiction over any litigation.

In the context of increasingly internationalized family life, subsequent migration of former partners may be anticipated and Brussels II Revised forms part of the EU's attempt to manage the consequences of such migration, including international child abduction. How responsibilities for care within the international family are conceptualized influences the legal response to family problems. However, this key element seems to have been missing from the EU's analysis of international child abduction when it sought to reinforce the application of the return remedy in Brussels II Revised. Despite the changes in the nature of child abduction, with increases in abductions by primary carer mothers, the EU's approach to regulating child abduction did not engage with the links between migration, family dissolution and care responsibilities. The return remedy and Brussels II Revised means that responsible parents do not remove their children without permission from the other parent or the court, even if their aim is to maximize their ability to care for the child. The control exercised over how the responsibility for post-separation care is carried out may effectively hinder the carrying out of care responsibilities in a specifically gendered way, tying women to a geographical location through their familial links. The assumed need to protect children's welfare through the return remedy ignores the need for informal care networks that women may have to facilitate such care, which is unavailable in the host state following the breakdown of their relationship. This externally imposed welfare standard fails to engage with the wider context of child welfare and the provision of care.

The legal regulation of family behaviour can affect the ability of individuals to carry out their caring responsibilities and this problem is particularly acute in cases of international child abduction. The return remedy is a right which does not necessarily ensure that individual responsibility towards a child can be carried out in the way a parent (usually the mother) would ideally wish. However, the impact of geographical distance on the other parent's relationship with their child, and differences in jurisdiction may outweigh these wishes. The desire to reinforce the application of the return remedy may be justifiable as it has other functions beyond returning a child 'home', including acting as a deterrent to further abductions and protecting the jurisdiction of the courts of the child's country of habitual residence over that child's welfare. However, when legislating the EU should have considered the social pressures that give rise to abductions, particularly by the primary carers of children. The failure to do so indicates that the EU does not currently have the expertise to analyse family-based migration phenomena to identify the causes and gendered effects of the law. Rather than acting upon assumptions, intervention in family law should be informed by the nature of the relationships involved in an attempt to reflect the complexities of international family life. These complexities need to be considered more carefully by the European institutions so that EU law, as well as accommodating more flexible and diverse forms of family life, adopts a realistic approach to the future regulation of both care responsibilities and migration following family dissolution.

## References

Ackers, L. 1998. *Shifting Spaces: Women, Citizenship and Migration within the European Union*. Bristol: Policy Press.

Ackers, L. and Stalford, H. 2007. Managing Multiple Life-Courses: The Influence of Children on Migration Processes in the European Union, in *Social Policy Review 19: Analysis and Debate in Social Policy*, edited by K. Clarke et al. Bristol: Policy Press, 321–42.

Antokolskaia, M. (ed.) 2007. *Convergence and Divergence of Family Law in Europe*. Antwerp: Intersentia.

Bailey, A. and Boyle, P. 2004. Untying and Re-Tying Family Migration in the New Europe. *Journal of Ethnic and Migration Studies*, 30(2), 229–41.

Beaumont, P. and McEleavy, P. 1999. *The Hague Convention on International Child Abduction*. Oxford: Oxford University Press.

Boyle, P., Cooke, T., Gayle, V. and Mulder, C. 2009 The Effect of Family Migration on Union Dissolution in Britain, in *Gender and Migration in 21st Century Europe*, edited by H. Stalford et al. Farnham: Ashgate, 11–21.

Calavita, K. 2006. Gender, Migration and Law: Crossing Borders and Bridging Disciplines. *International Migration Review*, 40(1), 104–32.

Carlier, J.-Y. and Sarolěa, S. 2007. Migrations and Family Law, in *International Family Law for the European Union*, edited by J Meeusen et al Antwerp: Intersentia, 439–60.

Collier, R. 2010. Fatherhood, Law and Father's Rights: Rethinking the Relationship between Gender and Welfare, in *Rights, Gender and Family Law*, edited by J Wallbank et al. Oxford: Routledge, 119–43.

Daly, M. 2005. Changing Family Life in Europe: Significance for State and Society. *European Societies*, 7(3), 379–98.

Dethloff, N. 2003. Arguments for the Unification and Harmonisation of Family Law in Europe, in*Perspectives on the Unification and Harmonisation of Family Law in Europe*, edited by K. Boele-Woelki. Antwerp: Intersentia, 37–65.

Diduck, A. 2003. *Law's Families*. London: LexisNexis Butterworths

Diduck, A. 2008. Family Law and Family Responsibility, in *Responsibility, Law and the Family*, edited by J. Bridgeman et al. Aldershot: Ashgate, 251–68.

Dyer, A. 2000. To Celebrate a Score of Years!*New York University Journal of International Law and Politics*, 33(1), 1–15.

Economic and Social Committee 2002. Opinion of the Economic and Social Committee on the Proposal for a Council Regulation concerning jurisdiction and the recognition and enforcement of judgments in matrimonial matters and in matters of parental responsibility repealing Regulation (EC) No. 1347/2000 and amending Regulation (EC) No. 44/2001 in matters relating to maintenance. OJ C 61/76 COM(2002) 222 final, 4 September 2002.

European Commission 2001. Proposal for a Council Regulation on jurisdiction and the recognition and enforcement of judgments in matters of parental responsibility COM(2001) 505 final, 6 September 2001

European Commission 2005. Green Paper on Applicable Law and Jurisdiction in Divorce Matters COM(2005) 82 final, 14 March2005.

Eurostat 2007. The Social Situation in the European Union 2005–2006. Online: Europa, available at <http: //ec.europa.eu/employment_social/social_situation/docs/ssr2005_2006_en.pdf> (accessed 26 November 2009).

Eurostat 2008. The Life of Women and Men in Europe. Online: Eurostat, available at <http://epp.eurostat.ec.europa.eu/cache/ITY_OFFPUB/KS-80-07-135/EN/KS-80-07-135-EN.PDF> (accessed 26 November 2009).

Fegan, E. 1996. Ideology After Discourse: A Reconceptualization for Feminist Analyses of Law. *Journal of Law and Society*, 23(2), 173–97.

Feijten, P. and van Ham, M. 2007. Residential Mobility and Migration of the Divorced and Separated. *Demographic Review*, 17(21), 623–53.

Fineman, M. 1995. Masking Dependency: The Political Role of Family Rhetoric. *Virginia Law Review*, 81(8), 2181–215.

Fineman, M. 2001. Contract and Care. *Chicago-Kent Law Review*, 76(3), 1403–67.

Freeman, M. 1998. The Effects and Consequences of International Child Abduction. *Family Law Quarterly*, 32(3), 603–42.

Freeman, M. 2001. Primary Carers and the Hague Abduction Convention. *International Family Law*, September, 140–50.

Hayes, M. 2006. Relocation Cases: Is the Court of Appeal Applying the Correct Principles? *Child and Family Law Quarterly*, 18(3), 351–72.

Herring, J. and Taylor, R. 2006. Relocating Relocation. *Child and Family Law Quarterly*, 18(4), 517–37.

Jones, J. 2011. The Responsibility of the EU: Familial Ties for All, in *Taking Responsibility: Law and the Changing Family*, edited by C. Lind, H. Keating and J. Bridgeman. Aldershot: Ashgate, 115–34.

Kulu, H. and Milewski, N. 2007. Family Change and Migration in the Life Course: AnIntroduction. *Demographic Research*, 17(19), 567–90.

Lamont, R. 2008. The EU: Protecting Children's Rights in Child Abduction. *International Family Law*, June, 110–12.

Lister, R. 2006. Children (but not Women) First: New Labour, Child Welfare and Gender. *Critical Social Policy*, 26(2), 315–35.

Lowe, N. 2007. The Current Experiences and Difficulties of Applying Brussels II Revised. *International Family Law*, November, 182–97.

Lowe, N. and Horosova, K. 2007. The Operation of the 1980 Hague Abduction Convention. *Family Law Quarterly*, 41(1), 59–103.

McEleavy, P. 2005. The New Child Abduction Regime in the European Union: Symbiotic Relationship or Forced Partnership? *Journal of Private International Law*, 1(1), 5–34.

McGlynn, C. 2006. *Families and the European Union: Law, Politics and Pluralism*. Cambridge: Cambridge University Press.

Morano-Foadi, S. 2007. Problems and Challenges in Researching Bi-National Migrant Families within the European Union. *International Journal of Law, Policy and the Family*, 21(1), 1–20.

Pěrez-Vera, E. 1980. Explanatory Report on the Hague Convention on the Civil Aspects of International Child Abduction 1980. Online: Hague Conference on Private International Law, available at <http://www.hcch.net/index_en.php?act=publications.details&pid=2779> (accessed 31 January 2007).

Pérez-Vera, E. 1982. Explanatory Report on the 1980 Hague Child Abduction Convention. Online: Hague Conference on Private International Law, available at <http://www.hcch.net/upload/expl28.pdf> (accessed 28 February 2011).

Piper, C. 2000. Assumptions about Children's Best Interests. *Journal of Social Welfare and Family Law*, 22(3), 261–76.

Reece, H. 2006. UK Women's Groups' Child Contact Campaign: 'So long as it is safe'. *Child and Family Law Quarterly*, 18(4), 538–61.

Ribbens McCarthy, J., Edwards, R. and Gillies, V. 2000. Moral Tales of the Child and the Adult: Narratives of Contemporary Lives under Changing Circumstances. *Sociology*, 34(4), 785–803.

Silberman, L. 2003. Patching Up the Abduction Convention: A Call for a New International Protocol and a Suggestion for Amendments for ICARA. *Texas International Law Journal*, 38(1), 41–65.

Silberman, L. 2005. Interpreting the Hague Abduction Convention: In Search of a Global Jurisprudence. *University of California Davis Law Review*, 38(4), 1049–86.

Silva, E. and Smart, C. 1999. *The 'New' Practices and Politics of Family Life, in The New Family?*, edited by E. Silva and C. Smart. London: Sage Publications, 1–12.

Smart, C. 1991. The Legal and Moral Ordering of Child Custody. *Journal of Law and Society*, 18(4), 485–500.

Stalford, H. 2003. Regulating Family Life in Post-Amsterdam Europe. *European Law Review*, 28(1), 39–52.

Stalford, H. 2005. Parenting, Care and Mobility in the EU: Issues Facing Migrant Scientists. *Innovation*, 18(3), 361–80.

Wallbank, J. 2001. *Challenging Motherhood(s)*. Harlow: Prentice Hall.

Wallbank, J. 2007. Getting Tough on Mothers: Regulating Contact and Residence. *Feminist Legal Studies*, 15(2), 189–222.

Windebank, J. 2001. Dual-Earner Couples in Britain and France: Gender Divisions of Domestic Labour and Parenting Work in Different Welfare States. *Work, Employment and Society*, 15(2), 269–90.

Worwood, A. 2005. International Relocation – the Debate. *Family Law,* 35(August), 621–7.

# PART III
# Acknowledging Caring Responsibilities?

# Chapter 10

# Grandparent Involvement and Adolescent Adjustment: Should Grandparents have Legal Rights?

Shalhevet Attar-Schwartz, Ann Buchanan and Eirini Flouri

## Introduction

Grandparents have always been central to supporting families (Buchanan and Ten Brinke 1997). However, given some recent socio-demographic trends, there is growing evidence that grandparents today are playing an increasing role in their grandchildren's lives (Tan et al. 2010). In recent decades many Western countries have witnessed a tendency for an ageing of the population and lower rates of fertility. This shift from a high-mortality/high-fertility to a low-mortality/low-fertility society has resulted in an increase in the number of generations alive at any one time and a decrease in the number of children within each generation. Thus, the number of individuals who will live part of their lives as members of three and four generation families is increasing (Harper and Levin 2005).

In addition, with growing numbers of dual-worker households and higher rates of family breakdown, grandparents are now playing an increasing role in their grandchildren's lives (Franklin 1997). The potential of the grandchild–grandparent relationship for the development of grandchildren is becoming increasingly recognized (Smith 1991). The study described in this chapter examined grandparent involvement among intact, lone-parent and stepfamilies and whether this had a different contribution to the emotional-behavioural and social adjustment of adolescents across different family settings. It was based on a nationally representative sample of 1,515 secondary school students (aged 11–16 years old) from England and Wales and on qualitative interviews with 40 adolescents.

As interest in the role of non-nuclear family members in children's and adolescents' lives has increased there has been a tremendous advance in research knowledge regarding intergenerational relationships in the past two decades. However, a considerable part of the existing literature focuses on the young child rather than the adolescent (for example, Hagestad and Speicher 1981; Thomas 1989). Adolescence involves various transitions that may modify a youth's relationships with parents and grandparents. Scattered empirical research findings about this modification are mixed (Creasey and Koblewski 1991). On the one hand, there are data to suggest that contact with grandparents tends to lessen during the transition from childhood to adolescence and beyond (for example, Atchley 1980). It has been suggested that the many challenges teens experience, including involvement in new relationships (particularly with peers) and in situations that demand more time and energy, may contribute to some sacrifice of the relationship they used to have with grandparents (Roberto and Stroes 1992; Bridges et al. 2007). Other studies show that the significance of grandparents and the desire for contact with them does not decline over the course of adolescence and adulthood (Kornhaber and Woodward 1981; Wiscott and Kopera-Frye 2000). In other words, older children may tend to spend less time with grandparents but still consider them to be attachment figures and important members of their social network (Matthews and Sprey 1985; Field and Minkler 1988; Kennedy 1990; Creasey and Koblewski 1991; Van Ranst et al. 1995).

The literature on grandparent–adolescent grandchild contact is guided mainly by the social ecological theory (Bronfenbrenner 1979), which suggests that to understand children's and adolescents' development and perceptions, we should take into account not only the characteristics and interactions of children and their immediate circles (such as their parents), but also experiences with family members outside the immediate family's residence and the wider environment in which they live (Lussier et al. 2002; Attar-Schwartz et al. 2009a). Grandparents often serve as a positive influence in the lives of their grandchildren by taking on various roles such as care-giver, playmate, advocate, advisor, mentor and friend (King et al. 2000). Many times they have caring responsibilities – even if these differ from those of parents. Yet, as will be discussed later, these responsibilities do not come with correlative rights (see Griggs et al. forthcoming). This lack of reciprocity means that grandparenting is very often a supererogatory activity, even more so than parenting is.

This theoretical framework suggests that grandparents are likely to influence grandchildren throughout childhood either directly (for example, by giving tutelage) or indirectly (for example, by supporting the parent).

One extension of the ecological framework has been Family Systems Theory in clinical research (Minuchin 1985; Lussier et al. 2002) which provides a psycho-social paradigm that emphasizes the importance of examining other family relations as affecting the child rather than focusing exclusively on the mother–child relationship to better understand child development and the ability of the family to adapt to change (Cox and Paley 2003; Ruiz and Silverstein 2007). In order to understand the dynamics of children's relationships with their multiple family members that exist within dyads, triads, and so forth, grandparents are critically important members of these family systems that should be taken into consideration (Troll 1996; Lussier et al. 2002).

## The Roles Grandparents Play in the Lives of Grandchildren

Previous studies indicate that grandparents have a variety of functions within their intergenerational families, especially in the lives of grandchildren. In Scotland, Hill et al. (2005) conducted one of the few studies to elicit the views of teenage grandchildren. They interviewed 73 older people with at least one teenage grandchild, and then some 58 young people in individual or joint interviews (with grandparents), or in group discussions. Ross (2006) noted that in the lives of young people grandparents have particular roles as *protectors* ('they are there when you are in trouble'; 'like second parents'); as *confidants* ('you can tell them things you cannot tell your parents'); as *supporters* mediating between generations; as *benefactors* helping with money, gifts and school fees; as *connectors* bringing together family history, family traits, and shared characteristics. Similarly, Kornhaber (1996) asserts that grandparents have instrumental roles in their grandchildren's lives by being *mentors*, *role models* and *nurturers* as well as playing the more symbolic role of *historian*, where they provide firsthand accounts of family histories, practices and rituals of the past. Bengtson (1985) also suggests that grandparents have five separate symbolic functions: being there; grandparents as national guards; family watchdogs (see also Troll 1983); arbiters who perform negotiations between members; and participants in the social construction of family history. Most of these grandparent roles contain both instrumental and emotional aspects which 'may be visualized along a continuum ranging from symbolic at one end to the interactive and instrumental at the other' (Kornhaber 1996, 88).

Traditionally there is a norm, widely accepted within the white Anglo-American societies, of non-interference by grandparents in the upbringing of their grandchildren (Hill et al. 2005). Harper and Levin (2005), however, demonstrate that this norm may apply with less force to grandparents of lone-parent families where grandparents can become *replacement partners* (as confidants, guides and facilitators), and *replacement parents* (as listeners, teachers and disciplinarians). It is also possible that where parents are working long hours, grandparents may be undertaking roles that are more traditionally associated with parents (Tan et al. 2010).

## Grandparenting and Adolescent Adjustment in Various Familial and Social Contexts

Research on the role of grandparenting in the family has been defined as a continuum with an emphasis on multidimensional and changing characteristics. As mentioned above, at the end of the continuum there may be no involvement or just indirect contact while at the other there is full-time care of grandchildren (Kivnick 1982; Cherlin and Furstenberg 1986; Wood and Liossis 2007). Grandparents with full-time care, at the far end of the grandparent involvement spectrum, present a mixed picture of the benefits for children, possibly because of unusual circumstances in which this takes place. Hunt (2001) in a review of the international literature on kinship care notes that it is not possible, due to the paucity of research evidence, to ascertain whether kinship care promotes the well-being of children. Studies in the US have shown significant emotional and general health problems amongst grandchildren raised by their grandparents (Casper and Bryson 1998). In the UK, recent research (Hansen 2006) comparing outcomes for toddlers in both formal care and grandparent care showed that the latter had the worst behavioural scores.

However, there is some research evidence that emotional closeness and informal involvement of grandparents are associated with reduced emotional and behavioural adjustment difficulties among children and adolescents (for example, Lussier et al. 2002; Ruiz and Silverstein 2007; Griggs et al. forthcoming). For example, Griggs et al. (forthcoming) found among UK adolescents that grandparent involvement was significantly linked with reduced psychological adjustment difficulties. These empirical findings were reinforced by qualitative interviews. In the interviews adolescents explained that time with grandparents represented an opportunity for relaxation, fun and treats but also time that they received attention and could share their thoughts and problems with a committed adult. Shared activities with grandparents may present opportunities to share problems and seek advice. In addition, it might also be that grandparents taking informal care of their grandchildren reduced parents' stress which in turn might affect their parenting. Some young people reported that it was easier to open up to their grandparents than to their parents, often because grandparents had shown themselves to be better listeners and more sensitive to the young person's concerns in the past.

It seems, therefore, as discussed above, that grandparent involvement may be linked to grandchildren's well-being either directly (for example, by tutelage) or indirectly (for example, by decreasing their parents' stress). Werner and Smith (1982) identified contact with grandparents as being one of the numerous protective factors for children at risk for maladjustment, in part because of the continuity in care that such a relationship provides during times of family transitions or stress.

In recent decades growing numbers of children and adolescents spend part of their childhood within families which do not include both of their biological parents, because their parents are divorced, remarried, or single (Dunn 2002; Office for National Statistics 2007; Attar-Schwartz et al. 2009b). Research consistently shows that children and adolescents in such families have on average higher probabilities of difficulties in their psychosocial, health and school adjustment than those growing up in two-parent biological families (for example, Amato and Keith 1991; Hetherington and Stanley-Hagan 1999; O'Connor et al. 2001; Dunn 2002). Research has documented a range of risk factors for this poorer adjustment, such as socio-economic difficulties, family conflicts, poor parental mental health, frequent changes in family situations, lack of social support for the mothers and decreased parental attention (Amato and Keith 1991; Hetherington et al. 1998; O'Connor et al 2001; Dunn 2002; Ruiz and Silverstein 2007).

A relationship with grandparents can be one of the more stable relationships in a child's changing world of adult relationships in non-intact family settings

(Ihinger-Tallman and Pasley 1987; Kennedy and Kennedy 1993) and there is evidence that adolescents may benefit from having them in their social networks as attachment figures and sources of emotional support (Ruiz and Silverstein 2007). Previous research has shown that patterns of contact between grandchildren and their grandparents vary in different family structures. For example, Kennedy and Kennedy (1993), in a study of 400 young adults in the US, found higher levels of grandparent involvement among young adults in single-parent families and step families than among those who grew up in intact families. This involvement included taking an active role in childrearing, as well as providing gifts and money during times of need. Evidence from the UK (Dunn et al. 2001) shows that children and adolescents report that in the weeks following parental separation, grandparents were the most frequent source of intimate confiding about family problems.

In the majority of cases of parental separation, the children reside with their mother (ONS 2007). Figures on the numbers of children of lone parents living in grandparent-headed households are hard to come by. In the study reported here (Attar-Schwartz et al. 2009a), further analysis of the data showed that only 0.7 per cent of the young people aged 11–16 lived in a grandparent *headed* household and about 5 percent lived with their parents and one of the grandparents (usually the maternal grandmother). Therefore, categorizing this small share of adolescents for subcategories of family setting might be not meaningful and it seems that there is room for a separate study aimed at investigating that issue.

Among non-intact families, paternal grandparents generally see less of their son's children. But maternal grandparents (especially grandmothers) often become much more involved in the care of the grandchildren during the years of single parenthood (Cherlin and Furstenberg 1986; Johnson 1988; Kennedy and Kennedy 1993; Dench et al. 1999; Lussier et al. 2002).

Only a handful of studies have examined the links between grandparenting and grandchildren's emotional and behavioural adjustment in different family settings. These studies have found that young people in non-intact families may be the main beneficiaries of a relationship with a close grandparent. In a recent study of 925 young adults (aged 18–23) by Ruiz and Silverstein (2007), based on the National Survey of Families and Households in the US, it was found that close and supportive relationships with grandparents reduced depressive symptoms, and that the association between grandparent social cohesion (including three dimensions: emotional closeness, frequency of contact and source of social support) and grandchildren's depression was significantly stronger for young people whose families of origin were absent a parent. Ruiz and Silverstein (2007) suggest that in the face of depletion of adult guardians in the household, grandparents serve as functional substitutes in reducing distress among young adults (see also Kennedy and Kennedy 1993). It should be noted, however, that their study, like some others, was retrospective and did not measure the concept of grandparent involvement per se (for example, Ruiz and Silverstein 2007). A recent study (Attar-Schwartz et al. 2009a) among a representative sample of about 1,500 UK young people is one of the few to examine this issue among adolescents. That study is described in this chapter.

## The Legal Context

In England and Wales, a grandparent has to seek leave (permission) from the court before making any court application (Children Act 1989, s.10). This applies to all section 8 orders (residence, contact, specific issue and prohibited steps orders, Children Act 1989). However, if a grandparent already has parental responsibility under a residence or special guardianship order (Children Act 1989, s.14A) there is no need to apply for leave of court to apply for a section 8 order. There are other circumstances in which grandparents might apply for a residence or contact order without leave (Children Act 1989, s.10(5)); if, for example, the child has lived with the grandparent for a period of at least three years in the last five, an application can be made without leave. Similarly an applicant can avoid the leave requirement if they have the consent of those with residence, or all those who have parental responsibility for the child. If the child is in care the consent of the local authority will suffice. Similar rules govern applications for special guardianship (Children Act 1989, s.14A).

Where leave is required the court is obliged to consider the nature of the application, the applicant's connection to the child and the risk of disruption to the child's life. If the child is looked after by a local authority, it must also consider the authority's plans and the parents' wishes and feelings (Children Act 1989, s.10(9)). Other factors such as whether or not the application is frivolous, vexatious or an abuse of process or whether or not there is a real prospect of success in the eventual application, may also be considered by a court called upon to grant leave (Grandparents Association 2009).

In England and Wales there is currently considerable pressure from grandparent groups for legal rights (Grandparents Association 2010) and indeed, the current government has recently initiated a Review of Family Law to examine this issue as promised in their manifesto (Conservative Party 2010).

In the US, all states have legislation providing for 'grandparenting visitation' subject to the welfare of the child (Hill 2001). Grandparents in every state in the United States have rights, in some circumstances (conditions vary from state to state), to be awarded custody of their grandchildren or to be awarded court-mandated visitation with their grandchildren. Recognition of grandparents' rights by state legislatures is a fairly recent trend, and most of the statutes have been in effect for less than 35 years (see, for example, Hawaii's grandparent visitation statute: Hawaii Revised Statutes § 571-46.3).

As a response to the debate on greater grandparental rights, a qualitative study by Douglas and Ferguson (2003) in the UK explored the role of grandparents in divorced families. This involved 113 interviews recruited from two samples obtained from divorce court records – 33 mothers, 16 fathers, 30 children, 21 sets of maternal grandparents and 15 sets of paternal grandparents. Douglas and Ferguson (2003) concluded that their study did not provide evidence that grandparents should have their special role recognized by the law.

However, the current situation in England and Wales falls short of the requirements set by the United Nations Convention on the Rights of the Child (1989). Article 5 states that:

> Parties shall respect the responsibilities, rights and duties of parents or, where applicable, the members *of the extended family* or community as provided by local custom, legal guardians or other persons legally responsible for the child, to provide in a manner consistent with the evolving capacities of the child, appropriate direction and guidance. (UN Convention on the Rights of the Child 1989)

It is estimated that one million children in England and Wales are unable to see their grandparents because families have either separated or lost touch. This means that many grandparents, especially paternal grandparents, feel they have lost a close and meaningful relationship (Grandparents Association 2010).

This situation also raises questions about the child's best interests which, under the Children Act 1989, are the paramount consideration in decisions affecting the upbringing of a child (s.1). The welfare principle is also the central doctrine informing decisions about children's upbringing under the UN Convention on the Rights of the Child 1989 (Article 3). This focus on the child's 'best interests' means that all care and visitation discussions and decisions are made with the ultimate goal of fostering and encouraging the child's happiness, security, mental health, and emotional development into young adulthood. Also central to the principles of the Convention (and indeed also the Children Act 1989) is the right of children to participate in decisions affecting their lives (see Children Act 1989, s.1(3)(a)). Therefore, the question asked in the following described study was whether grandparents have a contribution to the well-being of their adolescent grandchildren and whether they had a different contribution to the well-being of children in various family settings.

## UK National Study on Grandparenting and Adolescent Well-Being

The study on which this chapter is based focuses on the adolescents' perspective. It comprised two stages: (a) a survey of a national representative sample of 1,515 secondary school students in England and Wales; (b) in-depth interviews with 40 survey respondents. Below we describe briefly the data collection and sampling methods in each stage.

*Stage one: survey*

A total of 1515 adolescents aged 11–16 (school years 7–11) were recruited by a survey company from schools drawn from the School Government Publishing Company list using probability proportionate-to-size sampling. To ensure that young people of different ages participated, surveys were sent to specific school years, selected at random. A total of 70 schools participated in the study. Data was collected from the adolescents by an anonymous structured questionnaire in a classroom setting. The questionnaire included items regarding the background details of the adolescent and all living grandparents as well as different dimensions of the adolescent–grandparent relationship and adolescent well-being. Below we describe the measures used in the survey which are relevant to the current chapter.

*Adolescent emotional and behavioural adjustment* Adolescents' adjustment and prosocial behaviour were assessed by the Strengths and Difficulties Questionnaire (SDQ), a self-report 25-item scale measuring four difficulties (hyperactivity, emotional symptoms, conduct problems and peer problems), as well as prosocial behaviour (Goodman 1994; 1997).

*The closest grandparent* In this study we assessed the contribution of a close relationship with a grandparent to the adjustment of adolescents in various family contexts. Therefore, we were interested in examining the involvement of the closest grandparent. Elder and Conger's (2000) scale of grandparent–grandchild relationship was used to assess the emotional closeness of the adolescents to their grandparents. Adolescents assessed the quality of this relationship on a four-point Likert type scale (ranging from 1 = not at all to 4 = a lot) by indicating the extent to which: they could depend on their grandparent; they felt appreciated, loved or cared for by their grandparent; the grandparent helped them in significant ways; and they were close compared to other grandchildren to their grandparent. The total responses for each living grandparent were averaged: a higher mean score indicated a closer grandchild–grandparent relationship.

The grandparent who received the highest averaged score from the closeness scale was referred to as the '*closest grandparent*', and it was the involvement of these grandparents that we examined in this study. Additional criteria, as suggested by Elder and King (2000), were used when more than one significant grandparent emerged. These criteria were frequency of contact (the grandparent that they saw or talked to most was rated as the most significant), gender of grandparent (the same-sex grandparent was rated as the most significant), and lineage (maternal grandmother was chosen first, followed by maternal grandfather and then paternal grandparents).

*Grandparent involvement* The pattern of grandparent involvement was measured using a series of items about the direct and indirect influence of grandparents on grandchildren (King and Elder 1997; Elder and Conger 2000). The levels of grandparent involvement were determined by asking the adolescents to indicate the extent to which their grandparents had looked after them, participated in their social interests and school-related activities, had been mentor/advisor for future plans and problems, and provided financial assistance (Elder and Conger 2000). The extent of grandparent involvement was assessed using the summation of all these six items, ranging from 6 to 18, with higher scores indicating a higher level of grandparent involvement in adolescents' lives.

### *Stage two: qualitative interviews*

The purpose of the qualitative element of the research was to expand and help explain the 'how' and 'why' of the quantitative findings. It was an iterative process where the results from the survey influenced the focus of the interviews. Details of 60 young people willing to take part in qualitative in-depth interviews were collected during the survey process, permission being sought by the survey company from adolescents and their parents. Of these, a total of 40 interviews were conducted. These took place in the adolescent's home and were tape-recorded.

## Findings

### *Findings from the survey*

The main survey findings of the study showed that greater grandparent involvement was associated with more prosocial behaviour among the whole sample. In addition, as illustrated by Figures 10.1 to 10.3, while there were no differences in the levels of grandparent involvement across the different family structures, grandparent involvement was more strongly associated with reduced adjustment difficulties (namely fewer peer problems, fewer conduct problems and fewer total difficulties) among adolescents from lone-parent and stepfamilies than among those from two-parent biological families (Attar-Schwartz et al. 2009b).

### *Findings from the qualitative interviews*

Given that the findings from the survey data linked grandparent involvement with child adjustment and emphasized the importance of grandparents in times of parental separation, it was felt important to ask a representative group of young people what they thought about grandparents' legal rights.

This is the first study to report the views of young people on what they want from their relationships with their grandparents. Because of the potential importance of this research the findings from the interviews are presented below in great depth. The first section presented below considers whether grandparents should have rights to see their grandchildren, and the second whether grandparents should be involved in court disputes.

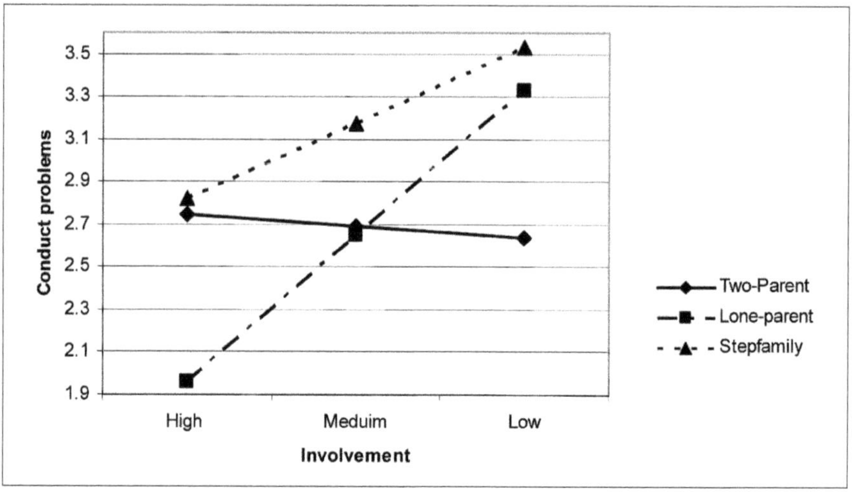


**Figure 10.1 Interaction between grandparent involvement and family structure in predicting conduct problems**

*Source*: Attar-Schwartz, S. et al. 2009, Grandparenting and adolescent adjustment in two-parent biological, lone-parent, and step-families. *Journal of Family Psychology*, 23(1), 67–75.

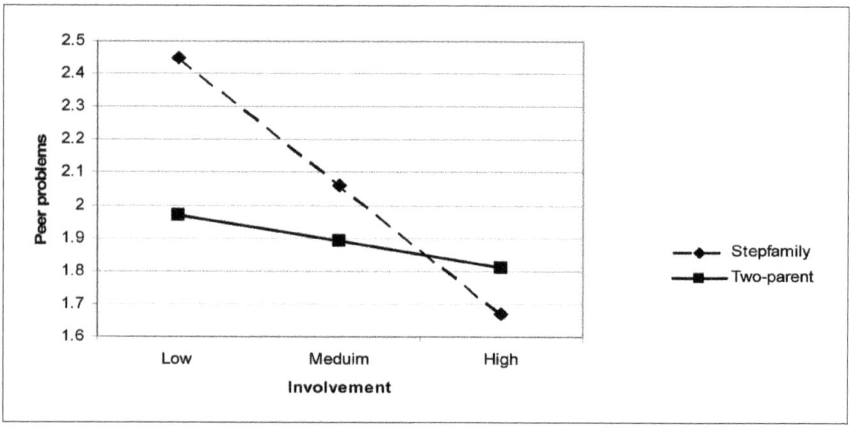


**Figure 10.2 Interaction between grandparent involvement and family structure in predicting peer problems**

*Source*: Attar-Schwartz, S. et al. 2009.

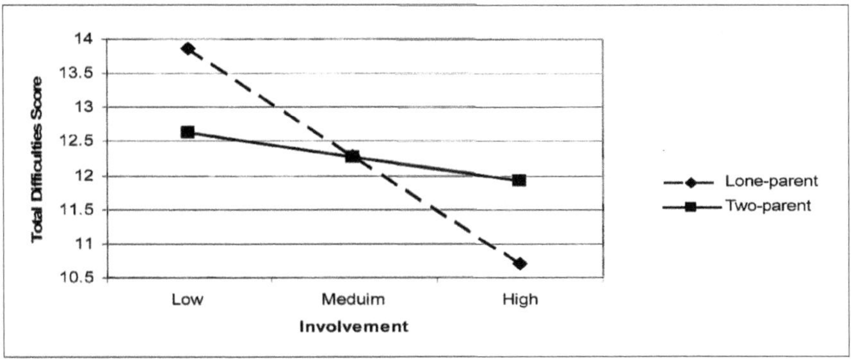


**Figure 10.3 Interaction between grandparent involvement and family structure in predicting total difficulties**

*Source*: Attar-Schwartz, S. et al. 2009.

*'Do you think grandparents should have rights to see their grandchildren?'* A significant group of young people strongly valued the extra support they obtained from their grandparents and the big role they played in their lives, and felt they would be missing out if they were not allowed to see them. When asked if it would be a problem if contact with grandparents was stopped, the following summarizes some of the responses:

> Yes, it will be, because it's part of someone's life they're just taking away.

> Yes, because I think it plays a big part in your life, because if you haven't got your mum to turn to it's someone else to turn to and it's not just your parents all the time, you've got different sort of people to turn to, like your grandparents.

> I think they should because grandparents are really important in the child's life because without them you wouldn't exist, because your mum wouldn't exist so they can't make you, if you know what I mean.

When asked more specifically whether they would be upset if contact with grandparents was stopped following their parents' separation or divorce, there was also a strong response because it was felt grandparents might help them talk things through:

> That would be a problem for me because … well yes I love them so I would be really upset if I couldn't see them.

> Yes I like seeing them … I'd rather have it, because they can help you can't they?

A second theme was that grandparents should keep in touch because they were different from other relationships. The main reason for that is that they were part of the family:

> Yes they should, because they're like grandparents so they're family so they should be able to have their own like, be able to be able to talk to them or keep in contact.

There were also strong feelings that parents should not be able to stop them seeing their grandparents.

> No they shouldn't be able to do that, (stop contact) no.

> Yes definitely they need to stay in touch, yes.

They felt they should have the legal right to see them:

> Because well it's their grandchild as well and it's part of their family, just to keep in touch and help them out, that kind of thing.

*'It's not the fault of children if parents row with grandparents'* A strong theme was that disputes between parents and grandparents were not the fault of grandchildren and should not result in the grandchildren losing contact with grandparents. The young people felt the children would suffer as a result. When asked what should be done about it some young people felt the law should be changed to ensure that grandparents could stay in touch with their grandchildren.

> (Children should not lose contact with grandparents) I think that's not fair, because it isn't the children's fault.

> I think they should get in touch because it's not their fault; it's not the grandparents' fault, and not the children's fault.

> Yes because that's like saying that you couldn't see your kids, that's unfair because they've had nothing to do with the divorce have they, so how is it their fault that they can't see their grandchildren?

> They should change it (the law).

*Contact even when parents do not agree* A significant number of young people felt they would want to keep in contact with grandparents even if their parents did not agree:

But even if your mum had a fight with your grandma, I think that the child should keep in contact with their grandma.

Personally, at this age I wouldn't be very happy if my parents didn't want me to see my grandparents, but I don't see in any way that they can stop me seeing them.

If my mum and dad broke up I would want to see my gran and granddad, but if I wasn't allowed to I would go and see them in secret and not tell anyone, because they're the ones that would help us more to get over something like that, than my mum or my dad. I wouldn't be able to live with not being able to go and see someone I really like.

*Grandparents as protectors* Another important point raised by the young people was that grandparents were the first line of defence if there were difficulties with parents. Many young people were aware that grandparents could act as their protectors, in extreme cases against the vagaries of their parents:

This might sound stupid, but if mum and dad are screw ups, at least the grandparents are good; they can point me in the right direction.

If there's something going on then I think they (grandparents) should step in or something and have a say, if something's going wrong.

Young people were pragmatic about the difficulties of family life:

Like if you and your mum or your dad have ups and downs you want someone to turn to. It's important for children to stay in contact with their grandparents, because if your mum and dad ever fall out and they're having trouble you can stay with your Nan, and sometimes Nan and granddads understand better than parents.

*In case of death* Two children mentioned that if their parents died they would like to go to their grandparents. They felt that, as family, grandparents would be able to share their pain at the death of a parent:

Well if my mum and dad do die, touchwood, then I would go to my Nan and granddad and I would preferably go to them than, because I'd rather be living with them than other family really.

I feel very strongly that they should (stay in touch) because they, like, they're sort of like a second mum if you're very close to them or a second dad, and they're sort of feeling your pain, whereas if you sort of go to a foster parent, they

> will like comfort you and everything but they're not like, you're not related to them or anything …heaven forbid if my parents died, I would want my grandma to be a very big part of my life.

*More ambivalent views regarding grandparents' legal rights* A minority of young people (five out of 40) had more ambivalent views about giving grandparents rights of contact, particularly if the grandparent might represent a danger:

> Well actually it's good and bad (contact with grandparents). They should actually keep it that way because if the grandparents are harassing the child or they're beating them or something then they would not want to see them.… But then on the other hand if the parents don't want the grandparents to see what the parents are doing then they could say no, (you can't see grandparents and that would be bad) … you can't really tell, you can't really judge, so it's kind of hard to say whether they should be given legal rights or not. But in any circumstances the grandparents still should be able to see the children.

But given that a grandparent presented no danger, young people felt contact should be allowed:

> I think they should be allowed to unless they've hurt them or something, I think they should be allowed, I think it's good for the children to see their grandparents and learn to get on with another generation.

> Personally, at this age I wouldn't be very happy if my parents didn't want me to see my grandparents, but I don't see in any way that they're going to stop me seeing them.

*In the final analysis it should be the young person's choice that ruled the day* Perhaps the strongest view was that in the final analysis, the young person should make the decision whether or not he/she wished to see their grandparent(s). As we have noted before, some young people even felt they would take the matter into their own hands and see their grandparents secretly.

> I think it should be more the kids' decision depending on their age. But obviously if the grandparents want to see the kids then I don't think the parent should just be able to say no … I think it depends on the kids' age because if they're really young then it's not really fair on them being brought up with one grandparent or no grandparents whatsoever, so I don't think it's fair.

> If my mum and dad broke up I would want to see my gran and granddad, but if I wasn't allowed to I would go and see them in secret and not tell anyone, because they're the ones that would help us more to get over something like that, than

> my mum or my dad. I wouldn't be able to live with not being able to go and see someone I really like.

## Should Grandparents be Involved in Court Proceedings Relating to Young People's Lives?

It was interesting that when it came to this question many young people were more pragmatic. While some said, yes of course, others could see the difficulties. Some of these young people had seen their own parents go through difficult conflicted court cases.

Some young people appeared to think it was normal for grandparents to be involved in a major family drama. But their perspective was very much that they might help them.

> Yes, because they are family and they might help me

> Well I think so, yes, because if there's like a major family problem, I mean they are a family member so I think they should be included.

> Because it's their grandchildren of course and because it's family, they understand what's been going on and everything and they can like, sort of like, how do you explain, help it out, like they can help you with it, they know like what to do and everything really, help you with it.

One teenager had a positive experience of grandparental involvement in his parent's divorce and had found it helpful:

> Yes, I think they should because my Nan helped out my mum in court and everything so she's made big decisions, and she's been really helpful through my life.

However, other young people had more reservations, especially those who had experienced their own parents' separation and divorce. They were aware of the limits to their grandparents' powers.

> (Grandparents) should be able to see us, but to say that they (our parents) can't get divorced then that's not up to them really.

> It depends whether it was about them or not, if it was them directly involved, but they would give advice and help out and make statements if that was the case.

Generally there was a view that they could be included but not to any great extent. It depended on the issues.

> *I think they should yes* [*be involved in the legal situation*], because it is kind of their business as well although it's like the parents mostly, but it is partly to do with them so they should be included.

Young people were very aware of the possibility of conflict and the problems of each grandparent supporting their side of the family. They felt the actual divorce was not their *grandparents*' business.

> I'm not saying it's a bad thing but I'm not saying it's a good thing. It's a bad thing because grandparents do like to help their children, but they might favour one side and a fight could start and stuff like that. So if you like let the children resolve things that would be better.

The teenagers were also aware that divorce concerned more than their well-being. There was property and money involved. Generally they felt grandparents were best kept away from the court battle.

> I think they should be informed about it but not actually be there.

In the individual interviews, all young people were asked whether they felt that grandparents should have *legal rights* to see their grandchildren. The overwhelming majority of young people felt strongly that they wanted their grandparents to stay in touch. Out of the 40 interviews, 35 young people expressed strongly that they wanted continuing contact with grandparents. Only five were uncertain or qualified their responses. One felt it was 'up to the parents', and another that, although she would like to keep in touch with her grandparents herself, she did know one grandmother who had stolen all her grandchild's money. A third mentioned that it should be up to the child as the grandparents may be 'harassing' the child. Overall young people were not especially concerned about their grandparents' rights but felt very strongly that it was *their right* to have continuing contact.

When, however, it came to involving grandparents in court decisions they were much more pragmatic. Here the responses were divided between those who felt grandparents should be involved 'because they are family and know you', and those who felt it would not help.

## Should the Positive Role of Grandparents be Better Recognized Legally?

The findings of the described study, as well as other studies, show that grandparent involvement is more strongly associated with reduced adjustment difficulties among children and adolescents who reside in non-intact families. Given the increasing proportions of children and adolescents growing up in non-traditional family structures, more attention may need to be paid to the role of grandparents as social supporters for children and adolescents *raised in* these changing and complex environments.

Those findings may indicate that grandchildren in lone-parent and stepfamilies are the chief beneficiaries of grandparent contact and that this contact is an important protective resource in their lives. Ruiz and Silverstein (2007) suggest that in the face of single parenthood and the new challenges imposed by forming a stepfamily, as well as new challenges faced by adolescents, grandparents may serve as functional substitutes in lessening adolescents' distress. These findings are in line with those of Werner and Smith (1982) who identified close contact with a grandparent as one of a number of protective factors for children born at risk for maladjustment, in part because of the continuity in care-giving that such a relationship provides during multiple transitions (see also Kennedy and Kennedy 1993). Studies also showed that grandparents were important confidants for young people in times of distress, such as parental separation and divorce, as well as during constructing a new family. In addition, they functioned as monitors of parental behaviours (for example, Kennedy and Kennedy 1993; Dunn and Deater-Deckard 2001).

However, although grandparents were identified in several studies as a potential resource and as potentially moderating the negative influence of parental separation and multiple family transitions (Cherlin et al. 1998; Ruiz and Silverstein 2007), currently grandparents' potential contribution to children's and adolescents' development is largely unacknowledged by professionals working with children and adolescents, as well as by legal forums and policy makers.

## Conclusion: The Case for Legal Rights for Grandparents

As discussed in this chapter, many grandparents have important caring responsibilities – even if these differ from those of parents. Yet, these responsibilities do not come with correlative rights (see Griggs et al. forthcoming).

Although it is recognized that, in individual cases, grandparent involvement may be a negative influence on the child, the findings that grandparental involvement is in general associated with better adjustment in young people might suggest that it is 'in the child's best interests' to ease the legal barriers preventing this involvement. A major legal barrier is the requirement for grandparents to apply for 'leave' of court before making any application about their grandchild. Grandparents are not eligible for legal aid and the costs of applying for this leave can effectively bar poorer grandparents from ongoing involvement with their grandchildren. When this is allied to findings that most young people wanted ongoing contact with their grandparents, and indeed see it as their right, a strong case is made to think afresh about this law. Young people felt that without access to their grandparents, they could be missing out on an important source of what we might call *social capital* (Putnam 2002). However, young people had some reservations about involving grandparents in legal disputes between divorcing parents. The paucity of research in that area leaves the dilemma of grandparents' legal rights still unsolved. Future studies should examine this issue more thoroughly and take into account the views of adolescents, grandparents and parents.

## References

Amato, P. and Keith, B. 1991. Parental divorce and the well-being of children: A meta-analysis. *Psychological Bulletin*, 110, 26–46.

Atchley, R.C. 1980. *The Social Forces in Later Life*, 3rd edition. Belmont, CA: Wadsworth.

Attar-Schwartz, S. et al. 2009, Grandparenting and adolescent adjustment in two-parent biological, lone-parent, and step-families. *Journal of Family Psychology*, 23(1), 67–75.

Attar-Schwartz, S., Tan, J.P. and Buchanan, A. 2009a. Adolescents' perspectives on relationships with grandparents: The contribution of adolescent, grandparent, and parent–grandparent relationship variables. *Children & Youth Services Review*, 31, 1057–66.

Attar-Schwartz, S., Tan, J.P., Buchanan, A., Flouri, E. and Griggs, J. 2009b. Grandparenting and adolescent adjustment in two-parent biological, lone-parent and step-families. *Journal of Family Psychology*, 23(1), 67–75.

Bengtson, V.L. 1985. Diversity, symbolism in grandparental role, in *Grandparenthood*, edited by V.L. Bengtson and J.R. Robertson. Beverly Hills, CA: Sage, 61–77.

Bengtson, V. L. 2001. Beyond the nuclear family: The increasing importance of multigenerational bonds. *Journal of Marriage and Family*, 63, 1–16.

Bridges, L.J., Roe, A.E.C., ALSPAC, Dunn, J. and O'Connor, G. 2007. Children's perspectives on their relationships with grandparents following parental separation: A longitudinal study. *Social Development*, 16, 539–54.

Bronfenbrenner, U., 1979. *The Ecology of Human Development*. Cambridge, MA: Harvard University Press.

Buchanan, A. and Ten Brinke, J. 1997. *What Happened When They Were Grown Up?* York: Joseph Rowntree Foundation/York Publishing.

Casper, L.M. and Bryson, K.R. 1998. *Co-Resident Grandparents and their Grandchildren: Grandparent Maintained Families*. Population Division Working Paper No. 26. Washington, DC: US Census Bureau.

Cherlin, A. and Furstenberg, F.F. 1986. *The New American Grandparent: A Place in the Family, a Life Apart*. New York: Basic Books.

Cherlin, A. J., Chase-Lansdale, P. and McRae, C. 1998. Effects of parental divorce on mental health throughout the life course. *American Sociological Review*, 63, 637–67.

Conservative Party. 2010. *The Conservative Manifesto 2010: Invitation to Join the Government of Britain*. London: Conservative Party.

Cox, M.J. and Paley, B. 2003. Understanding families as systems. *Current Directions in Psychological Science*, 12, 193, 196.

Creasey, G.L. and Koblewski, P.J. 1991. Adolescent grandchildren's relationships with maternal and paternal grandmothers and grandfathers. *Journal of Adolescence*, 14, 373–87.

Dench, G., Ogg, J. and Thompson, K. 1999. The role of grandparents, in *British Social Attitudes: The 16th Report*, edited by R. Jowell. Aldershot: Ashgate and National Centre for Social Research.

Douglas, G. and Ferguson, N. 2003. The role of grandparents in divorced families. *International Journal of Law, Policy and Family*, 17, 41–67.

Dunn, J. 2002. The adjustment of children in step families: Lessons from community studies. *Child and Adolescent Mental Health*, 7, 154–61.

Dunn, J. and Deater-Deckard, K. 2001. *Children's Views of their Changing Families*. York: Joseph Rowntree Foundation.

Dunn, J., Davies, L.C., O'Connor, T.G. and Sturgess, W. 2001. Family lives and friendships: The perspectives of children in step-, single-parent and non-step families. *Journal of Family Psychology*, 15, 272–87.

Elder, G.H. Jr. and Conger, R.D. 2000. *Children of the Land: Adversity and Success in Rural America*. Chicago: University of Chicago Press.

Field, D. and Minkler, M. 1988. Continuity and change in social support between young-old, old-old, and very old adults. *Journal of Gerontology*, 43, 100–106.

Franklin, D.L. 1997. Ensuring Inequality: The Structural Transformation of the African American Family. New York: Oxford University Press.

Goodman, R. 1994. A modified version of the Rutter parent questionnaire including extra items on children's strengths: A research note. *Journal of Child Psychology and Psychiatry*, 35, 1483–94.

Goodman, R. 1997. The strengths and difficulties questionnaire: A research note. *Journal of Child Psychology and Psychiatry*, 38, 581–6.

Grandparents Association. 2009. Children Law update, 29 April 2009. <http://www.grandparents-association.org.uk/images/section_8.pdf>.

Grandparents Association. 2010. <http://www.grandparents-association.org.uk>.

Griggs, J., Tan, J.P., Buchanan, A., Attar-Schwartz, S. and Flouri, E. forthcoming. 'They've always been there for me': Grandparental involvement and child well-being. *Children and Society*.

Hagestad, G.O. and Speicher, J.L. 1981. Grandparents and family influence: Views of three generations. Paper presented at the Biennial Meeting of the Society for Research in Child Development, Boston.

Hansen, K. 2006. Grandparental involvement in child-rearing and childcare. *CLS Cohort Newsletter*, Autumn, 2006.

Harper, S. and Levin, S. 2005. Family care, independent living and ethnicity. *Social Policy and Society*, 4, 157–69.

Hetherington, E.M. and Stanley-Hagan, M. 1999. The adjustment of children with divorced parents: A risk and resiliency perspective. *Journal of Child Psychology and Psychiatry*, 40, 129–40.

Hetherington, E.M., Bridges, M., and Insabella, G.M. 1998. What matters? What does not? Five perspectives on the association between marital transitions and children's adjustment. *American Psychologist*, 53, 167–84.

Hill, M., Ross, N., Cunningham-Burley, S. and Sweeting, H. 2005. *Grandparents and Teen Grandchildren: Exploring Relationships*. London: ESRC RES-000-22-0402.

Hill, T. 2001. What is a grandparent to do? The legal status of grandparents in the extended family. *Journal of Family Issues*, 22(5), 594–618.

Hunt, J. 2001. Family and friends carers: Scoping paper for the Department of Health. London: Department of Health. <http://www.dfes.gov.uk/childrenandfamilies/04016168%5B1%5D.pdf>.

Ihinger-Tallman, M. and Pasley, K. 1987. *Remarrying*. Newbury Park, CA: Sage Publications.

Johnson, C.H. 1988. *Ex Familia: Grandparents, Parents, and Children Adjust to Divorce*. New Brunswick, NJ: Rutgers University Press.

Kennedy, G. 1990. College students' expectations of grandparent and grandchild role behaviors. *The Gerontologist*, 30, 43–8.

Kennedy, G.E. and Kennedy, C.E. 1993. Grandparents: A special resource for children in stepfamilies. *Journal of Divorce and Remarriage*, 19, 45–68.

King, V. and Elder, G.H. 1997. The legacy of grandparenting: Childhood experiences with grandparents and current involvement with grandchildren. *Journal of Marriage and the Family*, 59, 848–59.

King, V., Elder, G.H. and Conger, R.D. 2000. Wisdom of the ages, in *Children of the Land: Adversity and Success in Rural America*, edited by R.D. Conger and G.H. Elder. Chicago: University of Chicago Press.

Kivett, V.R. 1985. Grandfathers and grandchildren: Patterns of association, helping, and psychological closeness. *Family Relations*, 34, 565–71.

Kivnick, H. 1982. Grandparenthood: An overview of meaning and mental health. *The Gerontologist*, 22(1), 59–66.

Kornhaber, A. 1996. *Contemporary Grandparenting*. Thousand Oaks, CA: Sage.

Kornhaber, A. and Woodward, K.L. 1981. *Grandparent/Grandchild: The Vital Connection*. Garden City, NY: Anchor Press.

Lussier, G., Deater-Deckard, K., Dunn, J. and Davies, L. 2002. Support across two generations: Children's closeness to grandparents following parental divorce and remarriage. *Journal of Family Psychology*, 16, 363–76.

Matthews, S.H. and Sprey, J. 1985. Adolescents' relationships with grandparents: An empirical contribution to conceptual clarification. *Journal of Gerontology*, 40(5), 621–26.

Minuchin, P. 1985. Families and individual development: Provocations from the field of family therapy. *Child Development*, 56, 289–302.

O'Connor, T.G., Dunn, J., Jenkins, J.M., Pickering, K. and Rabasah, J. 2001. Family settings and children's adjustment: Differential adjustment within and across families. *British Journal of Psychiatry*, 179, 110–15.

Office for National Statistics. 2002. <http://www.statistics.gov.uk/CCI/nugget.asp?ID=270&Pos=1&ColRank=2&Rank>.

Office for National Statistics. 2006.<http://www.statistics.gov.uk/pdfdir/bd0506.pdf>.

Office for National Statistics. 2007. Increase in families mainly cohabiting couples: Focus on families <www.statistics.gov.uk/focus/families>.

Putnam, R.D. (ed.). 2002. *Democracies in Flux: The Evolution of Social Capital in Contemporary Society*. New York: Oxford University Press.

Roberto, K.A. and Stroes, J. 1992. Grandchildren and grandparents: Roles, influences, and relationships. *Journal of International Aging and Human Development*, 34, 227–39.

Ross, N. 2006. Negotiating family transitions and relations: The perspective of teenagers and grandparents. Paper presented at the Promoting the Well-Being of Children: The Role of Grandparents and Kinship Care at University of Oxford, UK.

Ruiz, S.A. and Silverstein, M. 2007. Relationships with grandparents and the emotional well-being of late adolescent and young adult grandchildren. *Journal of Social Issues*, 63, 793–808.

Smith, P.K. (ed.). 1991. *The Psychology of Grandparenthood: An International Perspective.* London: Routledge.

Tan, J.P., Buchanan, A., Flouri, E., Attar-Schwartz, S. and Griggs, J. 2010. Filling in the parenting gap? Grandparental involvement with UK adolescents. *Journal of Family Issues*. Published online: <http://jfi.sagepub.com/cgi/content/abstract/0192513X09360499v1>.

Thomas, J.L. 1989. Gender and perceptions of grandparenthood. *International Journal of Aging and Human Development*, 29, 269–82.

Troll, L.E. 1983. Grandparents: The family watchdogs, in *Family Relationships in Later Life*, edited by T.H. Brubaker. Beverly Hills, CA: Sage.

Troll, L.E. 1996. Modified-extended families over time: Discontinuity in parts, continuity in wholes, in *Adulthood and Aging: Research on Continuities and Discontinuities*, edited by V. Bengtson. New York: Springer, 246–68.

United Nations Convention of the Rights of the Child. 1989. New York: UN.

Van Ranst, N., Verschueren, K. and Macroen, A. 1995. The meaning of grandparents as viewed by adolescent grandchildren: An empirical study in Belgium. *International Journal of Human Development*, 41, 311–24.

Werner, E.E. and Smith, R.S. 1982. *Vulnerable but Invincible: A Study of Resilient Children.* New York: McGraw-Hill.

Wiscott, R. and Kopera-Fyre, K. 2000. Sharing of culture: Adult grandchildren's perceptions of intergenerational relations. *International Journal of Aging and Human Development*, 51(3), 199–215.

Wood, S. and Liossis, P. 2007. Potentially stressful life events and emotional closeness between grandparents and adult grandchildren. *Journal of Family Issues*, 28, 380–98.

# Chapter 11
# Reflections on the Duty to Care for the Elderly in Portugal

Paula Távora Vítor

## Introduction

Modern industrialized societies face a challenge without precedent. Their populations are ageing and problems associated with the intergenerational imbalance that this causes are growing. Indeed, demographic data confirms that the group of 'elderly people' is not only increasing (due to the decline of mortality), but the numbers of younger people are also decreasing (because of reduced fertility) (Fernandes 2001, 40; Ribeiro 2005, 205). Self-evidently, the extension of life has its effects on family structure (Ribeiro 2005, 211). But these changes should not lead us into an unquestioning assumption that less attention is paid by families towards their elderly relatives (Jani-Le Bris 1993, 31). And, although it is true that fewer elderly people live with their adult children and that the proportion of the elderly living alone (in poverty, loneliness and circumstances of social exclusion) is larger than in the past (Fernandes 2001, 47), the stereotype of the isolated elderly person without any connection to her or his family is inaccurate (Fernandes 2001, 39–40; Ribeiro 2005, 212). Indeed, family still remains the essential setting for intergenerational exchanges (Fernandes 2001, 47; Tomé 2004, 52). This observation is reinforced by recent sociological studies that contradict the idea that the onset of the 'nuclear family' in the era of industrialization provoked a severance from the family of origin (Ribeiro 2005, 213, fn. 19). Neither the dominance of a smaller (nuclear) family nor the changes to it that have occurred in the last 200 years have led to the destruction of the links between parents and their children. On the contrary, parents and children have found new ways of relating.

This means that any stereotyped belief that families do not care for their elderly relatives is unfounded. Within the European context, families have been assuming their 'primary role' (Diduck 2008, 255), namely the care of elderly and dependent people, regardless of the diversity of family structures and social and political conditions which differentiate the traditions in different countries. This social behaviour is commonly characterized as the fulfilment of an ethical duty. In this chapter I shall address whether, apart from these social responsibilities, there is also (and ought to be) a legal duty to care for the elderly imposed on the family; if so, what is its content, source and nature.

## Family Responsibilities

### *Constitutional approach*

The 'principle of maintaining elderly people in their household[s]' is a feature of the European cultural milieu (Jani-Le Bris 1993, 51). Respect for human dignity and the right freely to develop one's personality demand the preservation of the elderly in their family and social environments rather than in institutional settings (Stanzione 1989, 451–2). The Portuguese Constitution (PC) is not blind to this requirement. Family is regarded as a 'fundamental element of society', and is considered to be a 'life phenomenon' and not only 'a juridical creation' (Canotilho and Moreira 2007, 856). Article 67, therefore, recognizes the family as the bearer of fundamental rights: '[t]he right to protection by community and the State and to the creation of all the conditions that permit the personal fulfilment of its members'.

This family protection includes the protection of the *unity of the family*, namely the right to coexist, or more specifically, the 'right of the family members to live together', which demands the creation of the conditions that allow family life (Miranda and Medeiros 2005, 407, 693). The reference to 'family life' must be understood in a broad sense. The main concern of article 67 is the spousal relationship. However, it is not its exclusive focus. The constitutional notion of family is flexible, open to different social conceptions and it includes the relationship between parents and their adult children (Miranda and Medeiros 2005, 690).[1]

Since article 67 creates social rights it imposes on the state the duty to develop specific activities (article 67(2)). Consequently, in order to protect the family, the state performs a series of different tasks, which include 'promoting the social and economic independence of family units' and 'the establishment of, and guaranteeing of access to, a national network of day-care centres and other social facilities for family support, and a policy for elderly people' (art. 67(2a) and (2b) PC).

The Constitution also addresses issues that concern 'Old Age' (or 'Third Age'), which is considered to be a category worthy of social protection guaranteed by the state (in article 72) (Canotilho and Moreira 2007, 884). It belongs, therefore, to the same category as article 67 ('social rights'). Article 72 grants elderly people the right of access 'to conditions of housing and of family and community life

---

1 In the German context, article 6(1) of the *Grundgesetz*, by which the state guarantees family protection, was the basis for a decision by the Supreme Administrative Court of Baden-Württemberg (VGHBW) that prevented an Albanian citizen from being deported on the ground that he had to take care personally of his mother. It was considered that family is a *Beistandgemeinschaft* (community of support), which justifies a family member who was in charge of another family member and who would only be able to take care of him/her in German territory being allowed to stay in the country (Henrich 1997, 7).

that respect their personal autonomy and prevent or surmount their isolation and marginal position in society'. These conditions require the 'familial integration of elderly people' and the creation of communal structures such as retirement homes or community facilities for social activities (Canotilho and Moreira 2007, 884). Therefore, family life appears as an essential dimension of protection in 'old age'.

In considering these constitutional regulations, we may conclude that the Portuguese Constitution does not approach this issue from the perspective of a 'familial duty to care for the elderly'. Here, a parallel can be made with the Spanish Constitution which, in article 50, refers to 'Old Age'. Debate in Spain has considered whether this article contains an exclusive imposition on public authorities to promote the well-being of elderly citizens 'independently from family relations' (Palma 2002, 148) or supposes an implicit recognition of the supporting function of family towards their elderly (Figuerruelo Burrieza 2004, 43, 45; Martínez Rodriguez 2004, 137). In Portugal the Constitution only addresses the issue within the framework of 'social rights' (which demand development of the activity of the state as a provider) and does not refer to 'family relations' themselves. In this way, according to the Constitution, the state is the entity obliged to promote the unity of the family (article 67); in particular, it must promote conditions that allow for a family life for elderly people (as defined in article 72). We must, therefore, look for a familial duty in other layers of the Portuguese system.

### *Becoming a familial duty – from the ethical to the legal regulation of care*

One of the social functions that family assumes is to provide for the satisfaction of the basic needs of its members, especially when they are not able to meet those needs themselves (Díez-Picazo and Gullón 2002, 36). In reality, notwithstanding the fact that there has been a growing assumption of traditional familial functions by other social organizations (Díez-Picazo and Gullón 2002, 40) the family has not renounced this responsibility. And the reason is almost self-evident; family conduct is most often rooted in ethical rules. These rules are sometimes appropriated by law and converted into juridical rules (Herring 2007, 668; Herring 2008, 53). Indeed an ethical imperative that sees family members seeking mutual support in situations of need usually precedes any parallel juridical duty. In this chapter I shall address the way in which ethical rules have been converted into legal precepts. That is to say, I shall analyse the shape given by law to the family's caring responsibilities and shall go on to consider the appropriateness of law's role in this respect.

I must, therefore, start with the family's responsibilities to care. However, it is not easy to define them. Even though 'responsibility is … a central concept of family relationships' (Lind et al. 2011, 7), it 'remains inadequately conceptualised' (Lind et al. 2011, 7) and its meaning is not univocal. Traditionally responsibilities have been seen as the 'corollary of rights' and the terms 'obligation' and 'responsibility' have been used interchangeably (Herring 2008, 42). Nevertheless, a distinction between these concepts may provide us with an important tool for understanding the regulation of family relations.

According to Eekelaar (2007, 129), the concept of responsibility goes beyond that of legal obligation and, once responsible behaviour is enforced, 'the fuller sense of responsibility is lost, for the behaviour, while remaining a responsibility, is now a legal duty' (Eekelaar 2007, 131). In the view of Lind et al., 'family responsibilities incorporate but are not confined to legally enforceable obligations and duties as determined by legal norms, properly called responsibilities when they exceed legal duties and obligations. In other words, whilst family responsibility includes obligations and duties, they are more than the sum of these' (Lind et al. 2011, 13).

In this chapter I shall adopt this broader meaning of responsibility; for me the concept of family responsibilities includes legal duties, which may or not be legally enforceable, but is more extensive than that. Indeed, there are some responsibilities which are not imposed as legal duties, but are allocated by law to family members. We might say that the law acts in an indirect way, assuming pre-existing family ethical and social values and rules, and taking advantage of its consequent behaviour, while accepting that there is not a strong enough foundation upon which to base a duty. As we shall see, this also occurs with duties of care. Paraphrasing Eekelaar (1991, 351) (where the author refers to the moral obligation to care for the children), there are situations in which there is a social practice that does not itself create a duty of care, but it may place a particular responsibility on some people rather than others. And the law is sometimes willing to appropriate that social allocation of responsibilities, in different ways.

Of course, the ethical content of family conduct determines that, regardless of the juridical regulation, real behaviour is motivated by other incentives. The intervention of law only occurs when there is a crisis (Díez-Picazo and Gullón 2002, 42). In the context of the care for a dependent elderly person, there will be a crisis when those who are responsible are not willing to assume that responsibility. In these situations, the state might intervene legislatively 'to *support* the maintenance of family relations' (Eekelaar 1984, 25), namely through the creation of legal rights and duties, such as a 'duty to care and support'.

What does an obligation to care and support mean? It might contain within its limits a wide range of behaviours that were thought not to be capable of legal definition. It might attempt to bring together different tasks that translate into a care-giving activity. Its existence is foreseen in abstract by law for certain familial relations (see below). But a satisfactory answer to the question needs a more concrete form. In order to provide that form one needs to ascertain the situation of need of the dependent person. This can range from minimal – if she or he is fundamentally autonomous – to a situation of almost total dependency which demands permanent support from a carer. One also needs to determine the prospective carer's means; the ability or availability to accompany the elderly relative or provide other forms of care may vary widely. Furthermore the ethical basis for such a legal duty may vary according to the family member to which the obligation to care is allocated. In effect, both the content and the source of a general duty to care will depend upon the person on whom the duty is to be imposed.

## Other Familial or Parafamilial Legal Duties

An adequate analysis of the potential 'duty to care and support' the elderly must clearly determine the boundaries of such a duty, especially with regard to other neighbouring responsibilities. The triple responsibilities identified by Herring (2008) as those of adult children towards their parents – consisting of financial responsibilities, decisionmaking responsibilities and caring responsibilities – provides us with a framework for analysis. I shall distinguish the duty to care for elderly relatives from the financial responsibilities and decision making responsibilities that may be imposed in law. In the Portuguese system the former are expressed in a legal maintenance obligation imposed on some family members while the latter can only be imposed in law on court-nominated guardians.

### *The maintenance obligation*

Portuguese law expressly creates an obligation to maintain people in situations of financial need which may be imposed on any of several family members (art. 2009 of the Civil Code). However, this expression of familial solidarity cannot be regarded as a 'duty to provide care and support', even though it may share important similarities with such a duty (Lima and Varela 1992, 263). Although the two duties have an analogous purpose – to assume responsibility for people in need – the nature of the *need* involved is different in each case. The maintenance obligation aims to respond to the economic needs of the dependent person (cf. article 2003 of the Civil Code) whereas the 'duty to provide care and support' deals with other aspects of need that do not demand pecuniary aid but rather emotional or day-to-day practical assistance.

There are, however, situations in which this distinction cannot be easily drawn. As a rule, the maintenance obligation is a pecuniary obligation paid monthly. However, the law allows it to be provided in other ways 'in the household and in the company' of the debtor (article 2005, nn.1 and 2 Civil Code) when the latter cannot afford to pay it. In cases like these the line that divides the pecuniary from the caring duties becomes less clear; there is no targeted pecuniary payment. Indeed, when the person in financial need is received into the debtor's household, she or he will become part of the network of personal solidarity that is implied in living under the same roof and will often benefit from the care provided by its other members. However, the right to be maintained will originate from a situation of economic need that does not demand aid to deal with other aspects of the dependant's life. Despite this, in practical terms, whoever needs financial assistance often also needs support in the performance of daily tasks. Thus, the 'duty to provide care and support' and the maintenance obligation often coexist in real-life circumstances. Nevertheless one must, in conceptual terms, separate economic need from the need for task oriented help so as to approach separately the two different duties to which they give rise.

The distinction between the maintenance obligation and the duty to provide care is also relevant in determining who is under an obligation to pay maintenance and who might be under an obligation to provide care and support. As far as the maintenance obligation is concerned, there is an extensive legal list of those who are obliged to make payments. That list includes not only spouses and former spouses and descendants and ascendants but also siblings and, under certain circumstances, uncles and stepparents (article 2009, Civil Code). However, the duty to provide care and support for a relative cannot be imposed on many of these individuals.

Finally, since it consists of a pecuniary payment, the maintenance obligation is enforceable as of right (article 1118, Civil Procedure Code) whereas the 'duty to provide care and support', given its nature, is not (Henrich 1997, 2–3; Herring 2008, 56).

*The duty of the guardian*

Elderly people may find themselves in situations of need that do not require financial help but rather relate to a diminished capacity to understand and to make decisions. Indeed, they may suffer from impairments that affect their mental competency. In those cases, the diminution or lack of capacity must be judicially acknowledged; the incapacitation must be declared and a legal representative – a guardian – must be appointed by the court.

The responsibilities of the guardian are directed to protecting the incapacitated person. However, they should not be confused with those implied by the obligation to supply care and support. The duty of the guardian is to provide for the interests of the incapacitated person, through legal representation, acting on behalf of that person and deciding in her or his place whenever decisions are required. This substitution or control over the decisionmaking process does not exist in the fulfilment of the 'duty to provide care and support' which may be directed to an entirely mentally competent person.

The beneficiaries of a guardian's activities are not the only people who need practical assistance. Nor even are all the people who suffer from diminished capacity entitled to a guardian. The guardian only acts on behalf of people who have undergone a judicial procedure that declares their legal incapacity which must be grounded in indicators of incapacity laid out in law: mental disorder, deafness and blindness, or even prodigality and the abuse of alcohol and other narcotics (articles 138 and 152, Civil Code). There are, therefore, several situations of dependency in old age (for example, those relating to physical well-being) in which there could be no recourse to the legal protection of a guardian.

Guardians are also not necessarily the people who have the ethical obligation to provide care and support for particular older people. In order to appoint a guardian the law (article 143, Civil Code) provides qualification guidelines. Within this list family members occupy a prominent and often privileged position (spouses, parents and adult children of incapacitated people). However, the qualifications also permit other persons (outside the family) to be vested with this function. The 'duty to provide care and support', on the other hand, only vests in family members.

## The Subjects

### *Elderly people*

Unlike children and young people who can generally be categorized as 'minors', 'elderly people' do not constitute an easily identifiable category. In the first place, 'elderly people' are adults. At what point do adults become 'elderly'? In the Portuguese system there are several allusions to the idea of old age, some referring to the period after 60 years of age, others to the period after 65 or 70 or 80. Settling the frontier of 'old age' or 'elderly' at 60 or 65 is, perhaps, more common than the older ages because of its easy association with the official retirement age (Stanzione 1989, 441; Herring 2007, 663). The Portuguese Constitution itself, as has been pointed out, uses the expression 'third age', a qualification of 'old age' that is grounded in the idea of the life course connected to production, being identified with post-working age. However, the use of this boundary has been subject to criticism based, on the one hand, on attempts to raise the retirement age, which provides the 'institutional definition of old age', and on the other hand, on early retirement (as well as prolonged unemployment) which point to the existence of a new phase, situated between the end of a working life and 'old age' itself (Fernandes 2001, 42, 44, 45).

In addition to the reference to 'age' or to 'old age' itself, we may also find certain rules that do not pertain solely to 'elderly people' but refer to categories in which they play an important role[2] (for example, widowhood or ascendants). Nonetheless, old age does not present itself as the basis upon which artificially to create an autonomous category, although some situations that arise from the ageing process can and should be taken into account by the law. Indeed, it seems very difficult to envisage the emergence of a homogeneous group (Herring 2007, 663) since old age does not necessarily imply feeble health that would cause

2 Even though the situations of 'feebleness' (articles 204 and 210, Criminal Code), 'dependency' (article 282, Civil Code) or 'invalidity' (article 63, n. 3, Portuguese Constitution) may be associated with old age, one must always bear in mind that it is inadequate to identify them.

dependency and is rightly not a basis upon which we might assume incapacity.[3] Accordingly, when identifying elderly people as the beneficiaries of the care and support provided by relatives, one must bear in mind that not every elderly person is dependent and that the level of dependency varies greatly. This leads to the conclusion that an elderly person is not entitled to a duty of care merely because of her or his age: a degree of need will also be necessary.

*Family carers*

Whenever we talk about care for elderly people there are, on the other side of the equation, the family carers. Within any family circle there are those more likely than others to provide support. Although family relationships range widely (to include the matrimonial relation, kinship ties, ties of affinity and of adoption – article 1576 of the Civil Code) the desire to allocate a caring role to each of them is not supported by the same ethical force. Family members can all be considered part of a 'solidarity community' (*Solidargemeinschaft*) (Henrich 1997, 1) and they often act accordingly. However, the law does not – and should not – treat them 'equally', even when they actually assume the same or similar responsibilities. The law associates the idea of an obligation to provide care and support for elderly relatives with defined categories of family members. Portuguese law refers to the existence of family *duties to care*: the 'duty of cooperation' and the 'duty to support' that the law imposes on spouses and on parents and children, respectively.

The content and the nature of these duties is, obviously, subject to debate. In order to analyse them, then, it will be necessary firstly to examine the duty of the spouse and then to consider the duty of children.

*The duty of the spouse* Article 1672 of the Civil Code establishes a list of duties which bind spouses mutually (Coelho and Oliveira 2008, 346). These include the so-called 'duty of cooperation' which is actually a duty of support. Indeed, its legal description indicates that spouses are obliged mutually to support and assist each other and to assume joint responsibility for family life (article 1674, Civil Code). This means that spouses need to support each other, providing spiritual support and physical or material aid to one another (Lima and Varela 1992, 263). The advent of dependency and illness would, therefore, be covered; arising from the duty's mutual basis one spouse has the obligation to assume the care of the other when she or he becomes dependent due to old age.

3 In the initial project of the Italian *amministrazione di sostegno*, 'elderly people' were target beneficiaries of this protection. However, such an idea generated great criticism and was subsequently abandoned. Emilio Vito Napoli has argued that the reference to old age associated with the restriction of capacity implies a lower conception of the human being connected with one life phase (Napoli 2002, 380), that is to say, that it associates incapacity directly with old age, without any further evaluation, and is thus discriminatory. Seealso Ferrando 2002, 129 and Bianca 2002, 121.

Data available about the actual care provided to elderly people demonstrate that, as a general rule, spouses are primary carers (Jani-Le Bris 1993, 72). The motivation behind this behaviour is generally attributed to *lifelong* spousal solidarity (Jani-Le Bris 1993, 85), a social value that is grounded in the '*presumptively perpetual* nature of marriage' (Coelho and Oliveira 2008, 211–12) and the bond assumed by each spouse when celebrating marriage.

The way spousal duties are fulfilled is not pre-emptively set out in law; it may be carried out in different ways according to the interests and capacities of the spouses; it depends on the particular circumstances of their relationship (Coelho and Oliveira 2008, 348). However, we may have a more accurate perception of how this care is provided when we consider other legal spousal duties. Indeed, among those listed in article 1672 one may find the duty of cohabitation. This duty involves the full sharing of house, bed and board (*tori, mensae et habitationis*) (Coelho and Oliveira 2008, 352); spouses should live together in the same house which they have mutually agreed to establish as their family home.[4] It is, therefore, no surprise that the spouse of the dependent person takes care of her or him while they continue to live together. It may even be that the spouses do not live together and that spousal care and support is being provided. Where, for example, one spouse is, due to illness, confined to a health institution but they intend to re-establish a common life as soon as they can (article 1782, Civil Code) the duty of cohabitation is not violated (Coelho and Oliveira 2008, 353) and the continued spousal provision of care is understandable. The duty of cooperation persists. And it may be fulfilled in a variety of ways ranging from direct care, to performing tasks at home that were once performed by the other spouse.

The duty to provide care can only be shaped by the needs of the person in need and the means of the person called upon to meet those needs (Lima and Varela 1992, 264). These obviously vary from situation to situation. In the case we are considering here the spouse of the dependent elderly person may also be elderly and may, therefore, also be dependent to a greater or lesser degree. This must feature in any assessment of the duty she or he owes the other spouse.

Finally, it must be stressed that the duty of cooperation is imposed on both spouses in the same manner. The principle of equality between spouses (article 1671, Civil Code; articles 13 and 67(3), Portuguese Constitution) requires this. It determines that spouses are reciprocally bound by legal duties. Thus, there are no

4 The Portuguese Civil Code imposes a duty of cohabitation on the spouses and, as an auxiliary obligation, it demands that the spouses determine where the family home will be, that is to say, the place where they will fulfil the duty of cohabitation. When agreeing upon the family's residence, the spouses have to take into account the circumstances defined by article 1673 of the Civil Code: the demands of their professional life and the children's interests, safeguarding the unity of family life. For instance, they have to consider their work location, the location of the children's schools, possibilities of contact of the children with other relatives, etc. Whenever the spouses fail to mutually determine the family home, the court is required to intervene and decide it (article 1673(3) of the Civil Code).

specific duties particular to women or to men (Coelho and Oliveira 2008, 346). And yet it is rare for men to perform caring roles even where the person in need is the wife of the man in question (Fernandes 2001, 41). Social behaviour is not fashioned by the demands of the legal system.

This leads to a final question: what are the consequences of the violation of the 'duty of cooperation'? Once fault-based divorce had disappeared from the Portuguese legal system (in 2008: Law 61/2008, 31 October) divorce can no longer be associated with the violation of a spousal duty. However, the new divorce law (article 1792, Civil Code) entitles a spouse who has suffered damage at the hands of the other to receive compensation. The full meaning of article 1792 is debatable and our courts still have not resolved the matter. Nevertheless, it is possible to imagine that the failure of one spouse to support the other would amount to (potentially serious) harm that could form the basis of a claim for compensation. And yet, despite the potential legal consequences associated with failure to meet this duty, it is not a duty which can be legally enforceable (on the same grounds that the support obligations of children towards their parents cannot be enforced, as I explain further below).

*The duty of children* In Portugal the parental tie gives rise to a series of reciprocal duties, including a 'duty of support' (article 1874(1), Civil Code). The legal rule does not distinguish between minor children and adult children and it imposes its duties regardless of cohabitation between these relatives. Yet, in spite of the legal imposition of *reciprocal* support, what it comprises is not clear, because the diversity of the situations involved may give rise to responsibilities that may vary widely, diminishing in intensity when children leave the parental home and reappearing powerfully when the parents get older (Pinheiro 2008, 275–6).

Social studies have shown the importance of exchanges between elderly parents or grandparents and their children or grandchildren. However, these exchanges assume different forms. It is more common that elderly people will aid their children and grandchildren financially and that these, in turn, will help their elderly relatives by performing tasks for them (Attias-Donfut 1995a, 13; Attias-Donfut 1995b, 71–6). Thus, the duty of support, which is only imposed by law on descendants in the first degree (that is, children) is also often actually assumed by other relatives, particularly descendants in the second degree (that is, grandchildren).[5]

Carers may also include people who are bound to the elderly person by affinity, that is, people who are married to a relative of hers or his. Taking into account that the group of carers is predominantly constituted by women, when care is assumed by descendants, the carers are usually the daughters of the dependent person and, to a lesser extent, daughters-in-law (Jani-Le Bris 1993, 66). This latter group does

5 The law does not impose a duty of personal support on grandchildren, although they may, as descendants, be obliged to pay maintenance to a grandparent as grandparents may also have to pay their grandchildren maintenance (article 2009, n. 1(b) and (c), Civil Code).

not owe any legal duty to parents-in-law. However, there may be a legal ground, although weaker, to the assumption of such responsibilities by these carers.

The activities of children-in-law as carers (usually daughters-in-law) may be captured by the duty of cooperation between spouses which refers to the assumption of the 'responsibilities intrinsic to family life' (article 1674, Civil Code). The responsibility is not, therefore, owed to the parents-in-law but to the other spouse. It is the spouse of the carer who has an obligation to care for the elderly dependent person (article 1784, Civil Code). In truth, according to Pires de Lima and Antunes Varela, the 'responsibilities intrinsic to family life' are associated with 'the personal duties that are not directly related to the spouses, such as the duties to raise and educate children and the duties to assist the relatives of one of them or any other person under their care' (Lima and Varela 1992, 264). However, they question why 'the law mentions responsibilities (instead of measures) and intends that the spouses will assume them together' (ibid). This question is an invitation to equate the legal nature of the behaviours involved. Indeed, the fact that Portuguese law has chosen the term 'responsibilities' rather than 'duties' shows that there are different legal concepts at work. The caring activities of the children-in-law are responsibilities that are undertaken, reflecting 'idealised family norms' (Lind et al. 2011, 4). The assumption of such responsibility is not the exact parallel of the legal obligation to care, but it has also not been completely ignored by the law. Its existence is recognized. This is not true of grandchildren who act as carers; although one might also say that they have conformed to the same 'idealised family norm', the law fails to acknowledge their activity.

To determine its content and nature the 'duty of support' owed by children to their parents must be further analysed. First, one needs to remember the family context of these relationships. In the traditional extended family, high birth rates ensured a large number of children and, consequently, the task of looking after the few people who attained old age was divided among these numerous children. In those circumstances it would not be difficult to develop and retain rules that would consider care-giving by children to be mandatory. Today, the possibilities for families to take care of elderly persons, namely by receiving them into their family homes, are more limited (Henrich 1997, 4)

It is true that the traditional scheme of caring for elderly dependants in Portugal, as in other southern European countries, most often involves cohabitation with carers (Jani-Le Bris 1993, 69). But it is not legally imposed. As with the spousal duty, the duty of children depends on the carer's means and the elderly person's needs. One may find different degrees of dependency that justify different levels of intervention by the carer. Only the most critical situations would require cohabitation; although cohabitation is not imposed by law in particular situations, one might ask whether or not law did demand it in order to comply fully with the 'duty to provide support'? One must still, in the first place, consider the carers' resources. If carers do not enjoy living conditions in their own residence which would enable them to house the dependent elderly person, cohabitation could never be demanded. But what would happen if the carer's residence did provide satisfactory 'living conditions'? One of the main characteristics of the modern model of the family is the absence of intergenerational cohabitation between adult children and their parents. In adulthood, as a rule, a person lives alone or as one of a couple, or in a family with minor children. Receiving an older parent into one's home compromises the right to privacy; it puts restraints on both the elderly person and the adult child to adapt her or his life to suit her or himself. This constriction of rights must, therefore, be grounded in the consent of both parties. These rights become a barrier to the imposition of a duty of cohabitation. The voluntary assumption of such a duty is all that remains; older people must be voluntarily brought into their children's homes. A duty along these lines is difficult to impose in law. Nevertheless, even in the situations in which there is no cohabitation, support can still be provided. Given the 'contextual nature' of family responsibilities, its form may differ (Lind et al. 2011, 10); it is possible, for instance, that children provide care by hiring and supervising the activity of healthcare professionals at the dependent person's home or paying frequent (working) visits to the elderly relative or by supplying meals.

In case of these assumed responsibilities we must, of course, wonder about the consequences of non-fulfilment: will these 'duties' be enforceable in law? Considering their nature, they are not directly enforceable. Apart from pecuniary obligations, namely maintenance obligations, there is a clear assumption, both in the legal texts and in court decisions that apply them, that if the responsibilities (including the duty of care) are fulfilled then the law's goals are achieved. If they are not fulfilled, the deeply personal nature of the responsibilities does not allow direct enforcement. Indeed, there are no known Portuguese cases in which enforcement was sought. Even if they existed, it is unlikely that the courts would impose a duty which is so highly personal in nature. And if they did try to enforce the duty it would have to be converted into a subsidiary compensation payment; the duty itself would remain 'unenforceable'. These forms of enforcement cannot create an environment in which the care-giving activity and the human relationships at their centre could 'develop and flourish in their own inexplicable ways' (Lind 2008, 271).

If the 'duty to provide support' imposed on children cannot and should not be legally enforced why has it been transformed into a legal precept? Perhaps the answer is that, in Dewar's words, the law has assumed the task of 'set[ting] the tone' for family behaviour 'rather than [conferring] measurable entitlements that one might expect to see enforced in a courtroom' (Dewar 1998, 474).

The grounds upon which to found a duty of children to care for their elderly parents are diverse. Some argue that children should honour their parents and their gratitude to their parents for having been cared for and raised justifies a duty of care (Wise, 2002, 567). However, a child may not always be in a situation that allows for parental support: 'what is required from the adult child depends on the parties' current needs and relationship, rather than simply upon how much was given during childhood' (Herring 2008, 49). Closely related to this justification is the idea of reciprocity (Wise 2002, 568; Herring 2008, 48). However, this idea has been subject to criticism; whereas the duty of a parent to a child arises from the fact that parents decide to bring the child into the world, the corresponding duty of children to their parents is 'less tenable' since 'children did not ask to be born' (Wise 2002, 568). Others choose the idea of the 'quality of the relationship' (English, referred to in Herring 2008, 49) as the basis for a duty of care. Nevertheless it is argued that it 'would be wrong to suggest that obligations are only dependent on the current relationship' (Herring 2008, 50). Finally, the nature of the parent/child bond itself and the unique position of the child to provide care are put forward as grounds (Herring 2008, 50). It may be argued, though, that this 'uniqueness' lies in no more than a 'romanticised notion of family care-giving' (Wise 2002, 571).

In the Portuguese context, the question is not what ground should be chosen, but rather what ground has been selected by law in the creation of a 'duty of support'. Indeed, the grounds to impose responsibility 'are contingent on context-specific factors, whether cultural or economic' (Eekelaar 2007, 114) and therefore must be analysed in the context of each legislative measure. In the Portuguese legal system this duty derives from the legal relationship of filiation. The social perception of the parent/child bond has allowed such a duty to be legally created. However, the 'quality of the relationship' is also relevant; where a parent has severely harmed a child it would be abusive to evoke a right to be cared for.

## Providing Support – Its Consequences for Families

In this chapter I have tried to demonstrate the way in which Portuguese law has allocated responsibility to care for elderly dependent persons to their spouses or their children by creating a 'duty to provide support' and a 'duty of cooperation'(although these responsibilities have different intensity and different parameters). Furthermore, it has been argued that, as a rule, other family members assume these functions, even when they are not legally bound to do so. In reality, family behaviour is primarily shaped by rules that are not imposed by law. Family law should, therefore, take these real responsibilities into account when structuring its regulation of responsibility. In this regard Portuguese law is problematic. On the one hand, the legislature has not ignored the caring behaviour of children and other relatives of elderly people; the system depends on their intervention to deal with dependency related problems (Tomé 2004, 64). On the other hand, the position of those who provide care (whether bound by a legal duty to do so or not) has not been sufficiently acknowledged and protected in Portuguese law.

Doing caring work entails costs for families (Fineman 2000, 20). Most of those costs are born by women.[6] And the changing context of the lives of women has increased those costs; women participate more in the labour market and yet they continue to perform the bulk of domestic labour. Furthermore, the social

6 About the role of women in the Portuguese context, see Fernandes 2001, 49, citing Paula Martins Gil. See also Hespanha 1995, 216.

security system still uses, as its point of reference, the model of 'independence and autonomy of the labourer, free and available to work uniformly during long hours' (Tomé 2004, 52, 57).

The consequences are not difficult to predict; the professional progression of women is compromised and sometimes even their continuing access to the labour market (Tomé 2004, 57, 59). This often brings financial hardships upon the carer, including not actively contributing to her own retirement pension (Jani-Le Bris 1993, 121; Perista 2005, 170). Additionally, one must consider the psychological costs (Fernandes 2001, 50) and the consequences for the health of the carer. The carer becomes a dependent person – there arises a 'derivative dependence' that makes her or him dependent on what limited institutional supports there are that facilitate care-giving (Fineman 2000, 20).

At a time when the law struggles to create equality of opportunities for women and men, this de facto situation cannot be ignored. Dealing with it is made more pressing when one considers that the carer is seldom in a situation that allows free choice; she is trapped. There are no adequate alternatives: the choice is stark, between the family or the retirement home. Given the 'traditional aversion to these institutions', even when the quality of the care they provide is unquestioned and they provide excellent security for elderly residents (Jani-Le Bris 1993, 59), family members still frequently choose to take care of their relatives themselves, even if it has negative effects on their economic and mental well-being.

## The Role of the Law Regarding Family Responsibilities to Care for the Elderly

The question arising from this analysis of responsibilities owed to, and performed for, elderly relatives seems self-evident: is imposing a legal duty of care on family members the best way to guarantee adequate care for people as they age? Should the moral duty that so many accept be converted into a legal obligation? On the one hand there is a danger of overloading 'informal carers'. Given that these people are mainly women who are not sufficiently recognized, compensated or supported this would be doubly invidious. And yet it may be argued that, since these obligations are already assumed by these subjects, it would be better to recognize them in the 'official' legal system of the state (Herring 2008, 53). Of course, the idea of converting the moral duty into a legal one has already been accepted in the Portuguese system; there is a legal obligation of support imposed on spouses and adult children of elderly people. But the duty is incomplete and it is limited to this small circle of relatives. Still, to the extent that it exists it does appear to support the view of Fineman that the state relies on a *mythically self-sufficient family* (Fineman 2004, 20, 31) and has chosen to *privatize dependency* (Diduck 2008, 257) through the instruments of family law.

The legal duties of spouses and children have been formalized in the Civil Code, which means that the legal system has expressly allocated to those family members the care of their dependants. However, the state has not chosen to reinforce or extend these duties. They are not legally enforceable. The law has not adopted a punitive approach. Nor, it is submitted, should that be done. Herring is surely right to suggest that 'a better option is for the State to seek to enable and encourage caring amongst family members, rather than [to] compel it' (Herring 2007, 670). In fact 'behaviour under compulsion is likely to be reluctant and possibly damaging to others' (Eekelaar 2007, 194).

It is not possible to rely solely on the families' efforts and capacity to face the dependency of their members. The law has acknowledged this at the highest level. According to article 67 of the Portuguese Constitution (no less) the state is expected to perform a series of tasks; it must create social facilities for family support and adjust taxes and security benefits to reflect family responsibilities. All these actions must be coordinated within the framework of a family policy and of a policy for the elderly. In order to reach these goals the state must act in two different capacities. It must provide services and social benefits and it must act as a lawmaker. The goal of its activities must be to ensure what Fineman has called, in the American context, the 'equitable distribution of the social assets' (Fineman 2008–2009, 15) in order to deal with vulnerability, for this is an 'enduring aspect of the human condition that must be at the heart of our concept of state and state responsibility' (Fineman 2008–2009, 8). In our system, public responsibility derives from the principle of the social state and is not limited to the economic contribution of the state. In addition the state must also create conditions that promote family integration and stimulate cooperation amongst family members. Of course, in the context of the care of the elderly, this ambition would be best achieved if the state addressed itself, not only to family regulation, but also to the regulation of the labour market and to the state of social security law (Tomé 2004, 52).

The Constitution itself assumes that the legislature must intervene in order to create the conditions which would enable people to achieve their social rights. If this work is not undertaken the Constitutional Court may declare the failure to be 'unconstitutional by omission' (article 283) (Canotilho and Moreira 2007, 856). This may lead to awards of compensation to those affected.

The state intervention that is advocated here may attract criticism from those who assert that 'state interventions in the family do not raise efficiency' (Becker and Murphy 1988, 4). However, it has also been argued that when granting incentives for families to care for their dependants, the state would benefit from the cost savings that would arise from the intervention of families (Henrich 1997, 7–8; Wise 2002, 584).[7] Additionally, one may argue that efficiency (and other market-related constraints) are not the only values to be considered by the state in its intervention. It has to implement other 'public values', namely 'equality,

7 In relation to the family reassuming its 'lost functions', such as caring for the elderly, as a present trend, see Oliveira 2004, 779.

justice and fairness', and thus protect vulnerable subjects (Fineman 2008–2009, 7–8) who, in this instance, are both dependent persons and carers.

It is submitted that the resolution of this issue can only be settled with the participation of the family, the state and civil society (Tomé 2004, 57; Miranda and Medeiros, 2005, 694). Indeed, everyone would benefit from family solidarity, supported by social solidarity. It is not possible, in the context of the present family structures, for the family to be the sole answer to dependency (particularly in old age).[8] It should be assumed that there is a 'collective or social debt' created by care-giving (Fineman 2000, 18) and that, therefore, the viable solution must be a mixed system of protection, centred both on the position of elderly dependent people and their family carers (Wise 2002, 565, 584).

## Conclusion

In this chapter I have analysed the way in which Portuguese law has converted moral rules that ground the social responsibilities of the family to care for their dependent members into legal rules. When it chooses not to ignore the responsibilities often assumed by family members, family law has addressed this issue in different ways. In relation to children-in-law, it has recognized their responsibilities, without imposing a family duty. As for children and spouses, it has created what is called a legal 'duty' of care. However, these legal duties are not enforceable in a traditional legal sense.

The Constitutional approach in Portugal has gone further and, it is submitted, has been more realistic and fairer than the family law approach. The Constitution has acknowledged the importance of family life for elderly people and has imposed an obligation on the state to support families by creating the conditions that allow family members to care for their dependent elderly. However, the rights granted by the Constitution will only be effective if the legislature intervenes. The law, therefore, retains its important role in the creation of a combined scheme of participation of the family, the state and civil society in the care of elderly dependent persons.

## References

Attias-Donfut, C. 1995a. Introduction. *Les Solidarités entre Générations, Vieillesse, Familles, État, Essais et Recherches*. Paris: Nathan, 5–23.

8 Among other reasons, this approach would fail to include 'the care of older persons who have never had children, or whose children are no longer living, live far away or cannot be located' (Wise 2002, 579).

Attias-Donfut, C. 1995b. Le double circuit des transmissions. *Les Solidarités entre Générations, Vieillesse, Familles, État, Essais et Recherches*. Paris: Nathan, 41–81.

Becker, G.S. and Murphy, K.M. 1988. The Family and the State. *The Journal of Law and Economics*, 31, 1–18.

Bianca, C.M. 2002. L'Autonomia Privata: Strumenti di esplicazione e limiti, in*La Riforma del'interdizione e dell'inabilitazione – (Atti del Convegno di Studi su 'Capacità ed autonomia delle persone' (Roma, 20 giugno 2002)*, Familia Quaderni, n.1, edited by S. Patti. Milan: Giuffrè, 117–24.

Canotilho, J.J.G. 2003. Direito Constitucional e Teoria da Constituição, 7th edition. Coimbra: Almedina.

Canotilho, J.J.G. and Moreira, V. 2007. *Constituição da República Portuguesa Anotada*. Coimbra: Coimbra Editora, vol. I.

Coelho, F.M.P. and Oliveira, G. 2008. *Curso de Direito da Família*, 4th edition. Coimbra: Coimbra Editora.

Dewar, J. 1998. The Normal Chaos of Family Law. *Modern Law Review*, 61, 467–85.

Diduck A. 2008. Family Law and Family Responsibility, in *Responsibility, Law and the Family*, edited by J. Bridgeman, H. Keating and C. Lind. Aldershot: Ashgate, 251–67.

Díez-Picazo, L. and Gullón, A. 2002. *Sistema de Derecho Civil. Derecho de familia. Derecho de Sucesiones*. Madrid: Tecnos, vol. IV.

Eekelaar, J. 1984. *Family Law and Social Policy*, 2nd edition. London: Weidenfeld and Nicolson.

Eekelaar, J. 1991. Are Parents Morally Obliged to Care for their Children. Oxford *Journal of Legal Studies*, 340–53.

Eekelaar, J. 2007. *Family Law and Personal Life*. Oxford: Oxford University Press.

Fernandes, A.A. 2001. Velhice, solidariedades familiares e política social – itinerário de pesquisa em torno do aumento da esperança de vida. *Sociologia, problemas e práticas*, 36, 39–52.

Ferrando, G. 2002. Protezione dei soggetti deboli e misure di sostegno, in*La Riforma del'interdizione e dell'inabilitazione – (Atti del Convegno di Studi su 'Capacità ed autonomia delle persone' (Roma, 20 giugno 2002)*, Familia Quaderni, n.1, edited by S. Patti. Milan: Giuffrè, 125–41.

Figuerruelo Burrieza, A. 2004. La protección constitucional de las personas mayores, in *Protección jurídica de los mayores*. Madrid: La Ley, 37–56.

Fineman, M.A. 2000. Cracking the Foundational Myths: Independence, Autonomy and Self- Sufficiency. *Journal of Gender, Social Policy & the Law*, 8, 13–29.

Fineman, M.A. 2004. *The Autonomy Myth – A Theory of Dependency*. New York and London: The New Press.

Fineman, M.A. 2008–2009. The Vulnerable Subject: Anchoring Equality in the Human Condition. *Yale Journal of Law and Feminism*, 20, 1–23.

Henrich, D. 1997. Zur Eröffnung des 3. Regenburger Symposiums für Europäisches Familienrecht, in *Familiäre Solidarität – Die Begründung und die Grenzen der Unterhaltspflicht unter Verwandten im europäischen Vergleich*, edited by D. Schwab and D. Henrich. Bielefeld: Ernst und Werner Gieseking, 1–8.

Herring, J. 2007. *Family Law*, 3rd edition. Harlow: Pearson.

Herring, J. 2008. Together Forever? The Rights and Responsibilities of Adult Children and their Parents, in *Responsibility, Law and the Family*, edited by J. Bridgeman, H. Keating and C. Lind. Aldershot: Ashgate, 41–61.

Hespanha, P. 1995. Vers une societé providence simultanément pré- et post-moderne, in Les Solidarités entre Générations, Vieillesse, Familles, État, Essais et Recherches. Paris: Nathan, 209–21.

Jani-Le Bris, H. 1993. *Responsabilidade familiar pelos dependentes idosos nos países das Comunidades Europeias*. Dublin: CLEIRPPA.

Lima, P. de, and Varela, A. 1992. *Código Civil Anotado*, 2nd edition. Coimbra: Coimbra Editora, vol. IV.

Lind, C. 2008. Conclusion: Regulating for Responsibility in an Age of Complex Families, in *Responsibility, Law and the Family*, edited by J. Bridgeman, H. Keating and C. Lind. Aldershot: Ashgate, 269–75.

Lind. C, Keating, H. and Bridgeman, J. 2011. Introduction: Taking Family Responsibility or Having It Imposed?, in *Taking Responsibility, Law and the Changing Family*, edited by C. Lind, H. Keating and J. Bridgeman. Aldershot: Ashgate, 1–21.

Martínez Rodríguez, N. 2004. Los mayores como beneficiarios de prestaciones familiares, in *Protección Jurídica de los Mayores*. Madrid: La Ley, 119–44.

Milone, L. (2001) Il disegno di leggen. 2189 sull'amministratore di sostegno, in*La Riforma del'interdizione e dell'inabilitazione (Atti del Convegno di Studi su 'Capacità ed autonomia delle persone' (Roma, 20 giugno 2002)*, Familia Quaderni, n.1, edited by S. Patti. Milan: Giuffrè, 105–16.

Miranda, J. and Medeiros, R. 2005. *Constituição Portuguesa Anotada*. Coimbra: Coimbra Editora, Tomo I.

Napoli, E.V. 2002. Una terza forma d'incapacità di agire. *Giustizia Civile, vol. LII*, Settembre, 379–83.

Oliveira, G. 2004. Transformações do Direito da Família, in *Comemorações dos 35 anos do Código Civil e dos 25 anos da Reforma de 1977, Vol. I – Direito da Família e das Sucessões*. Coimbra: Coimbra Editora, 763–79.

Palma, A. de. 2002. Respuestas de la Administración al envejecimiento de la población, in *El Envejecimiento de la Población y la Protección Jurídica de las Personas Mayores*. Barcelona: Cedecs135–51.

Perista, H. 2005. Usos do Tempo, Ciclo de Vida e Vivências da Velhice – Uma Perspectiva de Género, in *Direito da Infância, da Juventude e do Envelhecimento*. Coimbra: Coimbra Editora, 165–73.

Pinheiro, J.D. 2008. *O Direito da Família Contemporâneo*. Lisbon: AAFDL.

Ribeiro, J.S. 2005. Processos de Envelhecimento: A Construção de um Direito Emancipatório, in *Direito da Infância, da Juventude e do Envelhecimento*. Coimbra: Coimbra Editora, 203–29.

Stanzione, P. 1989. L'étà dell'uomo e la tutela della persona: gli anziani. *Rivista di Diritto Civile, Parte prima*, 439–54.

Tomé, M.J.V. 2004. Qualidade de vida: Conciliação entre o trabalho e a família. LexFamiliae – Revista Portuguesa de Direito da Família, Ano 1, no 1, 51–64.

Torrelles Torrea, E. 2004. La protección de las personas mayores en Cataluña: Perspectiva civil, in *Protección jurídica de los mayors*. Madrid: La Ley, 223–64.

Wise, K. 2002. Caring for our Parents in an Aging World: Sharing Public and Private Responsibility for the Elderly. *Legislation and Public Policy*, 563–98.

# Chapter 12
# Elder Abuse and Stressing Carers

Jonathan Herring

## Introduction

This chapter considers the woefully inadequate approach of the law to the issue of elder abuse. It is surprising, and somewhat embarrassing, how little has been written by academic lawyers on this issue. The law's response to the problem has been slow or even non-existent (Herring 2009). There are still no legal responses targeted specifically at the abuse of older people (Williams 2009).

Why? There are many explanations. This chapter focuses on one in particular. Elder abuse has been seen by many as a particularly tricky issue because it is usually caused by 'care-giver stress'. In the exhaustion and despair that caring can bring the carer has lashed out in anger or frustration. In such a case legal intervention is unlikely to help. Carers are not to be held responsible for the abuse. To reconfigure the caring responsibilities by removing an older person from their carer is unlikely to assist the older person and is unlikely to be what they want. The horrors of the nursing home are likely to be even worse than the unpleasantness of the occasional slap from the stressed carer. The solution lies, therefore, it is said, in offering support and advice to carers, rather than intrusive legal intervention. The responsibility of the state is argued to take the form of delicate social work intervention, rather than heavy-handed law.

This picture of elder abuse should be firmly rejected. Reliance on carer stress as the explanation for elder abuse has hampered the finding of an effective legal response to, and a proper understanding of, it. This chapter first summarizes the use that has been made of 'the carer stress explanation' in the literature; second, it demonstrates how, in fact, much elder abuse is a continuation of domestic violence; and finally it argues that the emphasis on carer stress has disguised the responsibility of societal attitudes and practices as a cause of elder abuse. Unless elder abuse is seen in the context of a patriarchal and ageist society its true nature and significance will not be appreciated and the responsibilities of carers and the state will not be properly understood.

Underpinning much of the argument of this chapter is a debate about responsibility. Who is responsible for elder abuse? The 'carer stress' argument seeks to explain elder abuse in a way which means those who carry out the abuse (the carers) are not responsible for their actions. In short, no one can be held to account for the abuse. This chapter will argue that in fact society and, in particular, ageism and patriarchy, are significant causes of elder abuse. The responsibility for elder abuse lies on us all.

## The Empirical Background

Before any of that, I provide a brief introduction to the notion of elder abuse. There is no consistent definition of it (Dixon et al. 2010). This should be neither surprising nor concerning. The meaning of the term will depend very much on the purpose for which the concept is to be used (Brammer and Biggs 1998). The Department of Health's (2000) guidance defined abuse as 'a violation of an individual's human and civil rights by another person or person'. That may be too wide, but it has become commonly used in practice and so will be adopted for the purposes of this chapter. Elder abuse can include behaviour which is physical, psychological, financial and sexual. It can include positive actions and neglect (Cooper et al. 2008).

Determining the extent of elder abuse is extremely problematic. This is partly because of the difficulties in definition, but also due to reluctance of victims to disclose it or label it as such. We now have the benefit of a major recent study of elder abuse in the UK carried out for Comic Relief (O'Keeffe et al. 2008). It found that 2.6 per cent of people aged 66 or over who were living in their own private household reported misuse involving a family member, close friend or care worker in the past year. When neighbours and acquaintances were included as possible perpetrators the prevalence rate increased to 4 per cent. That latter percentage would mean that 342,400 older people have been subjected to some form of mistreatment in the past year. Focusing on mistreatment by family members, close friends or care workers; 1.1 per cent of older people had suffered neglect; 0.7 per cent financial mistreatment; 0.4 per cent psychological; 0.4 per cent physical mistreatment and 0.2 per cent sexual. Seventy-six per cent of those who reported mistreatment said that the effect on them was serious or very serious. The researchers found these figures to be on the conservative side as they did not include care home residents and some of those most vulnerable to abuse lacked the capacity to take part in the survey. Also, even among those interviewed there may have been those who, for a variety of reasons, did not wish to disclose abuse.

As mentioned, the law has no particular legal interventions directed towards elder abuse. Instead, the government has preferred to focus on protection of vulnerable adults, rather than specifically older adults. Hence, for example, the Safeguarding Vulnerable Groups Act 2006 is designed to protect all vulnerable adults (Association of Directors of Social Services 2005). I shall be mentioning some of the problems with this approach later. Having provided a summary of the nature of elder abuse, I turn now to consider the central theme of this chapter: the extent to which elder abuse can be explained by the stressful circumstances that the carers find themselves in.

## 'Care-Giver Stress'

In the public imagination elder abuse is popularly regarded as caused by carer stress (Pritchard 2007). This claim has been described by academic specialists in the field as a 'persistent characterization' (National Centre on Elder Abuse 2002) and 'widely accepted' (Bennett et al. 1997, 54; Pillemer and Finkelhor 2006). A good example of the carer stress explanation is the following statement from an influential organization in the United States, the National Centre on Elder Abuse (2008, 3):

> Although it is known that in 90% of all reported elder abuse cases, the abuser is a family member, it is not known how many of these abusive family members are also caregivers. Researchers have estimated that anywhere from five to twenty-three percent of all caregivers are physically abusive. Most agree that abuse is related to the stresses associated with providing care.

Linda Woolf (1998), considering the causes of elder abuses, lists the following as the first factor explaining elder abuse:

> Caring for a non-well older adult suffering from a mental or physical impairment is highly stressful. Individuals who do not have the requisite skills, information, resources, etc. and who are otherwise ill-prepared for the caregiving role may experience extreme stress and frustration. This may lead to elder abuse and/or neglect.

The American Psychological Society (1999, 2) in their booklet on the issue claim:

> Caregiver stress is a significant risk factor for abuse and neglect. When caregivers are thrust into the demands of daily care for an elder without appropriate training and without information about how to balance the needs of the older person with their own needs, they frequently experience intense frustration and anger that can lead to a range of abusive behaviors.

Supporters of the carer stress explanation emphasize that, of course, not all carers respond to stress in the same way, but it is the response to the stressful situations which determines whether abuse occurs (Nolan 1993).

Much work has been done in seeking to expound on these claims and explain the theory in more detail (Nerenberg 2002). It has been said that care-giver stress causes depression and mood disturbances which lead to abuse in uncharacteristic outbursts of anger (Garcia and Kosberg 1992). Emphasis is placed on empirical evidence that carers who have to live with the dependent are particularly likely to be abusive (Nerenberg 2002) as compared with those who do not. Indeed some research suggests that the greater the number of hours per day the carer must care, the greater the risk of abuse (Bendik 1992). Further, it has been claimed that the lower functioning the 'victim', the higher the likelihood of abuse (Coyne et al. 1993). Carers of those suffering from dementia are particularly prone to commit abuse (Dyer et al. 2002). 'Victims' who are violent towards care-givers are more likely to suffer abuse at the hands of the care-giver (Coyne et al. 1993). Evidence has been produced which, it is said, shows certain forms of behaviour by the victim cause the carer stress, which can lead to abuse. Such behaviour includes verbal aggression, refusal to eat or take medications, calling the police, invading the care-giver's privacy, noisiness, 'vulgar habits', disruptive behaviour, embarrassing public displays and physical aggression (Pillemer and Suitor 1992). Others refer to the 'difficult personality' of the dependant causing carer stress and hence abuse (Phillips 1986, 197). As can be seen, there are real dangers of the arguments leading to the abused person being said to be the real cause of the abuse.

Despite its hold on the public imagination and the emphasis placed on it during the early years of research into elder abuse, most recent studies downplay the relevance of carer stress as a cause of elder abuse. There is now a substantial body of research suggesting that care-giver stress plays a very minor role in causing elder abuse (Pillemer 1993; Bennet et al. 1997, 54; Brandl and Raymond 1997; Bergeron 2001; Brandl and Cook-Daniels 2002). The House of Commons Health Select Committee (2004, para. 36), when looking at the issue of elder abuse, received evidence from several bodies working in the field that carer stress was rarely a factor in elder abuse. Help the Aged in its evidence stated: 'few incidents of abuse are committed by loving, supportive people who have lashed out as a consequence of the burden of their caring responsibilities' (House of Commons Health Select Committee 2004, para. 36). This is certainly not to say that the evidence suggests that carers do not suffer stress, quite the opposite. It is clear that caring is extraordinarily hard work (Gainey and Payne 2006). But there is no evidence that the stresses of caring are linked to abuse in any significant way.

## Significance of Seeing Elder Abuse as Carer Stress

In this chapter I do not intend to investigate in detail the dispute over the role of care-giver stress. I shall take it that the prevailing view of the last few years is correct and that it plays only a small role. What, however, I do want to do is to bring out the significance on policy of the 'care-giving stress' explanation.

Seeing elder abuse as caused by care-giving stress has a number of significant consequences. The image created is of a victim who is vulnerable and problematic (McDonald and Collins 2000). They are not responsible for what is happening to them. We cannot expect them to help themselves, indeed it is their behaviour and condition which has created the stressful situation. The care-giver stress model easily leads to blaming the older person, rather than the perpetrator, for the abuse. It suggests that the best response to elder abuse would be to offer support and assistance to the carer, and medical support to the dependant, rather than offering protection or services to the person being abused (Bergeron 2001). Indeed, as

Simon Biggs (1994) points out, the carer stress model neatly fits into the logic of community care, with the support of carers in the home with a care package being the solution to the problems facing the older person. The care-giver stress model also clearly indicates that criminal punishments are not appropriate because the abuser is not to blame and is responding in an understandable way to an extremely difficult situation (Pain 1999).

There are two other, even more important, consequences of explaining elder abuse as caused by carer stress and these will take up the rest of this chapter. The first is that it ignores the fact that a significant portion of 'elder abuse' is in fact domestic violence that has been going on for a considerable time. The carer stress model sanitizes elder abuse as a sad situation, rather than recognizing it as a grave interference in human rights (Herring and Choudhry 2006). It pigeonholes elder abuse into a specific category of its own, rather than seeing it as part of the broader picture of prevailing violence against women. Secondly, the care-giver stress explanation hides all the wider social factors which contribute to the practice, perpetuation and lack of recognition of elder abuse. In particular, it disguises the significance of ageism and patriarchy (Whittaker 1996). There is no better indication of the failure to appreciate the significance of gender in the context of elder abuse than the very existence of the 'carer stress' theory itself. The fact that the vast majority of those caring are women, but the vast majority of those abusing are men should have immediately demonstrated that the link between stress and abuse was not as strong as had been assumed (Hines and Malley-Morrison 2005).

## Elder Abuse and Domestic Violence

One survivor of elder abuse described her experience in this way:

> I stayed with him for 39 years. It was a long time to put in, but I wasn't brave enough to leave. … We moved down here and he only lived for another two years. …And then I was free. I don't know whether you ever saw Penelope Keith in *To the Manor Born*, the episode where she went to her husband's funeral? She came out of the church and said to her friend, 'Is there anybody looking?' Then she threw her hat in the air, jumped with joy and shouted, 'Hooray, hooray!' That was exactly how I felt. (Sargent and Mears 2000, 21)

As this indicates, some elder abuse is simply the continuation of a violent relationship.

There is now ample evidence that a significant portion of elder abuse is simply the continuation of abuse that has been going on in one form or another throughout the relationship (Nolan 1993; Cooney and Mortimer 1995; Penhale 1999; Brandl and Cook-Daniels 2002; Lundy and Grossman 2004). Old age, it seems, can make domestic violence visible in a way which was not apparent earlier in the relationship (Koenig et al. 2006). The Comic Relief Survey found that mistreatment was performed by partners in 51 per cent of cases and interpersonal abuse carried out by them in 57 per cent (O'Keeffeet al. 2008). Of course, it cannot be assumed that because the elder abuse is carried out by partners it is continuing domestic violence. However, the authors of the survey concluded that the implication of their data was that either these cases of interpersonal abuse by partners are 'the elderly graduates of domestic violence or they have a condition, such as dementia that sometimes gives rise to violent behaviour' (O'Keeffe et al. 2008, 2).

Linda Vinton (1992, 18) argues: 'Abuse is not primarily about old age at all but about certain damaging patterns which have continued into old age. This applies mainly to situations within the family; for example elder abuse is sometimes simple marital violence which has continued into old age. ' It is, therefore, not surprising that many of the factors that indicate a risk of elder abuse are the very ones that also indicate a risk of domestic violence: living situation, social isolation, cognitive impairments, physical impairments, substance abuse and relationship dependency (Mowlam et al. 2008). Women suffering elder abuse at the hands of spouses report similar patterns of conduct as those suffering domestic violence, with constant criticism and controlling behaviour, leading them to threatening and violent actions (Mowlam et al. 2008, 5.1.1.). Similarly reasons given for not reporting elder abuse match those given by victims of domestic violence: including fear of reprisal or retaliation, misplaced loyalty or gratitude, dependency on the partner and confusion (Bitondo-Dyer et al. 2003). The links between elder abuse and domestic violence can be taken further. Many of the themes of the early theoretical work on domestic violence can be seen in the treatment of elder abuse: denial of the problem; blaming the victim; failure to provide adequate legal protection; and individualizing the problem (Pain 1999). It seems indeed true to suggest that work on elder abuse is in a similar place to where work on domestic violence was 20 years ago (Mornington 2004).

Elder abuse should be seen as part of the wider debates on domestic violence; violence against women; racist abuse and anti-social behaviour (Biggs 1996). It is revealing that the self-completion questionnaires on domestic violence and intimate partner abuse from the British Crime Surveys of 1996 and 2001 were not offered to women over the age of 59. This reveals the way that elder abuse has been hived off into its own special category. The age of the victim of domestic abuse should have no effect on its categorization (Rathbone-McCuan 2000). Domestic violence is domestic violence, whatever the age of the victim.

It is remarkable that the substantial amount of work that has been done in the area of domestic violence to demonstrate the way that societal attitudes cause and reinforce domestic violence, finds no echo in much of the writing on elder abuse (Desmarais and Reeves 2007). Just as with domestic violence, unequal gender and power relations create a context within which male violence against women can continue unacknowledged and unchallenged (Johnson et al. 2010). In the context of elder abuse we have the additional factor of ageism whereby elder people are stigmatized and marginalized in society in a way which enables abuse to take place and hinders an effective challenge to it (Nelson 2002).

## Gender and Elder Abuse

Until recently gender played a relatively small part in the analysis of elder abuse. Indeed, in a 1996 literature review McCreadie (1996) found only one study of elder abuse that mentioned the significance of gender. Since then much more attention has been played to it (for example, Aitken and Griffin 1996; Hightower 2010). There now appears a general acceptance that women are significantly more likely to be victims of violent elder abuse than men (Bergeron 2004) and that most protagonists are men (Mears 2003). The Comic Relief survey found that 80 per cent of cases of interpersonal abuse were carried out by men; with women only responsible for 20 per cent of incidents (O'Keeffe et al. 2008). While it is, of course, important to appreciate that elder abuse does occur to men and where it does it may have a particular significance and require a particular response (Desmarais and Reeves 2007), this should not overlook the fact that men make up the substantial majority of abusers (Crichton et al. 1999).

What can we tell from the fact that the majority of physical abusers of elderly people are men and their victims are women? Action on Elder Abuse (2004, 2) suggests not much: 'The fact that more women than men are identified as suffering abuse is likely to reflect the reality that women live longer than men and are consequently more likely to be living alone. It may also be that men are also less likely to report being abused. 'This is not convincing, not least because there is no evidence of a change in the gender ratios among younger victims or perpetrators. Further the links previously mentioned with domestic violence provide a powerful reason for thinking that the gendered arrangement of elder abuse is extremely significant.

There has been extensive literature on the way that patriarchy enables, reinforces and protects men who carry out domestic violence (Vinton 1991; Salazar et al. 2003; Madden Dempsey 2009). This indicates that the societal and structural inequalities against women are reflected in and reinforce unequal relationships at home (Glendenning and Decalmer 1993). As Michelle Madden Dempsey (2007, 934) writes:

> the patriarchal character of individual relationships cannot subsist without those relationships being situated within a broader patriarchal social structure. Patriarchy is, by its nature, a social structure – and thus any particular instance of patriarchy takes its substance and meaning from that social context. If patriarchy were entirely eliminated from society, then patriarchy would not exist in domestic arrangements and thus domestic violence in its strong sense would not exist. … Moreover, if patriarchy were lessened in society generally then *ceteris paribus* patriarchy would be lessened in domestic relationship as well, thereby directly contributing to the project of ending domestic violence in its strong sense.

The failure to appreciate the significance of gender in elder abuse means that approaches to combat it focus on the vulnerability of the victim rather than the structural inequalities within the relationship and more broadly within society (Madden Dempsey 2006). It may also explain the relatively little public attention the issue receives. Older women, it is said, become invisible in our society. That may be why their abuse is too (Smith and Hightower 2001).

## Ageism and Elder Abuse

The arguments made above should not lead us to conclude that elder abuse is no more than a version of domestic violence, because that would be to ignore the significance of the age of the parties and particularly the power of ageism. Ageism creates preconceptions and norms of the behaviour and attitudes expected of older people (Herring 2009, Chapter 3). These are reinforced by a range of subtle means including characterizations in the media, advertising, language and social norms. Those who transgress these norms are subject to ridicule.

Society portrays older people as lacking capacity or being of doubtful capacity. This can lead to services targeted at older people as primarily appropriate for those of marginal capacity and emphasizing dependency (Biggs 1996). This can restrict their access to power, public spaces and their role in the community. These all have significant impact on elder abuse. First, ageism works hard to keep older people in their homes or restricted to a few specific public places. This means that more time is spent at home and therefore the scope of intimate abuse is increased. Further, the lack of access to support from others, or public services, means that elder abuse goes undetected. Society's strictures can mean that older women become dependent on their partners both economically and socially and this vulnerability can itself foster elder abuse.

Second, ageist attitudes create and reinforce attitudes among older people about themselves. The ageist notion that older people are a 'waste of space' and always complaining about things, deters victims of elder abuse seeking help or indeed even leads them to believe that the behaviour is not abusive (Herring 2009). Such attitudes belittle and sap the confidence of those suffering abusive relationships.

Third, the lack of alternative facilities for older people both in terms of housing and social support can make the alternatives to the abusive situation as terrifying as the abuse itself. Financial barriers to seeking help or leaving the relationship can be even greater among older women than younger victims of domestic violence (Straka and Montminy 2006).

Fourth, there is evidence that older people, in general, are more likely to remain with abusers than younger women (Wilke and Vinton 2005). Indeed, as we have seen, many have lived with the abuse for many years. Older women are likely to be influenced by the attitudes and values that they were raised with (Straka and Montminy 2006). These mean that, in general, there are increased levels of religious belief (Straka and Montminy 2006); a sense of powerlessness; a stronger commitment to 'privacy of the family' (Zink et al. 2006); and a belief that one should make sacrifices for 'the good of the family' (Buchbinder and Wintstein 2003, 24). It has even been suggested that some older women have come to regard abuse as normal (Brandl and Cook-Daniels 2002). These all deter victims of elder abuse from seeking help (Macdonald 2000). One study of services for older abused women in Scotland found shame and embarrassment as significant factors inhibiting women from seeking help (Dunlop et al. 2005).

Fifth, there are ageist attitudes about men that affect perpetrators. Is elder abuse in part an attempt by men to assert power in the home when ageism means they are losing it in other areas of their life (Biggs et al. 1995, 21)? We cannot know, but it is interesting to note the evidence that perpetrators of abuse tend to be those who are themselves highly dependent on the victim (Ogg and Munn-Giddings 1993).

Finally, there are the difficulties some women face in accessing services designed for younger victims of domestic violence (Scott et al. 2004). Older women find that shelters do not offer them the kind of environments they are seeking and they are rarely used by older women. Services for victims of violence are often targeted at younger women and, among older women, there is a lack of awareness and wariness of official support (Straka and Montinimy 2006). Of course, there are also quite a number of victims of elder abuse who lack capacity to seek help or intervention.

## Intersecting -isms

A proper understanding of elder abuse requires not only an appreciation of ageism and sexism, but also of the way the two intersect (Madden Dempsey 2009, Chapter 7). And not just these social forces, but racism, homophobia and disability discrimination can all have an impact on a case of elder abuse (Turell 2000). Cohen (1984, 11) has written:

> The elderly in our society are generally rejected, but we are particularly disdainful of older women. The discrimination begins in infancy and escalates as we become mature women. But it doubles as we grow older, for then we are not only women, but old women, perceived as unattractive, unneeded, and parasitical.

As she indicates, in elder abuse we have structural inequalities based on age and sex within the relationship and within society which do not just operate independently, but also combine to reinforce each other and produce unique inequalities of their own. Nancy Levit (2002, 228) writes:

> On an experiential level, one person might belong to several identity groups (such as gender, race, ethnicity, socioeconomic status, and sexual orientation); moreover, individuals' experiences comprise several identity facets intersecting

> at once. … A black woman, for instance, experiences not just racism and sexism, but the … burden of intertwined racism and sexism, which is its own unique (and perhaps particularly virulent) form of discrimination.

Such attitudes about older women affect the behaviour of the perpetrator as well as the victim. It also affects the response of officials to elder abuse. A powerful example of this can be seen in research into police practices in cases of elder abuse in Rhode Island, USA. There it was found that the police were reluctant to arrest old men who were seen as frail and not capable of doing a serious injury; while older women tended to be regarded as unreliable and confused, and therefore unlikely to be effective witnesses in court (Klein et al. 2004).

Racism and other forms of discrimination can also combine. There is evidence, for example, that older black women find official services irrelevant to the context of their lives and alien to their lifestyles (Aitken and Griffin 1996). Similarly there are special issues for lesbian, gay, bisexual and transgendered elders who are victims of abuse (Morrissey 2010).

## The Way Ahead

With the above points in mind it is possible to consider a more effective response to elder abuse to one based on carer stress. It will only be possible to sketch out a few proposals here. I shall be particularly brief where others have discussed the issues at length.

First, there is a need for an effective public protection regime to authorize state intervention to protect those victims of elder abuse who are unable to access the legal support system. We have a sophisticated legal framework setting out the obligations on local authorities to protect children in need and to authorize protective measures where children are in need, but there is no equivalent for older people. The House of Commons Health Affairs Committee (2004, 1) noted the (quite appropriate) attention in the media which had been paid to the torture of Victoria Climbié, but noted that

> few knew about Margaret Panting, a 78-year-old woman from Sheffield who died after suffering "unbelievable cruelty" while living with relatives. After her death in 2001, a post-mortem found 49 injuries on her body including cuts probably made by a razor blade and cigarette burns. She had moved from sheltered accommodation to her son-in-law's home – five weeks later she was dead. But as the cause of Margaret Panting's death could not be established, no one was ever charged. An inquest in 2002 recorded an open verdict.

In 2002 John Williams wrote an article entitled 'Public Law Protection of Vulnerable Adults: The Debate Continues, So Does the Abuse'. It still does, and it still does (Williams 2002; 2009).

Second, we need to utilize the criminal law to demonstrate clearly the severity of elder abuse, in the same way that there have been moves to do so in relation to domestic violence. It seemst hat the police are involved in cases of elder abuse only rarely and that where they are there have been complaints that they do not take it sufficiently seriously (Fitzgerald 2006). The existence of age-hate crime is unrecognized in the criminal law

Third, we need an effective set of refuges and local support systems for victims of elder abuse (Blood 2004). As already mentioned, the limited facilities available for victims of domestic violence tend to be targeted at younger women and there are very few that seek to address the needs of older women (Pritchard 2000).

Fourth, ultimately the challenge to elder abuse must come from changing wider attitudes within society. We need to combat the wide range of forces that enable and reinforce ageist attitudes within society (Social Exclusion Unit 2005). Lack of social inclusion, lack of access to information and lack of remedies can all contribute to the social circumstances that enable elder abuse to take place (Department of Health 2005; Dixon et al. 2010). Failure to integrate older people into mainstream society adds to the problems (Schuyler and Liang 2006). As Higgs (1995, 535) has pointed out 'older citizens, active or not, are presented as one of the causes of social crisis through their disproportionate demands for welfare resources'. Older people have been seen as taking resources from needy younger people or adding to their tax burden (Ng 1992). Until society fully respects and treasures its older members, negative attitudes about them will persist and these will be reflected in and reinforced by elder abuse.

Fifthly, there is the issue of dependency (Harbinson and Morrow 1998). The government has stated that a primary goal of policy is to combat dependency among older people (HM Government 1998, para. 11. 3). In *Safeguarding Adults*, there was a move away from protecting towards safeguarding and away from vulnerability to risk to independence. *Safeguarding Adults* explains that this 'means all work which enables an adult "who is or may be eligible for community care services" to retain independence, wellbeing and choice and to access their human right to live a life that is free from abuse and neglect' (HM Government 1998, para. 11. 4). The report explains the shift away from vulnerability because that concept 'can be misunderstood, because it seems to locate the cause of abuse with the victim, rather than in placing responsibility with the actions or omissions of others' (HM Government 1998, para. 11. 7).

I have argued that this is misguided (Herring 2009, Chapter 10). To some, the dependency among older people is itself a result of government policy, societal structures (Townsend 2006) and the failure to acknowledge older people's full citizenship. This may well be so, but I want to focus on the assumption that dependency is something undesirable. Diane Gibson (1995, 709) comments:

> The problem, then, is not the problem of dependency per se. It is the problem of how dependency within social policy is constructed, at both the individual and the societal level. At the individual level, it is the lack of alternatives coupled

> with the discretionary control over whether the assistance is given which renders a particular exchange an undesirable one. At the societal level, it is the labelling of particular groups of people in particular circumstances, most notably those who have neither alternatives to escape the situation or the political power to do anything about the way in which they are treated which allows the construction and application of the particular social label "dependent".

Dependency itself is not undesirable. Dependency is often regarded as causing a loss of freedom and dignity. This is not, and should not, be so. We are all, or virtually all, dependent on others; and others are dependent on us. It is true that at different stages of life the extent and nature of dependency may vary. Further, it is often far from apparent in a caring relationship who is dependent on whom. As Michael Fine and Caroline Glendinning (2005, 619) argue:

> Recent studies of care suggest that qualities of reciprocal dependence underlie much of what is termed "care". Rather than being a unidirectional activity in which an active care-giver does something to a passive and dependent recipient, these accounts suggest that care is best understood as the product or outcome of the relationship between two or more people.

In truth there is often give and take in the 'carer' and 'cared for' relationship. Their relationship is marked by interdependency. The 'cared for' provides the 'carer' with gratitude, love, acknowledgement and emotional support. Indeed often a 'carer' will be 'cared for' in another relationship (Herring 2007).

The individualistic model of dependency which some of the government publications regarding old age appear to promote is undesirable and unrealistic. Older people who are dependent on others for their care should not be regarded as having failed in achieving a good old age. The problem is that too often older people in need of care are regarded as having nothing to offer. The best way ahead is to emphasize inter-dependence (Biggs 1994). We need to find and emphasize the ways that even those who need substantial levels of care can contribute to society and others. We need to find ways of valuing them. The notion that independence will prevent elder abuse is clearly misguided. Indeed it is those who are most disconnected from society and from friends who can be most at risk of abuse. Care work needs to be valued, acknowledged and rewarded effectively (Herring 2007). That involves making it part of the wider community's responsibility. Care of those unable to care for themselves should be seen as one of society's most important tasks. If care were taken more seriously, many of the problems of elder abuse would diminish.

Finally, we must recognize that elder abuse is not a single phenomenon and is a complex one. It must be tackled on many fronts. The government's current approach is to incorporate responses to elder abuse within protection of vulnerable adults. This fails to deal with those aspects of elder abuse which are a result of age, rather than vulnerability. As I have argued elsewhere, a significant portion of elder abuse reflects ageist attitudes (Herring 2009). It should be obvious that elder abuse can encompass a complex range of behaviours: it can include ongoing domestic violence; abuse of care-givers by care recipients (Phillips et al 2000); community harassment (Biggs 1996); an inhibiting fear of violence in public spaces (Meyer and Post 2006); an aspect of alcohol misuse (Campbell Reay and Browne 2001); retaliation by adults of abuse they suffered as children (Campbell Reay and Browne 2001); and abuse of grandparents by grandchildren they are caring for (Kosberg and MacNeil 2005). As argued above, these are all bolstered by patriarchal and ageist power structures, when providing practical assistance in individual care responses will need to be tailored to the circumstances of the individual case.

## Conclusion

This chapter has considered the role played by the myth that care-giver stress is a major explanation for elder abuse. While acknowledging the enormous toll that caring can take, it has been argued that it plays little part in explaining elder abuse. Indeed the emphasis placed on carer stress as an explanation has meant that the real issues surrounding elder abuse have received insufficient attention. It has been often overlooked that elder abuse is, in fact, domestic violence that has continued over the course of the whole relationship. Further, carer stress has been used to individualize the problem of elder abuse and focus attention on the problems created by the 'dependent' and 'vulnerable' older person, rather than the abuser and on the wider social forces that reinforce and enable the abuse to take place. Responsibility for the problem of elder abuse is therefore placed on the older person themselves or the carer. However, neither can be held to account for the abuse.

Elder abuse, it has been argued, is a caused by a complex mix of social and personal factors. Ageism and patriarchy are powerful forces which underpin and sustain the structural inequalities that enable the violence to be perpetuated. Seeking to promote independence, as some government publications have done, is unlikely to be an effective response to elder abuse. Older people, like us all, are dependent on others for their well-being; and have people dependent on them. This is to be celebrated, not disparaged. We need to find ways of recognizing our interdependence with each other. Younger people are as dependent on older people as older people are on younger people. We need to promote and enable older people to live in a set of relationships which enable them to live fulfilling and satisfying lives, free from abuse. Older people are often ignored in our society. Their voices are not heard and they are regarded as 'out of touch' and 'past their best'. Their care is delegated to carers who receive little acknowledgment or reward for the work they do. Their abuse is left unacknowledged and unchallenged.

## References


Action on Elder Abuse. 2004. *Hidden Voices: Older People's Experience of Abuse*. London: Action on Elder Abuse.

Aitken, L. and Griffin, G. 1996. *Gender Issues in Elder Abuse*. Thousand Oaks, CA: Sage.

American Psychological Society. 1999. *Elder Abuse and Neglect: In Search ofSolutions*. Washington DC: American Psychological Society.

Association of Directors of Social Services. 2005. *Safeguarding Adults*. London: Association of Directors of Social Services.

Bendik, M. 1992. Reaching the breaking point: Dangers of mistreatment in elder caregiving situations. *Journal of Elder Abuse & Neglect*, 4, 39–60.

Bennet, G., Kingston, P. and Penhale, B. 1997. *The Dimensions of Elder Abuse*. Basingstoke: Macmillan.

Bergeron, L. 2001. An elder abuse case study: Caregiver stress or domestic violence? You decide. *Journal of Gerontological Social Work*, 34, 47–63.

Bergeron, L. 2004. Abuse of elderly women in family relationships: Another form of domestic violence against women, in *Handbook of Women, Stress, and Trauma*, edited by K. Kendall-Tackett. Aldershot: Routledge.

Biggs, S. 1994. Failed individualism in community care. *Journal of Social Work Practice*, 8, 137–49.

Biggs, S. 1996. A family concern: Elder abuse in British social policy. *Critical Social Policy*, 16, 63–88.

Biggs, S., Phillipson, C. and Kingson, P. 1995. *Elder Abuse in Perspective*. Milton Keynes: Open University Press.

Bitondo-Dyer, C., Connolly, M.-T. and McFeeley, P. 2003. The clinical and medical forensics of elder abuse and neglect, in *Elder Mistreatment: Abuse, Neglect, and Exploitation in an Aging America*, edited by R. Bonnie and R. Wallace. Washington DC: National Academies Press, 339–81.

Blood, I. 2004. *Older Women and Domestic Violence*. London: Help the Aged.

Brammer, A. and Biggs, S. 1998. Defining elder abuse. *Journal of Social Welfare and Family Law*, 20, 285–304.

Brandl, B. and Cook-Daniels, L. 2002. Domestic abuse in later life. *The Elder Law Journal*, 8, 302–35.

Brandl, B. and J. Raymond, J. 1997. Unrecognized elder abuse victims: Older abused women. *Journal of Case Management*, 6, 62–8.

Buchbinder, E. and Wintstein, T. 2003. 'Like a wounded bird': Older battered women's life experiences with intimate violence. *Journal of Elder Abuse and Neglect*, 15, 23–44.

Campbell Reay, A. and Browne, K. 2001. Risk factor characteristics in carers who physically abuse or neglect their elderly dependants. *Ageing & Mental Health*, 5, 56–62.

Cohen, L. 1984. Small Expectations: Society's Betrayal of Older Women. Toronto: McClelland and Stewart.

Cooney, C. and Mortimer, A. 1995. Elder abuse and dementia–A pilot study. *International Journal of Social Psychiatry*, 41, 276–83.
Cooper, C., Selwood, A. and Livingston, G. 2008. The prevalence of elder abuse and neglect: A systematic review. *Age and Ageing*, 37, 151–60.
Coyne, A., Reichman, W. and Berbig, L. 1993. The relationship between dementia and elder abuse. *American Journal of Psychiatry*, 150, 643–6.
Crichton, S., Bond, J., Harvey, C. and Ristock, J. 1999. Elder abuse: Feminist and ageist perspectives. *Journal of Elder Abuse & Neglect*, 10, 115–30.
Department of Health. 2000. *No Secrets*. London: The Stationery Office.
Department of Health. 2005. *Safeguarding Adults*. London: Department of Health.
Desmarais, A. and Reeves, K. 2007. Gray, black, and blue: The state of research and intervention for intimate partner abuse among elders. *Behavioral Sciences and the Law*, 25, 377–91.
Dixon, J., Manthorpe, J., Biggs, S., Mowlam, A., Tennant, R., Tinker, A. and McCreadie, C. 2010. Defining elder mistreatment. *Ageing and Society*, 30, 403–20.
Dunlop, B., Beaulaurier, R., Seff, L., Newman, F., Malik, N. and Fuster, F. 2005. *Domestic Violence Against Older Women*. Miami, FL: Florida International University.
Dyer, C., Connolly, M. and McFeeley, P. 2002. The clinical and medical forensics of elder abuse and neglect, in *Elder Abuse: Abuse, Neglect, and Exploitation in An Aging America*, edited by R. Bonnie and R. Wallace. Washington DC: National Academy Press.
Fine, M. and Glendinning, C. 2005. Dependence, independence or inter-dependence? Revisiting the concepts of care and dependency. *Ageing and Society*, 25, 601–31.
Fitzgerald, G. 2006. The realities of elder abuse, in *Ageing, Crime and Society*, edited by A. Wahidin and M. Cain. Cullompton: Willan.
Gainey, R. and Payne, B. 2006. Caregiver burden, elder abuse and Alzheimer's disease: Testing the relationship. *Journal of Health and Human Services Administration*, 29, 245–59.
Garcia, J. and Kosberg, J. 1992. Understanding anger: Implications for formal and informal caregivers. *Journal of Elder Abuse & Neglect*, 4, 87–100.
Gibson, D. 1995. Dependency: The career of a concept, in *Dependency, Re-Examining the Social Construction of Elder Abuse and Neglect*, edited by S. Graham. Sydney: University of New South Wales.
Glendenning, F. and Decalmer, P. 1993. Looking to the future, in *The Mistreatment of Elderly People*, edited by P. Decalmer and F. Glendenning. Newbury Park, CA: Sage Publications.
Harbinson, J. and Morrow, M. 1998. Re-examining the social construction of 'elder abuse and neglect' – A Canadian perspective. *Ageing and Society*, 18, 691–711.
Herring, J. 2007. Where are the carers in healthcare law and ethics? *Legal Studies*, 27, 51–73.

Herring, J. 2009. *Older People in Law and Society*. Oxford: Oxford University Press.

Herring, J. and Choudhry, S. 2006. Righting domestic violence. *International Journal of Law, Policy and the Family*, 20, 95–119.

Higgs, P. 1995. Citizenship and old age: The end of the road. *Ageing and Society*, 15, 535–50.

Hightower, J. 2010. Abuse in later life: When and how does gender matter?, in *Aging, Ageism and Abuse*, edited by G. Gutman and C. Spencer. Amsterdam: Elsevier, 17–29.

Hines, D. and Malley-Morrison, K. 2005. *Family Violence in the US*. Thousand Oaks, CA: Sage.

HM Government. 1998. *Better Government for Older People*. London: HMSO.

House of Commons Health Committee. 2004. *Elder Abuse*. London: The Stationery Office.

Johnson, F., Hogg, J. and Daniel, B. 2010. Abuse and protection issues across the lifespan: Reviewing the literature. *Social Policy and Society*, 9, 291.

Klein, A., Tobin, K., Salomon, A. and Dubois, J. 2004. *A Statewide Profile of Abuse of Older Women and the Criminal Justice Response*. Washington DC: US Department of Justice.

Koenig, T., Rinfrette, S. and Lutz, W. 2006. Female caregivers' reflections on ethical decision-making. *Clinical Social Work Journal*, 34, 361–72.

Kosberg, J. and MacNeil, G. 2005. The vulnerability to elder abuse for grandparents raising their grandchildren: An emerging global phenomenon. *Journal of Elder Abuse and Neglect*, 15, 33–53.

Levit, N. 2002. Theorizing the connections among systems of subordination. *University of Missouri–Kansas City Law Rev*, 71, 227–49.

Lord Chancellor's Department. 1997. *Who Decides?* London: Lord Chancellor's Department.

Lundy, M. and Grossman, S. 2004. Elder abuse: Spouse/intimate partner abuse and family violence among elders. *Journal of Elder Abuse and Neglect*, 16, 85–102.

Macdonald, L. 2000. *Out of the Shadows: Christianity and Violence against Women in Scotland*. Edinburgh: Centre for Theology and Public Issues, University of Edinburgh.

Madden Dempsey, M. 2006. 'What counts as domestic violence? A conceptual analysis. *William and Mary Journal of Women and the Law*, 12, 301–85.

Madden Dempsey, M. 2007. Towards a feminist state: What does 'effective' prosecution of domestic violence mean? *Modern Law Review*, 70, 908–35.

Madden Dempsey, M. 2009. *Prosecuting Domestic Violence: A Philosophical Analysis*. Oxford: Oxford University Press.

McCreadie, C. 1996. *Elder Abuse: Update on Research*. London: Age Concern.

McDonald, L. and Collins, A. 2000. *Abuse and Neglect of Older Adults: A Discussion Paper*. Washington DC: National Clearinghouse on Family Violence.

Mears, J. 2003. Survival is not enough: Violence against older women in Australia. *Violence Against Women*, 9, 1478–89.

Meyer, E. and Post, L. 2006. Alone at night: A feminist ecology model of community violence. *Feminist Criminology*, 1, 207.

Mornington, District Judge. 2004. *Responding to Elder Abuse Behind Closed Doors*. London: Age Concern.

Morrissey, C. 2010. Abuse of lesbian, gay, transgender, and bisexual elders, in *Aging, Ageism and Abuse*, edited by G. Gutman and C. Spencer. Amsterdam: Elsevier, 45–51.

Mowlam, A., Tennant, R., Dixon, J. and McCreadie, C. 2008. *UK Study of Abuse and Neglect of Older People: Qualitative Findings*. London: Department of Health.

National Center on Elder Abuse. 2002. *Preventing Elder Abuse by Family Caregivers*. Washington DC: National Center on Elder Abuse.

National Center on Elder Abuse. 2008. *A Fact Sheet on Carer Stress and Elder Abuse*. Washington DC: National Center on Elder Abuse.

Nelson, T. 2002. *Ageism*. Cambridge, MA: Massachusetts Institute of Technology Press.

Nerenberg, L. 2002. *A Feminist Perspective on Gender and Elder Abuse: A Review of the Literature*. Washington DC: National Committee for the Prevention of Elder Abuse.

Ng, E. 1992. *Children and Elderly People: Sharing Public Income Resources. Ottawa*: Canadian Social Trends.

Nolan, M. 1993. Carer–dependant relationships and the prevention of elder abuse, in *The Mistreatment of Elderly People*, edited by P. Decalmer and F. Glendenning. Thousand Oaks, CA: Sage, 148–59.

Ogg, J. and Munn-Giddings, C. 1993. Researching elder abuse. *Ageing and Society*, 13, 381–414.

O'Keeffe, M., Hills, A., Doyle, M., McCreadie, C., Scholes, S., Constantine, R., Tinker, A., Manthorpe, J., Biggs, S. and Erens, B. 2008. *UK Study of Abuse and Neglect of Older People Prevalence Survey Report*. London: Department of Health.

Pain, R. 1999. Theorizing age in criminology: The case of home abuse, in *British Criminology Conferences*, edited by M. Brogden. London: British Criminology Society, 1–12.

Penhale, B. 1999. Bruises on the soul: Older women, domestic violence, and elder abuse. *Journal of Elder Abuse & Neglect*, 11, 1–22.

Phillips, L. 1986. Theoretical explanations of elder abuse: Competing hypotheses and unresolved issues, in *Elder Abuse: Conflict in the Family*, edited by K. Phillemer and R. Wolf. Dover, MA: Auburn House, 197–215.

Phillips, L., Torres de Ardon, E. and Briones, G. 2000. Abuse of female caregivers by care recipients: Another form of elder abuse. *Journal of Elder Abuse & Neglect*, 12, 123–43.

Pillemer, K. 1993. The abused offspring are dependent: Abuse is caused by the deviance and dependence of abusive caregivers, in *Current Controversies on Family Violence*, edited by R. Gelles and D. Loeske. Newbury Park, CA: Sage, 237–49.

Pillemer, K. and Finkelhor, D. 2006. Causes of elder abuse: Caregiver stress versus problem relatives. *Journal of Health Human Services Administration*, 19, 245–64.

Pillemer, K. and Suitor, J. 1992. Violence and violent feelings: What causes them among family caregivers? *Journal of Gerontology*, 4, 165–72.

Pritchard, J. 2000. *The* Needs of Older Women*: Services for* Victims of Elder Abuse and Other Abuse. Bristol: The Policy Press.

Pritchard, J. 2007. *Working with Adult Abuse: A Training Manual*. London: Jessica Kingsley Publishers.

Rathbone-McCuan, E. 2000. Elder abuse within the context of intimate violence. *University of Missouri–Kansas City Law Review*, 69, 215–26.

Salazar, L., Baker, C., Price, A. and Carlin, K. 2003. Moving beyond the individual: Examining the effects of domestic violence policies on social norms. *American Journal of Community Psychology*, 32, 253–64.

Sargent, M. and Mears, J. 2000. *Older Women Speak Up: Older Women Are Empowered by Telling our Stories of Violence in the Home*. Sydney: University of Western Sydney.

Schuyler, D. and Liang, B. 2006. Reconceptualizing elder abuse: Treating the disease of senior community exclusion. *Annuals of Health Care Law*, 15, 275–96.

Scott, M., McKie, L., Morton, S., Seddon, E. and Wasoff, F. 2004. *Older Women and Domestic Violence in Scotland: '...and for 39 years I got on with it'.* Edinburgh: Health Scotland.

Smith, M. and Hightower, J. 2001. *Silent and Invisible. What's Age Got to Do With It?*Vancouver, BC/Yukon: Society of Transition Houses.

Social Exclusion Unit, 2005. *Excluded Older People*. London: The Stationery Office.

Straka, S. and Montminy, L. 2006. Responding to the needs of older women experiencing domestic violence. *Violence against Women*, 12, 251–67.

Townsend, P. 2006. Policies for the aged in the 21st century: More 'structured dependency' or the realisation of human rights? *Ageing & Society*, 26, 161–79.

Turell, S. 2000. A descriptive analysis of same-sex relationship violence for a diverse sample. *Journal of Family Violence*, 15, 281–93.

Vinton, L. 1991. Abused older women: Battered women or abused elders? *Journal of Women and Aging*, 3, 5–19.

Vinton, L. 1992. Battered women's shelters and older women. *Journal of Family Violence*, 7, 63–72.

Whittaker, T. 1996. Violence, gender and elder abuse, in *Violence and Gender Relations: Theories and Interventions*, edited by B. Fawcett, B. Featherstone, J. Hearn, and C. Toft. London: Sage, 78–93.

Wilke, D. and Vinton, L. 2005. The nature and impact of domestic violence across age cohorts. *Affilia*, 20, 316–28.

Williams, J. 2002. Public law protection of vulnerable adults: The debate continues, so does the abuse. *Journal of Social Work*, 2, 293.

Williams, J. 2009. State responsibility and the abuse of vulnerable older people, in *Responsibility, Law and the Family*, edited by J. Bridgeman, H. Keating and C. Lind. Aldershot: Ashgate, 81–105.

Woolf, L. M. 1998. *Ageism: Myths and Biases against Aging and Older Adults*. Crestwood, MO: Crestwood Community Center.

Zink, P., Jacobson, C., Regan, S., Fisher, B. and Pabst, S. 2006. Older women's descriptions and understandings of their abusers. *Violence Against Women*, 12, 851–65.

# Chapter 13
# Intensive Caring Responsibilities and Crimes of Compassion?[1]

Heather Keating and Jo Bridgeman

In this chapter our focus is upon recent criminal cases where a parent has killed or assisted the death of a child, who may be an adult, and at the time of death that child was suffering from severe disabilities, debilitating injury or chronic illness. We include within our discussion cases where the parent has provided assistance that has enabled the child to commit suicide, although not those where the assistance has taken the form of accompanying them abroad in order to be assisted to die. We thus explore the relationship between criminal and family responsibilities through an examination of recent cases where parents have acted to end their child's real,[2] or imagined, suffering in what could thus be understood as an altruistic or compassionate act. In doing so, it will be necessary to consider the nature of both family responsibilities and responsibility as understood by the criminal law, the reasons given by the parents[3] and the way in which the criminal law categorizes and responds to such behaviour. It will be suggested that the current categorization into murder, manslaughter on the grounds of diminished responsibility, and assisting suicide, while appropriate for some cases, does not allow for the full story of other cases that we explore to be both told and taken into account. It will be argued that there is a gap in the options available to the courts and that consideration should be given to how best this gap might be bridged.

We start with a brief account of two cases from January 2010 which prompted our discussion of, and reflections on, these cases within the context of the legal regulation of family responsibilities. Frances Inglis was convicted of the murder of her 22-year-old son, Thomas, and sentenced to serve at least nine years of her life sentence. Sixteen months earlier, Thomas had sustained severe head injuries

---

1 We are extremely grateful to Jonathan Herring for his many constructive and insightful suggestions on an earlier version.

2 We do not, therefore, consider cases of infanticide. While this offence (which also acts as a partial defence to murder) may be used in the context of maternal killing of severely disabled infants, the focus of infanticide is upon the mother's mental condition arising from the effects of giving birth (see Clarkson et al. 2010, 697–701).

3 We should note the limitations of our data. Our discussion of criminal trials is reliant upon media accounts for detail about the cases. We could have explored, but do not have the space to do so here, the ways in which the media constructs the accused and their reasons for killing.

in a fall from an ambulance. He was able to communicate by blinking and by squeezing of hands although his prognosis was uncertain. His family had been advised that an application could be made to court for a declaration that it was lawful to withdraw food and water. That seemed, to his family, to offer a cruel, slow and ghastly death (Pidd 2010) although it should be noted, as he was not in a persistent vegetative state, this course of action will only be approved by a court if the patient has given informed consent or if an incompetent patient's condition is 'so intolerable as to be beyond doubt' (*W Healthcare Trust v H and Another* [2004] EWCA Civ 1324). Frances Inglis had, very soon after the accident, formed the view that her son would not want to live like this. Within 10 days of his accident she tried to obtain heroin to administer to him with the aim of ending his life (Bannerman 2010a). She researched on the Internet the quantity of heroin that would be required to kill him and purchased it. Following an earlier attempt to end his life for which she was on bail, upon condition that she did not visit her son, Frances Inglis barricaded herself in his nursing home room and administered the fatal dose (Bannerman 2010b).

The second case concerns Kay Gilderdale, who pleaded guilty to aiding and abetting the suicide of, but denied attempting to murder, her 31-year-old daughter Lynn (Laville 2010b). She was found not guilty of the charge of attempted murder and received a 12-month conditional discharge for assisting her daughter to die (Laville 2010b). Lynn had become ill with ME at the age of 14. Within six months she was paralysed and within nine she could neither speak nor swallow. Lynn was fed through a tube and bedridden, she had numerous micro-fractures due to loss of bone density and her major organs and hormone system were breaking down (Swain 2010). Lynn had spoken to her parents of her intention to end her life; she had had a Do Not Resuscitate Order placed on her medical notes and a 'living will' drafted to the effect that she did not 'want doctors to do anything more to prolong her life' (Laville 2010a). In the early hours of one morning in December 2008 Lynn had summoned her mother to her. Seeing that Lynn had removed the morphine from the syringe which administered it over a 24-hour period and attached it to the line to administer it directly into her veins, Kay tried to persuade her daughter not to end her life. Lynn insisted it was time and asked her mother for help. Kay fetched two more syringes of morphine which Lynn administered in the same way. With a resistance to morphine built up over such a long period of use, this massive overdose did not appear to kill her. Kay crushed up sleeping tablets and sedatives, dissolved them in water and administered them via the naso-gastric tube. Concerned that her daughter should not feel any pain she also administered Lynn's usual dosage of drugs. Over 28 hours after Kay was first called by her daughter, Lynn died (description of events of Lynn's death taken from interview with Kay Gilderdale in Swain 2010).

As well as being intrigued by the complexities of these criminal cases and the debates and discussions prompted by them, we were curious to explore what an ethic of care perspective could contribute to consideration of the responsibility for actions which, in the abstract, appear to be the antithesis of caring and the rejection of family responsibility. Commentators who are critical of the employment of a care perspective as an analytical tool have argued that it is essentialist believing that a care perspective aligns care with a distinctly female voice. Even though Carol Gilligan's observation of a different approach to moral problem solving than that offered by then dominant perspectives in moral development was based upon empirical studies with women whom, she noticed, had previously been excluded, she was careful to point out that she was seeking to identify a contrasting approach and not to make an observation about the sexes (Gilligan 1982, 2). From her radical feminist perspective, Catharine MacKinnon has argued that the ethic of care is the 'articulat[ion] of the feminine' and may encourage 'women [to] identify… with what is a positively valued feminine stereotype', in other words, that women use the language of care because that is the only activity for which they are valued within society (Dubois et al. 1985, 74–5).[4] Furthermore, it has been suggested that to focus upon a caring ethic or caring activity is to perpetuate and enhance a connection between women and care, reinforcing women's oppression and subordination to men. And, that to focus upon caring is inevitably to valorize care. Whilst critics continue to associate care with a feminine approach, those who argue for recognition of care do so with the aim of enhancing the value of care (Herring 2007a) or argue for the integration of care and justice (for example, Held 1995; West 1997; Kittay 2002; Kittay in this volume). As Carol Gilligan herself argued:

> The moral imperative that emerges … is an injunction to care, a responsibility to discern and alleviate the "real and recognizable trouble" of this world. … [The other] moral imperative appears rather as an injunction to respect the rights of others and thus to protect from interference the rights to life and self-fulfillment. Development … would therefore seem to entail an integration of rights and responsibilities through the discovery of the complementarity of these disparate views. (Gilligan 1982, 100)

To ignore the contribution of a caring perspective is to ignore the counterbalance to a selfish, individualistic, rights-orientated approach offered by considerations of context, connection and responsibility. It is to perpetuate the invisibility of care, to maintain the pretence that care is not required by us all and to fail to accord value to care and to the providers of care.

These cases came to our attention as high profile cases in which parents were being required to explain themselves within a framework into which only some of them could fit and then only partially, and which, in our view, raised questions which were not being articulated about the visibility and value of care, the limits of public responsibility to care and the obstacles presented to carers as well as whether the law is in need of reform to reflect our moral judgement about parents who kill out of compassion.

4 Although as the chapters in this volume amply demonstrate, caring activity is not valued.

## Filicide

The behaviour that is the subject matter of this chapter is extraordinary. Statistically, homicide is an uncommon event; and, although it is largely a 'domestic' crime (where in approximately 70 per cent of cases the killer and victim were known to each other), filicides (killings by parents of their children) are more uncommon still. Because of the small numbers involved there can be variation from year to year, but in 2008, for example, official statistics for England and Wales reveal that of the 651 cases recorded as homicide, 50 involved child victims under the age of 16. Of these a parent was recorded as the principal suspect in 56 per cent of cases (in 24 per cent of cases no principal suspect had yet been identified) (Smith et al. 2010, 15). There are, on average 32 filicides each year in England and Wales (Flynn 2009, 7). The NSPCC is of the view that child homicides are under-represented in recorded crime figures (preferring to include child deaths resulting from a wider range of neglect or abuse than is the case with recorded figures) (NSPCC 2009). What can be said with certainty, however, is that a child is much more likely to be killed by a family member, that is, someone with the responsibility to care for them, than by a stranger.

There have been a number of studies around the world which have explored maternal and paternal killings. Whilst they provide valuable insights, caution is required: there is no one standard definition of filicide – so some studies only consider child victims under the age of 16 or 18 whilst others do not impose an age limitation. Some include only biological parents (Friedman et al. 2005) whilst others also include step-parents (Liem and Koenraadt 2008). Many studies look at maternal or paternal killings but only a few consider both and potential differences between them (Flynn 2009, 19). Finally, the rarity of filicide makes it difficult to obtain representative samples and studies use different methods for obtaining data (Flynn 2009, 19). But given this, it does seem that younger children are more at risk of homicide than older children and this also tallies with official crime statistics where children under the age of one are most at risk (Smith et al. 2010, 16). Findings as to whether mothers or fathers are more likely to kill their children are inconsistent (see Morris and Wilcynski 1993), but it does seem that there is a very strong relationship between neo-naticide and mothers and that this skews the overall figures so as to give the impression that mothers are more likely than fathers to kill their children. If this group of killings is removed, then fathers are more likely to kill than mothers (Flynn 2009, 19). This supports an earlier analysis of children murdered by their parents between 1995 and 2001 that revealed that 160 of them had been killed by their fathers and 136 by their mothers. In addition, 56 children had been killed by step-parents: 54 by stepfathers and two by stepmothers (letter from Home Office, May 2002, cited in Yarwood 2004, 9).

Over 40 years ago, Resnick identified the motives for filicide as (1) altruistic, (2) acutely psychotic, (3) accidental filicide (fatal maltreatment), (4) unwanted child, and (5) spouse revenge filicide (Resnick 1969). This typology has been influential but has been subject to modification by later researchers. Studies suggest that parents who kill often express the view that the killing was altruistic: this was true of almost half of the parents in Resnick's US study and in Marleau et al.'s small study of paternal killings in Canada (1999). However, here too caution is needed. For example, Resnick's definition of 'altruistic' killers included both parents who killed children to release them from suffering and filicides associated with suicide (where the parent desired to end his or her own life but would not abandon the child). Other studies have categorized suicidal parents as mentally ill rather than as altruistic (Flynn 2009, 28). In d'Orban's study, only those where the child's suffering was real were classified as mercy killings and this accounted for 1 per cent of killings (d'Orban 1979; see also Dell 1984). In Bourget and Gagne's study of maternal filicides in Canada, none of the cases were considered to be mercy killings (Bourget and Gagne 2002; Flynn 2009, 28).

One factor that appears consistently in the studies is that of mental illness. In Bourget and Gagne's study a 'psychiatric motivation' was found in 85 per cent of the cases (most commonly depression) and in Friedman's study 70 per cent of mothers and 30 per cent of fathers had had previous contact with mental health services (Friedman et al. 2008). As the cases included in this chapter reveal, in some cases the illness results from the long-term strain of caring for a severely disabled child, while in others the illness has been a recurring part of the parent's life.

The information obtained by typological research is valuable but 'it is important to state that parents kill children for various reasons and it is misleading to consider filicide as having a single motivation or cause. In reality the individual circumstances of any homicide are complex' (Flynn 2009, 36). This is amply borne out by the cases included in this chapter.

Although much publicity has been given recently to instances of assisted suicide, as far as *official* figures go, this too is a rare event. Official statistics reveal that there were between seven and 13 offences recorded in England and Wales in each of the last four years (Walker et al. 2010, 30). Beyond this, lies an unknown figure;[5] but what we do know is that, between 1999 and 2009, 134 people travelled from Britain to Dignitas in Switzerland,[6] there to end their lives, and that a further 800 people have become members of Dignitas so as to seek assistance in dying (Campbell 2009).

## The Criminal Law

Given the cases that form the basis of our study, it is important to be aware of the distinctions currently drawn under English criminal law. The category of homicide

5 Including, of course, deaths in hospitals, of which at least some may have involved end of life decisions which included the taking of steps to assist the patient to die (Seale 2006).

6 <www.guardian.co.uk/news/datablog/2010/feb/25/assisted-suicide-dignitas-statistics> (accessed 17 May 2010).

consists of murder, manslaughter and infanticide. A further offence, of particular relevance to this chapter, is that of assisting suicide.[7]

Murder is defined as the unlawful killing of a person with malice aforethought (which means that the defendant must have intended to kill or to cause grievous bodily harm) (*Cunningham* [1982] AC 566) and carries a fixed penalty of life imprisonment. Manslaughter is an extremely broad offence. Carrying a maximum penalty of life imprisonment, it includes killings where the accused lacks malice aforethought but the prosecution proves, for example, that he or she intended some harm to the victim. Manslaughter also includes killings with malice aforethought but where a partial defence reduces liability to manslaughter; one such partial defence is that of diminished responsibility, created by section 2 of the Homicide Act 1957. In order for murder to be reduced to manslaughter under section 2 (recently amended by the Coroners and Justice Act 2009)[8] the defence (upon whom, exceptionally, the burden of proof rests) must prove that at the time of the killing the person charged with the killing was suffering from an abnormality of mental functioning which arose from a recognized medical condition, substantially impairing his or her ability to do one or more things (to understand the nature of his or her conduct; to form a rational judgement; to exercise self-control) and providing an explanation for his or her acts. Expert evidence continues to be necessary under the new law. There is room to hope that psychiatrists will in the future be able to provide testimony within their range of expertise (as to whether, for example, the person could form a rational judgement given his or her medical condition) rather than being called upon to determine questions of moral responsibility as happened under the old law. Guided by medical testimony, juries will be called upon to determine whether the killer's recognized condition substantially impaired her ability to do any of the things listed above. If the plea is successful the court has discretion as to the appropriate sentence, and, as some of our case studies illustrate, low sentences have been imposed.

Historically, the plea of diminished responsibility has often been accepted by the prosecution in relation to long-term carers who kill their terminally ill spouses with consent (Law Commission 2005, para. 8.84). The Law Commission has commented that the defence 'provided a practically convenient method for the prosecution, defence and the court, by agreement, to dispose of cases where nobody would wish to see the imposition of a mandatory life sentence. This has been achieved by a sometimes strained and sympathetic approach to the medical

7 Section 5 of the Domestic Violence, Crimes and Victims Act 2004 creates the offence of causing or allowing a child or vulnerable adult to die. While this offence is used against parents who kill (or do not intervene to prevent another killing), it is not the most likely charge in relation to altruistic killings and is not considered further in this chapter. But see Herring (2007b) where arguments analogous to those made here concerning the role and relationship of individual and state responsibility are made.

8 These provisions came into effect in October 2010.

evidence and the language of the statute' (Law Commission 2003, para.1.55).[9] James Lawson's plea of guilty to the manslaughter, on the grounds of diminished responsibility, of his 22-year-old daughter, Sarah, who had suffered from depression for 10 years and attempted suicide three times in the week before she died, was accepted. Melody Turnbull also pleaded guilty to manslaughter on the grounds of diminished responsibility. In her case there were two counts because she had killed two of her children, Robert, aged 23 and Richard, aged 20. Both boys had had cerebral palsy, were blind, incontinent, could neither speak nor stand and each had the mental capacity of a six-month-old baby (Levin 2001). Melody reached breaking point when the lease of their house was due to expire without suitable accommodation having been found. Fearing that they would be separated and her sons taken into care, she first drugged the boys and then smothered them. At her trial she was sentenced to three years' probation. The view taken by the Ministry of Justice in its impact assessment of the new legislation is that 'given the nature of the changes ... we do not expect any significant shifts in the numbers or types of cases which benefit from the partial defence of diminished responsibility, and our analysis of the 2005 cases supports this conclusion' (Ministry of Justice 2009, 6). However, it has been convincingly argued that the new wording has narrowed the defence (Miles 2009, 8–9; Mackay 2010, 302) and the worry must be that this may reduce its usefulness in the types of cases we are considering.

It is worth emphasizing two features of English law at this stage. First, homicide may result from a positive act (such as asphyxiation) or from an omission or failure to act in circumstances where a duty to act exists. Parents owe a duty to their children to care for them under common law and under section 1 of the Children and Young Persons Act 1933. A parent who deliberately fails to do so with the result that the child dies may be convicted of murder (as, for example, in *Gibbins and Proctor* [1918] 13 Cr. App. R. 134) or manslaughter if the failure was grossly negligent (*Adomako* [1995] 1 AC 171; *Evans* [2009] EWCA Crim 650). However, the distinction between acts and omissions is highly significant in one respect: the withdrawal of treatment by doctors of severely disabled or ill patients is not homicide (*Airedale NHS Trust v Bland* [1993] AC 789).

Secondly, while the surrounding circumstances or reasons given by parents may be absolutely critical in our study, and may be relevant to decisions to prosecute (say, for assisted suicide) and in relation to sentencing, motive itself is irrelevant to the legal determination of a killing as murder. Thus, a parent who intentionally kills his or her child (where no defence, such as diminished responsibility, exists) in order to bring an end to the suffering of the child will be guilty of murder: there is no special category or defence of 'mercy killing'.

9 There is evidence that women defendants are more likely to succeed with a plea of diminished responsibility than men but there has also been sustained criticism of the way in which some defendants are forced to couch their defence in terms of their mental illness in order to avoid a conviction for murder: see Allen 1987; McColgan 1993; Morris and Wilcynski 1993.

Unlike the above, where the accused causes the death, section 2 of the Suicide Act 1961 (as amended by the Coroners and Justice Act 2009[10]) criminalizes the actions of someone who 'does an act capable of encouraging or assisting the suicide or attempted suicide of another' if that act was intended to encourage or assist suicide or an attempt at suicide. Thus, although committing suicide is not a crime (the offence was abolished by section 1 of the 1961 Act), helping another person to do so is. The amended offence is complete whether or not the suicide or attempted suicide actually occurs: it has, thus, become a conduct rather than a result crime (Hirst 2009, 875). However, the change to the law is not intended to lead to a change in the types of cases which are prosecuted (Starmer 2009), as failed efforts to aid could formerly be punished as attempts in any event. The offence carries a maximum penalty of 14 years' imprisonment but the consent of the DPP is necessary before a prosecution can be brought.

Assisting suicide has come under increasing scrutiny over the last decade, not least because of the increasing coverage given to those who assist family members to travel to Dignitas in Switzerland but also due to the efforts of both Diane Pretty and Debbie Purdy. Diane Pretty sought an undertaking from the DPP that her husband would not be prosecuted if he were to assist her suicide. The DPP felt unable to give such an assurance so Mrs Pretty sought a declaration from the courts, basing her claim on Articles 2, 3, 8, 9 and 14 of the European Convention on Human Rights and Fundamental Freedoms. The House of Lords held that the DPP is unable to give an undertaking to people that they will not be prosecuted and that s.2 of the Suicide Act was not incompatible with the Convention (*R (on the application of Pretty) v DPP* [2002] 1 AC 800). Some eight years later, the House of Lords was required to revisit the issue when Debbie Purdy argued that, if the DPP could not provide an assurance against prosecution, at least the DPP should be required to provide clear guidance as to the factors which would be taken into consideration in deciding whether to prosecute. The House of Lords accepted Debbie Purdy's argument, holding that the right to respect for private life under Article 8 of the Convention was engaged and that this meant that guidance had to be available so that individuals would know in advance how to conduct themselves so as to avoid breaking the law (*R (on the application of Purdy) v DPP* [2009] UKHL 45).

As the then current Code for Prosecutors failed to give sufficiently precise guidance, the DPP was required to revise it, producing an offence-specific guide. The DPP conducted a public consultation (at the same time issuing interim guidance), followed by revised guidance published in February 2010. The new policy identifies 16 factors which make it more likely that a prosecution will be brought: they include that the victim was under 18, that the victim had not reached a voluntary, settled, clear and informed decision to commit suicide and that the suspect had pressured the victim into committing suicide. The policy also identifies five factors which make a prosecution less likely: these include that the suspect

10 In force 1 February 2010.

was wholly motivated by compassion, that the actions of the suspect constitute acts of minor assistance only and that the actions of the suspect can be characterized as reluctant encouragement in the face of a determined, voluntary, settled, clear and informed decision to commit suicide (Director of Public Prosecutions 2010). Kay Gilderdale had been convinced that the guidelines, which were under discussion when she was charged, would lead to charges being dropped against her (Swain 2010). However, the charge which proceeded to trial, and of which Kay was acquitted, was attempted murder, not aiding and abetting suicide to which she pleaded guilty.

## Responsibility in the Criminal Law

We have previously explored the concept of responsibility in the criminal law as theorized by Hart, Gardner, Duff, Tadros and Cane (Bridgeman and Keating 2008; Lind et al. 2011). We do not wish to repeat ourselves here, so briefly summarize this as the ability to respond: according to Hart this involves 'the ability to understand what conduct legal rules or morality requires; to deliberate and reach decisions concerning these requirements and to conform to [and thus take control of] decisions when made' (Hart 1967, 360). Gardner has argued that it is part of being a self-respecting person

> to be able to give an intelligible rational account of herself, to be able to show that her actions were the actions of someone who aspired to live up to the proper standards. … She wants it to be the case that her actions were not truly wrongful, or if they were wrongful, that they were justified, or if they were not justified, that they were at least excused. (Gardner 1998, 590)

There is no dispute that when a person is involved in the death of another they should have to account for themselves. But does the law hear what they say? Does it see the position they were in? Is it capable of recognizing the complexity of the truth? Or do they have to account for their actions within a framework into which some may only partially fit? As the cases cited here reveal, there may be instances in which the *unreasonableness* of the defendant's conduct in killing makes a verdict of manslaughter by virtue of diminished responsibility an appropriate verdict,[11] even if it may only reveal a partial truth (focusing as it does, of course, upon the individual responsibility of the parent rather than a wider view). If one considers again the case of Melody Turnbull, one might well conclude that the decision to

11 However, if the Law Commission's proposals for a radical reform of the law of homicide were to be implemented, killing on the grounds of diminished responsibility would be designated 'second degree murder': it must be highly questionable whether this would be the appropriate label for parents who have killed in order to end their children's suffering (Law Commission 2006).

kill her two severely disabled sons because she feared they would be taken into care and that they would then not be cared for was appropriately described as diminished responsibility: irrational and born out of desperation, utter exhaustion and illness. It was one she bitterly regretted afterwards (Levin 2001, 28). On the other hand, if we had comprehensive information about her experiences of caring for her sons for over two decades and their complete dependence upon their parents, it might be that we could understand her fears for their care, at least, as being well grounded.

But what of the case of James Lawson? Were the facts appropriately reflected by the verdict of manslaughter on the grounds of diminished responsibility? The judge accepted that James thought he was acting in his daughter's best interests. His daughter, Sarah, had a long history of depression and self-harm and had attempted suicide three times in the week that James Lawson watched his daughter take an overdose and then smothered her with a pillow (Gysin 2001). On the facts, is it appropriate to describe the killing as irrational? Was it a *reasonable* compassionate act, albeit one where the father was close to or at the breaking point? The same questions can be asked of the circumstances of Kay Gilderdale. Had the prosecution been able to prove that Kay's actions had caused her daughter, Lynn's, death, Kay would have been charged with murder. It seems very probable that a diminished responsibility plea would then have been put forward which would have been accepted. Yet Kay acted on the basis of what her daughter wanted in an act of compassion that was starkly at odds with what she herself wanted. In an interview given after her trial she described how she acted as she did knowing it was what her daughter wanted, however much it was not what she wanted:

> I have never had a moment's regret. … If I had, I don't think I would be able to cope. I know I did what Lynn needed and now she is at peace. I never wanted her to go. I wanted her to stay. By helping her, I was going against what I was feeling and doing what I knew she wanted. The hardest thing that anybody can ever do in life is to watch their child die, when all you want to do is keep them here and make them better. (Swain 2010)

In cases such as these, there is very likely to be medical evidence upon which a plea of diminished responsibility can be built. As Ost has commented, cases such as James Lawson's

> illustrate the reality that although the courts have to work within the constraints of the criminal law, they are willing to invest the defence of diminished responsibility with a certain degree of elasticity in order to encompass situations where a spouse or relative faces tremendous pressure and kills their loved one to relieve suffering. Furthermore, the courts appear to recognize that in these circumstances, the suffering in question is felt by both the person who kills and the person who is killed. (Ost 2005, 360)

However, recognition of the suffering of both parent and child is not extended to every case.[12] Seeing her acts as deliberate and uncaring and failing to appreciate the hurt she was feeling, when remanding Yvonne Freaney to a psychiatric clinic, Judge Nicholas Cooke QC told her: 'There's evidence you have been harming yourself. Whatever has happened, that is not the way forward' (Salkeld and Faulkner 2010).

By accepting a plea of diminished responsibility the law may reduce the complexity of the story to such an extent as to at least distort the truth. And in other circumstances, if the test were to be stretched to accommodate 'deserving' cases, even less truth would be revealed about the full circumstances of the killing. As Gardner has pointed out, the essence of diminished responsibility is that the person's actions were *unreasonable*. But where the killing is one motivated more by compassion (than by illness) to save the loved child from further suffering, we might respond by saying 'I can understand why you did it' – in other words, the actions of the parent are *reasonable* (adapting Gardner's argument in relation to the plea of provocation, Gardner 1998, 591), although this does not make them right.

Tadros has argued that there 'is a strong case for treating these cases [assisted suicide and mercy killings] as distinctive' (Tadros 2008, 59). He comments:

> What we can say about these cases is that the defendant had a genuine and plausible, even if ultimately faulty, conception of how to respond appropriately to the autonomous desires of the victim,[13] and hence a genuine and plausible, if ultimately faulty, conception of respect for the life of the victim. That seems to me fundamentally distinct from, for example, cases of reckless killing or killing with diminished responsibility, where the defendant is insufficiently motivated by respect for the victim's life, however that is conceived. (Tadros 2008, 59–60)

Currently, if there is insufficient or no medical evidence to support a diminished responsibility plea, the law is incapable of hearing the reasons offered by the parent: it is murder. Such a case is that of Frances Inglis who killed her son, Thomas. Frances was grief stricken, believed that her son's life had ended when he sustained brain damage and that she was releasing him from hell. As she explained, she did not consider her actions to be murder:

---

12 Ost goes on to consider the case of *Latimer* [2001] 1SCR 3 where the Canadian Supreme Court rejected the defence of necessity to a charge of second degree murder by a father of his daughter who had a severe form of cerebral palsy, was quadriplegic and in severe pain; she discusses whether the landmark case of *Re A (conjoined twins)* [2000] 4 All ER 961 raises the possibility of such a defence here to mercy killings, favouring such a development in the context of medical mercy killings (2005, 366–70).

13 Tadros includes cases where, for example, the victim is in a persistent vegetative state and cannot consent: 'we must take into consideration what the victim would have wanted as a way of respecting their rational will over their life, but also the true value of what remains of their life regardless of how they would have come to see it' (2008, 59).

> I don't see it as killing or murder. The definition of murder is to take someone's life with malice in your heart. I did it with love in my heart, for Tom, so I don't see it as murder. I knew what I was doing was against the law. I don't know what name they would call it but I knew that the law would say it was wrong. I believed it would have been Tom's choice to have been allowed to die rather than have the intervention to keep him alive. (Pidd 2010)

The reports suggest that she was hysterical, not coping and was unable to accept the doctor's positive outlook for Thomas (Grice 2010, 25). Yet she was also capable of planning his death: researching how many grammes of heroin would be needed to kill her son and then obtaining both needles and the drug. While the concept of premeditation has no place in the law of murder, her behaviour led the judge to describe it as a 'calculated and consistent course of criminal conduct' (Grice 2010, 25). Unlike the cases of James Lawson and Kay Gilderdale, Frances was not acting in direct response to the wishes of her child, although she clearly believed she was acting in his best interests (nor was she actively caring for him at the time as he was in a nursing home). In the face of the medical view of Thomas' condition and her state of mind, one might view her actions as irrational, but she fell outside the scope of the diminished responsibility plea. She was thus convicted of murder with its mandatory life sentence.

Joanne Hill was also convicted of murder and sentenced to serve a minimum term of 15 years' in prison. The prosecution presented the killing of Naomi, who suffered from a mild form of cerebral palsy, as a selfish act by a mother who was ashamed of her daughter. Joanne's plea of manslaughter on the grounds of diminished responsibility was rejected by the jury, yet there was evidence that Joanne had suffered such severe post-natal depression that it seems her doctors would have sectioned her had she not gone voluntarily into hospital. She subsequently drank heavily and often did not even acknowledge Naomi. Just days before she killed Naomi, she asked her husband, Simon, if he would agree to Naomi being adopted. At the time she drowned Naomi her defence claimed that she was suffering from depression and some six months after doing so she was still being held in a secure mental hospital (Craven and Tozer 2008, 4). On one level one could perhaps say that this was simply a case where the medical evidence was disputed but it is worthy of rather more reflection than that. This seems to have been an irrational, unreasonable killing that is very different from the actions, of say, Kay Gilderdale. Even if a partial defence of mercy or compassionate killing existed, this would surely fall outside it. But was it murder? It is interesting, at the least, to note that in both Frances Inglis' and Joanne Hill's cases there was no long-term history of devoted care to draw upon.[14]

---

14 A further case, which resulted in a finding of manslaughter by diminished responsibility is that of Andrew Wragg, who killed his 10-year-old son, Jacob, who suffered from an incurable condition, Hunter's syndrome. Andrew Wragg had returned from three months in Iraq working as a security officer to pay off debts. He told his wife that he 'had

It is to the subject of caring responsibilities we now turn as we examine whether other accounts of responsibility offer insights which responsibility as accountability neglects.

## Caring Responsibilities: Invisible, Private and Ignored

The criminal law approaches these cases through an atomistic, rights-orientated, individual justice, framework. Defendants in the criminal courts are treated as autonomous individuals who choose to act and make choices to maximize individual interests (West 1987), and who look to the law both to protect their freedom and to protect them from conflict with others:

> [A]ccording to liberal legalism, the subjective experience of physical separation from the other determines both what we value (autonomy) and what we fear (annihilation). We value, and seek societal protection of, our autonomy: the liberal insists on my right to define and pursue my own life, my own path, my own identity, and my own conception of the good life free of interference from others. Because I am me and you are you, I value what I value, and you value what you value. The only value we truly share, then, is our joint investment in autonomy from each other; we both value our right to pursue our lives relatively free of outside control. We can jointly insist that our government grant us this protection. We also share the same fears. I fear the possibility – indeed the likelihood – that our ends will conflict, and you will frustrate my ends and in an extreme case cause my annihilation, and you fear the same thing about me. I want the right and the power to pursue my own chosen ends free of the fear that you will try to prevent me from doing so. You, of course, want the same. (West 1988, 8–9)

What this individualistic account leaves out is the connections which may exist between persons, such as parent and child, as result of which separation from the other is perhaps feared rather than desired and the instinct is to protect rather than harm.

Parents who take such drastic action put themselves at the mercy of the criminal process and of the construction of events in which they are portrayed as

---

looked into his [Jacob's] eyes and seen that he had no future' (Woolcock 2005, 11). The accounts of Jacob's condition and of the events of the days before he died given by Jacob's mother, his primary carer, and father became increasingly distant as did the animosity between them, and Jacob's mother became the main prosecution witness (Payne 2005, 13). Suspending his sentence, the trial judge Mrs Justice Anne Rafferty, told him she considered that Jacob's mother had been complicit in the killing and that she believed he would not have killed his son if he did not think his wife agreed with what he was doing (Woolcock and Hoyle 2005).

a cold, callous killer who sought to rid themselves of the unremitting burden of caring for a vulnerable dependant. It forces those who wish to refute this account either to rely upon diminished responsibility; internalizing the diminution within themselves as their inability to cope or to present themselves as self-sacrificing; sacrificing their freedom in order to release their child. The family of Frances Inglis, for example, described her as a 'courageous and compassionate mother' who 'sacrificed herself to end her son's life in the most humane way possible' (Bannerman 2010b). Inevitably, the criminal law focuses upon individual responsibility for past conduct with responsibility being understood as the ability to provide a rational account of the reasons for chosen and voluntary actions. Yet, the criminal law's approach to responsibility is not the only framework through which we should explore questions of responsibility in such cases. After all, these are cases in which family responsibilities intersect with criminal responsibility. We want to step back, to consider responsibilities for caring within families so that we can seek better to understand the factors which have placed these parents in a position where they were either so desperate that they could neither see right from wrong, or they followed the wrong course because it felt like the only way.

We have argued elsewhere for an understanding of 'responsibility in family life as both historic … and prospective … contextual and relational' (Lind et al. 2011, 10 referencing Cane 2002, 5, 31). As we observed, traditional accounts conceive of responsibility as relational in the sense of being owed by one to another arising from agreement or a particular role or determined by morality or law. Others have argued that responsibilities are relational in the sense that they arise from relationships with others rather than from agreements, moral norms or legal obligations. Carol Gilligan, for example, has contrasted responsibility as 'personal commitment and contractual obligation' with responsibility as response meaning, 'taking charge of yourself by looking at others around you, seeing what you need, seeing what they need, and taking the initiative to respond' (DuBois et al. 1985, 44). A relational account of responsibility focuses upon *response to the other* in the relationship, in contrast, for example, to the account given by Hart, above, of *response to legal rules or moral norms*. Responsibility is thus understood as 'interpersonal responsiveness', that is, responding to those to whom they are connected, to 'particularity and context' (Fiore and Nelson 2003, ix). Responsiveness to others then, importantly, is contextual and situated. Alongside the abstract determinations of rights-based approaches, we need to explore the particular: 'genuine moral dilemmas arise because the chief concern of moral deliberation is to respond appropriately to the persons with whom we are connected in various ways' (Lindemann Nelson 1999, 124). One of the distinguishing features between the cases under consideration is the extent to which there was responsiveness to the particular needs of the child, whether articulated by them or interpreted by their parent (although, as this is of limited relevance within the current legal framework,[15] the accounts we are relying upon provide us with insufficient information to enable us to elaborate on this point here). What we do wish to focus upon here is the invitation, indeed demand, of a relational approach to recognize that the ability of any one individual to respond to another to whom they are connected is not solely determined by their willingness or ability. Caring activity occurs within a time and place. What is expected of the individual depends upon social ordering, cultural expectations and public provision. The ability of the individual to care is affected by the support that is available to them as carers and, conversely, upon the obstacles which they are required to overcome in their caring. To explore this we must consider the social, cultural and political context for long-term intensive caring activity.

*The invisibility, gendered nature, and lack of value, of care* As Jonathan Herring has reminded us, caring is considered voluntary and informal, it is marginalized, viewed as unimportant, is unnoticed, unrecognized and invisible (Herring 2007a, 66). Participation in the public realm continues to be conditional upon the absence of any constraints arising from relationships, the needs of others or dependencies. Consequently, the nature and extent of dependency and care that occurs in the private domain can be ignored, remain unacknowledged. So too can the responsibility of others to support those who care. Despite the dependence of the functioning of the public realm and of society upon the work of those who care, maintaining the invisibility of this essential work perpetuates the lack of value accorded to caring activity.

The essential work of care is predominantly done by women; within families, it is predominantly mothers who fulfil day-to-day caring responsibilities (Cain, Kittay, Manhas, Herring, Newnham, George, and Lamont in this volume). When a child requires long-term and intensive caring because of severe disabilities, injuries sustained in an accident or debilitating illness, their day-to-day care is, most often, provided by their mother (Read and Clements 2002, 29). Social expectations establish for these mothers an imperative to care arising from 'accidents of our embeddedness in familial and social and historical contexts' (Held 2006, 14–15). In an effort to ensure their child receives the best possible care – which requires that caring acts are performed in a caring manner – mothers often undertake that care themselves. To meet the complex needs of their child they may develop a range of new skills which extend beyond mothering, to include nursing, medical technician, therapist, interpreter, entertainer, teacher. Frequently, the father's primary responsibility is to provide financially for the family. In some cases, including some of those considered here, the child's father, whilst *caring about* their child, separates themselves from their family leaving the responsibility to *care for* with the child's mother (using Joan Tronto's characterization 1993,

15 For example, the judge in suspending James Lawson's sentence of imprisonment took into account that 'at all times' James had believed he was acting in Sarah's best interests and out of love (Gysin 2001).

105–7). Given that mothers caring for children with disabilities have identified their partner as the greatest source of support (Read and Clements 2002, 30), it is reasonable to assume that having sole responsibility for caring increases the stress, isolation and sense of overwhelming responsibility (Dobson et al. 2001, 31). In some cases, the demands were so great, such as those faced by Melody and Ron Turnbull in caring for their sons, Robert and Richard, that shared care was the only option.

*Privatization of care* In her study of families caring for young children with disabilities, parents told Janice McLaughlin of their experiences of abandonment by family and friends, of 'refusals to care and rejections from both formal actors and agencies' and minimal public provision of care, which 'channelled' responsibility for care to the child's mother and to the private sphere (McLaughlin 2006, 1.3, 5.1). Advances in medical knowledge and technology, policies of community (meaning home) care, geographical dispersal of families, and withdrawal of friends and family (McLaughlin 2006, 5.6) provide the background to the privatization of intensive caring activity. Given the focus of the criminal law upon the actions of the individual, we are not able to consider the extent to which the mother was supported in her care by the state and caring professionals, by the community or family and friends. Nor is she asked to explain the extent to which others turned their backs on the family's needs, to which they were disowned or excluded from social occasions (Dobson et al. 2001, 27; McLaughlin 2006). Studies of families caring for children with disabilities reveal the extent of financial deprivation and lack of practical, material and emotional support available to them (Dobson et al. 2001). These cases raise most directly unasked questions about the limits of the practical and emotional support provided to carers by an uncaring society (with legislation directed to carers affording only limited assistance, Carers (Recognition and Services) Act 1995, Carers and Disabled Children Act 2000, Carers (Equal Opportunities) Act 2004) and the limits of public responsibility for the care of those with complex needs. Frequently, these cases are reported as if public responsibility to treat, care or support is simply not relevant, as if these are personal tragedies which the individual and their families must deal with. In others, the story is one echoed in studies of parents caring for children with disabilities, of inadequate services, inconsistent services and services which fail to meet their needs (Dobson et al. 2001; Read and Clements 2002, 35), which adds to the stress of caring (Wray and Wray 2004, 204), and reinforces the sense that the responsibility to care is confined within the family (Anderson and Elfert 1989). For example, Melody and Ron Turnbull had cared for their sons, both of whom had cerebral palsy, were blind, incontinent, could neither speak nor stand and each had the mental capacity of a six-month-old baby, with never more than a couple of hours' continuous sleep at night (Levin 2001), for the two decades of the boys' lives. Both Melody and her husband sought to secure the very best quality of care for their sons and this meant that there were difficulties with doctors, social services (who, for example, suggested at points that residential care might be a better option) and housing staff (over the provision of suitable accommodation for the family). They felt treated by social services as passive recipients of services and not as parents who were most directly concerned for their children's well-being and who had become experts in their children's needs as they cared for them all day, every day. Social services would not listen to what they wanted for their sons and they would not accept what they considered to be unsuitable provision; the result was no provision. Mencap, in their study, *No Ordinary Life*, noted the conclusions of the independent review of the care of Richard and Robert Turnbull that their deaths were not anticipated. The Mencap report continues:

> The experiences of parents recounted in this report challenge that view. If services had recognized the massive caring task the Turnbulls faced, the impact on their own health and wellbeing, and the evident lack of appropriate help available, it is hard to see how this event would have taken them so completely by surprise. (Mencap 2001, 33)

Melody Turnbull explained her actions: 'The truth is I could not take anymore and I knew they could not cope without me' (Mencap 2001, 33). In the abstract that seems questionable but put into context becomes understandable. The care given to Sarah Lawson by the NHS was the subject of an independent review (Durham 2001, 3). This review concluded that her care had been fragmented, management of her needs poor and that there had been a lack of communication between the different agencies involved (Frith 2004, 9). It also noted that there was no consideration given to the extent to which her parents were coping with the demands of caring for Sarah; enquiries would have revealed that her father had depression and 'was in an increasingly desperate state of mind over his daughter' (*The Independent* 2004, 30).

When caring is invisible and when it goes without question that caring responsibilities will be fulfilled by the family, there is no scope for admitting the difficulties of caring and, with past experiences of refusals of care, finding a way of asking for, or securing, support. We are not suggesting that the state loses moral warrant to prosecute such parents on the basis of a prior failure of these families by the state, rather that to respond by punishing the parent without any recognition of the wider circumstances perpetuates the invisibility of caring responsibility, the privatization of care and the lack of value accorded to caring.[16] Questions about the responsibility of the state to families with intensive caring needs continue to be avoided. Caring for children is currently predominantly a personal responsibility of parents but do the community, society and state not only fail to support parents expected to provide long-term intensive caring but actually place obstacles – environmental obstacles, discriminatory attitudes, disdainful responses – in their way?

16 We thank Jonathan Herring for posing this question.

*Obstacles to the provision of care* The turning away from families caring for a severely disabled member or a child with a debilitating illness is a reflection of attitudes to illness and disability which reinforce the responsibility to care as a private, parental duty. One parent in the study by Dobson et al. said 'It was as if we didn't exist. Nobody wanted to know us' (Dobson et al. 2001, 28), although in public they and their child come under a penetrating and critical gaze. Discriminatory attitudes, disdain, hostility towards, and even bullying of, the long-term sick and disabled abound. The experience of another parent of 'harsh stares and unthinking questions' (Dobson et al. 2001, 27) was echoed by Yvonne Freaney who, when discovered by police holding the hand of her dead 11-year-old, severely autistic son, Glen, told police: 'At least now nobody can point fingers at him'.[17] Ron Turnbull is noted to have said, 'At the end of the day people thought my sons were worthless, utterly worthless, and we were too. I thought they were very special' (Mencap 2001, 5). They retreated from the outside world because of the stares, nudges and hurtful comments (Braid 2001). There was evidence before the court that Joanne Hill blamed herself for her daughter, Naomi's, disability about which she was 'acutely embarrassed'(Craven and Tozer 2008, 4). As Alice Maynard, Chair of Scope, observed, this case highlighted the wider issue that 'society continues to portray disability in a negative light, creating shame and stigma around impairment' (Craven and Tozer 2008, 4).

Currently, few making judgement will really have insight into what is involved in caring in such circumstances, the isolation, the expectations or the obstacles. Something of the reality of the experience is summarized in the Mencap report, *No Ordinary Life*, who were told by parents of:

> [T]he daily battle these families have had to get even basic and essential needs met. … [T]hose parents who used residential respite services, only to find their son or daughter dehydrated at the end of the visit, or with pressure sores. … [T]he health services who would not listen to parents and left one young man in terrible pain, commenting that 'this is just the way they are sometimes'. … [T]he delays and confusion, and the lack of priority accorded to families who are carrying out what we have demonstrated to be a massive caring task, many without a functional level of sleep. … [T]he social isolation experienced by a great many of the parents, where previous relationships with friends, relatives, and all too often partners, have faded away. [T]he struggle to cope with the competing needs of other children. In short, parents have learned bitterly and painfully that very few people know how to help. (Mencap 2001, 32–3)

The current response of abandoning parents to care, 'channeling' as Janice McLaughlin terms it, the responsibility to the privacy of the home, rendering it

17 The report also details that she had recently separated from her husband and had been living with Glen in a series of temporary accommodations (Salkeld and Faulkner 2010).

invisible and then castigating them for what, may, in the circumstances, in their marginalized and secluded position (McLaughlin 2006), have seemed to be the right, or the only, thing to do is to ignore social and public responsibility for the vulnerable and their carers. The just response of a caring society to such cases would surely be to ask honest questions about the limits of social and public obligations to support parents to fulfil intensive caring responsibilities.

## The Just Response of a Caring Society?

As the case studies reveal, the stories of parents who resort to the compassionate killing of their child are complex. Their circumstances are all different, their experiences and reasons for the action they took varied. The decision may have been born out of the exhaustion that comes from years of intensive caring, despair, a profound need to protect the child from further suffering, a respect for the child's own wishes or a sense that this is what the child would have wanted. The decision may, of course, also result from the mental state of the parent. It would be naive to think that there may not be other reasons and mixed motives for some parents; a sense of shame, perhaps, or a focus upon what is best for them rather than their child.

The law has developed according to certain paradigms, punishing, justifying and excusing as an 'emblematic example of law's common correspondence with a male point of view' (Conaghan 2002):[18]

> The Rule of Law generally and legal doctrine in its particularity are coherent reactions to the existential dilemma that follows from the liberal's description of the male experience of material separation from the other: the Rule of Law acknowledges the danger of annihilation and the Rule of Law protects the value of autonomy. … It neither recognizes nor values intimacy, and neither recognizes not protects against separation. (West 1988, 58–9)

Neither does it recognize the complexities of intimacy and connection.

As we have noted elsewhere, family responsibility, while incorporating legal duties and obligations, is more than the sum of these (Lind et al. 2011, 13). Certainly many of the parents we have considered have cared for their children day and night, day in day out, year after year, doing much more than their legal duty. At this interface between family responsibilities and criminal responsibility, then, in rightly holding parents to account for their actions, somehow the law has to hear and make sense of these stories and determine which killings are appropriately labelled as murder (with a mandatory life sentence) and which should escape this degree of censure. Courts have to decide if the person who kills a loved one is a

18 Describing the sex discrimination and tort case of *Waters v Metropolitan Police Commissioner* [2000] 1 WLR 1607.

threat to society and whether punishment would serve any purpose (see Ost 2005, 361). And in doing so the law must protect the vulnerable: those whose condition is such that they are either incapable of making their wishes known or could be made to feel such a burden to those caring for them, upon whom they may be completely dependent, that they are willing to sacrifice themselves. We need to be very wary about any law which weakens this protection or seems to lessen the value of life (see Hayes 2005, 307). Yet currently, the law appears to leave both carer, and cared for, vulnerable (Biggs and Mackenzie 2006).

Yet, the only way the law may respond currently where the charge is one of murder (rather than assisting suicide) is by way of the diminished responsibility plea. Some commentators take the view that this is the most appropriate response because the decision to take a loved one's life is likely to be guided by emotion and not by reason (Ost 2005, 370). While this may be true in some instances, it does not seem to be wholly appropriate for others that we have explored, nor, under the revised diminished responsibility plea, may it continue to be possible. But it is not enough that a murder conviction is avoided. Nor is it enough that in many instances a low sentence is given. Gardner has argued that the gist of an excuse is that the person lived up to the standards of character which were demanded of her (Gardner 1998, 597–8). Could it not be said that the act of care involved in the compassionate killing by a parent of a child may, in some circumstances at least, live up to the standard of character expected? This is not to suggest that the killing is even partially justified, but that consideration should be given to a separate partial defence of mercy/compassionate killing which operates as an excuse and enables us to say that we understand why the parent acted as he or she did. Indeed, Melody Turnbull's husband, Ron, who had shared the care of their two sons, has said 'Nothing can justify what Melody did, but I understand' (Braid 2001, 1–2). When caring remains invisible and undervalued; when caring is kept out of sight in the private sphere; when discrimination against the sick and disabled abounds, there is little attempt to understand.

This means that, as the Law Commission has recommended, there should a public consultation (similar to but broader than the recent one on assisted suicide) on whether there should be a new tailor-made offence or partial defence to murder of 'mercy killing' based on 'acting out of compassion'. As the Law Commission stated, 'there would need to be a much wider debate before concluding that the concept of "compassion", as a motive, is in itself a sufficiently secure foundation for a "mercy" killing offence or partial defence' (Law Commission 2006, para.7.29) but there does already seem to be some support for it being regarded as a different form of homicide (Mitchell 1998, 468). And this wider debate must confront societal expectations, the value of care, the limits of public responsibility to care and societal obstacles to caring. And although our focus has been upon parental killings, consideration would also have to be given to how the relationship between the parties would be delineated. If any such law were to be enacted, there would, of course, be hard cases but that might be a price worth paying for a law that 'preserves the moral significance of the defendant's motive in the light of facts about the victim's life' (Tadros 2008, 60) and is more reflective of the complexities of the circumstances driving parents who take this most ultimate of steps; where responsibility means both accountability and response to all those around us.

## Addendum

Since writing this chapter, Francis Inglis' appeal against her murder conviction has been heard. The judgment provides further insight into Francis Inglis's view of what had happened and should happen: it seems she was so desperate for the facts about her son to be told that she would not consider entering a plea of guilty on the basis of diminished responsibility (*Inglis* [2010] EWCA Crim 2637, [42]). After acknowledging that 'on any view this case is a tragedy', Lord Judge CJ stated that

> we must underline that the law of murder does not distinguish between murder committed for malevolent reasons and murder motivated by love. Subject to well established partial defences, like … diminished responsibility, mercy killing is murder. … How problems of mercy killing, euthanasia and assisting suicide should be addressed must be decided by parliament, which, for this purpose at any rate, should be reflective of the conscience of the nation. In this appeal we are constrained to apply the law as we find it to be. (*Inglis* [2010] EWCA Crim 2637, [37]–[39])

Accordingly, the appeal against conviction was dismissed. Lord Judge then considered the appeal against the minimum term of nine years' imprisonment, believing it to be the first murder case involving a mercy killing to have come before the court. His Lordship described the combination of aggravating factors (the elements of planning, the vulnerability of the victim and the abuse of position of trust) and mitigating factors (such as the belief that the murder was an act of mercy) as involving 'one of the most difficult sentencing decisions faced in this court (at [61]) but concluded that the minimum term should be reduced to five years' imprisonment.

## References

Allen, H. 1987. *Justice Unbalanced: Gender, Psychiatry and Judicial Decisions*. Milton Keynes: Open University Press.

Anderson, J.M. and Elfert, H. 1989. Managing chronic illness in the family: Women as caretakers. *Journal of Advanced Nursing*, 14, 735–43.

Bannerman, L. 2010a. Jury heckled over murder verdict for mother who 'acted out of love'. *The Times*, 21 January, 7.

Bannerman, L. 2010b. 'I am not a murderer, I'm a mother', says Frances Inglis; Bewildered family plan to fight on for 'compassionate killer'. *The Times*, 23 January.

Biggs, H. and Mackenzie, R. 2006. End of life decision-making, policy and the criminal justice system: Untrained carers assuming responsibility [UCARes] and their uncertain legal liabilities. *Genomics, Society and Policy*, 2(1), 118–28.

Bourget, D. and Gagne P. 2002. Maternal filicide in Quebec. *Journal of the American Academy and the Law*, 30, 345–57.

Braid, M. 2001. Why I had to kill my boys. *The Independent*, 3 March, 1–2.

Bridgeman, J. and Keating, H. 2008. Introduction: Conceptualising family responsibility, in *Responsibility, Law and the Family*, edited by J. Bridgeman, H. Keating and C. Lind. Aldershot: Ashgate, 1–17.

Campbell, D. 2009. 800 Britons in waiting list for Swiss suicide clinic. *The Observer*, 31 May.

Cane, P. 2002. *Responsibility in Law and Morality*. Oxford: Hart.

Clarkson, C.M.V., Keating, H.M. and Cunningham, S.R. 2010. *Clarkson and Keating: Criminal Law, Text and Materials*, 7th edition. London: Sweet and Maxwell.

Conaghan, J. 2002. Law, harm and redress: A feminist perspective. *Legal Studies*, 22, 319–39.

Craven, N. and Tozer, J. 2008. Evil mother killed my little princess. *Daily Mail*, 24 September, 4.

Dell, S. 1984. *Murder into Manslaughter; The Diminished Responsibility Defence in Practice*. Oxford: Oxford University Press.

Director of Public Prosecutions 2010. Policy for Prosecutors in Respect of Cases of Encouraging and Assisting Suicide.

Dobson, B., Middleton, S. and Beardsworth, A. 2001. *The Impact of Childhood Disability on Family Life*. York: Joseph Rowntree Foundation.

d'Orban, P.T. 1979. Women who kill their children. *British Journal of Psychiatry*, 134, 560–71.

DuBois, E.C., Dunlap, M.C., Gilligan, C.J., MacKinnon, C.A. and Menkel-Meadow, C.J. 1985. Feminist discourse, moral values, and the law – A conversation. *Buffalo Law Review*, 34, 11–87.

Durham, M. 2001. Sarah made regular attempts at suicide. But a nurse just told her to find a hobby. *The Independent*, 16 May, 3.

Fiore, R.N. and Nelson, H.L. 2003. Recognition, responsibility and rights: An introduction, in *Recognition, Responsibility and Rights: Feminist Ethics and Social Theory*, edited by R.N. Fiore and H.L. Nelson. Lanham, MD: Rowman & Littlefield Publishers Ltd.

Flynn, S. 2009. *Filicide: A Literature Review*. Manchester: University of Manchester.

Friedman, S.H., Horowitz, S.M. and Resnick, P.J. 2005. Child murder by mothers: A critical analysis of the current state of knowledge and a research agenda. *American Journal of Psychiatry*, 162, 1578–87.

Friedman, S.H., Holdon, C., Hrouda, D.R. and Resnik, P.J. 2008. Maternal filicide and its intersection with suicide. *Brief Treatment and Crisis Intervention*, 8, 283–91.

Frith, F. 2004. Mental Health Crisis: How a father was driven to kill his own daughter. *The Independent*, 27 July, 9.

Gardner, J. 1998. The gist of excuses. *Buffalo Law Review*, 1, 575–98.

Gilligan, C. 1982. In a different voice: Psychological theory and women's development. Cambridge, MA: Harvard University Press.

Grice, E. 2010. Cold blooded killer or a loving mum. *The Daily Telegraph*, 22 January, 25.

Gysin, C. 2001. Mercy for man who killed sick daughter; father who smothered depression victim is given a suspended jail term. *Daily Mail*, 9 June, 22.

Hart, H.L.A. 1967. Varieties of responsibility. *Law Quarterly Review*, 83, 346–64.

Hayes, M. 2005. Criminal trials where a child is the victim: Extra protection for children or a missed opportunity? *Child and Family Law Quarterly*, 307–28.

Held, V. 1995. *Justice and Care: Essential Readings in Feminist Ethics*. Boulder CO: Westview Press.

Held, V. 2006. *The Ethics of Care: Personal, Political, and Global*. New York: Oxford University Press.

Herring, J. 2007a. Where are the carers in healthcare law and ethics? *Legal Studies*, 27, 51–73.

Herring, J. 2007b. Familial homicide, failure to protect and domestic violence: Who's the victim? *Criminal Law Review*, 923–33.

Hirst, M. 2009. Assisted suicide after Purdy: The unresolved issue. *Criminal Law Review*, 12, 870.

Kittay, E.F. 2002. When caring is just and justice is caring: Justice and mental retardation, in *The Subject of Care: Feminist Perspectives on Dependency*, edited by E.F. Kittay and E.K. Feder. Lanham, MD: Rowman & Littlefield Publishers, 257–76.

Laville, S. 2010a. Mother gave her daughter a cocktail of lethal drugs after she begged for ME suffering to end, court told. *The Guardian*, 19 January.

Laville, S. 2010b. As mercy killer is freed, judge asks: 'Why was she in court?': Trial of mother who helped daughter die reopens debate on assisted suicide. *The Guardian*, 26 January.

Law Commission. 2003. Partial Defences to Murder. Consultation Paper No. 173. London.

Law Commission. 2005. A New Homicide Act for England and Wales. Consultation Paper No. 177. London.

Law Commission 2006. Murder, Manslaughter and Infanticide. Law Com No. 314. London.

Levin, A. 2001. Fatal Embrace – the mother who loved her sons so much she had to kill them. *Daily Mail*, 3 March.

Liem, M. and Koendraadt, F. 2008. Filicide: A comparative study of maternal versus paternal child homicide. *Criminal Behaviour and Mental Health*, 18, 166–76.

Lind, C., Keating, H. and Bridgeman, J. 2011. Introduction: Taking family responsibility or having it imposed?, in *Taking Responsibility, Law and the Changing Family*, edited by C. Lind, H. Keating and J. Bridgeman. Aldershot: Ashgate, 1–21.

Lindemann Nelson, H. 1999. Always connect: Towards a parental ethics of divorce, in *Mother Troubles: Rethinking Contemporary Maternal Dilemmas*, edited by J.E. Hanigsberg and S. Ruddick. Boston: Beacon Press, 117–35.

Mackay, R. 2010. The Coroners and Justice Act 2009 – partial defences to murder: (2) The new diminished responsibility plea. *Criminal Law Review*, 290–302.

Marleau, J.D., Poulin, B., Webanck, T., Roy, R. and Laporte, L. 1999. Paternal filicide: A study of 10 men. *Canadian Journal of Psychiatry*, 44, 57–63.

McColgan, A. 1993. In defence of battered women who kill. *Oxford Journal of Legal Studies*, 13(4), 508–29.

McLaughlin, J. 2006. Conceptualising intensive caring activities: The changing lives of families with young disabled children. *Sociological Research Online*, 11(1), available at <http://www.socresonline.org.uk/11/1/mclaughlin.html> (accessed 24 May 2010).

Mencap. 2001. *No Ordinary Life*. London: Mencap.

Miles, J. 2009. The Coroners and Justice Act 2009: a 'dog's breakfast' of homicide reform. *Archbold News*, 6–9.

Ministry of Justice. 2009. *Impact Assessment: Homicide.* Available online at <www.justice.gov.uk/publications/coroners-justice-bill.htm> (accessed 18 March 2010).

Mitchell, B. 1998. Public perceptions of homicide and criminal justice. *British Journal of Criminology*, 38(3), 453–72.

Morris, A. and Wilcynski, A. 1993. Parents who kill their children. *Criminal Law Review*, 31–6.

NSPCC Evaluation Department and the NSPCC Safeguarding Information Service. 2009. *Child Killings in England and Wales*. Available online at <http://www.nspcc.org.uk/Inform/research/briefings/child_killings_in_england_and_wales_wda67213.html> (accessed 17 May 2010).

Ost, S. 2005. Euthanasia and the defence of necessity: Advocating a more appropriate legal response. *Criminal Law Review*, 355–70.

Payne, S. 2005. Jacob's mother denies attempt to blacken her husband's name. *The Daily Telegraph*, 4 March, 13.

Pidd, H. 2010. 'Better he is in heaven than hell on earth.' Mother guilty of murdering disabled son. *The Guardian*, 21 January.

Read, J. and Clements, L. 2002. *Disabled Children and the Law*. London: Jessica Kingsley.

Resnick, P.J. 1969. Child murder by parents: A psychiatric review of filicide. *American Journal of Psychiatry*, 126, 325–34.

Salkeld, L. and Faulkner, K. 2010. 'At least now nobody can point at him'. *Daily Mail*, 19 May.

Seale, C. 2006. National survey of end-of-life decisions made by UK medical practitioners. *Palliative Medicine*, 20, 3.

Smith, K., Flatley, J., Coleman, K., Osborne, S., Kaiza, P. and Roe, S. 2010. *Homicides, Firearm Offences and Intimate Violence 2008/09*. London: Home Office.

Starmer, K. 2009. House of Commons Public Bill Committee on the Coroners and Justice Bill (4th sitting) (5 February 2009). Available at <www.parliament.the-stationery-office.co.uk/pa/cm200809/cmpublic/cmpbcor.htm>.

Swain, G. 2010. 'I held her arm as she fell asleep for the final time. How can they say I murdered Lynn when I just loved her so much?' *Daily Mail*, 28 January.

Tadros, V. 2008. The limits of manslaughter, in *Criminal Liability for Non-Aggressive Death*, edited by C.M.V. Clarkson and S. Cunningham. Aldershot: Ashgate, 35–60.

The Independent. 2004. Leader column: We must confront our fears and face up to this tragic epidemic of self-harm. *The Independent*, 27 July, 30.

Tronto, J. 1993. Moral Boundaries: The Political Argument for an Ethic of Care. New York: Routledge.

Walker, A., Flatley, J., Kershaw, C. and Moon, D. (eds). 2010. *Crime in England and Wales 2008/9*. London, Home Office.

West, R. 1987. The difference in women's hedonic lives: A phenomenological critique of feminist legal theory. *Wisconsin Women's LJ*, 3, 81–145.

West, R. 1988. Jurisprudence and gender. *University of Chicago Law Review*, 1–72.

West, R. 1997. *Caring for Justice*. New York: New York University Press.

Woolcock, N. 2005. Father toasted 'mercy killing' of son. *The Times*. 1 March, 11.

Woolcock, N. and Hoyle, B. 2005. Fomer SAS soldier is cleared of murdering severely disabled son. *The Times*, 13 December 2005, 4.

Wray, D. and Wray, S. 2004. Andrew: A journey – A parents' perspective. *Child: Care, Health & Development*, 30(3), 201–6.

Yarwood, D. 2004. *Child Homicides: Review of Statistics and Studies* (compiled for Dewar Research). Available at <www.dewar4research.org/docs/chom.pdf> (accessed 16 May 2010).

# Chapter 14
# Sufficiency of Home Care for Extraordinary Children: Gender and Health Law in Canada

Kiran Pohar Manhas

## Introduction

> Care is at the very root of women's history, as it is around care that the main part of women's destiny is woven. It has been the main focus of their activity and has therefore influenced what has been expected of them. It even shapes the destiny of those women who, today, do not wish to be burdened with it. (Colliere 1986, 95)

The gendered division of labour cannot be ignored (Armstrong and Armstrong 2004). While women were obliged 'to assure the continuity of life', men were required to repel death (Colliere 1986). This set the stage for a valuation of cure over care. These distinctions assured a lowly status to home-based healthcare which involve long-term caring rather than acute curing.

Long-term home and community care are some of the 'fastest growing components of the health care system' in Canada (Royal Commission on the Future of Health Care in Canada 2002, 171). There is no single definition of home care. Generally, home care involves 'an array of services that allow individuals who suffer some mental or physical incapacity to live at home and receive the care they need' (Royal Commission on the Future of Health Care in Canada 2002, 173). It ranges from personal care and home-making support to professional services (ibid). Home care has been endorsed for reasons that include public preference, technological advances, perceived financial savings, and suggested benefits to patients and family related to independence and quality of life (ibid).

With advances in home care in Canada comes a new population of children. These children have significant physical or developmental disabilities but are able to live at home (Peter et al. 2007). The novelty of this population stems from the fact that as recently as a decade ago, these children would not have survived their disabilities or could not have lived outside an institution (Peter et al. 2007). Although able to live at home, many of these children rely on medical technologies or significant medical care (Goldberg et al. 1994). For these children with *extraordinary* care needs (ECNs, also known as *complex* or *special* care needs), the relocation to home enables them to experience many facets of a 'traditional childhood' such as playing with siblings, going to school, or enjoying recreational activities. However, this experience is anything but 'traditional' given the extraordinary reliance on technology and care providers. Home care results in increased burdens of caring responsibility upon already over-burdened formal and informal care-givers, who are primarily female (Status of Women Canada 1999; Peter 2000; Armstrong and Kits 2001; Canadian Policy Research Network 2005). In *One Hundred Years of Caregiving*, Armstrong and Kits (2001, 12) summarized the literature on the gendered distribution of care-giving:

> The clear answer to the "Who provides [care?]" question is women. As daughters, mothers, partners, friends, or as volunteers, women are the overwhelming majority of unpaid primary caregivers and spend more time than men in providing care. Women are much more likely than men to do personal care and offer emotional support. Men's contributions are more likely to be concentrated in care management or household maintenance, shopping or transportation. In other words, women are more likely to provide the care that is daily and inflexible while men provide care that can be more easily planned and organized around paid work. And men are more likely than women to get formal help when they do provide care, on the assumptions that they must have paid jobs and that they lack the skills necessary to provide care.

Literature on the social, ethical consequences and effect upon health of home care, especially for the elderly, is easy to find. It is difficult, however, to detect legal scholarship in this area, and more so in the pediatric context (Peter et al. 2007). The interests of women and children are not served by this gap.

This chapter will begin to address this gap using a feminist legal analysis. First, the legislation governing the funding of home care services in Canada is analysed to expose gender bias. The analysis then turns to the small subset of relevant case law. This critique focuses on two cases given their unique directness and saliency to the issue of sufficiency of provincial government funding for home care for children with ECNs. In *Dassonville-Trudel (Guardian ad litem of) v Halifax Regional School Board*, 2004 NSCA 82 (*Dassonville-Trudel*), the Nova Scotia Court of Appeal (NSCA) considered a mother's call for increased funding for the home care of her autistic daughter. This case looked at family income and the question of whether child protective services were required if funding was not increased. The second case, *McQueen v Nova Scotia (Coordinator for Home Care)*, 2006 NSSC 127(*McQueen*), concerned a 35-year-old woman with cerebral palsy, and her mother, who appealed against the denial of home care funding to facilitate her de-institutionalization. The Nova Scotia Supreme Court (NSSC) relied heavily on the mother–daughter dynamic in its decision.

This legal analysis exposes the pervasive subordination and oppression of women and children in deliberations about extraordinary care and home settings through an examination of the public–private divide and its ability to subordinate women and an undercurrent of gender bias. The outcomes of these cases are not entirely negative; rather they represent a mix of small victories and major losses for these complainant families – victories presented as small forms of recognition of the over-reliance on the 'private' realm, and of the inherent susceptibility of these children and their mothers. Opportunities to rectify biases do, therefore, exist. There is room within the law, especially the common law, to promote greater equity in the distribution of care responsibilities for children with ECNs. Avenues for legal reform to aid mothers and their children in attaining sufficient home care support are plausible if the small victories are recognized and harnessed. Such avenues are discussed in the critique of each case.

## The Legislative Framework

Canadians prize healthcare and expect equal access to it (Brown 1993). Canada has attained some national uniformity on healthcare through a delicate balance of federal and provincial legislative authority. This uniformity is far from complete. The constitutional division of powers in Canada provides the provinces with the bulk of the authority over health matters (Constitution Act, 1867, 30 & 31 Vict., c. 3 (U.K.), ss.91 and 92). The federal government's health-related jurisdiction is limited to the military, marine hospitals, First Nations' populations and national public health issues.

A spending power, nonetheless, 'allows the federal government to indirectly fund programs of social insurance by making financial grants to the provinces that the provinces can then use to pay for the programs' (Lahey 2007, 25). The federal Canada Health Actaims to realize universal accessibility and characterization of healthcare across the country by laying out criteria for the provinces to meet in their implementation of provincial health insurance programmes (Canada Health Act, R.S.C. 1985, c. C-6 (CHA); Lahey 2007). Provinces are motivated to follow these criteria because federal funds are available to compliers.

Section 7 of the CHA outlines the five hallmarks of Canada's highly revered public healthcare system: public administration, comprehensiveness, universality, portability and accessibility. These attributes apply only to 'insured health services' that include hospital services, physician services and surgical-dental services provided to insured persons (CHA s.2). The 'equal accessibility' provision for *healthcare* in the CHA relates to services provided in hospital or by physicians. But *care required to improve the health* of individuals and the population entails many more services and care provided in various locales and by various practitioners. This distinction reinforces the separation between *care* and *cure*, between *nurses* and *doctors*, and ultimately between *women* and *men* (Colliere 1986).

Home care is specifically excluded as an 'insured health service' in the CHA, but is included in the definition of 'extended health care services' (CHAs.2). Provinces are open to determine the level and form of publicly funded home support provided in their jurisdiction. There are no requirements for universality, comprehensiveness, accessibility, portability, or public administration for extended healthcare services (Gray 2000). This results in a 'patchwork' of different home care programmes across Canada (Gray 2000, 178). The patchwork is further extended and complicated intra-provincially as rural–urban differences also play a role in the availability of resources (Armstrong and Armstrong 2004). Generalizations about home care support become impossible. The diversity of conditions, illnesses, families, patients, and settings that could be involved in home care further compound this difficulty. At best, two generalities arise. First, each province and territory offers some form of assessment, case management and funding support under a public home care programme. Secondly, public home care support is severely complicated and diverse in organization, implementation and realization.

*Myriad parties, unclear responsibilities*

The exclusion of home care from the CHA has complicated the legislative governance of pediatric home care. In Alberta, for example, four provincial ministries are involved with pediatric home care: the Ministry of Health and Wellness, the Ministry of Education, the Ministry of Children and Youth Services and the Ministry of Seniors and Community Supports. With multiple governmental bodies involved, the organization and delivery of home care becomes increasingly confusing. The question of 'who is responsible?' is increasingly difficult to answer.

The practice of home care is further complicated by the myriad parties involved. In Alberta, a non-exhaustive list of parties involved in the care of a child with ECNs living at home includes the parents, the siblings, the extended family and friends, the community-based home care team, the hospital-based experts (in areas such as pediatric care, acute care and critical care), the administrative team monitoring the disbursement of provincial funds and the public medical and social programmes for children with disabilities (including Alberta Aids to Daily Living (AADL) and Family Support for Children with Disabilities (FSCD)). Different professions and training colour these parties, such as medicine, nursing, respiratory therapy, occupational therapy, social work and home care aid workers. Communication and clarity of roles, expectations and responsibilities is necessary. However, this is not always available (Kirk 2001; Peter et al. 2007).

There is a process to the initiation and delivery of home care. Despite their differences, this process is relatable between provinces. In Alberta, an agreement (the 'Care Agreement') between the provincial government and the family (as represented by the parent or guardian) outlines the amount of provided public aid, the government's responsibilities, and the family's responsibilities (Family Support for Children with Disabilities Act, S.A. 2003, c. F-5.3, s.4 and Alta. Reg. 140/2004, ss.3–6). Governments do not enter into Care Agreements unless the families (usually mothers) undertake a threshold level of responsibilities (Mitchell, Personal Communication, January 13, 2007). The power imbalance between the state and families threatens the fairness of the Care Agreement's allocation of responsibilities.

Home care legislation directs dispute resolution regarding the Care Agreement to mediation and arbitration, followed by appeal to administrative review boards and then appeal to the court system (FSCD Act, S.A. 2003, c. F-5.3, ss.6 and 7 and Alta. Reg. 140/2004). The power and effectiveness of the appeals process has received little scrutiny. This is deeply unfortunate. Legislators rely on this process to equalize the power imbalance between families and government, hopefully striving for fairness. However, uncertainty marks its effectiveness and oppressive trends pervade its application.

The devaluation of care work is evident in the exclusion of home care from Canada's public healthcare system. The distribution of responsibilities is complex, convoluted and resistant to input from persons outside government. The literature is also clear. The overwhelming majority of the care-giving responsibilities fall on mothers and families, with some supplemental support from the public sphere (Lantos and Kohrman 1992; Bjornsdottir 2002; Armstrong and Armstrong 2004; Wang and Barnard 2004; Kirk et al. 2005). This chapter considers whether these trends are recognized, redressed or supported by adjudicators, including the judiciary.

## Case Law: Insufficiency of Government Home Care Support

Many people have responsibilities for the care of children with ECNs living at home. The family and the government, however, represent the two major parties fulfilling care-giving responsibilities for these children with the former represented predominantly by the mother and the latter by the public healthcare system. The tension between mothers and the public healthcare system about how care should be allocated in home care conjures the division between public and private sectors, and its injurious consequences for women.

Feminist scholarship has long recognized 'the ideological division of life into apparently opposing spheres of public and private activities, and public and private responsibilities' (Boyd 1996, 162). The foundations of this division are considered highly gendered, rooted in neo-liberal political ideology, and quite detrimental to children and families:

> We have a historic and highly romanticized affair with the ideal of the private and the individual, as contrasted with the public and the collective, as the appropriate units of focus in determining social good. After all, the very concept of the private defines the domain of the individual – an unregulated space where individual freedom reigns and in which each would-be-king can construct his castle. If a child is part of that private landscape, it is deemed a private matter, not the occasion for public subsidy or support. Children are like any other item of consumption, a matter of individual preference and individual responsibility. (Fineman 2001, 1403)

The proverbial castle remains family and home, while the public and collective have focused on markets and institutions (Boyd 1996). Women also have historically been relegated to private domains, which excluded them from recognition, valuation, participation in and assistance from the male-dominated public realm (MacKinnon 1982). Productivity, and hence value, has been limited to the public institutions (MacKinnon 1982). The public/private division obscured injustice and unfairness within the private realm of family and home (Boyd 1996).

The public/private dichotomy augments the inherent vulnerabilities of these families and children. Cardona (2004, 37) defined vulnerability as 'an internal risk factor of the subject or system that is exposed to a hazard and corresponds to its intrinsic predisposition to be affected, or to be susceptible to damage'. The families of children with ECNs have a heightened predisposition for needing medical care (for the child and to address the stress and exhaustion of care-givers), divorce, debt and social isolation (Williams et al. 2005; Carnevale et al. 2006; Carnevale 2007). A myriad factors contribute to these inherent predispositions, such as the child's physical state, latent emotional instability in the family, a family's precarious economic position, and the social stigma associated with children with ECNs (Wang and Barnard 2004). The Care Agreement generally favours the state and, hence, tends to augment the susceptibility of the family and child to the detrimental consequences of inadequately moderated care-giving burdens.

The appeals process for Care Agreements represents an avenue through which to contest the disparities in resources, powers and burdens between mothers and government in pediatric home care. However, the two cases explored here demonstrate the limits to achieving fairness, that is the removal of oppressive tactics such as exploitation and powerlessness (Young 1990). *Dassonville-Trudel* and *McQueen* buttress the public/private distinction, especially as it relates to the allocation of responsibilities, and augment the vulnerabilities of these children and their mothers. This critique will first focus on the facts and issues of each case. After such introduction, the findings of each case will be discussed to distinguish the small victories and major losses. The critique will conclude by exposing the undercurrent of gender bias through these judgments.

### *The facts and issues*

The facts and issues of *Dassonville-Trudel* and *McQueen* set the stage for the elaboration and discussion of the judicial appeals process in funding disputes between mothers and daughters, on one hand, and the public home care programs, on the other.

*Dassonville-Trudel* In *Dassonville-Trudel*, a mother (Joyce Dassonville) appealed to the NSCA on behalf of herself and her daughter Dominique from a judgment of the Supreme Court of Nova Scotia (*Dassonville-Trudel (Guardian ad litem of) v Halifax Regional School Board* (2002), 205 N.S.R. (2d) 88; *Dassonville-Trudel (Guardian ad litem of) v Halifax Regional School Board*, 2004 NSCA 82). Nine-year-old Dominique suffered from a severe form of autistic spectrum disorder (ASD). Her extreme ECNs made her almost 'unmanageable' (*Dassonville-Trudel* 2004, at [2]). She required constant supervision, was not toilet trained, had a penchant for violent behaviour, and was unable to communicate (*Dassonville-Trudel* 2004, at [3]). Ms Dassonville argued that the financial assistance the family received from the 'In-Home Support Program' (the Program) of the Department of Community Services (the Department) was inadequate. The family requested additional funding for intensive toilet training, an in-home security system, and other special needs.

The tensions between the parties were complicated by fluctuating assessments of family income. Initially, in 1998, the family had been denied the Program funding because their dual income exceeded the maximum allowable under the Program Guidelines. In June 2000, Ms Dassonville deliberately left her employment, removing employment constraints on her care-giving and entitling the family to financial assistance.

One year later, Ms Dassonville began receiving a modest income through some legal consultation work and, once more, the family's income disentitled their Program eligibility. The family appealed this disentitlement at the NSCA. Despite these changes in their financial situation, the reality remained that, with or without public funding, Dominique's family felt inadequately equipped to care for her.

Ms Dassonville contended that without further, appropriate funding 'the family could not continue to provide for Dominique, who would then be a "child in need of protective services" within the meaning of s.22 of the Children and Family Services Act'(R.S.N.S. 1989, c.5, 'CFSA', *Dassonville-Trudel* 2004, at [7]). The situation was quite dire for Dominique's mother; either she secured more publicly funded home support or she would have no choice but to give up her child entirely to governmental protective services.

At trial, Coughlan J dismissed all of Ms Dassonville's applications. Coughlan J used the moderately deferential standard of review (SOR) – reasonableness *simpliciter* – to review the Department's decisions. Judicial deference prevailed because of the Department's relative expertise about what families with children with disabilities needed, the resource-allocative nature of the decisions, and the highly factual nature of whether a child was in need of protective services.

Ms Dassonville argued on appeal that Justice Coughlan's SOR choice was erroneous and that the following decisions by Coughlan J were unreasonable:

a. the Program Guidelines explicitly did not allow funding of the requested home security system and the intensive toilet training;
b. the income limits in the Program Guidelines excluded the appellants from the Program; and
c. the Department's determination that Dominique was not 'a child in need of protective services'.

*McQueen* The applicant in *McQueen* was Alison McQueen, a 35-year-old woman with cerebral palsy who desired to move from a community-based institution to her own personal dwelling purchased using proceeds from her late father's estate. The facility, where she had lived for four years, included 24-hour attendant care and supervision of up to six residents completely funded by the Department of Community Services (DCS). Outside the institution, public home care support at the level Alison required fell to the Department of Health (DOH). Alison self-referred to the DOH in October 2004 and indicated her intention to move to a personal residence in 20 days. At this time, she requested an eligibility assessment for home care services. Because Alison 'did not have an overall permanent care plan in place at [the date of the assessment with Continuing Care Coordinator], … the Coordinator was unable to specifically determine Ms McQueen's unmet needs at that time' (*McQueen* 2006, at [9]). This stopped the DOH from pursuing Alison's requests further. The Coordinator testified that, instead, Alison was invited to return to the DOH upon gathering more information and organizing an overall care plan. Alison testified no such invitation was made.

Alison applied for and received some assistance from the 'Employment Support Income Assistance (ESIA), a program which provided financial assistance to individuals who chose to remain at home with family' (*McQueen* 2006, at [10]). Meanwhile, the DOH 'understood that Alison's mother was living with her' (*McQueen* 2006, at [10]).

After struggling for about six months with only her mother's care-giving support, Alison commenced the Supreme Court proceedings. She challenged the exercise of ministerial discretion and/or the failure to exercise the same that left her without the requested home care support. Her claim contained the detailed home care support she needed to thrive in the community. These supports included about three hours daily of ADL; about four hours daily of attendant care (to help with grocery shopping, meal preparation, and the organization and attendance of social and recreational activities); attendance of medical appointments; live-in support; a supportive room-mate; and aid with coordination of her entire care plan. She estimated the monthly costs to be about $3400.

In July 2005, after Alison had lodged her claim, the DOH agreed to reassess her needs. The DOH cited a change in her circumstances since they last met which meant that Alison now qualified for funding. Relying significantly on the presumption of a great deal of informal care-giving by Alison's mother, the DOH provided: one and a half hours daily for personal care and exercises; a (single) follow-up assessment by an occupational therapist; and one and a half hours daily of light housekeeping. Alison's previous reliance on 24-hour care and the permanency of Alison's disability appeared unpersuasive and marked the DOH-proposed home care services with shades of inadequacy. Ms McQueen could not decrease her care-giving to her adult child.

Upon persistence with the litigation, a further government reassessment was conducted, which expanded the public home support services provided. These services, at a cost of $1, 290.30 a month, included: evening meal preparation assistance three days a week; two hours daily of personal care service (assistance with showering; bed-making; cleaning washroom related to bathing); training and assistance with daily range of motion exercises; one and a half hours, every two weeks, of light housekeeping (cleaning washroom, kitchen and main living space; laundry); thirty minutes daily assistance with light breakfast preparation; use of a hospital bed; and occupational therapist assessment and follow-up visit. Nevertheless, Alison and her mother continued their litigation as expressed in their initial complaints.

*The findings: small victories, major losses*

The judicial findings for both *Dassonville-Trudel* and *McQueen* can only be described as small victories coupled with major losses for the complainant families. These mother–daughter dyads could see glimmers of recognition in the determinations, but such appreciation was overshadowed by major losses in their arguments.

*Dassonville-Trudel: willing to give up care-giving to care for one's child* The judicial determination of Ms Dassonville's appeal discussed four major issues identified above. First, writing for a unanimous NSCA, Bateman JA thoroughly analysed the SOR determination for this case. At the time of this case, Canadian jurisprudence recognized three choices for SOR: patent unreasonableness (the most deferential to administrative decisionmakers like Program administrators); correctness (which accorded no deference to administrative decisionmakers and left the court to complete its own determination fully); and reasonable *simpliciter* (which fell between the previous two).

Bateman JA found many factors favoured the highly deferential standard of patent unreasonableness. These included the need to make difficult decisions regarding the allocation of scarce resources, the lack of legal interpretation required, the Department's greater expertise in initially recognizing children that need protective services and the myriad factors to consider in initiating protective proceedings. Nevertheless, the NSCA used reasonableness *simpliciter* because the Minister supported such an SOR in the governmental submissions. The Dassonville-Trudels experienced a small victory: the NSCA opened the door to the most deferential SOR (which would delimit any hopes for change on appeal), but did not walk through that door.

However, Bateman JA's SOR determination supports a higher level SOR for future appeals on the allocated public home care support. Even before outlining its determinations in these circumstances, the NSCA facilitated subsequent courts' *refusal* to review similar funding decisions with any ability to alter outcomes. When funding decisions are consistently preserved from critique at the appeals level by the judiciary, the suitability of this recourse is doubtful. This represents a major loss for women and children with ECNs.

*Dassonville-Trudel* (2004, at [27]) promotes the courts' failure to challenge the permissive nature of Program-enabling legislation:

> [the impugned provision] … neither requires the Minister to provide services, nor obliges the Minister to enter into an agreement with the parents of the child with special needs. The criteria for determining whether a family is unable to provide the services required by the child, the nature of the services covered by the Department and the manner of delivery of those services is not directed by the statute. The provision of Program funding to families involves a balancing of limited funds as against limitless needs. It is a polycentric issue … [T]he very broad grant of discretion considered in conjunction with the polycentric nature of the issue favours the most deferential approach to the Minister's decisions [emphasis added].

The social biases obliging mothers to provide care cannot be easily dismantled by the judiciary. Judicial deference further militates against minimizing the vulnerability of these women and their children. The courts framed an issue as unfortunate when they should have said unfair. Judicial deference aims to distinguish the expertise of the courts from that of the legislature. However, where discrimination and unfairness are pervasive, the courts and their allegiance to impartiality should be allowed to exert their competence. Unfortunate situations beg for sympathy and empathy, while unfair circumstances necessitate remedy. The current usage of judicial deference in home care allocation decisions impedes such remedies.

Next, the NSCA considered the requests for additional funding. Using the reasonableness *simpliciter* standard, Bateman JA provided some (albeit small) victories for the family. The implications of these victories for other mothers are unknown. The NSCA found the Department unreasonable in determining that the Program Guidelines explicitly excluded the funding of the intensive toilet training and home security. This decision was considered 'an unreasonable exercise of statutory discretion [as it] rigidly appl[ied] the Guidelines without consideration of the particular circumstances of the family' (*Dassonville-Trudel* 2004, at [38]). The Court then reassessed the previous appraisals of family income and the child's need. Although he recognized the appropriateness of means tests, Bateman JA asserted:

> As for the family's financial eligibility, I am of the view that the Guidelines were applied in an irrational way and that their application without regard to the actual needs and circumstances of this family was an unreasonable exercise of the statutory discretion. While I speak of an unreasonable exercise of statutory discretion, … it is my view that, on both issues there was, in effect, a failure to exercise discretion. (*Dassonville-Trudel* 2004, at [38])

Following the unanimous Supreme Court of Canada (SCC) judgment in *Maple Lodge Farms Ltd v Canada*, [1982] 2 S.C.R. 2, at 6 (S.C.C.), strict adherence to guidelines was discouraged as that 'would be to elevate ministerial directions to the level of law and fetter the Minister in the exercise of his discretion' (*Dassonville-Trudel* 2004, at [39]).

Bateman JA advocated a contextualized approach considering both income and needs:

> The In-Home Support Program Guidelines, insofar as they impose a family income cut-off, if rigidly applied, fail to take into account the individual circumstances of the families in need. A family with an income above the Guidelines maximum is denied assistance, although the child in question may have extraordinary needs which far exceed the parents' financial ability to respond. Such a family may, in fact, be more in need of assistance than is one with an income below the Guidelines amount, but whose child has more moderate special needs (*Dassonville-Trudel* 2004, at [42]).

Consideration of context and relationships, which accords with the 'ethics of care' advocated by Carol Gilligan (1982), rather than the blanket application of general rules, offers a response more reflective of reality.

In his contextualized analysis, Bateman JA examined the sequence of requests and denials between Dominique's mother and the Department. The gendered devaluation of care pervades the Department's responses to Ms Dassonville's many funding requests. Ms Dassonville's initial demands were much broader than the psychological intervention for toilet training and the in-home security system. She requested additional respite, funding for parental travel to educational conferences, funding for a communicative abilities assessment as well as funds for Dominique's restricted dietary needs. Dominique's mother estimated the respite costs alone as about $71,000 annually. In response, the Department increased the family's total monthly funding from $300 to $600, and refused the one-off funding requests. Several factors influenced the Department's decision including fiscal responsibility and the scarcity of resources where need is limitless. In October 2000, the Department further increased Dominique's monthly in-home support to $825. However, this was still well below Ms Dassonville's stated level of need. A mother's knowledge of her child's care needs were disregarded. Consequently, as explained above, the appeal and quest for fairness continued. Notably, the appeal was narrow in scope, limited to the process of refusing to fund the toilet training programme and a home security system, as well as assessing the family income.

Using the Guidelines, the Department indicated the toilet training, as an intensive treatment, could not be covered by the Program; and the security system was not covered under the Program. The services eligible under the Guidelines included core services (for example, respite care), enhanced support (such as additional respite or extremely high medical costs), and special needs (expenses and professional fees related to the child's disability and not covered by an insurance plan).

A clear, contextualized analysis of the Guidelines found the Minister's refusal unreasonable. Contrary to the Department's position, the Guidelines could support the funding requests by Ms Dassonville. The NSCA thus allowed the appeal and quashed the two funding refusals. The Court remitted the requests for intensive toilet training and the in-home security system to the Department for reconsideration, within its statutory mandate.

This small victory was still to be overshadowed. The judgment could aid the Department in continuing its refusal to provide funds to provide support for Dominique's unique needs. Bateman JA's statements left the Department well within its statutory mandate to use 'ministerial discretion' to decide *not*to fund these requests. Further invocations of fiscal responsibility would likely seal the deal for future judicial deference, and would avoid finding support in the guidelines. The underlying unfairness would then remain unresolved.

Without the toilet training and in-home security system, Dominique's care needs remained extreme and extraordinary. Progress was unattainable, especially in areas of personal security and safety. The care-giving demands on Dominique's mother would only increase as Dominique grew in age and size. The gendered demands of care-giving, the documented inadequacy of provincial home care support, judicial deference, and ministerial discretion would likely perpetuate injustice.

Third, the court examined the Department's decisions relating to family income and Program eligibility. When originally approved in 2000, the Department excluded Ms Dassonville's income from the first six months of 2000. As she was unemployed at the time of the income assessment, Ms Dassonville's income while previously employed became irrelevant. However, this same half-year's income was used to exclude the family from the Program in 2001. Bateman JA correctly recognized this inconsistency and found the Department clearly mistaken it its income calculations. It conjured allusions to arbitrariness and unfairness in the process of Program inclusion and exclusion. Bateman JA found the disqualification of the Dassonville-Trudels incorrect. A victory for the family!

The NSCA advocated a contextual and flexible approach to permit 'a true picture of family income' rather than the strict application of guidelines. The Department did not adequately consider dramatic changes to the family income over a year, and did not exhaust their statutory discretion, which resulted in a 'failure to exercise that discretion in light of the actual needs and circumstances of this family' (*Dassonville-Trudel* 2004, at [64]). Ms Dassonville's appeal was allowed and the income-based decision to disqualify the family was quashed.

The family's eligibility was remitted to the Department for 'consideration using correct annual income figures running from the commencement of the Special Needs Agreement, subject to the family providing accurate income information' (*Dassonville-Trudel* 2004, at [69]). Unfortunately, the remit left open the possibility that the Department could disqualify the family again. The

Court limited its judicial determination to whether the Department had 'genuinely considered the requests [of the family regarding their income circumstances] on their merits in exercising the discretion permitted under the statute', and 'not whether [the Department] had ... done so the result would have been the same' (*Dassonville-Trudel* 2004, at [66]).

The perpetuation of injustice is less pronounced here compared to the remitting of the additional funding decisions. It would be utterly unreasonable for the family to remain disqualified. Any realistic interpretation of their income in 2000 and Ms Dassonville's changing employment status could not permit disentitlement. Nonetheless, this victory is small given the larger context of historical inadequacy in home care funding for children like Dominique and that Ms Dassonville continued to have to forgo a skilled career outside the home to facilitate the family's eligibility.

Finally, the appellate decision examined the reasonableness of the Department's assessment that Dominique was not in need of protective services. Since the fall of 2000, the Department had been actively monitoring the family from a child-protection perspective. Dominique's needs were recognized as 'placing considerable strain on the family and that Ms Dassonville, in particular, was experiencing significant stress' (*Dassonville-Trudel* 2004, at [72]). The NSCA ultimately dismissed their concerns, perceiving a history of maternal indecision on the sustainability and suitability of Dominique's care. Bateman JA agreed with the trial judge: the Department acted reasonably in not placing Dominique in protective services. A closer examination of this perceived indecision suggests the courts incorrectly assessed the situation.

In April 2001, the Department approached Ms Dassonville about placing Dominique 'in a situation outside the family home', but her mother would not consider it (*Dassonville-Trudel* 2004, at [72]). Three months later, however, she self-referred to the Dartmouth District Office claiming Dominique was in need of protective services. When the Department responded a week later, Ms Dassonville indicated 'she would not surrender Dominique into the Department's care, if asked to do so. She said she had made the referral *out of desperation*, hoping to obtain additional services to assist with Dominique's care' [emphasis added] (*Dassonville-Trudel* 2004, at [72]). Ms Dassonville then sent a letter requesting the Department's position on initiating protection proceedings in August 2001.

The majority of the SCC in *New Brunswick (Minister of Health and Community Services) v G. (J.)* [1999] 3 S.C.R. 46 recognized that state removal of a child from parental custody constituted a serious interference with the psychological integrity of the parent. It is no small matter for a mother to consider placing her child in protective services. In *New Brunswick*, state interference with a parent–child relationship correlated to significant stigmatization, loss of privacy, and disruption of family life, which triggered the parent's right to the security of the person entrenched in the Canadian Charter of Rights and Freedoms, found in the Constitution Act, 1982, being Schedule B to the Canada Act 1982 (U.K.), 1982, c. 11. The magnitude of the parent–child bond makes a mother's equivocation on the state removal of her child realistic and reasonable, despite her own self-referral. She should have been greeted with compassion, understanding and positive assistance from the government, not the opposite. The state took indecision to mean Ms Dassonville – and hence the Department also should – no longer considered Dominique in need of protective services. The connection to a Charter right should have militated against judicial deference by the NSCA. In *Dassonville-Trudel*, the gravity of the request and the circumstances surrounding it appeared inconsequential and were not considered. The opportunity to clarify the connection between government support and adequacy of care for a child with ECNs was lost.

If the SOR of correctness had been used in this judicial review, the actual circumstances of Dominique and her mother could have been given due consideration. Lack of choice and extreme anxiety undergirded Ms Dassonville's request to place her child in protective services. Such drivers went unnoticed or were inconsequential to the administrative and judicial decisionmakers. The brevity of the judicial discussion of this issue suggests disregard for her circumstances. The reasonableness *simpliciter* SOR thwarted fairness for Dominique and her mother and obscured the unfairness of the balance between public and parental responsibilities for care in ECN contexts.

The undesirable finding that Dominique indeed required protective services could have exposed the insufficiency of the public home care support. Only such an embarrassing and disheartening decision could effect real change for home care programmes in Nova Scotia, and the rest of Canada. Or, if using the correctness standard, Bateman JA found Dominique did not need protective care, the judicial analysis would have guided families and government on the legal distinction between real and perceived inadequacy of public home care. And, it would inform the balance of responsibilities between mothers and the state. Such guidance is necessary. How much public assistance can families expect in the care of their extraordinary children? How much care-giving burden is mothers' alone? The answers to these questions are unknown. Yet the opportunity to shed light on them was lost in *Dassonville-Trudel*.

Alternatively, the desperate circumstances of mother and daughter in *Dassonville-Trudel* should have coloured the entire judicial decision, even on the reasonableness *simpliciter* standard. Ms Dassonville was harshly torn between her fervent need for Dominique to have adequate care and her equally ardent desire to keep Dominique at home. The reasonableness analysis did not consider the funding denial's precipitation of such struggle and despair.

It appears that only if Ms Dassonville could traverse 'the brink' and give her child up to the state, could she have secured more complete care-giving. This severance seems counter-intuitive to the law's prioritization of preserving family unity. Ms Dassonville was 'stuck between a rock and a hard place'. The vulnerability of her position led to two ghastly, mutually exclusive choices: a complete family unit including Dominique or adequate care for Dominique. A cohabitating family and an appropriately cared for child with ECNs appear incompatible given the outcomes and implications of *Dassonville-Trudel*. The wretchedness of this predicament is almost incomprehensible.

### *McQueen*: The Power yet Weakness of Litigation

The brief judicial determination in *McQueen* also consisted of small victories for mother and daughter trumped by major losses. First, the rejection of Alison's first self-referral to the DOH is astounding for its reasoning. Alison was dismissed from any consideration of home care support because she had not organized her own permanent care plan. It is disturbing and disingenuous that Alison was expected to assess her own needs and formulate a care plan. Needs assessment and care planning are clearly within professional expertise and responsibility.

The limits of public provision placed Alison in an unacceptable position. On the one hand, she could have complete access to the services required but she was limited to living in a public institution. On the other hand, she could live in her own personal home, but she would have to forgo some of the care she required. The desire for development, growth and independence for those with corporeal dependencies appears thwarted, not promoted, by the current framework of public home care programmes. Persons with intensive ECNs seem obliged to forgo independence of spirit due to dependence of body. Some may argue that at least 'adequate' care is available somewhere, or that economic efficiency necessitates those needing continual care to be housed together. However, the universal need for familial and social connection makes mandatory living in the public sphere intolerable and unfair.

While Alison turned to the ESIA programme for assistance, the DOH considered her care needs met by her mother. The assumption of maternal care-giving appeared to absolve the DOH. No one followed up with Alison despite knowledge that she had not secured any care plan to support her transition from 24-hour institutional care to independent living. Clearly, 24-hour institutional care was equated to care by a single mother. The risks and burdens of sole care-giving for these women were augmented, disregarded and possibly exploited by the DOH. The reality of this desertion was missing from *McQueen*.

Next, the facts in *McQueen* highlighted a small victory for Alison and her mother. The initiation of this claim demonstrated the power of litigation to redress wrongs and power imbalances. Only after Alison lodged her claim did the DOH reassess her needs (in July 2005). In this case, litigation helped re-balance the input of public entities versus private individuals in the allocation of responsibilities for home care.

The DOH cited a 'change' in her circumstances since they last met to trigger reconsideration of Alison's eligibility. The changes suggested were that she lived alone; that she appeared to have improved her ability to function independently; and that she had a back-up plan for care involving her mother and friends. Inconsistencies abound in these purported changes. First, her initial meeting with a

DOH representative was on the date she moved into her current apartment, and she had lived nowhere else after leaving the institution. Second, if she was functioning more independently than before, Alison would have needed less government assistance, not more. And, third, the care plan Alison requested in 2004 strongly suggested that she did not want, nor plan for, her mother to be burdened with her care, even as back-up.

In assessing needs and allocating funds, the DOH relied significantly on the presumption of a great deal of informal care-giving by Alison's mother. Given her reliance on 24-hour care and the permanency of her disability, inadequacy marked the home care services proposed by the DOH. A small victory for Alison arrived in that a further government reassessment was conducted, which expanded the public home support services provided from the initial assessment. It was highly unlikely that the DOH would have reconsidered the scope of public responsibility had Alison and her mother not begun litigation proceedings.

Alison's victories ended here, however. The state aid continued to rely heavily on informal care-givers. Alison's consistent requests for aid in attending social activities and in finding a room-mate strongly suggest her pool of potential informal care-givers was limited. She had her mother. But Alison continued to ask for an unrelated room-mate to relieve her mother from being everything for Alison at all times. Alison requested a live-in support person to act as back-up when home care was unavailable. This encompasses the third issue identified in this legal critique: public responsibility for the care of children with ECNs at home relies on mothers, and disregards the value of non-familial kinship.

The services provided by the DOH were more home-focused than community-focused. They could (somewhat) facilitate Alison living in her apartment, but not living in her community. No allowances were made for how Alison would navigate and function beyond her apartment doors. Alison could not escape the social exclusion commonly associated with the structure of home care, despite her protests and requests (Aronson and Neysmith 2001). This minimization of the import of relationships and communities counters most feminist and relational conceptions of the world (Gilligan 1982; Minow and Shanley 1996; Aronson and Neysmith 2001).

The DOH argued that socialization was provided by the Home Support Workers when they came to fulfil their duties. Such socialization would be minimal at best. They were at Alison's abode for a short time and had numerous tasks to complete. What a limited conceptualization of socialization! What about interactions with peers in age or circumstance? What about participating in developmental activities outside the home, as able-bodied individuals do? The government's perception of public responsibility diminished the value of the home care support provided to Alison and her mother. The government relied on Ms McQueen to cover its failures to care and it did not complete its mandate to assist Alison with living and thriving *in her community*.

Finally, the judicial determination in *McQueen* consisted of a final, significant loss for Alison and her mother: the judiciary failed to equalize the power difference between government and individuals in the allocation of public versus private responsibility. Alison's initial Originating Notice referred to the actions of the DOH and DCS in 2004, whereby they denied her eligibility for any public home care services. After initiating her claim, Alison was reassessed by the DOH and DCS on two occasions and some services were provided. Alison felt the services remained inadequate, so she continued her claim. However, Alison did not amend her application to include the 2005 government decisions.

The original application impugning the 2004 funding denial was considered the 'only' issue in front of the Court. Alison acknowledged the events of 2005 in a Supplementary Affidavit sworn 11 April 2006. This (likely) mis-step on the part of Alison and her counsel (if she had any) to update or reformulate her application led to the evocation of the doctrine of mootness. The government claimed the application was moot because the 2005 funding decisions overtook the 2004 events. Edwards J wholeheartedly took up the government's argument to indicate no live controversy existed between the parties. The myriad issues implicated in this application were divested from thoughtful judicial consideration. Edwards J further suggested that any amended application would have been 'difficult if not impossible to sustain' because Alison could no longer allege a denial of services (*McQueen* 2006, at [24]).

At issue in *McQueen* (2004, at [2]) was not simply the claimed 'unlawful, unreasonable, in bad faith and made for extraneous purpose' denial of consideration for home care services for Alison in October 2004. The sufficiency of public support for families where children had ECNs, and the extent of parental versus public responsibility, were the questions the Court had to consider. A complete juridical analysis of Alison's predicament would have truly enlightened this area, no matter the outcome. The legal issues in *McQueen* shape communal responsibility in the care of those with chronic, significant care needs – an issue rarely discussed in Canadian law. The gendered division of labour deserves some judicial recognition. Society's continual reliance on the free labour of women, especially mothers, must be exposed, especially with the lack of similar expectations on men and fathers.

Alison continued her litigation, but she acknowledged the events of 2005 in her submissions. It is likely she did not fully comprehend the possibility and implications of the doctrine of mootness. The obstinacy of the legal system likely impeded true justice for Alison; her chance to be heard in an adjudicative setting was frustrated.

The doctrine of mootness could have been set aside if 'the social cost of continued uncertainty in the law' was recognized. Edwards J thought this did not apply as '[a] ruling on the 2004 request will not assist "others in similar circumstances", as the special needs of each and every applicant for services for the disabled is unique on its own set of facts and the eligible criteria is very fact reliant' (*McQueen*, at [26]).

Much is contentious about the trial judge's decision not to hear Alison's application on mootness. The utilization of the term 'private reference' alludes back to the persistent public/private divide that has subjugated women. In *McQueen*, a disabled woman and her care-giver mother were particularly isolated by the court's unwillingness to traverse the public/private divide. The judiciary is necessary to redress the imbalance between the popular and the individual. Unfortunately, the Court in *McQueen* was insensitive to the consequence of this role.

Given the dearth of jurisprudence in this area, it was uninformed to suggest that 'others in similar circumstances' would not be aided by the judicial treatment of this case. Individual variety aside, commonality exists such as the need for public assistance to survive and thrive, and the need for fair and flexible entry into and adequate care within home care programmes.

A concrete reprimand of the government's conduct in 2004 would have ensured no future family in need of home care services could be so quickly denied and abandoned. Without such precedent, these circumstances could continue to arise. The knowledge, costs and connections necessary to enter the litigation arena may be too great a barrier for most members of this vulnerable population. This would leave many individuals without any recourse: an unequivocal injustice.

### *Undercurrents of gender bias*

The critique of these judgments thus far has focused on inadequacies: the inadequacy of public home care support, and the inadequacy of the judicial review process to recognize, reconsider, or rectify such support insufficiencies. The imbalance between family victories and losses exaggerates these inadequacies. Undercurrents of gender bias have been noted and touched upon already, but this analysis aims to expose further such underlying bias.

The primary mode by which gender bias was revealed in *Dassonville-Trudel* and *McQueen* was in the heavy reliance on overwhelming and disproportionate responsibilities on the mothers of children with ECNs. In doing so, the ideological distinction between public and private domains remained exploitive and inconsiderate of women and their circumstances. Moreover, inherent vulnerabilities of these women and their children were inflated. Whether the gender bias was social or legal in origin, the judiciary's non-response signals inadequacies in the adjudicative options available to families involved with home care support programmes.

In *Dassonville-Trudel*, Dominique's *mother*, not father, left lucrative employment to care for their child. Ms Dassonville earned considerably more over six months ($27,981.99) than her husband ($12,374.64). Nevertheless, Ms Dassonville left her lucrative employment in June 2000 to care for Dominique. There were likely many reasons compelling her to leave paid employment. Yet, the care-giving work, as in most cases, appeared the most compelling and trumped her greater earning potential outside the home. This begs the question whether any *real* choice exists for mothers when *deciding* to forgo paid employment to care for their child? 'Women family members [are] expected to supplement home care services without pay and at great personal expense in terms of their own health, incomes, benefits, career development and pension accumulation, while men [are] not under as much pressure to do so' (Armstrong and Kits 2001, 9).

One year later, Ms Dassonville began receiving a modest income through some legal consultation work, and once more the family's income disentitled their Program eligibility. Thus, Dominique, her mother and family were socially punished when Ms Dassonville expanded her role beyond the archetypal care-giver and mother. Perhaps if she had taken a less remunerative position, her family would not have been disentitled from public support. However, the oppressive connotations of that option cannot be ignored: skilled, lucrative employment outside the home was incompatible with public support of in-home care.

The family appealed this disentitlement at the NSCA. Nevertheless, the changes in their financial position and thus eligibility for financial assistance should not hide the reality that, with and without public funding, Dominique's family felt inadequately prepared to care for her.

Similarly, in *McQueen*, the government's persistent reliance on the presumed informal care-giving of Alison's mother was palpable and furthered the injustice. A single mother of an adult child was still held responsible for round-the-clock care of that 'child's' home care needs. This single mother was equivalent to a fully staffed, 24-hour-care institutional setting. The vulnerability of these women was utterly amplified. The decisionmakers (government and judicial) disregarded the need for non-parental socialization, which fostered social isolation. Ultimately, *McQueen* disregarded any remotely relational conceptualization of society, where relationships and connections are paramount and where care-givers as well as care recipients have needs.

Another feature of the undercurrent of gender bias was related to the public/private dichotomy. Whilst the philosophy and existence of home care support programmes could be applauded for countering the public/private partiality, its incompetence in meeting the care needs of these mother–daughter dyads suggests superficial, rather than remedial, surpassing of the public/private bias.

Certain responsibilities, such as care-giving, are overwhelmingly emphasized as the mother's alone (Armstrong and Kits 2001; Armstrong and Armstrong 2004). In *Dassonville-Trudel*, it is clear Dominique's mother undertook another arduous role as an advocate. The expansion of mothers' roles into advocacy may be lauded as countering the delegation of women away from the public eye and in the home. The common disregard of women's voices and concerns in society hinders the utility of women advocates. It is intrinsically unfair that women must do 'all the heavy lifting'. Mothers caring for children with ECNs are already over-burdened because public aid is insufficient. Why must competent advocacy be added to their long list of tasks?

A downward spiral begins: one's child is not receiving enough care so the mother must advocate for more assistance in care-giving, but that takes time away from her care-giving and the child is left with even less adequate care. The traditional 'double day' of women turns into a 'triple day'. Paid work and care-giver work is compounded with advocacy work. If the judicial appeals process were sure to redress the social biases against women, then the additional role of active child advocate would not be so tragic; effective advocacy would lead to real social and systematic change, and care-giving would become more valued and equitably shared in society and families. However, the results of *Dassonville-Trudel* suggest the 'triple day' for mothers of children with ECNs does *not* have a foreseeable expiration date. Maternal advocacy regarding the rebalancing of public and parental responsibilities for care is not fully effective in the legal system.

The *McQueen* decision highlights both the power and weakness of litigation to aid mothers and their children with ECNs to garner sufficient home care support. Only through initiating a legal action could Alison and her mother agitate the government into action. However, the pervasiveness of the public/private divide was utterly unavoidable in this case, and was perpetuated by the final decision. The government's feet are firmly planted in the public sector. When Alison wished to move into a non-institutionalized (i.e. private) residence, the public aid she, and her mother, so desperately relied upon would not accompany her. These are choices an able-bodied person or her family need never make: that fact alone suggests unfairness.

Another signal of the gender bias relates to the gendered devaluation of care pervading governmental responses. Boyd (1996, 166) recognized 'labour … viewed as "women's work" or domestic labour tends to command lower compensation than that viewed as "men's work", even if it is performed by a formally recognized employee'. Moreover, '[t]he gendered work aspect of the public/private divide thus reproduces itself also within each of the two spheres, with women performing "women's work" that is relatively undervalued in each sphere' (Boyd 1996, 166).

In *McQueen*, Alison was abandoned to navigate the complex intricacies of establishing a care plan. Moreover, the huge discrepancies between the funding requested and that provided suggest the devaluation of care directs the balance of public versus parental responsibility in home care. Care work, deemed primarily female, continues to be devalued in the public sphere through low compensation, minimal subsidization, and minimal professional import or assistance.

In *Dassonville-Trudel*, the Department's responses to Ms Dassonville's many funding requests appear to have also been influenced by the gendered devaluation of care. Ms Dassonville's initial demands were much broader than the psychological intervention for toilet training and the in-home security system. She requested additional respite; funding for parental travel to educational conferences; funding for a communicative abilities assessment; as well as funds for Dominique's restricted dietary needs. Dominique's mother estimated the respite costs alone as about $71,000 annually. In response, the Department increased the family's total monthly funding from $300 to $600, and refused the one-off funding requests. Several factors influenced the Department's decision including fiscal responsibility and the scarcity of resources where need is limitless.

The Department's devaluation of care work screams for change in societal views about care-giving. Linda McClain (2001) suggested considering care as a public value and re-conceptualizing child-rearing as social reproduction. Public valuation brings collective responsibility. This would 'make more explicit the relationship between resources and responsibilities, i.e., fostering responsibility by providing resources that help parents and caregivers better provide care' (McClain 2001, 1680). Social reproduction brings caring to the forefront by focusing on 'the task of nurturing children and ensuring their moral development and education … to prepare them to take their place in the wider culture, as responsible, self-governing persons' (McClain 2001, 1683).

Although children with ECNs may never be conventionally 'self-governing', they should not be excluded from the perceived benefits of social reproduction. As Eva Feder Kittay (1995, 8) expressed it:

> At some stage in the lives of each of us we face at least one period of utter dependency; and, with accident and disease forever a danger to the most independent of us, we are all, at least potentially, dependents. … While we are all dependent on some form of care or support, at least minimally, and although dependencies vary in degree, those that involve the survival or thriving of a person cut most deeply through the fiction of a social order presumably constituted by independent equal persons.

For them to thrive, or even survive, children like Dominique (and Alison) need adequate care. Without it, they would be lost to society and their families, and most significantly to themselves. A just and fair society could not permit such loss.

In October 2000, the Department further increased Dominique's monthly in-home support to $825. However, this was still well below Ms Dassonville's stated level of need. A mother's knowledge of her child's care needs was disregarded. Consequently, as explained above, the appeal and quest for fairness continued. Notably, the appeal was narrow in scope, limited to the process of refusing to fund the toilet training programme and a home security system, as well as of assessing the family income.

This critique of *Dassonville-Trudel* and *McQueen* recognizes that the judiciary has not escaped the influence of gender bias that is pervasive in society. Children with ECNs who wish to live at home with their families are impeded by this partiality. Public responsibilities are garnered in a fashion that prioritizes and exploits maternal responsibilities, that valorizes the public/private distinction, and that devalues care work.

## Conclusion

Home care is more and more appreciated as integral to the care regimes for children with ECNs. These children and their mothers are some of the most vulnerable in society. They are physically, emotionally, socially and economically very susceptible to injury even if all the community support in the world were available. The fact that they do not receive sufficient care triggers contentions of unfairness. No one is capable of adequately caring for another continuously for days, weeks, and years on end. However, a group of people making a concerted effort might manage.

Each province has included home care programmes in their healthcare systems, due to political and social pressure rather than legal imperatives. These programmes are inconsistent, inter- and intra- provincially. These programmes dictate if and how care will be delivered. The limited bargaining power of children and families (especially mothercare-givers) augments vulnerabilities and questions the fairness of the homecare contracts. How can we ensure that children get the care their unique needs require? How can we ensure families are supported to care for their children to the best of their ability, without risking the detriment of the child's or mother's health? The adjudication process represents one of the last vestiges for equalizing this significant power imbalance.

Unfortunately, both *Dassonville-Trudel* and *McQueen* suggest that judicial deference to 'policy' decisions related to resource allocation trumps individual, and population, concerns for justice and fairness. Social biases against women, such as the relegation to and devaluation of care-giving work, appear insulated from legal reprimand through judicial deference. There were small victories in each case, such as the promotion of the contextual and flexible approach in *Dassonville-Trudel* and the power of litigation to re-evaluate a refusal to care in *McQueen*. However, each positive was negated by the preference for the *status quo*, which thrusts 'double' or even 'triple' days on women, especially mothers of extraordinary children.

The court did not really address the issue at the heart of these debates: can children be permitted to live in their home and community while still retaining complete coverage of their care needs? In both *Dassonville-Trudel* and *McQueen*, the children and their mothers were faced with choosing between separation and adequate care. The courts ignored the greater issues, approaching the claims through very narrow lenses.

One cannot argue that the law itself was incapable of addressing the larger issues, because it was and is. Available avenues were not pursued. The doctrine of mootness could have permitted the court to examine the sufficiency of care issue in *McQueen*. The standard of review of correctness would have allowed the court to assess whether Dominique was adequately cared for at home, by her family and home care programme in *Dassonville-Trudel*. Most importantly, in both cases, fairness could have been advocated through the judicial acknowledgement (if not condemnation) of gender bias.

The Court's adjudicative role did not redress the power difference between government and vulnerable children and their mothers. These vulnerable populations must now wait for another of their own to recognize the injustice of inadequate home care support and the overwhelming burden placed on care-givermothers. This subsequent advocate must also possess the resources (social, political and economic) to pursue the adjudicative route. These steep demands coalesce with recognized barriers of access to the legal system and the precedents established by *Dassonville-Trudel* and *McQueen*. Together, they obscure how long, if ever, these families will have to wait for true progress. For children whose very survival requires competent and attentive care, this wait is likely much too long. The judiciary must take up more contextual approaches which value fairness more than judicial deference to help these mothers and children along.

## References

Armstrong, P. and Armstrong, H. 2004. Thinking It Through: Women, Work and Caring, in *Caring For/Caring About*, edited by K.R. Grant et al. Aurora, ON: Garamond Press Ltd, 5–43.

Armstrong, P. and Kits, O. 2001. *One Hundred Years of Caregiving*, Ottawa: Law Commission of Canada.

Aronson, J. and Neysmith, S.M. 2001. Manufacturing Social Exclusion in the Home Care Market. *Canadian Public Policy*, 27(2), 151–65.

Bjornsdottir, K. 2002. From the State to the Family: Reconfiguring the Responsibility for Long-Term Nursing Care at Home. *Nursing Inquiry*, 9, 3–11.

Boyd, S.B. 1996. Can Law Challenge the Public/Private Divide? Women, Work, and Family. *Windsor Yearbook of Access to Justice*, 15, 161–88.

Brown, M.G. 1993. Rationing Health Care in Canada. *Annals of Health Law*, 2, 101–19.

Canadian Policy Research Networks. 2005. *A Healthy Balance: Caregiving Policy in Canada Backgrounder*. Ottawa: Canadian Policy Research Networks Inc.

Cardona, O.D. 2004. The Need for Rethinking the Concepts of Vulnerability and Risk from a Holistic Perspective: A Necessary Review and Criticism for Effective Risk Management, in *Mapping Vulnerability: Disasters, Development and People*, edited by G. Bankoff, G. Frerks, and D. Hilhorst. London: Earthscan Publishers, 37–51.

Carnevale, F.A. 2007. Revisiting Goffman's*Stigma*: The Social Experience of Families with Children Requiring Mechanical Ventilation at Home. *Journal of Child Health Care*, 11(1), 7–18.

Carnevale, F.A., Alexander, E., Davis, M., Rennick, J. and Trioni, R. 2006. Daily Living with Distress and Enrichment: The Moral Experience of Families with Ventilator-Assisted Children at Home. *Pediatrics*, 117, 48–60.

Colliere, M.F. 1986. Invisible Care and Invisible Women as Health CareProviders. *International Journal of Nursing Studies*, 23(2), 95–112.

Fineman, M.A. 2001. Contract and Care. *Chicago-Kent Law Review*, 76, 1403–40.

Gilligan, C. 1982. *In a Different Voice: Psychological Theory and Women's Development*, Cambridge, MA: Harvard University Press.

Goldberg, A.I., Gardner, G. and Gibson, L.E. 1994. Home Care: The Next Frontier of Pediatric Practice. *Journal of Pediatrics*, 125, 686–90.

Gray, J. 2000. Home Care in Ontario: The Case for Co-Payments. *Health Law Journal*, 8, 177–97.

Kirk, S. 2001. Negotiating Lay and Professional Roles in the Care of Children with Complex Health Needs. *Journal of Advanced Nursing*, 34(5), 593–602.

Kirk, S., Glendinning, C. and Callery, P. 2005. Patient or Nurse? The Experience of Being the Parent of a Technology-Dependent Child. *Journal of Advanced Nursing*, 51(5), 456–64.

Kittay, E.F. 1995. Taking Dependency Seriously: The Family and Medical Leave Act Considered in Light of the Social Organization of Dependency Work and Gender Equality. *Hypatia*, 10(1), 8–29.

Lahey, W. 2007. Medicare and the Law: Contours of an Evolving Relationship, in *Canadian Health Law and Policy*, edited by J. Downie, T. Caulfield, and C. Flood. Markham, ON: LexisNexis Canada Inc., 1–67.

Lantos, J.D. and Kohrman, A.F. 1992. Ethical Aspects of Pediatric Home Care. *Pediatrics*, 89(5), 920–24.

MacKinnon, C.A. 1982. Feminism, Marxism, Method and the State: An Agenda for Theory. *Signs*, 7(3), 515–44.

McClain, L.C. 2001. Care as a Public Value: Linking Responsibility, Resources, and Republicanism. *Chicago-Kent Law Review*, 76, 1673–732.

Minow, M. and Shanley M.L. 1996. Relational Rights and Responsibilities: Revisioning the Family in Liberal Political Theory and Law. *Hypatia*, 11(1), 4–29.

Peter, E. 2000. The Politicization of Ethical Knowledge: Feminist Ethics as a Basis for Home Care Nursing Research. *Canadian Journal of Nursing Research*, 32(2), 103–18.

Peter, E., Spalding, K., Kenny, N., Conrad, P., McKeever, P. and Macfarlane, A. 2007. Neither Seen Nor Heard: Children and Homecare Policy in Canada. *Social Science & Medicine*, 64, 1624–35.

Royal Commission on the Future of Health Care in Canada. 2002. *Building on Values: The Future of Health Care in Canada – Final Report*. Ottawa: National Library of Canada. Available at <http://dsp-psd.pwgsc.gc.ca/Collection/CP32-85-2002E.pdf> (accessed 7 July 2008).

Status of Women Canada. 1999. *The Changing Nature of Home Care and its Impact on Women's Vulnerability to Poverty*, edited by M. Morris et al. Ottawa: Research Directorate – Status of Women Canada.

Wang, K.W.K. and Barnard, A. 2004. Technology-Dependent Children and their Families: A Review. *Journal of Advanced Nursing*, 45(1), 36–46.

Williams, A.P., Spalding, K., Deber, R.B. and McKeever, P. 2005. *Prescriptions for Pediatric Home Care: Analyzing the Impact of the Shift from Hospital to Home and Community on Children and Families*. Toronto: M-THAC Research Unit. Available at <http://www.teamgrant.ca/M-THAC%20Greatest%20Hits/M-THAC%20Projects/All%20info/Pediatric%20Home%20Care%20-%20Bonus%20Track/Publications/p8452.pdf> (accessed 18 January 2007).

Young, I.M. 1990. *Justice and the Politics of Difference*. Princeton, NJ: Princeton University Press.

# Chapter 15
# Why We Should Care About Global Caring[1]

Eva Feder Kittay

> When the girl I take care of calls her mother Mama, my heart jumps all the time because my children also call me "Mama". When I pack her lunch … that's what I used to do for my children … I think I should be taking care of them instead of another child … If I had wings, I would fly home to my children … Just for a moment, to see my children and take care of their needs, help them, then fly back over here to continue my work. (Parreñas 2001, 119)

## Setting the Problem

Arlie Hochschild, in the essay she provocatively entitled 'Love and Gold', speaks of an interview conducted by Rhacel Parrenãs. Hochschild writes: 'Vicky Diaz, a college-educated schoolteacher who left behind five children in the Philippines, said, "the only thing you can do is to give all your love to the child [in your care]. In my absence from my children the best I could do in my situation is to give all my love to the child." Without intending it, she has taken part in a global heart transplant' (Hochschild and Ehrenreich 2002, 22, quoting from one of the interviews in the excellent study by Parreñas). This 'global heart transplant' (GHT, for short), that is, the transfer of love and care from one's own child to a child one is paid to care for in a foreign land is the moral focus of the present chapter.

The migrants I am talking about here are mothers or daughters – the women on whom the responsibility to care for children, the ill or disabled, and the elderly has largely fallen, and who themselves take responsibility for ensuring the welfare of dependants. They leave their families for extended periods for wages which, while considered low by the standards of the 'receiving' wealthier nations, are lucrative compared to what they can garner at home in the 'sending' nations. Their wages are mostly sent back to improve the conditions of the families they leave behind. They understand themselves to be acting as good mothers and daughters, fulfilling their responsibility to care for their families, not through intimate daily contact, but by providing sorely needed material benefits.

In this chapter I argue that the moral sense of unease inherent in Ehrenreich's dubbing of this form of global migration involves a harm most fully captured by

---

1 This chapter is a shortened and revised version of 'The Moral Harm of Migrant Carework: Realizing a Global Right to Care', 2009, *Philosophical Topics*, 37(1), 53–73. I would like to thank Edward Minar, editor of *Philosophical Topics*, for granting permission to reprint the article in this altered form.

an ethics of care, an ethics that emphasizes responsibilities that arise from our relationship to others. Although other forms of injustice figure in the harm, it is the hardships these women face in fulfilling their deeply felt responsibilities to care, along with the compromised situation of their dependants, that call for demanding a global *right* to care. Although the phenomenon of migrants leaving their own families behind to do carework for others is not new, the global dimensions of the migrations, and the extended absences the geographic distances impose, force us to look at issues of responsibility in the family in a new way, providing fresh ways to think about our responsibility to families globally.

First, considering the condition of migrant care workers underscores the responsibility of feminist theory to explore the impact when changing expectations concerning gender and work rub against old expectations that remain in place even as new ones emerge. The women of whom I speak exemplify this converging of old and new gendered familial responsibilities: as they *defy* the traditional gender roles of the caring mother or dutiful daughter insofar as they leave behind children and relatives who need care, they simultaneously *enact* the traditional gender role of care-giver by 'pouring',[2] as they say, love into their charges. As the need for their labour in wealthier parts of the globe is also, in some measure, due to the success of feminism in propelling more women into the labour market, feminists have a special responsibility to work toward a more just situation with respect to care labour and its impact on families from poor nations.

Second, the situation of these migrant women forces us to reconsider what it means for a mother to fulfil her responsibility to care for her children, for a daughter to fulfil a responsibility she understands that she has to care for her ageing, ill or disabled relatives.[3] That is, the exigencies of their lives require them to understand their responsibilities to care for dependent others in non-traditional ways. I shall argue that we need to formulate a right to care, one that acknowledges their reality.

In doing so, we find a new way to reconnect an ethic of rights to an ethic of responsibility which, as Carol Gilligan, and many feminist philosophers have maintained, is an ethics based on care and connection (Gilligan 1982; Card 1990). For the harm, I shall argue, in the global heart transplant is a harm to relationships. Thus while certain connections we have to others render us responsible to them, we also should be able to claim the right to meet those responsibilities. Thus the situation discussed here calls for a wider recognition of social responsibility for care work, not simply as it is viewed as a nationally bounded issue, but as a global one.

2 Parreñas 2001. Parreñas relates that the Filipina women in her study speak of 'pouring love' into their charges, something they do not mistake for the love they have for their own children (183).

3 In speaking of a mother's responsibilities or a daughter's responsibility it is easy to assume that I affirm that these are gendered responsibilities. Let me be clear: I do not believe these *ought to be* gendered responsibilities; but in our deeply gendered world, they largely, though not exclusively, remain gendered responsibilities and the families, including the women themselves, view them this way.

We can begin by thinking of the migration of women care labourers as *a global movement of the scarce resource of caring labour* from those parts of the world where there is a need for cash to those parts of the world where there is both a demand for care-givers and a willingness to pay for their services. To think of care as a commodity has an oxymoronic ring. Care, when it is worthy of the name, generally involves an emotional bond between the care-giver and the particular person for whom one cares. In certain circumstances, the affective component of care may be an instilled virtue that can be extended to others more or less impartially (for example, the good nurse), but more often it is the sort of care that flows from an affective bond, one we tend to call 'love'. The suggestion is that not only carework, but *love* is displaced and makes the transnational journey, transmuting the nobler element, love into the baser one, gold. If speaking of care as a 'scarce resource' is more ominous than thinking of the migration of workers, as Mary Zimmerman claims, we need to ask what about this is so disturbing (Zimmerman et al. 2006, 18).

There can be little doubt of injustice if wealthy nations solve their *care crisis*, as the greater demand for careworkers than these nations can supply internally has been called, by eviscerating the care structures in poor societies. There also can be little doubt that women in the wealthier nations have been able to enter the workforce in greater numbers because of the availability of non-domestic careworkers. One needs only to survey parks, childcare facilities, and eldercare homes to see the demographic make-up of those who do the waged caring labour in the US. Thus not only have feminist aspirations necessitated more paid care work, the availability of this new labour pool has also facilitated the feminist agenda. Still more reason to insist that feminists have a special responsibility to examine the moral implications of this transformation.

If there is in fact an injustice, we have to ask who exactly is harmed? The children deprived of their mothers? Yet they benefit from the remittances and tend to be better off (financially and educationally, that is) than those in families where there is no migrant mother; daughters, especially, benefit. The mothers? But they leave without overt coercion; they decide to remain at the job rather than return home. Some women escape bad and abusive marriages, and may find themselves with a lighter work load than at home. The sending nation? One UN report, however, claims that 'migration for remittances' is the most successful anti-poverty programme, one that has suffered in the current global recession. The UN reports that the sending nations benefit from the inflow of cash, so much so that there is an active effort to promote policies of migration in nations such as Indonesia and the Philippines.[4] In the words of one defender of globalization, Jagdish Bhagwati: 'The migrant female worker is better off in the new world of

---

4 *Marketplace* 2007. According to Dilip Ratha and Maurice Schiff of the World Bank Group, 'Remittance flows are more than twice as large as total development aid and represent the largest source of foreign exchange for numerous countries' (Ratha and Schiff 2009).

attachments and autonomy: the migrants' children are happy being looked after by their grandmothers, who are also happy to be looking after the children; and the employer mothers, when they find good nannies, are also happy and they can work without the emotionally wrenching sense that they are neglecting their children' (Bhagwati 2004, 78). Everyone's happy … why worry?

Yet the idea of a mother leaving her children for a decade at a time to care for the children of others; or leaving her own ailing parents to care for the elderly in a wealthier nation has a morally unsavoury cast.[5] The moral problematic, I suggest, is not easily captured in our standard moral categories. I shall consider now a number of possible ways to diagnose the moral harm. First, I shall consider casting it as gender injustice, and as a violation of rights. These are resources taken from the language of justice, and each figures in the analysis. But the moral harm is most precisely captured by an ethics of care, an ethics that only occasionally finds its way into legal discourse.

## The Gender Question

It is difficult to imagine the GHT in a world with full gender parity in the family and in the workplace. Even though the demand for care-givers is, in part, driven by the widespread movement of women into the workplace, the demand for *female* domestics to replace the care labour of these women is itself a function of gender biases about whose responsibility it is to care for children, the elderly, the sick and the disabled. Furthermore, the difficulties such as children's pain of separation from their mothers is also influenced by gendered expectations. Anca Gheaus also points out that the expectation in some societies that other female relatives participate in caring for children may even put additional pressure on mothers to migrate, knowing that there will be a female relative who will be available to do hands-on care. But these relatives do not ordinarily act as parents and the loss of a mother in day-to-day activities remains a loss that is experienced by the children (Gheaus forthcoming). Parreñas and other researchers consistently report that children express strong preferences for the father rather than the mother to go abroad should a parent need to leave home to send back remittances (Parreñas 2001, 146). Unabated patriarchal attitudes of sending nations contribute to expectations that leave children feeling more abandoned by their migrant mothers than by their migrant fathers. Although the women bring in the major portion of the family

5 It is an interesting and important question whether the length of time that mothers remain away from home matters to the moral analysis. Women who migrate from Eastern Europe to Western Europe do not spend the same length of time away from their families as do women who cross continents. The burdens and rewards may be different. But many of the same problems are reported in studies of Romanian migrants and their families, see Gheaus forthcoming.

income, gendered patterns of care have not been altered in these countries, and fathers rarely take the place of the mother in the home.

In the receiving nations, gendered workplace rules are the reason that women, when they migrate, return at less frequent intervals than men. And despite bucking gendered social expectations in the sending nation, in the receiving nation the women take on traditional female roles, with lower pay, lower status and greater vulnerability for sexual exploitation.

Yet one does not have to be an apologist for globalization to admit that migration can have benefits for the women themselves. It is not necessarily an unalloyed evil for all the women involved, although all suffer from the lost intimacy with their children. Gender injustice may contribute to the harms, but as some harms are balanced by gains women make, gender injustice can only be part of the diagnosis.

## Human Rights and the Right to Care

Given the importance of the care-giving experience in the lives of all individuals, both as givers of care and receivers of care, it is interesting that care-giving has been viewed primarily as a responsibility and not as a right: a right to fulfil the responsibilities we feel so keenly and which have such importance to those who mean so much in our lives. The right to benefit from and participate in care-giving, especially familial care-giving, has not been stressed along with other capacities, freedoms, and opportunities that make up the human rights paradigm. Should we not develop a language of rights that incorporates both a right to be cared for and a right to care for those to whom we have special attachments, commitments, obligations and responsibilities?[6]

On the one hand, it appears obvious that we ought to formulate a 'right' of some sort. All children, it would seem, have a right to adequate care. But is that a right to be cared for by one's parent? By one's mother? Similarly it would seem that all frail elderly have a right to decent care and treatment. But is it a right to be

6 It is worth saying a brief word about my understanding of the difference between obligation and responsibility. The source of an obligation is some moral or legal principle that binds my action to certain duties. A responsibility may arise from an obligation. I am responsible for fulfilling my obligations. A responsibility may also arise not out of a principle or law, but out of a relationship I have to another and to the expectations we each have of each other within that relationship. I may not be obliged to help a friend in need, but I may well feel a responsibility for that friend's well-being, since friendship is often a source of such feelings ('after all, what are friends for' we say), and so feel that it is my responsibility to assist the friend in her need. A parent has a duty toward her child, a duty recognized in law. But a parent will also feel a responsibility toward a child that arises not out of law, nor even out of a general moral obligation to care for one's child, but out of the expectations that the child has toward this particular parent and the particular relationship that the parent has to her child or children. Both obligations and responsibilities need protection in a right to care.

cared for by a specific individual, by the individual who is (or feels herself to be) most responsible for the care of this elderly person? By the person the frail elderly person holds responsible for her care? Must the care be delivered in one's own home? Will any passable level of care discharge the right to receive care? Does the obligation or responsibility that is the correlate to the right fall only on family members or does the state owe anything either to the one with the right to be cared for or the one who has a right to give care?

Still another difficulty comes from defining what activities count as care. A case in point is seen in the phenomenon of 'the global heart transplant'. *Being cared for*, by, and *caring for* those that matter to us are generally thought to involve face-to-face activity, particularly for those who cannot fulfil their needs without such care (Bubeck 1995). In formulating a *right to be cared for* or a *right to give care*, however, the demand for 'face-to-face interaction' is too stringent. True to the gendered stereotype of the self-sacrificing mother, many women interviewed speak tearfully of their children's unwillingness to understand that migrating was a sacrifice they performed in order to benefit their children and provide a good life for them. The face-to-face care, they believed, could be provided by others: kin, hired domestics, and sometimes (but not reliably) the father. But it is the absence of adequate resources, not distance as such, that they see as the greater obstacle to properly caring for their families.

These considerations may allow us to formulate a more relevant conception of care, but more specifically a conception of care that could conceivably function in formulating a right to care. Steven Darwall writes that caring for someone means desiring what is good for the person *for his own sake* (Darwall 2002, 7). A right to care would pertain to those who are dependent on another for care, that is, to those who cannot reasonably be expected to satisfy their own interests. We can say then that care, in a sense relevant to a right to care, involves: *attending to those interests of another that the person in need of care cannot reasonably be expected to satisfy on his or her own, and to attend to these interests for the sake of the one in need of care.*

In some sorts of care, as I noted, who does the caring is less important than how the care is administered; while in other situations of care, the attachment of the persons in the caring relationship is of great importance. It matters who gives care and for whom one cares. What motivates the care is, in some cases, as important as how well the care is carried out. Care, when worthy of the name, generally involves an emotional bond between the care-giver and another individual. As Folbre points out, this bond frequently serves as the 'intrinsic motivation' beyond the material compensation that commonly motivates work.[7] This bond gives rise to a sense of responsibility for the well-being of another, a sense of *respons*ibility which makes us *respons*ive to the other's needs. A right to do caring labour to

7 Folbre 2003. Even when the carework is paid for, in the case of caring which includes this intrinsic motivation as well as the economic incentive, we are not simply transmuting the love into gold.

collect a paycheque is scarcely different from a right to work at whatever work we choose. It is not a right to care as such. The care that needs the protection of rights is the right to care for and be cared for by those with whom we stand in significant relationships of affinity, where the care arises out of an intrinsic motivation to care for the other for his or her own sake.

To capture the sense of care we want in a right to care, we need the distinction between *caring for* and *caring about*. 'Caring for' *involves a set of activities required to attend to the well-being of another* – this we may say is a practice of care – while 'caring about' *involves an attitude, which in the strongest case is such that the other's well-being is requisite to our own* – this is the attitudinal conception of care.[8] Both need to figure in defining the sense of care we are searching for. Thus we can define caring for in the fullest sense as *attending to those interests of another that the person in need of care cannot reasonably be expected to satisfy on his or her own, and that this person is one whose welfare is a critical aspect of my own welfare and yet we attend to these interests for the sake of the one in need of care*. Under this definition, mothers who try to fulfil their responsibility to care for their children, and to ensure that they are well cared for, by working abroad to send home remittances, all the while sacrificing their own desire to be with their children, may be said to be *caring for* their children.

Robin West has argued that we have a right to care, what she calls a '*doulia right*' (West 2004, 98). West, one of the few theorists who have attempted to develop a right to care, builds on the conception of doulia that I have developed in previous work. Doulia (after the post-partum carer, a *doula* who cares for the mother so that she can care for her newborn baby), is a principle that claims that some third party, often the state, must support those doing dependency work, so that the dependency worker does not herself have to sacrifice her own well-being in order to discharge her duties to her dependants. The term dependency work is limited to meeting the needs of one who is in a condition that Martha Fineman and I have called 'inevitable dependency' (Fineman 1995; Kittay 1999). Dependency work also delimits certain practices of care, namely those devoted to meeting needs that are a direct consequence of the dependency and that are, for the most part, hands-on: dressing, feeding, fundamental points of healthcare, instruction and socialization, as well as the emotional needs that accompany this dependent state. Thus we can say that procuring the necessities that are a pre-condition for meeting those needs is part of caring, but it is not the hands-on care that the term dependency work delimits. These are among the supports the dependency worker requires of a 'provider' who 'provisions' the dependant and dependency worker so that both can survive and thrive.

This suggests that, in defining a right to care, we need a clause about the need for a carer to be supported in her caring for dependants, allowing her to meet her own needs as well as those of her dependant as she cares. That is, we need a right

---

8 See also Fischer and Tronto 1990 for a related but somewhat different way to parse the different senses of 'care'.

to care to be backed by a right to the material means to carry out such care. A right to care then, would have two parts, where the first part has two clauses:

1. The right to care for a dependant is:

   a. A right to be able to express and manifest an attitude of care by being able to engage in the practices of care toward certain particular persons. These are persons

      i. who are dependent on another to meet essential needs because they cannot fulfil these needs on their own and which must be met if these individuals are to survive and thrive;
      ii. whose welfare we care about and want to care for, for their own sake, and because our own sense of well-being is greatly diminished when these persons are not well cared for.

   b. Doulia rights. To be able to engage in the care practice of dependency work with provisions adequate to meet the needs of the dependant and without depleting the resources of the dependency worker or otherwise making it impossible for the dependency worker to meet her/his own urgent needs.

2. A right to be cared for is:

   a. A right to be cared for when we are unable to meet our own essential needs;
   b. A right to be cared for by one who cares for us in the sense of 1 above.

Formulating a right to care helps clarify certain things: This formulation of care does not preclude activities such as procuring the economic means for the dependant to survive and thrive. The migrant mothers of whom we speak are then not denied a right to care in the sense of 1a, where practices of care include procuring the means for benefiting the dependant. But these women could be said to lack doulia rights precisely because they are not supported in their efforts to do the hands-on dependency work for the dependants closest to them.

Yet this right to care still leaves many questions unanswered: who is authorized to define care practices for the purposes of fashioning 'a right to care'? If we formulate a right to care that recognizes the labour of these migrant mothers as caring for their families, then we respect the interpretation they themselves give to their choice. But such a right does little to grant them the wherewithal by which they can avoid the pain to themselves and to their children of these extended absences and the problematic of commodifying the loving care that is implicit in the diverted mothering in which they participate.

Furthermore, what public entity is to secure these rights? Whose responsibility is it? We can imagine that the state from which these women originate has a responsibility to its citizens to ensure that they have the possibility of discharging this duty in a manner consistent with the well-being of the dependant and the care-giver. But such state provisioning most likely requires resources the state lacks. If the migrations take place then, does the receiving nation have any duties that are correlates of these rights?

Finally, for the purposes of our inquiry here: whence come such rights? That we may have certain rights to receive certain goods and services essential to our ability to survive and function is not in question if we accept a statement of universal rights such as the UN Declaration of Human Rights.[9] That we have a right to a family is also already in the UN Declaration and does not require the formulation of a specific right to care.[10] The only justification for clauses such as 1a ii or 2b can, I suggest, come from a care ethics that has gone global.

## The Contributions of a Care Ethics

Among the values and practices associated with an ethics of care are attentiveness to others; attention to context; the concrete specificity of individuals; responsiveness to another's need; an emphasis on human vulnerability and dependence; and perhaps above all, a relational understanding of the self. I shall deal here with two of these: (a) the relational self, and (b) the acknowledgment of human dependency.

### *Relationality*

It is the emphasis of care ethics on relationality that really gets to the heart of the moral problem with GHT. The harm is the special harm that care ethics highlights: the threat to relationships. What is lost in the migration of the mother for extended periods of time? The daily care can be and usually is executed more or less satisfactorily by kin or domestics. The mothers normally do continue to love their children – in fact their work is in the service of their love for their children. While the mothers speak of 'pouring' the love into the charges in their care, they do not speak of pouring their love into their own children. The term apparently is a way of making a distinction between how one loves one's own child and how one loves

9 For example Article 25 of the Universal Declaration of Human Rights 1948 states: 'Everyone has the right to a standard of living adequate for the health and well-being of himself and of his family, including food, clothing, housing and medical care and necessary social services, and the right to security in the event of unemployment, sickness, disability, widowhood, old age or other lack of livelihood in circumstances beyond his control.'

10 The Universal Declaration of Human Rights 1948, Article 12, states: 'No one shall be subjected to arbitrary interference with his privacy, family, home or correspondence. ... Everyone has the right to the protection of the law against such interference or attacks.'

a charge. Perhaps the idea of 'pouring love into' another is an image that captures the less-than-fully relational nature of that love. Such love is less something that binds care-giver and charge in some lasting arrangement; it is rather a temporary bond one creates with another. The love of a parent to a child ordinarily binds a parent to a child (or, say, a daughter to an elderly parent) in such a way as to bond their interests and well-being, making the boundaries of self porous. When the contact between the people who stand in such relationships is blocked, the relationship's cathartic potential goes unrealized. That energy is instead released by 'pouring' the love into another child – her ward. The relationship with the ward does not have the commitment that binds one for life. It is a relationship formed only to be broken. And so it is not a relationship that one can genuinely invest in fully. It is 'relationship like' – but only that. At the same time, the relationship in which one is fully invested becomes frayed. The mothers speak of not recognizing their children, of the children not recognizing them.

A care ethics focuses both on the nature of the connection and the specificity of who relates to whom. It is these connections, as Gilligan so perceptively observed, that give rise to responsibilities that we feel morally bound by.[11] As close relationships of dependency care are not (easily, at least) fungible, children receiving physical daily care from kin, domestics and fathers are receiving these intimacies from someone other than the individual with whom they formed these caring relationships and, not insignificantly, the one with whom they expected to form this relationship. Similar remarks can be made about the care an adult child may wish to give to an ailing elderly parent or other close relation. Relationships formed through dependency needs generally will, especially when backed up with societal expectations and social norms, be the source of deep attachments and a deep sense of responsibility to a singular other. Treating these relations as fungible is deeply antithetical to all but the most professional care (for example, of a nurse's relation to a patient). If care ethicists are correct in their understanding of the self as relational – that is, an understanding of a self-identity that incorporates one's relationships into the construction of identity rather than standing apart from identity – then such a relational self will incorporate those close dependency relations into its very identity. The relational self of the carer will understand fulfilling the responsibilities that arise out of these relationships as crucial to their self-identity as a moral agent worthy of self-respect.

Correlatively, the relational self of the one in need of care will form expectations from another that, when realized, will confirm the moral worthiness of the self, but when disappointed will undermine that sense of self-worth. From the perspective of the cared for, the very preservation and development of self, as well as our self-understanding, depends on this other and on her responsiveness to our needs and expectations. Clearly then, whomsoever you relate to in these crucial ways – *that*

11 See Carol Gilligan 1982, especially at 73, and 132 for Gilligan's observations that the women in her study who cast moral problems in terms of care and connection chose to speak a language of responsibility.

individual – is incorporated into your own self-identity. If you are the vulnerable dependant, it is *this* individual and her relationship to you that forms the very ground of your being – at least that is how a young dependant would experience it.

Again, it is not that another cannot perform the tasks that make up the repertoire of caring activities – they can and, under good circumstances, can do it effectively and with kindness and affection. But when the relationship forged through dependency is disrupted and different actors are substituted, a relational conception of the self would predict a disturbance in one's self-understanding as well as a rupture in relationship that cannot always be mended.

Broken connections, broken relationships are the harms that Carol Gilligan found her subjects most wanted to avoid (Gilligan 1982). Migrant mothers make the attempt to sustain these relationships with their own children but relationships forged in intimacy are difficult to maintain across distance, especially for a dependent child whose ways of knowing and relating to her mother reside in the intimacies of daily care and daily emotional sustenance. Some mothers find it too difficult emotionally to be employed in childcare; others assume such work and transplant their hearts.

Why should fathers not be able to take over? Why are fathers permitted to leave with greater impunity than mothers. Within essentially patriarchal societies, fathers rarely do, in fact, take over and fathers rarely establish relations based on such dependency care. In the role of breadwinner, the fathers' relationship is at a remove from face-to-face dependency care, although it may well be a form of care. But as it is at a remove, it is (more) fungible and less intimately intertwined with either the father's or child's identity.

Societal expectations, of course, contribute both to the mothers' and the children's pain, and these expectations are forged in patriarchy. If relationships are to be maintained, these societal expectations must be renegotiated. Many of us have had to do just this in our own lives. But extended absences are a set-up for frayed relationships and without the solidity of firm relationships it is unlikely that such societal expectations and patriarchal norms can be renegotiated.

Furthermore, even though the mothers themselves do not cease to care about and love their children, care as a practice and as an ethic requires that care, as Nel Nodding says, has 'to be completed in the other' (Noddings 1984, 4; Kittay forthcoming). If the children feel neglected and uncared for, even the intention and the understanding of the mother that her activity is in the service of her care for her children, the outcome may not *be* care if their labours are not taken up as care by the children. Without the negotiations that can render the appropriate interpretation by the children of the absence as a form of care, not a form of neglect, the mother's intent to care is undermined.

*Dependency and vulnerability*

The final point I wish to make about the contribution of a care ethics concerns its recognition of inevitable human dependency (as well as interdependency) and our need to receive and to give care as a central feature of our ethical life.

An ethics of care, then, would stress the importance of valuing caring relations in a multitude of ways: one of which is financial. In addition, an emphasis on dependence asks that we recognize the vulnerability caring relations impose on the care-giver and on her sense of herself as a person who fulfils her responsibilities, that is as a person who can be self-respecting. John Rawls highlights self-respect as the primary good we require regardless of what conception of the good we may hold. Rawls's view holds that a just society provides the social bases of self-respect. Thus, even on Rawlsian grounds, providing the means by which a person can fulfil the responsibilities needed to be self-respecting may require providing the means by which women can fulfil their roles and that dependants can see themselves as worthy.[12]

## Conclusion

Let us step back and ask again about the dilemmas posed in the first part of this chapter. These were based on a (not so hypothetical) hypothetical premise: that a welfare state needed the labour of migrants to provide care services to its members. That same condition may pertain even in the more utopian feminist welfare state. That is, even a state that tried to honour the requirements of an ethics of care might nonetheless be dependent on the labour of migrants to provide some of that care. One could speculate that were labour conditions of careworkers substantially to improve, more citizens – hopefully men as well as women – would be drawn to carework. With fewer work opportunities in these societies, the attraction of (relatively) well-paid care work in a foreign land would not exert the same pull – a pull that now works in tandem with the push of poverty in the native land. Were such a day to come, mothers in poor nations might still seek employment in these wealthier nations, seeking out the least desirable and low paying work. Under the relative utopian conditions of a caring and just society, the generous welfare provisions would make even these poor paying jobs attractive. Insofar as remittances from abroad do have a positive impact on poverty in the sending nations, would it actually be 'caring' to deny migrants (even those who leave behind dependants to whom they would, in better circumstances give hands-on care) the opportunity to come to the affluent nations to work? As long as there remains a large differential in income and opportunity between nations, and as long as these conditions conjoin with hierarchical gender roles, the moral quandary

12 I owe this insight in large measure to Cara O'Connor whose dissertation is devoted to developing this point.

of the migrant mother may still be with us. Perhaps societies guided by a care ethics and by an understanding of the harm (and benefit) of transnational families would look to helpful policies that minimize ruptures to important relationships. Good immigration policies, with family reunification a priority, might encourage permanent emigration among some workers. For those who chose a transnational family life, it would be a choice made in the context of working conditions that permitted frequent and lengthy 'vacations', widely available services for the children whom they could bring along while they were working abroad, benefits that would travel back with them to their home lands, and so forth. Such gains need not await the ideal state, but can be achieved only when we are willing to acknowledge inevitable dependency and give full weight to the value of the labour, and the attachments, and responsibilities it entails.

## A Brief Coda

As such transnational migration, at least on a broad scale, is caused by structural injustice, an ethics of care must join with an ethics of justice. The way, ultimately, to enable robust relationships of care is to alter the economic and political inequalities that drive this migration. This is not to close the doors to migrants but to alter the conditions that drive women (as well as men) to split apart their families in order to secure a brighter future for their children.

In the end then, it seems as if the *most caring* thing those of us who reside in these receiving nations ought to do may be to fight for more just global distributive and redistributive policies that would reduce the great disparities in wealth, rights, and capabilities between the populations of wealthy and poor nations. Short of such a scheme of justice, we can only mitigate – not remove – the harms elucidated by a care ethics that is 'the global heart transplant'.

## References

Bhagwati, J. 2004. *In Defense of Globalization*. Oxford: Oxford University Press.

Bubeck, D. 1995. *Care, Gender, and Justice*. Oxford: Clarendon Press.

Card, C. 1990. Gender and Moral Luck, in *Identity, Character, and Morality: Essays in Moral Psychology*, edited by A.O. Rorty and O. Flanagan. Cambridge, MA: MIT Press, 199–218.

Darwall, S. 2002. *Welfare and Rational Care*. Princeton, NJ: Princeton University Press.

Fineman, M.A. 1995. *The Neutered Mother, the Sexual Family and Other Twentieth-Century Tragedies*. New York: Routledge.

Fischer, B. and Tronto, J. 1990. Towards a Feminist Theory of Caring, in *Circles of Care*, edited by E.K. Abel and M.K. Nelson. Albany, NY: SUNY Press, 35–62.

Folbre, N. 2003. *Caring Labor*, A transcription of a video by Oliver Ressler, available at <http://www.republicart.net/disc/aeas/folbre01_en.htm> (last accessed 20 July 2010).
Gheaus, A. forthcoming. Care Drain: Who Should Provide for the Children Left Behind? Manuscript available from author.
Gilligan, C. 1982. *In a Different Voice*. Cambridge, MA: Harvard University Press.
Hochschild, A. and Ehrenreich, B. 2002. *Global Woman: Nannies, Maids, and Sex Workers in the New Economy*. New York: Henry Holt and Company.
Kittay, E.F. 1999. *Love's Labor: Essays in Women, Equality and Dependency*. New York: Routledge.
Kittay, E.F. 2009. The Moral Harm of Migrant Carework: Realizing a Global Right to Care. *Philosophical Topics*, 37(1), 53–73.
Kittay, E.F. forthcoming. The Completion of Care, in *Care and the Professions*, edited by A.M. Gonzalez, C. Iffland and E.F. Kittay.
*Marketplace*2007, Poor People Supporting Poorer People. Available at <http://marketplace.publicradio.org/>, 17 October 2007 (last accessed 18 July 2010).
Noddings, N. 1984. *Caring: A Feminine Approach to Ethics and Moral Education*. Berkeley, CA: University of California Press.
Parreñas, R.S. 2001. *Servants of Globalization: Women, Migration, and Domestic Work*. Stanford, CA: Stanford University Press.
Ratha, D. and Schiff, M. 2009. Migration and Remittances. Review of Reviewed Item. World Bank Group News and Broadcast. Available at <http://web.worldbank.org/WBSITE/EXTERNAL/NEWS/0,contentMDK: 20648762~menuPK:34480~pagePK:64257043~piPK:437376~theSitePK:4607,00.html> (last accessed 18 July2010).
West. R. 2002. The Right to Care, in *The Subject of Care: Feminist Perspectives on Dependency*, edited by E.F. Kittay and E.K. Feder. Lanham, MD: Rowman and Littlefield, 88–115.
West, R. 2004. The Right to Care. *Boston Review: A Political and Literary Review*, April/May.
Zimmerman, M.K., Litt, J.S. and Bose, C.E. 2006. Globalization and the Multiple Crises of Care, in *Global Dimensions of Gender and Carework*, edited by M.K. Zimmerman, J.S. Litt and C.E. Bose. Stanford, CA: Stanford University Press.

# Index

**Bold** page numbers indicate figures.

For Product Safety Concerns and Information please contact our EU
representative GPSR@taylorandfrancis.com
Taylor & Francis Verlag GmbH, Kaufingerstraße 24, 80331 München, Germany

www.ingramcontent.com/pod-product-compliance
Ingram Content Group UK Ltd.
Pitfield, Milton Keynes, MK11 3LW, UK
UKHW022018230926
475702UK00029B/1988

*9781138260627*